tainted life

tainted life

marc almond

sidgwick & jackson

First published 1999 by Sidgwick & Jackson
an imprint of Macmillan Publishers Ltd
25 Eccleston Place, London SW1W 9NF
Basingstoke and Oxford
Associated companies throughout the world
www.macmillan.co.uk

ISBN 0 283 06340 8

1 3 5 7 9 8 6 4 2

A CIP catalogue record for this book is available from
the British Library.

Tattoo photography by Lesley Howling.
All other photographs from the collection of Marc Almond.
Every attempt has been made to locate the
holders of copyright material.

Typeset by SetSystems Ltd, Saffron Walden, Essex
Printed and bound in Great Britain by
Mackays of Chatham plc, Chatham, Kent

To Langy

Contents

Contents

Intro

The taxi driver keeps looking in his rear-view mirror at me. I know he's going to speak. I know he's going to ask me *that* question. I know this because they always do. What always amazes me is the way they ask it, like they're the first to have thought of it.

'You're him, aren't ya? Uhhmm, don't tell me . . . Marc Almond! When you gonna be on the telly again?'

Then he phones his wife on the mobile.

'You'll never guess who I got in the back, Sandra. You won't believe it. Marc Almond! No, no him. Yeah, Marc Almond. Say hello to me wife would you, Marc? Go on.'

He then hands me the mobile phone.

'You wouldn't sing something to her, would you? Go on, sing a bit of that song – how's it go?'

1

'Lost little childstar, alone on the stage'

I hate the beginnings of autobiographies. If you're like me you may prefer to skip to Chapter 4 or 5 for those tales of fame, drug hell and debauchery. You want to know if those rumours are true, where the money went, and what it is he or she was really feeling in those public moments.

But, as I sit down to write my own story, I realize that that would be too easy: it would mean ignoring the early triggers of inspiration and motivation, and the things that shed light on so much of what I became and why I acted in the way I did. So skip ahead if you want, but first of all I'm going to need to explore the beginning after all.

The opening scene must be set, and where better than Southport, a small coastal town in the north-west of England? 'Sunny Southport by the sea', as we Sandgrounders like to call it – a lovingly local term for the natives of a place that has, like most Victorian seafront towns, seen better days. In fact in Southport the sea rarely seems to come in, loitering instead on the horizon like a dirty grey strip. Out of this protruded the distant black outline of a wrecked ship; replaced now by an ugly great oil platform that mars the view. The sea may reluctantly creep in during the lonely hours, but I suspect few have ever seen it. As it retreats, it leaves a ragged tideline of bones and shells, sea-smoothed pieces of sculptured wood, armless dolls, green bottles and hundreds of old knotted condoms.

As Southport is near the Liverpool estuary, the meeting point for the open sewer pipes of the surrounding area, swimming is a hazard. In fact, Southport has occasionally enjoyed the distinction of being 'one of Britain's filthiest beaches'. The famous sand hills, where many a virgin has been deflowered, are left unkempt and wild, sliced in half by a long road that stretches from one end of the town to the other. The once beautiful, proud pier is now neglected and rusted, and stands out of the sea like an old dinosaur skeleton. The whispering ghosts of young women in low-cut floral dresses – the girls who strengthened a thousand front-line soldiers' resolves – haunt the promenade. By the beach stands a cluster of outdated rides, bingo booths and 'Hook-a-duck' stalls, the Tunnel of Love and Pirate Caves painted with gaudy pictures of buxom women at the mercy of toothless buccaneers. But this pleasure beach's roller coaster no longer thrills. It seems that time has passed the whole thing by, the advancing sands of the beach ever threatening to close in and reclaim it. The outdoor Lido with its art-deco décor and its majestic globe atop the café building – the place where I spent many of my childhood years with my sister and cousins in the school holidays – has long gone. Whatever stands there now could never match the beautiful building of so many young memories. Or is it the memories that can't be bettered? The floral gardens on the promenade don't seem so well tended, and the boating lake has been closed down; does the rickety train still circle the sad papier-mâché prehistoric reptiles in the 'Land of the Dinosaur' ride, now even more redundant in this Spielberg age?

A trip into town takes you to Lord Street, once a proud showpiece with sparkling lights, canopied with glass Victorian verandas over café fronts, 'high-class goods' shops and furriers for rich old ladies who haunt the patisseries – all now in need of a rejuvenating lick of paint. Take a walk down Liverpool Road to Hillside and you'll see huge houses from a bygone age of elegance and money, now old people's retirement homes and cramped flats.

The misguided good intentions of local politicians who diverted money away from this 'millionaire's village' failed to help the rest of Merseyside much, but left Southport much the worse for wear. So it remains, like Miss Havisham and her wedding dress, awash with a faded splendour that imbues it with a slightly seedy air of decayed decadence. Southport, however, seemed once to me to be the most beautiful and special place in the world, full of chattering spirits and magic, and a beach that stretched on into for ever. A place of secrets and subtext, like that white-picket-fence down in David Lynch films. The carpet of respectability was what you saw first, but when you peeked underneath you found sleaze and cobwebs.

A middle-class boy with so many secrets, who felt unloved and unappreciated, I keep Southport in my heart and soul. Whenever I smell the sea or a flower shop or coffee éclairs, candyfloss or frying doughnuts I think of it. When I feel sad I think of its desolation and isolation – the wild gorse dunes that hem the beach, the peeling façades, its loneliness when the streets are wet and grey with winter drizzle.

*

I began life one early Southport morning – in birth-certificate terms, on 9 July 1957 at Southport Maternity Hospital. Sex: male. Parents: Sandra Mary Almond (formerly Dieson) and Peter John Sinclair Almond, Second Lieutenant in the King's Liverpool Regiment. Named: Peter Mark Sinclair Almond. Born in Cancer, with Leo rising.

I was brought up at my grandparents' house in a 'dead posh' part of town called Birkdale. It was a beautiful house that then seemed to be huge but was, as one discovers later in life about so many childhood things, really quite average in size, set in an elegantly kept garden tended by a Mr Downs. My father never seemed to be around, as he was then still in the army, and though my mother was there I always thought of my grandparents, Peter and Gladys Dieson, as my second parents. It seemed to me that when my father appeared he always brought with him trouble.

My grandfather was a tall, handsome Norwegian we called 'Papa', who loved to joke and tease, poking gentle fun in a mixture of English and his mother tongue. My grandmother was a small, elegant lady who loved to spoil her grandchildren. She and Papa taught us to speak properly and say 'barth' for bath and 'parth' for path, to remain seated at the tea table until everyone had finished, and to never answer back. Certain people were 'common'. Black people were foreigners, and were never talked about unless in hushed tones as 'darkies'; they existed principally in Enid Blyton books. I was fifteen before I spoke to an *actual* black person. We weren't allowed to watch *Coronation Street*, because it was considered too common, with too many 'flamin' 'ecks'. Later, after grandpa died, grandma seemed to grow more modern and liberal in her views, moving to the tune of today more than anyone else in the family, even as she ended her days in her late nineties as a resident in one of those dreaded old people's homes that adorn every street of a town like Southport.

With my sister, Julia, who was two years younger than me, I had on the whole an early childhood of laughter, games and learning, spending summer days with our cousins Stephen, Gary and Fiona, playing in the garden, splashing in the paddling pool, making dens out of sheets and deckchairs or dressing up in old clothes from the drawer kept for dusters. Prancing about in my grandfather's old shirts and my grandma's old cardigans and pinafores (even her old bloomers), we made up theatrical shows before being chased with the garden hose for a good soaking. I watch those early innocent memories on home movies with bewilderment, and ponder on how those days slipped away, and where they went.

I became a sickly child, afflicted by asthma and bronchitis brought on by house dust and our pets, Whisky the cat and Candy the labrador. Too much excitement also induced attacks, during which I'd turn blue, unable to breathe, wheezing and coughing until a nurse came to administer an injection to calm my panic. To help my breathing, my grandfather used to walk along the beach carrying me on his shoulders – long walks along the tideline taking in the fresh sea air, him singing the old Bing Crosby song 'Take my hand, I'm a stranger in Paradise'. At other times he took my sister and me swimming at the Victoria Baths to strengthen my chest. Afterwards we drank hot chocolate, then, as we drove home, I'd look for the secret stash of Murraymints kept in the car's glove compartment. These memories contrast sharply with the reality of him many years later as a victim of debilitating Alzheimer's disease. To see this proud and handsome Norwegian patriarch being spoon-fed and crying (in one of the retirement homes that line Liverpool Road) will always haunt me. For their part, the beautiful tiled Victoria Baths have now been turned into a wine bar and disco.

So I wheezed and sneezed my way through childhood. It wouldn't be until around the age of eleven or twelve that I settled down to enjoy a Christmas without illness – the intense excitement would build up and bring on an asthma attack. Nonetheless, Christmases would still be fun.

Grandpa would hand out the presents – my sister and I always had piles of them. One year I received a red plastic Dalek suit – I was obsessed with Doctor Who. The plastic smelt new and unfamiliar, and I spent all day tottering around the house pestering everyone with the Dalek arm (nothing more than a sink plunger). I loved also Lego and Britten zoo animals, and fervently collected them, as well as Action Men figures when they first came out. But above all else was my collection of books – endless books that I couldn't get enough of. Drawing books with crayons and paints, children's adventure stories such as Enid Blyton's *Famous Five* and *Secret Seven*, Andersen and Brothers Grimm fairy stories, *Just So Stories* and the illustrated Bible. I was fascinated by the stories of angels and Sodom and Gomorrah. One fairy story featured a dragon that was chopped to pieces, his flesh strewn over the countryside. The picture annuals of Rupert the Bear, and the tale of a strange pig called Toby Twirl who found a magic flying box and was always coming up against evil child-snatching witches. *Struwwelpeter* with its cover showing a long-haired boy fleeing, pursued by a pair of scissors that cut off people's thumbs. Disturbed but intrigued, I would go to bed and dream about these stories, imagining myself one of the characters in them.

This make-believe came to fill the place of friends. I found it hard to make friends, to communicate with other people (and even harder when, just as I did, I would be whisked away from school because my father's change of jobs – or lack of one – took us away). The alternatives were books and drawings – and, later on, music. So I became attached to toys and animals, imaginary friends. My favourite companion was a monkey called Jacko, a stuffed toy with a plastic moulded face without whom I wouldn't venture anywhere. I was often seen pedalling around on my blue tricycle with Jacko sticking out of its bag. When I outgrew him he was given away, but I still find myself searching stalls at Camden Market, trying to find another. I even called my pet African Grey parrot after him. Perhaps I never really did outgrow him.

I also used television as a means of escape. My favourite shows were *Torchy the Battery Boy*, *Fireball XL5*, *Ten Town* (about a group of children who lived in a town made of wooden boxes) and *Four Feather Falls*, featuring a puppet dog called Dusty. This imaginary friend became a reality when I named our next dog after him. From a very early age I also loved drawing and painting. My grandfather would give me piles of paper pulpboard from his Norwegian paper business, on which I would scribble and doodle and colour monsters, witches, dragons and brightly coloured faces. I'd also construct houses from cereal packets and paint them, and at Christmas I loved to decorate twigs with glitter and shiny decorations to give to my grandmother. Isolated in my own world though I was, these substitute friends and activities allowed me to develop and flourish. To me this world was real – a place to escape to from the traumas that began to surround me.

*

We left my grandparents' house when I was about four, and went to live on a modern housing estate in Starbeck, on the outskirts of Harrogate. This was the first of many such moves – from Southport to Starbeck, back to Southport, then to Horsforth near Leeds, and then back again to Southport.

Life in Starbeck couldn't have been more different from life in Southport. I started infant school, which terrified me (as always happened in a childhood of starting new schools). On the first day I made my mother stand outside the school all day to wait for me, so I could see her at break times (though I'm sure she went home in between). But I did manage to draw a portrait of Miss Stracken, my teacher, which I took home to my proud mother.

At primary school I was always getting into trouble for playing tricks and running away. Once I taunted a girl for being fat, so she pushed me on to the pavement, scraping my knees. During a hide-and-seek game, the same girl crept up on me and knocked me down, and my head hit the corner of a concrete step. I staggered through the school, looking pale and ghostly, trailing blood. My distraught mother rushed me to hospital, and I was given stitches in my forehead – a scar splits my left eyebrow to this day.

I played endless tricks at home too, especially on my sister. Alone with her, I would throw her dinner or cereal on to the floor and then shout, 'Look what Julia's done!' I would pull the heads off her dolls and again blame it on her; being too young to talk back, she would inevitably be chided for it. What a charming child! Nowadays, a lot of my problems – being unable to sit still or concentrate, always hyperactive, constant misbehaviour, learning problems with arithmetic – would be diagnosed as a type of dyslexia. But perhaps there was something more deep-rooted that made me such a 'little monster with an angel's face'.

At that time I was what you could call a cute child: a wide, smiling, cheeky face with a missing front tooth; hair a sandy colour, with a cowlick at the front. This lick was the cause of endless annoyance to me – I could never have the haircut I wanted. My mother, even today, frowns upon my latest hair colour, my tattoos or the piece of metal on my face, saying 'When you were little you were such a lovely boy – lovely skin and a sweet face' – as if to say, 'What the hell happened?' What did happen? What happened was that I accumulated all the baggage of a Tainted Life, prompting me to love 'alternative' things – tattoos, facial jewellery, more outlandish, less 'normal', hairstyles and colours – all in an endless search for individuality, for an identity, for attention. All because the person we think we are is someone we don't really like at all.

When I was six I had an early kind of sexual experience. I was playing in the garage with Paul, the boy from next door. Paul was the same age as me, and we often played together, making dens or scooting around on our tricycles. And, as children do, we started to mess about. We'd innocently pull our pants down and I'd smack his bottom, then he'd smack mine – that was it. But a few days later when we did the same thing under a rug in the back garden I looked up and saw his mum staring angrily over the fence. Ashamed and embarrassed, I blushed a deep red. I knew whatever it was I was doing was wrong. After that day I was terrified to be in her presence in case she would tell my mother, and she would give me looks as if to say, 'You naughty boy – I know what you were doing and I may just tell.' I lived in fear of that for so long, and couldn't bring myself to look her in the face. She *knew*, and I felt guilt for the first time.

At six I still suffered from asthma every time I was excited or upset. I started to go to physiotherapy classes to learn to control my breathing and relax. Whenever I had a bout of wheezing, my mother would administer a Bronchipac, a foul-tasting pill, which made me retch – I can still summon up the taste of it to this day. But I did love the spoonful of Scott's Emulsion and the Haliborange tablet I was given each morning.

We would still spend the summer in Southport, where I became more and more inquisitive. I used to love what my grandma called 'rooting' – 'Stop rooting!' she'd say as she'd catch me exploring drawers and cupboards for secret treasures, which I'd pinch to keep in my little treasure box of old beads, half-melted pieces of sealing wax, some of my father's army badges and my grandfather's old Masons' medal. Obsessed with 'rooting', I was always finding something new – one day even an art-deco powder compact and a gold fan. Nor was this inquisitive nature confined to the house. When we went out on excursions I would often wander off. On one occasion I wandered into the Rolling Barrel at the Southport funfair and knocked myself unconscious. More frightening for all concerned was the day I was taken to Southport Zoo by my grandma. When she turned her back for a moment I was gone. She finally found me in the orang-utan enclosure, offering the ape my ice lolly. The keeper had left the cage door open, and I had gone in to give the ape a hug. By the time the keeper quietly crept into the cage and slowly removed me from the ape's clutches, the orang-utan seemed to have adopted me. My grandmother was distraught, and I got told off in no uncertain terms.

After a couple of years in Starbeck we moved back to Southport, and I started again at another primary school. Once more the ordeal was terrifying – new surroundings, having to try again to make friends, having to fit in. Yet constantly moving house and changing schools has held me in good stead, enabling me to adapt to strange surroundings and foreign situations. That there is a side to me that takes over and makes the whole survive, like a hermit crab taking on a new protective shell. I am after all a Cancer.

*

At home discontent began to bubble away below the surface between my mother and father – rows, dissatisfaction, developing into unremitting tension. They tried to keep it from my sister and me, but we always knew it was there. I remember on several occasions unwittingly coming between them.

I see my father only in a half-light – an elusive figure, flitting in and out of my early life, away either in the army or as a travelling salesperson. He was a handsome man, with a touch of the Dirk Bogarde, yet he always seemed to carry a dark cloud – the one that shadows addicts, bringing blackening troubles that express themselves in resentment, anger, self-pity and lack of self-worth. I see that shadow sometimes when I look in the mirror and it scares me.

As the years went by, my sister and I would dread his coming home. More often than not he would be drunk, would shout at me, slap me across the face, or – worse of all – threaten to send me away to boarding school. There was always an edginess to him, a dark anger behind his eyes as secretive as those bottles he hid away. I wasn't aware of my father's drinking at this time; it wasn't until my early teens that I began to understand the signs of alcoholism. But my sister and I became closer in the domestic chaos, drawing together, playing and cuddling. And yet I would still tease and torment her – learning perhaps how some people behave towards women. What seed had I inherited? Where were these mannerisms learned?

I made my theatrical debut at this time, as an Eskimo in the school play, a picture of cuteness and innocence dressed in a fluffy white outfit. Success led to a more 'serious' part as Merry Hump in the school production of *Merry Hump and Grumpy Hump* opposite schoolfriend Paul John as Grumpy Hump. With a papier-mâché hump tied to my back, I set out to show that, if you were kind and nice and naturally merry, you would lose your hump. If you were mean and nasty and grumpy then you would remain crippled for life.

I loved being in the school plays, on stage, with all the attention and applause. Only one thing stood in the way of bigger and better roles: my stammer. It wasn't yet as bad as it would be, when I hit the awkwardness and hyper-awareness that accompanies early teens. But, as home life worsened, the affliction also intensified. I would dread more than anything else that time in lessons when I was required to read out loud. As the moment approached, my scalp would prickle and sweat would run down my back. The more paralysed with fear I became, the more I knew I wouldn't be able to get that first word out – especially if it began with a certain letter. There would be a silence as my turn came round – a silence so long, so overpoweringly loud that I'd have to almost sing the first word to get it out. I learned then what many therapists were later to discover: that you cannot stammer when you sing – which is how I eventually reconciled my love of performing on stage with having a speech impediment. I realized in time that my stammer, together with my inability to concentrate and remember things, meant that I would never be an actor. But these were still early days, before the age when children are at their cruellest. In due course my stammer would become a licence to mock and imitate – 'A-A-A-A-A-A-Almond' – and a class would collapse in hysterics.

I had my first crush, aged seven, on a girl called Ingrid Tebay. I sent her notes, and thought about her constantly. And it was her name that stuck with me later when I needed to invent an imaginary girlfriend at secondary school in Leeds. 'My girlfriend's called Ingrid and she lives in Southport,' I used to explain when asked why no one ever saw her. 'I see her in the holidays when I go home to stay with my grandparents.' It sounded impressive, the name exotic enough to be believed, and it served its purpose. When confronted by other boys as to why I didn't want a girlfriend in Leeds, I would point out that I was loyal to Ingrid. To think, she went out with me for all those years and didn't even know it!

Even had I wanted to, I doubt I could have found many friends who wanted to share my loves and dreams, so I continued to develop my own company. Other boys were into sports and rougher games, and didn't take to dressing up as Robin to play with me – especially when I always insisted on being Batman, with what I considered the better outfit. My sister and I were forced to be friends with the children of a family called the O'Driscolls, who lived across the road from our house in Farnborough Road – my mother was a friend of their mother. Becky and Ricky, the two children, always gave me the impression they never cared for us, but we were forced into each other's company. Ricky was a sports type, and audibly groaned whenever I appeared.

But at the back of the O'Driscolls' home, over a wall, was an overgrown orchard, where a small cottage stood. It had been abandoned years earlier, still full of furniture, all of which was now smashed. Upturned chairs, bric-a-brac, faded photos and discarded old clothes were strewn around. It was as though the occupants had fled in the night, or died. Our imaginations had them buried under the floorboards. Tramps and other unruly children had since ransacked it. One particular room appeared to have been a makeshift laboratory, now with broken test tubes and Petri dishes, as though once occupied by an insane professor or witch, who in our minds must have carried out experiments, or dark spells. How we loved to explore that cottage, crunching over the broken glass, looking for treasure – a rusty brooch or a dusty old book – scaring and daring each other to go into the darkened kitchen or the musty upstairs bedrooms! Once I went there alone to explore, intrepid but fearful. Upon opening the door to the kitchen I saw a man crouched on the floor – a tramp looking for shelter, dishevelled in appearance. He stood up, shouted and chased me outside. I turned and ran, my heart beating, this strange, evil-looking man pursuing me. I struggled over the wall and ran shaking all the way home. I didn't tell anyone what had happened but he, and that moment of intense fear evoked by him, visited my dreams for a long time afterwards. Decades later this image came back to me during my periods of withdrawal nightmares.

*

One day I arrived home from school and was told that we were moving, again. My father had changed jobs and found employment as a salesman in a small town called Horsforth, just outside Leeds. I felt worried, and withdrew into my books; I didn't relish having to make new friends over again, nor the distance of Horsforth from the sanctuary of my grandparents and those sunny afternoons and week-ends spent in their back garden, or simply walking on Southport beach with my grandfather.

We moved to a modern maisonette above a newsagent in Hors-forth's Town Street. I started immediately at the local junior school in Featherbank. It felt to me even then that this was a move down in the world, with the house cramped and lacking privacy. There were a few happy moments, though, the memory of which stands out all the more. I actually enjoyed myself at Featherbank School. My favourite teacher was Miss Bunn (who actually wore her hair up in a big bun), who taught drama enthusiastically – encouraging us all to be growing trees or waking mushrooms.

I made several friends, too. A boy called Ian, who wasn't at my school but lived near my home, was from South Africa; his family were followers of the Bahá'i religion. Their house was filled with fascinating African artefacts – wooden masks and carvings, strange-smelling animal skins, tom-tom drums, and an elephant's foot made into a stool. I wanted to touch and examine them all. Once I lifted up a spear and all hell broke loose – I'd touched the sacred spear given to Ian's mother by an African chief. She claimed I had caused a curse to fall on the family. Terrified, I ran back home, and the friendship was over.

My parents made me join the Cubs, which I sorely resented. Escaping Southport had at least meant leaving the Sea Scouts behind. Now I was made to wear that itchy green jumper, that stupid neckerchief and woggle, that humiliating cap. I suspected that my parents thought the Cubs would instil some masculine discipline into their fragile son. But I loathed the Cubhouse, those ridiculous rhymes, the games with Scoutmasters in short pants and loud, over-jolly voices who should have known better. Once a month was Church parade and, on an inevitably wet Sunday, we had to march through the streets of Horsforth. Once again I faked my way through to survive, opting for the less challenging badges – for rewarding tasks like book-reading or first aid. I once again found my forte in the form of theatrical presentations, cast first as Albert in the story of Albert and the Lion. The following year I had the unforgettable role of Queen Elizabeth I – no doubt because, with my feather haircut, I was the most feminine-looking boy in the troop. At ten, I stood in my flouncing dress and wimple in our living room, rehearsing, my face made up with white powder and red lipstick. Soon after I was allowed to drop out.

Featherbank Junior School was mixed, and most of the boys of ages ten upwards were obsessed with sex. One day a boy in the class informed us that his brother had this thing called 'spunk', which came out of his penis. We were enthralled as he described this elastic-type stuff, which his brother kept in a jam jar under the bed. Most couldn't wait until they too had some of this stuff, and many of them were constantly looking for the opportunity to find out if they were yet blessed. I didn't find any myself until a year or so later, when I was playing with myself in the toilet and started feeling dizzy. Something then shot across the room, nearly bowling me over. Thrilled yet fearful, I couldn't wait to repeat the experience, to see if it was real, and if indeed it would happen again. Another secret to feel guilty about, the results of my experiments, encrusted on a handkerchief, were hidden in a 'private' drawer. One day I came home and found the handkerchief washed and ironed by my mother. Destroyed with shame and embarrassment, I was sure my mother must have examined it, discovered the stains, *known*. How dare she go into my private things and, worse, discover my secret? I felt unable to look her in the face for some time. Sex and sexuality were already becoming associated with shame and guilt, and a barrier of communication began to go up between my mother and me.

By aged ten I was beginning to be more sexually curious, which led to another incident that caused humiliation and embarrassment. In an episode of *The Saint* with Roger Moore, one of his adversaries was a stripper called Selena. I became obsessed with Selena, and fascinated by strippers and striptease. I started to draw pictures of naked women in suspenders and little breastpieces, peeking from behind curtains. I so wanted to meet a real stripper – see a strip show. In fine early-adolescent tradition, I began to cut out and collect photos of women in bras and corsets from the Freeman's mail-order catalogue. I also loved to look at the men's underwear section – and most particularly the bulges in the Y-fronts – but as yet I hadn't developed the courage to cut them out, too. I still felt a need to be drawn to female sexuality, which seemed to be the normal way of things. I didn't know yet about the other path, and thought that my curiosity about naked or semi-naked men was a phase everyone has but shouldn't do anything about, it being linked to shame, to be put out of one's mind at every opportunity. But perhaps I *knew*. After all, I would always burn a deep red at any mention of homosexuality on the television, or when watching the caricatures that were Larry Grayson or John Inman. I even remember one particular episode of *Steptoe and Son* that had Harold courted by a flamboyant antique dealer – was this how all these sorts of men were: effeminate, lecherous predators?

My Selena drawings were kept with the Freeman's models in my bedside table. Then one day I came home from school and was greeted by my grandmother, who wanted a word. You *know* when they *know*, and you panic, and prickly heat and nausea overcome you. She looked at me so seriously – a stern look of concern and disappointment – as she brandished the drawings of Selena (complete with intimate details) and Freeman cut-out photos. I wanted to die, to just be plucked up and deposited in some other place, far away. And my grandmother of all people – the one woman I thought so much of, and whom I adored – was the one to have found this secret stash! She told me how *dirty* they were, but promised not to inform my mother if I destroyed them.

I listened to my parents' record collection; I couldn't yet afford records of my own. The most contemporary record they possessed was *With the Beatles*, as well as my mother's singles of 'Let's Dance' by Chris Montez and 'Zambezi', a twist track, as well as Chubby Checker's 'The Twist'. I also delved into my father's jazz records by Dave Brubeck, and discovered a strange, gargle-voiced singer called Eartha Kitt. And I was really turned on by the psychedelic sounds starting to be played on the radio and the pop TV shows. I loved the promotional film that accompanied the Stones' 'Jumping Jack Flash', the band dressed in feathers and make-up, totally glam. I was also a fan of the Monkees, and their mad, surreal TV show. I duly discovered Radio Luxembourg and Radio Caroline, hiding like so many other adolescents at the time under the bed sheets, trying to keep the cheap radio tuned into the faint reception and the volume down for fear of my parents hearing.

More legitimately I watched every pop show from *Thank Your Lucky Stars*, *Ready Steady Go!* and *Juke Box Jury* (which always followed *Doctor Who*) through to *Top of the Pops*. All in enigmatic black and white. Particular memories stay with me – Sandie Shaw in a chequered dress dancing in bare feet; the glossy lipstick of Kathy Kirby; the pockmarked beauty of a young Eric Burdon with the Animals; a skinny Mick Jagger dressed in a long jumper, shaking maracas; the space sounds of the Tornadoes, hip-shaking black-suited boys with greasy hair, and beehived girls, twisting and jiving. A ponytailed man dressed in a white frilled shirt, looking like a high-wayman, swashbuckling among the adoring audience, sang in a rich, deep voice a song from *West Side Story*. I was moved by three brothers singing in harmony, the good-looking one – Scott – at the front with dark glasses and outstretched arms, fragile and shaking. A shy, suited young man sang 'Twenty-four Hours from Tulsa', pain-fully innocent-looking. How I wanted to be one of these people singing one of these songs! Their performances thrilled me as a ten-year-old, made me dream a more fanciful dream.

My school work suffered progressively the more I lay awake at night. I went to school with dark shadows under my eyes and a head full of sounds – sounds that I hoped would block out the arguments that took place between my parents into the early hours. It would start with my mother continually nagging my father about something or other – his drinking or his lazing around – and arguing would then ensue and escalate. My mother's dissatisfaction and frustration with my father would often result in her losing her temper with my sister or me over the slightest thing. Once I was taken ill at school with a stomach bug; I hoped I would get home in time to make it to the toilet, but I failed. I was dreading facing my mother, mainly because of the humiliation associated with such a mishap. I arrived in the house with my trousers a mess. I tried to explain that I was ill and it was an accident, but my mother went hysterical, slapping and thrashing me. She pushed me against the wall, and I banged my head badly. For a while afterwards I walked on eggshells, wary of her and of my father finding out. Naturally my mother felt compelled to tell him of my misfortune, and in turn he too went berserk. Such understanding parents.

Another lasting traumatic experience was the day when, near home, I climbed a wall which happened to back on to a slaughter-house. I witnessed in horror a young calf led out and shot in the head with a bolt gun. Its legs gave way beneath it, and it dropped, dead weight, to the floor. I was horrified, and couldn't enjoy eating meat again. Yet death and the image of it became something of an obsession. I was fascinated by dead birds and carcasses of animals. When my hamster died, I kept digging it up to inspect it before reburying it, fascinated by the process of decomposition. Years before, I had seen a man collapse in the street in Blackpool. The inevitable crowd gathered round, and we all watched as ambulance men tried to revive him. I remember his body going into spasm as they applied electric shocks over and over again until they finally gave up, covering him in a sheet. Another time, at Southport Fair, I had watched an elderly man climb on to the waltzer. When it came to a halt he was slumped, lifeless, in one of those semicircular chairs. He had died of a heart attack.

Perhaps that is where my fascination and fear of death germinated. The mystery of it, that levelling inevitability, almost comforting in its lack of discrimination. I love to walk through graveyards and read all the headstones, knowing that all of us will one day be reduced to no more than a name – gone the way of all flesh. I would so much like to believe in reincarnation, the soul living on, but I'm too sceptical. When you listen to people who claim to have been reincarnated, they've always been Cleopatra, Mesopotamian royalty, one of Casa-nova's lovers – no one has been a slum dweller or a toilet cleaner, which is more probable. The odds seem too stacked against my coming back with any sort of privileged life – a limbless beggar in a Bombay slum is more likely. But I'm as afraid of death as I am fascinated by it, just as I am afraid of ageing. I never want things to die, just as I never want things to change. I am sure that death is the end, and we end up as dust in the ground, in the black void, in the eternal nothingness – and perhaps we should be thankful for it. I've had so many brushes with death that I've also developed a belief that some sort of spirit or guardian angel must watch over me and protect me in some way.

*

You'll know by now that being established meant time to move again. Perhaps I should warn you that there are at least three more moves before the end of this chapter, so don't get too settled. We moved back to Southport for a bit while my parents waited to move into another house back in Horsforth. This time we found ourselves in a dingy flat belonging to my father's parents, Nana and Grandad, and I started back at Farnborough Road Junior School, having completely lost contact with all my old schoolfriends.

The depressing flat proved the ideal catalyst for family arguments and bad moods, especially since we all had to sleep in one room. Julia and I slept on makeshift camp beds, which we shared with cockroaches. I became the focus of my father's ugliest and most resentful moods. I became a constant source of irritation to him. His behaviour was always reliably unpredictable, depending on whether he had had a drink or not. I would often get slapped across the face for the slightest thing, and grew very wary of annoying him. In such circumstances you learn to move about in silence, trying not to have your presence felt, to be indiscernible. Those moments preceding the anger were the worse, as I waited in uncertainty and trepidation. So I began to loathe and hate my father with a vengeance. My sister remained more in his favour, yet even she was not exempt from his wrath. And though my mother made an attempt to intervene; the distance between us grew, too.

I all the more looked forward to the time we spent at my grandparents', especially as it became apparent that they too couldn't stand my father. I always got the feeling that they had never liked or approved or him – that between them there was a secret. In my early teens my father said to me, after one particular row, that I was never planned or really wanted, and that in fact he and my mother had had to get married because of me. Despite my mother's denials, it all seemed to make sense. There would be talk of loans of money my grandparents had made to my father, inevitably ending with rows and my father storming out. My father had obviously been incapable of supporting my mother with a child. And their now-nightmare marriage was all precipitated by me. What a wonderful burden for their child to bear!

Then it was time to move back to Horsforth, to a house in Brownberry Drive – located in a better area, it was a pleasant enough house. I had a small but quiet room of my own overlooking the garden, and adorned the walls with pictures, including a large Spanish poster advertising a bullfight. The bold lines and colours told me something of mystery and drama, as well as savagery. Those pictures in turn were replaced by ones of rock stars; music was beginning to take over.

I took my eleven-plus back at Featherbank Junior School, somehow muddling through it, struggling with arithmetic but letting flow on the essays and English, even though my writing was appalling. It was amazing that I managed to write anything at all – I had long since lost the thread of lessons. But then a strange thing happened which set things on a different course. We were told that no one had passed the exam in my class, but two people were considered borderline cases – a girl, whose name I forget, and me. I could barely believe it. We had been selected to be sent, along with a dozen other children, for a series of tests, and if accepted would be offered the opportunity of attending a better school.

When the appointed morning arrived we sat a writing and arithmetic test, and in the afternoon did creative painting and drawing on a selected theme. I was determined to do well and, though I muddled through the morning, I felt pleased with the afternoon. This was a chance, as it turned out, to go to Aireborough Grammar School (just outside Leeds) – a school reserved for bright and successful children. It was a far preferable alternative to where I was otherwise heading, Benton Park in Rawdon, where gangs roamed and beat people up, and initiation involved your head being put down the toilet – children are such charming creatures! I knew there was every possibility that if I went to Benton Park I might not survive; I would be beaten up by the rough kids from the Yeadon or Guiseley estates the moment they heard my soft posh voice or my stammering speech impediment. I knew I had to survive.

Perhaps the guardian angel I always believed in was looking over my shoulder the day they gave out the results. I had passed. I was on my way to Aireborough Grammar. But perhaps there had been a mistake, for I discovered the school far exceeded my learning capabilities, and for the next few years I came to utilize every survival technique imaginable. I became adept at diving and dodging and skiving. I was the class fool, always the one brought to the front to illustrate a difficult equation, there for the amusement of all, always the one to make a joke or disrupt the lesson. My speech impediment was soon noticed and picked up on. Apart from my stammer, I also pronounced my Rs softly. 'Say "prune",' somebody said to me. 'Pwune,' I replied – and that was it. I was nicknamed Pwune. For difficult lessons I learned a trick that would get me out of bother: I would quietly cause myself to hyperventilate until I blacked out, to be rushed to the sick bay. I loved to lie in that sick bay for hours. I told everyone I had a hole in the heart, thinking the other pupils would be more kind towards me if I had a life-threatening disability.

My fantasies weren't restricted to my health. I thought I liked girls – or at least I wanted to; I hung around with girls at school, and talked about girls in the presence of other boys. Of course, there was always Ingrid safely ensconced back in Southport. But I also felt drawn towards certain boys, and began a series of crushes. In my first year I had a close friendship with a boy called Paul – we were inseparable. We used to go for long walks, and when no one was watching we would stop and kiss (often for the longest time), telling each other everything. Once we went on a first-year school trip to

London – my first visit – and I was thrilled to attend the museums and waxworks, to walk out on the streets and experience the bustle and noise of the city. I remember, in our small hotel in Paddington, on a portable black and white television, watching Neil Armstrong land on the moon. Four of us boys had to share a room. I actually shared a bed with Paul, and, strangely, it seemed the most natural thing in the world. We hugged each other, and Colin, one of the other boys, seemed most interested in our closeness, almost envious, and said nothing to the others. Years later I was to have sexual experiments with Colin too during cross-country runs, when we stopped to masturbate and see which of us could come first. But, just as that was to cease, so things with Paul also came to a halt. He told me he couldn't see me any more. I suspected his parents had grown fearful of our closeness and nipped it in the bud. I resented him for a while after that, even siding with the other boys against him.

Ironically, because of my tales of Ingrid and the tall stories I wove, I actually acquired a reputation as one for the girls. Once a friend called Chris Halliday and I went out looking for girls together after school – Chris even asking my advice on whom he should pull. I of course gave him my worldly knowledge on the subject, and upon meeting a couple of local girls he disappeared into a bush with them. I naturally stayed and waited for him, unable to participate because of my unwaivering loyalty to Ingrid. Chris, of course, was the one I really wanted. He always accepted me at school, and gave me time. I was smitten. Once both Chris and Colin came to call for me after school, and I was hopeful that something more adventurous might happen. But I thought girl hunting was most likely on their minds, and my father was in one of his moods, so I was afraid to accept their invitation for fear of annoying him. As they walked back up the drive I wondered in the pit of my stomach if I had missed a chance. Perhaps I had; they didn't call for me again.

There was experimentation with girls too, though. Gillian Lax was the class beauty, with her long flaxen blonde hair and blue eyes. She and her friend Tina Mitchell were considered the class man-eaters: both were known to be sexually advanced beyond their years. Once I spent a lunchtime with them in the long grass out in the fields behind the school. I took out my penis, and we began to play with it – at which point another boy crept up to the scene and spoilt the mood and nothing more happened. A second encounter with Gillian occurred at a party in her house. We locked ourselves in the bathroom, she pulling down her skirt and I undoing my trousers. However, due to the commotion and lewd comments by revellers outside the bathroom door, I found myself unable to get an erection. But at least I felt I had wanted it to happen. I succeeded in losing my virginity a year later, at thirteen, to a girl called Hilary – a big-boned, galumphing, sweaty girl who towered over me. I fumbled through it, somehow managing to fulfil the necessary requirements. For a while I even thought I loved her, that she was special – until I found out to my horror that Colin had done it to her too, one afternoon in Bluebell Woods.

I was occasionally physically bullied at school, once or twice quite seriously. I was also completely hopeless at sports, especially football and rugby, ever among the last to be picked for a team. The familiar 'Oh no, sir, not Almond!' would be heard as I was forced upon reluctant team-mates, who always put me well out of the way, where they thought I could do the least damage to the final score. Rugby was worse than football – my shirts stretched out of shape where I'd wrapped my hands in the hem to keep warm on those cold and joyless afternoons. Eventually I opted for cross-country, in which I could take leisurely walks until within view of the school gates, when I would smear mud on my knees and sprint the home run, ensuring I was enough out of breath to convince the teachers of a valid effort. Of course cross-country had for a time the further attraction of stolen moments with Colin, too. I also loved swimming, and was at one point even selected to be in the swimming team.

*

My wayward behaviour and poor performance continued as home life steadily deteriorated. My sister and I started finding the hidden alcohol bottles – in the piano, behind cushions, and even once, when returning from my grandparents', in my bed. The rows escalated, culminating in violent fights. My sister and I would sit on the stairs until the early hours, shaking and crying, waiting for the moment when we could try to intervene. The sound of crashing furniture, doors slamming, the noise of somebody falling over was unbearable. Night after night there would be more screaming and crying, my father beating my mother, pulling her hair out, and occasionally turning on us – more often than not on me. In bed I would be afraid to sleep, listening intently to the muted hollering, permanently on guard, fearful of the argument encroaching into my room, and wanting to rush down and protect my mother.

Once my father did burst into my room and attempted to suffocate me with the pillow. On another occasion the violence got so out of hand that I tried to call the police, but he grabbed the phone from me and hit me across the head with the receiver, knocking me unconscious, and causing a slight laziness down the right-hand side of my face. He was always drunk, but never a drunk, never swaying or staggering; only the occasional slur gave it away. Intoxicated humour would inevitably turn into a vile tirade of abuse and violence – mostly focused on me, because he saw me as the source of his shortcomings, failings and resentments, his pain, his entrapment. I yearned for the time at school as much I resented it – a few hours' escape before returning to the insanity of home life. When my mother got a job at the doctor's surgery to earn extra money (and no doubt to get herself away) my father became still more resentful, hot on the heels of losing his own job.

One day my art teacher, Mrs Green, wanted to speak to me in private. My father had stormed drunkenly into the school and demanded to see her, wanting to know if I was a homosexual. I was thirteen years old. My art teacher, an Afro-haired Bohemian type with embroidered smocks, had told him that he should accept me for whatever I was – she must have thought she was doing the right thing. Taking me aside she asked me if there was anything I wanted to tell her about my home life, and that I could always come to her with my problems. Then she asked me if my father was an alcoholic or violent. Like so many abused children do, I clammed up, explaining that everything was just fine. But one day I flipped and ran crying from school. The PE masters chased me for what seemed like miles, caught me, and returned with me. 'Come on, boy, what's the matter?' They shouted, with that lack of sensitivity that only games masters can muster. I just cried. I didn't know where I was running to.

In many ways I blamed my mother. Why couldn't she divorce my father and let us get on with a normal life? After all, this wasn't a case of an occasional fight or family row: this was night after night after night, day in and day out. It was bound to affect me, to damage me. Incredibly, during this time my mother decided to take in a student to stay in the spare room. Perhaps she saw this as a way to force my father to curb his behaviour. The student's name was Claire – she was a lovely Irish girl sent to us, I thought, from heaven. In the beginning my father would moderate his behaviour when she was around, but eventually the alcohol won through. On one occasion he even burst into her room, threatening and shouting at her.

Soon afterwards she moved out, understandably, and went to the Trinity College Residential Hall near us in Horsforth. She was a fan of folk music and loved Paul McCartney and Simon and Garfunkel. During her short stay with us she brought new records into the house, and even took me to the occasional college concert. Music once again became my focus and refuge. I began to buy records with every bit of

money I could obtain. The first album I purchased was the soundtrack
to the stage musical *Hair*, because I loved the cover so much – a
picture of an Afro-haired man lit up by psychedelic electricity. I was
particularly taken by a song called 'Sodomy'. I played it wondering
what the words meant, sensing they were risqué; when I eventually
found out exactly what it was about I never played it again out loud
– but at every opportunity in private. I also seized on *Benefit* by
Jethro Tull, *Deep Purple in Rock, Led Zeppelin III* and *Fire and
Water* by Free. This was the time of progressive rock. The first single
I bought was 'Green Manalishi' by Fleetwood Mac, the second 'All
Right Now' by Free. The third was a strange little song by an odd
young man with corkscrewed hair and glitter on his cheeks: Marc
Bolan's 'Ride a White Swan'. I'd heard it one day on the John Peel
show, and I loved it more than anything I had ever heard before: it
was tinny, it was short, and the singer had a voice not unlike Larry
the Lamb, but something about it was very special – and had quite
an effect on my musical taste.

It was actually John Peel who helped me through the hard times –
with his evening shows and his Sunday-afternoon slot. I had rushed
out and bought the maxi picture single of 'Ride a White Swan' – the
first person in the school to do so – and from then on I followed
everything Marc Bolan did. When the record was a hit, I watched
him on *Top of the Pops*. He wore a kind of breastplate, and was
heavily made up with glitter on his cheeks. In honesty I was squirming, with an uncomfortable sensation in my stomach as my disapprov-
ing parents watched it with me. My father's stare was invested with
distaste. In its blurred sexuality, Marc Bolan's appearance was truly
shocking to this world, and this was the first time I'd seen anyone on
television flout such taboos. The same atmosphere was probably to
reoccur in so many other living rooms when I was to do the same
thing myself less than ten years later, the last thing in the world I'd
have imagined myself doing then. I became an obsessed fan, along
with my friends Jane Nicholson and Julie Stafford: we carried the
torch for Bolan between us. I was really the only male fan of Bolan's
at school – he was definitely a girl thing; most boys wouldn't dare
own up to liking this frail, glittering elf who shook his curly hair and
screwed up his face, stamping his feet when he sang. Slade were much
more of a lads' thing, but to me they were impostors, looking and
sounding ugly. Bolan's songs were about secret worlds with strange
magical creatures, full of sense in their surreal absurdity – you just
had to be able to look at things through his eyes.

T-Rex were regulars on John Peel's show, and it was John Peel I
had to thank for introducing me to a musical world, from the

accessible to thoroughly out-there experimental, and to find out more about this world I started buying music papers. A new one called *Sounds* had just come out; I remember buying the first issue because it had a free black-and-white poster of Jimmy Page. My head was filled with songs and singers, albums that I wanted to buy and concerts I longed to go to. Sadly, my dinner money would only stretch so far.

Every lunchtime at school I would sit and talk with my friends Jane and Julie about music and records. Whenever we got the chance we'd skip school to go back to Jane's house and blast out 'Lucky Man' by Emerson, Lake and Palmer. Our musical snobbery hadn't set in yet; music culture wasn't yet divided into the cool and the uncool. Later we'd divide the era into 'AB' and 'BB' – 'After Bowie/Bolan' and 'Before Bowie/Bolan'. 'BB' it was OK to have what would later be referred to as the old farts – the ELPs, the Yeses and the Tulls – in your collection. 'AB', of course, everyone would deny that they'd ever had these bands' albums. One of the seniors at school, John Sessions, started a record club – at lunchtimes, everyone would bring their favourite albums in and John would DJ. Favourites were The Who's *Live at Leeds*, ELP's first album, and a strange, sinister track called 'Killer' by Van de Graaf Generator, with Peter Hammill's demented voice veering precariously between sneer and opera, and truly disturbing in a way I'd never heard before.

I got into trouble when we sneaked some lager into the record club and stupidly left the cans behind. It wasn't long before they were traced to me, and I was placed on special report. I was also once taken to the headmaster for allegedly bringing drugs into school – someone had reported me. They were actually for my hay fever, but I do recall the unsympathetic head asking me, 'Have you ever tripped?'

When my teenage hormones started to go crazy, I broke out in the worst acne of all time. My face was a mass of spots, giving me a new name among my fellow pupils – Acne Carriage. My hair was slightly long, and my feather cut was always greasy. What's more, I began to wake up with a mess in my pyjamas that always followed a sexual dream. We had been taught about sex in the first year by our plain-speaking English teacher, Mrs Coles. She had described 'little boys' sticks' going into 'little girls' slots'; I had gone red and tried not to laugh. We had been told about wet dreams, but it was still a shock when they happened, and the pyjamas had to be sponged before my mother saw them. What was worse was that I went through a period of wetting the bed – I think partly out of fear of the fights and rows that still pervaded our family life, and partly for the comfort the warmth of the urine brought my unconscious body. I'm glad to say it was short-lived.

I seized on any opportunity to get out of the house as much as possible. I found a part-time job as a stable boy at a local riding school. I loved horses, much as I adored all animals; I watched TV's *Follyfoot* religiously. What's more, *Follyfoot* often used horses from the stables where I worked. I never actually got paid for cleaning the stables and polishing the saddlery, but was given riding lessons, and was even allowed to take out rides. At thirteen years old this was a dream come true, galloping across the fields and woods. I didn't let my allergies and asthma prevent me from spending my time at the stable; after all, my PE master hadn't allowed my asthma to preclude me from sports.

I was also beginning to be allowed to get away in the evenings – homework began to slip down the list of my parents' cares and concerns; no doubt they were relieved to have me out of the house. I joined a youth theatre group, where I learned about movement, dance, jazz and a touch of ballet, though I failed to develop any sort of coordination. I managed to get a series of small parts in the productions, but my stammer still prevented me from taking on substantial roles. However, I did secure a walk-on part in an American television production, set in Dickensian England. It was filmed at Kirkstall Abbey Museum, in its replica of a Victorian street, and I played a street urchin who thieved a wallet from a man's pocket.

Being allowed to stay out at night also meant I began to go to concerts – any I could. If I'd heard a band on John Peel, I wanted to see them in the flesh. I was lucky to live between Leeds and Bradford, for most of the big bands and artists stopped at either one or the other on their tours. Leeds University always had the best. I went to my first concert there.

One day Jane and Julie came to me with the news that T-Rex were to play Bradford's St George's Hall. We went straight after school to get tickets, and when the actual day came we skipped school early so that we could wait outside the stage door for Marc to arrive. Outside, touts were selling cheap posters and programmes – we had no idea they were bootlegs, reviled by the artist: to us they were simply mementoes we could afford. After waiting the longest time in the cold, listening to the sound of drums and bongos from the hall – Mickey Finn testing his sound – and just as we imagined that we'd missed Marc himself, a long black car drove up and he stepped out. I remember he was tiny, dressed in a red velvet jacket decorated with large cherries. I was in awe, unable to comprehend that he was actually there in person in front of me. He looked unhappy and swept past us, knocking aside the posters we proffered for signing. His famous corkscrew hair brushed past my face. I didn't care that we'd been snubbed. I had seen him close up, and in the flesh.

Spending evenings out, I at last began to feel like an individual, and started to be quite flamboyant in my dress. I had wanted to be a suedehead, and at one point was desperate for Sta-Prest trousers and a Crombie, complete with brolly and handkerchief – I believed they would make me the envy of the other boys at school, or at least their equal, and imbue me with masculinity. But all those clothes proved too expensive. I opted instead for the affordable hippie look: purple loons with flare-sleeved T-shirts, psychedelic cravats bought from Leeds Market or Lewis's. I cut darts out from my jeans and inserted starry material to give them a wider flare. I began to wear black flared cords to school and a black jumper, removing my blazer badge. This all-black look lasted to the end of my school days. When I was pulled up by a teacher, I would say that my parents couldn't afford new regulation school clothes. That my home life was not as it should be was general knowledge, together with the natural consequence that I was somewhat strange, so the teachers left me alone.

I became friends with another boy at school, Frank Catteraul, a mad Jethro Tull fan who revelled in being the 'school freak' and 'hippie', his hair longer than anyone else's. We'd roam the playground at lunchtime to shouts of 'There go the freaks!' We despised the others in return, and laughed to ourselves about them – we didn't feel anything in common with the rest of the school anyway. Though he could never understand my liking Bowie and Bolan, we were both intrigued by a new band we were reading about who mixed the Velvet Underground with sci-fi synthesizer sounds and fifties B-movie references: Roxy Music. The singer – a greasy, sleazy, leather-clad man called Bryan Ferry – fascinated me. Theirs was a name to be dropped, despite the fact they didn't even have a record out.

I still got pushed about and threatened from time to time, and the words of abuse remained constant – 'puff'/'bender'/'bummer'/'queer'/ 'weirdo'/'freak' – sometimes as a whisper, often as a shout, and occasionally in unison as several people would chant. They hurt far more than words should, and often I would cry in private. I learned as best I could to adapt, but I am still hurt as much now as I was then by personal jibes. My friends today tell me that I'm still in that school playground, battling to survive.

*

One day during the school holiday in 1972 my mother sat my sister and me down and told us the news that we had wanted to hear for years: she was divorcing my father. We could barely contain our joy. But it meant that we would have to move back to Southport to live with my grandparents, to leave behind my school and such friends as I'd made. Almost overnight we left. I was sad to go in many ways, as I was at least settled at Aireborough Grammar, but the relief of not having an abusive, violent, alcoholic father made everything else insignificant. Those last few months in Leeds had been hell; my father had got hold of my sister's and my savings accounts, and had spent all the money on alcohol: our savings, donated by our grandparents every Christmas or birthday, had been squandered away. Added to this, my mother had discovered my father had been having an affair with her best friend. That was the final straw.

For a while I tried to keep in contact with my old friends, whom I had left without time even to say goodbye, but it became increasingly difficult as I spent so much time trying to fit into my new school and environment. It was basically the same pattern as before, except that by now I was so hopelessly behind with my schoolwork that I was put down a year. When I discovered that if I didn't attend the first registration of a class no one would know I was absent, I never registered for quite a few. I found places to hide out and read, or spent extra time in the art room. I managed to gravitate towards other class outsiders, and made a few good friends.

Tim Winter was another boy who lived with a divorced mother, and he too found solace in T-Rex, David Bowie, Roxy Music – and the innovative Alice Cooper. I was first drawn to Tim after seeing him on the school bus proudly displaying his copy of Alice Cooper's *School's Out* under his arm (he told me he was wearing the 'Free Paper Panties' that came with it under his school uniform). Alice, who had performed on *Top of the Pops* brandishing a sword and dressed in black with running black-panda eye make-up, united all the school weirdos and disaffected youth – chiefly Tim and me. We spent nights round at Tim's, while his mother made cream cakes for us (not wise for youths with acne problems), playing records and dancing around the room.

Stuart Walton, a strangely androgynous boy, was the spitting image of Brian Eno. He shared our twisted, cynical view of the world. During our marathon record-playing sessions in Tim's bedroom we formed what could be called my very first band: Distorted Operetta. Tim played his Bontempi organ, while Stuart and I wrote lyrics and sang. We recorded songs on Tim's tape-to-tape machine, even managing to double-track. The songs were basically twenty-minute jam sessions, with Stuart and I writing typically school-poetry stuff about 'going insane at the end of the world'.

Sadly, though, we all fell out once I became friendly with a boy called Simon, a member of the notorious school gang. I had actually been introduced to Simon through Tim; we became friends through music – and also through several schoolboy sexual-discovery sessions. It was a helpful friendship: I was then accepted by the rougher members of the school. Formerly someone who was bullied, I felt I could now at last walk tall, but this friendship alienated me from my other friends, and a great deal of spiteful, vicious name-calling resulted. Laughing about it years later with Tim and Stuart, we decided that it was little more than a case of handbags at fifty paces: we were all class survivors. A competitiveness had always existed between us – who had the records first, who was the biggest fan of whichever band. But our tastes had also bonded us: at our school we were the first to discover Iggy Pop, Nico, the New York Dolls, Wayne County, Enó and Alice Cooper, while everyone else was still buying their Yes albums. We read the music papers and leaped at everything about Bowie or Lou Reed or anyone associated with them.

I grew my hair long, and sometimes put red streaks in it with Indian ink. I always wore black – and just a touch of eye make-up. I was treated with amusement by the teachers, and by now was written off academically. I had class battles with Mr Davies, the English teacher, and Mr Cook, the physics teacher, for being defiant and insolent – battles of wills which often ended with me being slapped or sent out. All my learning now took place outside school, where I digested books and watched endless movies. I was increasingly passionate about films: musicals, horror, thrillers – any movie, though I was particularly taken with horror at this time.

We were still living with my grandparents, and it must have been hard on them, living with a music-mad teen who was going off the rails. And my sister was now showing signs of waywardness herself. I also began thieving. My friends and I devised a way of stealing records from record shops. We'd enter with a few albums under our arms, making sure we were seen, but slip more albums in between those and leave quickly. In those days the records were left in the sleeves in the racks. Surprisingly, we never got caught, and my record collection expanded rapidly. I also stole pop posters – a local store had a blind spot by the poster rack, and I would spend a nerve-racking five minutes stuffing a David Bowie poster down my trouser leg.

I always went about in a T-shirt and flimsy jacket, whatever the weather: I'm sure it was this that contributed to my feeling strangely ill one day at school. I felt cold and dizzy, even nauseous. As the day progressed I felt worse and worse, soon vomiting, until finally I collapsed in a blackout. And it wasn't an act this time. I was rushed to hospital, where I was diagnosed with pneumonia and complications. I had developed pleurisy, my lungs filled with fluid. It took six weeks off school to get well enough to return – during which time school work was impossible. I was left susceptible to chest and lung infections for the rest of my life. Lying at home at my grandparents', listening to music, I began to notice changes in my grandfather's health too – he had become short-tempered and absent-minded, acquiring an obsession with switching TV channels over and over, unable to make a decision or relax. I know now that it was the early stage of Alzheimer's.

My mother bought a small house in Crowland Street, just below the gasworks, and we moved once again. A new man came into our lives, someone she'd known for a long time: Richard. He was the complete opposite of my father, thoughtful, and generous – at last, someone she deserved. The house was five minutes from school, and eventually I just went into morning and afternoon registration and then went home, often waiting behind the wall until my mother went to work.

At Christmas I was given an Afghan coat that smelt the whole house out but fulfilled my dream: I was a fully fledged hippie. I started painting my nails – just on one hand: black or purple – and wore eye make-up, with my hair way down my shoulders. At this time my mother was enjoying her new love, and as I was an unruly teenager there really was little she could do to change me. I went to visit my old friend Frank Catteraul a couple of times in Leeds – once for an overnight stay, when we went to a Roxy Music concert. It was their first show without Eno. We hated Bryan Ferry's new tuxedo and bow-tie image, and though I liked the *Stranded* album I felt that Eno had taken the music with him when he left the band.

On another occasion when I went up to see Frank he introduced me to a girl called Christine, a young hippie with long blonde hair – she turned out to be the sister of the girl he was seeing. His parents were away, and we spent a night at his house running around nude, even taking a naked walk down the local village street at three in the morning. Christine and I bought long, matching tapestry coats and wore glitter stars round our necks, and she became my girlfriend for a while. Sometimes she came to visit me in Southport with Frank, but my mother didn't approve of them at all. Odd that my mother didn't approve of a girl I was seeing: later she would have approved of any girl that came along!

I started going into Liverpool to see concerts – Lou Reed on his *Berlin* tour, Captain Beefheart, Cockney Rebel. One special day, David Bowie was at the Liverpool Empire. It wasn't easy being a Bowie fan at school, laying yourself open to taunts and even violent attacks. A year or two earlier he had appeared on television with his full make-up and orange hair; during a performance of 'Starman' on *Top of the Pops* he had put his arm around the lead guitarist Mick Ronson. Next day, all hell broke loose in the playground. Bowie was a *queer*, and if you liked him then you must be queer too – not such odd logic, perhaps. He had just released *Aladdin Sane* – performing in a one-legged, one-armed suit, with a gold circle on his forehead. He was taking it all as far as he could. When he split up with the Spiders (much to the dismay of Tim, Stuart and me, because we loved Ronson as much as Bowie), he went for a white-soul style. *Aladdin Sane* had thrilled us with its fantastic lyrics. And Bowie also, along with the great Alex Harvey, introduced us to a Belgian singer/ songwriter called Jacques Brel, who wrote about death and sex, whores and the gutter, and he too was to have a profound influence on my music.

The three of us set off for Liverpool that night on the train from Southport, silver streaks in our hair and make-up on our faces. It wasn't long before we got the attention of a couple of guys who came to sit beside us. They flirted and laughed, asking questions about 'sexuality'. Naturally, we remained coy and guarded, but laughed along with them, hoping that good humour would defuse a hostile situation. However, as the train pulled into Bootle station they stood up, produced an empty bottle, and brought it down on my head, causing me to crash to the floor. They then began laying into us with their fists. I wasn't hurt too much, but we all had bloody noses and heads.

That night at the concert, as Bowie went through his strobe routine with Mick Ronson, kneeling to perform fellatio on the guitar, I found myself climbing over the barrier and reaching up to the stage. I stood for a while, silver glitter paint and sweat running down my face as Bowie sang 'Rock 'n' Roll Suicide'. As he sang 'C'mon give me your hand', I reached up and he took my hand. I was touched by my God – 'Hail, hail the idol.'

By complete contrast, my friend Tim and I went to see another singer in Southport Floral Hall that same year. We walked into the sound check unhindered, and took a seat to watch Marc Bolan, now a little overweight, sit alone and cross-legged on the stage with an acoustic guitar. Nobody cared as people milled around the audito- rium – such lack of awe for this former pop god! Outside, a notice indicated that plenty of tickets remained unsold. Tim and I still had stars in our eyes, though, and watched, the realization of Marc's fall from grace only slowly dawning as he went through his motions.

I went through the motions, too – of doing my 'O' levels. I sat in silence, not able to answer any of the questions, filling sheets of paper with nonsense, practising my signature on them, so at least I wouldn't have the shame of handing in an empty paper. I eventually gained two 'O' levels – Art and English. The headmaster of King George V School called me to his office and announced that he was at a loss to know what I could do with my life. Perhaps, he suggested, I could get a job with the council. Refusing to take part in the end-of-year photo, I threw my books across the playground. The relief of leaving was enormous. For a sexually confused, academically disadvantaged, physically challenged child with a dysfunctional home life and a speech impediment, the miracle was that I had made it through at all. And I had even made a few friends in the process. It had to be up from here on. Didn't it?

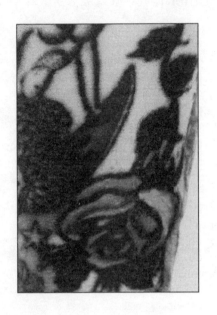

2

'Mother loves to be concerned'

As I ran across the school playing field away from my past, I felt happy and full of hope – perhaps more than any other time. I had just been accepted for a place on the General Art and Design course at Southport Art & Technical College. It was a dream come true, but it so nearly didn't happen at all. Despite having a promising portfolio, there was a mandatory requirement of five 'O' levels. Still, I knew that in exceptional circumstances this entry requirement could be waived, so it was with a mixture of trepidation and hope that I'd gone for my interview with Mr Bottomley, the principal, and two or three of the tutors. I loved art – the only thing, apart from music, that really meant anything to me. If I wasn't accepted I had no idea what else I could do. I had thought about drama college, but I knew that with my stammer I wouldn't stand a chance. At the interview I showed my portfolio, made up largely of work I'd done at home, and tried my best to convince the tutors that I deserved a place in the college. Luckily they were swayed by my work – or perhaps by my enthusiasm – and it was one of the best days of my life when I opened the letter of acceptance for the course. If I proved to be good enough, I could go on to a one-year foundation course.

I still had the summer before me, and some cash to earn, and I managed to get a job at Bevan's Fruit Drinks Factory. My grandfather knew the owner, a Mr Goddard, which must have helped. I started by working in the laboratory, assisting in the creation of fruit flavours. I say 'assisting', although the job involved little more than scrubbing the surfaces and cleaning the floors and test tubes – the rest of the time I stared dreamily out of the window. My mind was always elsewhere, and one day I managed to drop an entire tray of test tubes and Petri dishes, causing my demotion to the factory floor. Each day I would finish up a shade of orange or green or pink, depending on which particular barrel needed scraping. My mouth continually tasted sweet and sickly, and the regular blasts of preservative CO_2 sent me wheezing and rushing for the asthma inhaler.

But it was while working at Bevan's that I got a place in my first real band. Working alongside me in the factory was a tall, slim, would-be rock star called Robert, with the rugged looks of Roger Daltrey and corkscrewed hair like Marc Bolan's. He wore a gold earring, velvet jacket and tight jeans – showing off the biggest crotch I had ever seen. At lunchtimes he would sit cross-legged with a guitar, singing songs from *Cosmic Wheels*, the new Donovan album. I had just turned seventeen, had hair over my shoulders, and wore flared jeans, hippie T-shirts, love beads around my neck, and traces of eye-liner. Robert and I became good friends, hanging out together and on occasions listening to the new Bryan Ferry album or *Goat's Head Soup* by the Stones. Robert was in need of an adoring fan, and, well, I became that fan. One day he invited me to a rehearsal by his band, Andromeda. 'In fact,' he said, 'you can sing backing vocals if you like.' Just like that! I was so thrilled to be asked to be part of this god's band that I didn't give him a chance to change his mind. I rushed out and bought a microphone and a stand – a solid pneumatic stand with three feet, the same type I still use to this day for good luck.

I was immediately at ease with the rest of the guys, who didn't resent me joining – they too seemed to idolize Robert (who sang lead), doing whatever he said, hanging on his every philosophical word. The guitarist had a red Bowie-type haircut and called himself (surprisingly) Ziggy. Rehearsals took place every Sunday in an old poultry shed, ankle deep in chicken shit; the smell was unbearable. Yet it was with pride that I took my place at the back and doubled Robert's choruses, adding some tone-deaf ooohs and aaahs. I'd had no training in singing, but I loved it. I'd been in the school choir, occasionally taking solos, but that was about all. I did once shock the class at Aireborough Grammar by standing up in lessons (during a discussion about running away from home – something I knew about) and singing, unaccompanied, a version of the Beatles' 'She's Leaving Home'. When the song finished there was a stunned silence before the class burst into applause with a new respect for me – the hero, or the fool? A similar fearlessness allowed me to dance like an idiot in the aisles at concerts (back in those schooldays in Leeds) while my friends Jane and Julie slunk in their seats, pretending not to know me. Maybe singing and performing could be a way to make people respect me, admire and even – dare I have thought it? – *like* me.

Andromeda's set consisted of several Bowie songs, some Beatles and T-Rex, and a couple by Free and Bad Company – each member contributing their choices. As yet, I wasn't allowed that privilege. Besides, the excitement was so much for me that I'd lose my voice after a couple of numbers. (I didn't learn about technique until well into my professional career.) We played a couple of local gigs, me banging a tambourine at the back.

My chance to be up front came quite unexpectedly, as chances do. One day Robert stormed out after a temperamental argument. He announced that he was packing it all in, and left – his aura close behind. It was then that I was asked by the others if I would like to be the lead singer. I needed no persuasion – in fact, I felt like the character Eve in the 1950 film *All About Eve*, waiting quietly in the wings for my chance. A new guitarist, Steve, joined, and we began playing more local gigs.

Our set still comprised of covers – 'The Devil's Answer' by Atomic Rooster and Doors numbers joining the old favourites. I had moved on from T-Rex, feeling that *Zinc Alloy* was the last Bolan album that I really loved, and I felt betrayed by Bryan Ferry, who was moving further away from Eno with his covers albums. I still liked Bowie, though not enamoured of his new plastic-soul direction. I was now listening to American bands who sang about sex, drugs and death – the darker side of glam rock. I had actually discovered the Doors on holiday at my cousin Carol's home in Wales when I was twelve. She was older than me, and I found in her record collection an album called *Waiting for the Sun* with a song on it about sex and lizards entitled 'Not to Touch the Earth'. A pale Jim Morrison, dressed in black, was on the cover, and on the record he sang in a croon – eerily warm and yet at the same time deathly. His sound was sexual, and had awakened something in me. Now, five years later, I got to sing some of those songs. I would pretend to be Morrison or Bowie, actually wanting to be everybody – anybody so long as it wasn't me.

For our first gig I wore my purple satin loons and a panne-velvet flare-sleeved shirt, with black nail varnish and silver eye make-up. The sparse audience was gobsmacked, especially when I jumped from the stage and kicked my mike stand across the floor. We rehearsed like crazy, and began to get a small circle of friends who always came to see us, including a stocky Hell's Angel called Glen. He became friends with me, and looked out for my well-being. I spent afternoons round at his flat listening to Hawkwind and heavy metal, drinking cans of lager and smoking joints beneath a Stars and Stripes flag. I thought I was in *Easy Rider*, and revelled in the role.

Alcohol and joints. The first joint was the scariest – should I? shouldn't I? Would it make me an addict? What if I was sick? What if I became crazed? I took a drag and inhaled, coughed, and tried again. Nothing. Another drag. Then, whoooaaaa! It was the beginning.

*

The summer passed slowly, as only teenage summers can, eager anticipation slowing time down. I couldn't wait to get to art college and indulge all my Bohemian fantasies, whims, pretensions and desires to my heart's content and with licence. September arrived. I wanted to make an impression on my first day, so turned up as 'freaky' and 'arty' as possible in my Afghan coat and long scarves, clad all in black. The truth was I was as nervous as hell, feeling fearful, lost and alone. I looked for someone to tag on to, and found another boy from King George, Huw Feather – a large, stocky Jewish boy with a theatrical flair who wore the biggest pair of platform shoes in the world. He'd bought them from Clobber in Southport! Huw was stylish and well versed in all the latest trends, read *Vogue, Harpers* and all the glossy design magazines, collected comics and art deco, and seemed to know about everything that I considered to be worth knowing about. While we had been at the same school, we hadn't really been in the same circles. Huw remembers me selling him a James Taylor album; I remember him as one of the individuals who were occasionally mean to me. Although Huw was doing the foundation course and I merely General Art and Design, we shared a love of theatre, camp and all things outrageous. But Huw's musical tastes were in complete contrast to mine: the Pointer Sisters, Labelle and American soul. Nonetheless, this friendship was that port in a storm.

The most startling surprise for me was how different the tutors at the art college were from those at school. They rarely if ever talked down to you. I found myself actually wanting to hear what they had to say! Sue Halliwell was a vivacious blonde with a great sense of humour and a flirty smile. Sue could chat and joke with you (she even loved to share a drink and camp around), but woe betide the student who didn't work. Work you had to, or you were out. Most of the other boys in the class fancied her like mad, but I just loved to be outrageous with her, and once drove along good old Lord Street standing up in the back of her sports car smoking a joint, a red feather boa flying in the wind. Years later Granada Television made a documentary about me and I recreated that very scene – except this time driving down the beach, and with the joint no more than a giant rolled-up piece of paper (honestly).

Then there was Max Eden. Max was the epitome of the brilliant/ mad/genius artist. With a shock of grey hair and a dashing moustache, he had been friends with the great expressionists, and a pupil at one time of Dali. Max often thrilled us with stories of his adventures in the art world. Everybody hero-worshipped him. Years later my cousin Stephen, a working artist and painter himself, attended the same college and Max was still there, as inspiring as ever. Between Sue and

Max, I came to learn so much about art, and under their guidance my own work began to improve and develop.

My determination at college (I so wanted to do that foundation year) forced me to abandon the band. I don't remember clearly how it ended, but enthusiasm waned, as did the rehearsals. My days became filled with art classes and my nights with revelling in Southport's Bohemian underbelly. After college I headed to the pub with my colleagues, discussing the merits of such and such, seeing how many barley wines we could consume before collapsing. And, it being art college, my drinking drifted into lunchtimes, and I sometimes returned to classes in the afternoon intoxicated, occasionally stoned, and then more often than not both. I still wasn't necessarily a *happy* person though: happiness is a trait like many others – to a degree it must be learned.

I became friendly with a girl called Carol, who wore thick black eye make-up like the silent-film vamp Theda Bara, an Indian tilak, stars all over her face, turbans and Chinese gowns. Her face was always deathly pale, giving her the appearance of being on drugs, and more often than not she *had* been dabbling. She talked in a hippy, trippy, distant manner, a million miles from reality, staggering into class trying hard not to laugh. We drank, smoked and fell about together, and spent hours in the storage cupboard fumbling with each other, eventually emerging red-faced and covered in black lipstick.

Having already discovered hash, I bought little bits whenever I could. Soon afterwards I progressed on to pills. A hippy boy invited me to a party at his house one evening, and handed me a white Mandrax tablet. 'Here,' he said, 'try this.' I swallowed the pill, lay on the sofa, and watched the light bulb on the ceiling travel round and round in ever-decreasing circles. Suddenly I felt an overwhelming nausea and ran out to the front lawn, where I vomited in the cold night air. It didn't put me off, and the next time I simply tried not to mix too much alcohol with whatever the drug was. Can you believe that I would be so reckless after all I had witnessed with my own father and his chronic addiction? But no one knew then that addiction is passed on through generations. Even if I had known, what difference would it have made? I was seventeen, just growing up, and experimenting as teenagers do. I didn't have a job, and thought myself free of responsibilities. I was making new discoveries about myself and the place in which I lived – that sunny Southport could be seedy Southport, with its underbelly of cheapness and trashiness behind the conversative façade, the veneer of respectability disguising a corrupt core.

During that summer before going to art college, I spent afternoons down on Southport beach, fascinated by a particular area just off the Birkdale entrance. In the sand hills, where a maze of gorse bushes and long grass grew, it was apparent that certain activities went on. I was initially mystified as to why so many men stood about in the dunes or around the bushes, or lay about in the long grass. They seemed to be standing guard, watching, waiting, anticipating. It didn't take me too long to put two and two together: it was a meeting area for homosexuals – and it fascinated me. Suddenly I saw the world through different eyes – things that most people would pass by and fail to notice I could now see. Men looking for other men; boys looking for other boys. Later I told Huw about this area, and we laughed and joked, for ever after referring to it as 'fairyland'. If you walked around the area you would occasionally see sexual acts taking place, or watch other people lying flat in the grass, spying on others' sexual activity. I also learned about cottaging: men cruising and picking up other men in public toilets – a pastime that was extremely common in Southport.

In time I found out that Southport had gay bars too – or, more accurately, bars frequented by gays. It even had a small gay club (though it was very much a case of 'Knock three times and ask for Blanche'), which I learned about from an eighteen-year-old boy with a bleach-blond bouffant who called himself Vicky. I'd met him one day on the beach. Furthermore, I discovered that Southport had a healthy swingers scene. This revelation came from a hairdresser called Philip – an individual who revelled in the fact (although whether it was a fact I was dubious) that he was bisexual. At this stage I too thought myself bisexual, as I'd had experiences with both sexes. In all honesty, I wasn't that sure of the boundaries of my sexuality at all.

Philip was a camp, moustached, flamboyant individual. He dressed creatively in outré suits, and decorated his flat in browns and creams – the colours of 1975. It was Philip who introduced me to American disco music for the first time. I must admit I wasn't instantly taken by it, but several tracks became important – 'In the Bush' by Musique and 'Spacer' by Sheila B. Devotion, as well as 'Let's All Chant' by the Michael Zager Band. The disco bug would hit me much harder later on. But, more interestingly then, it was Philip who tried to introduce me to the world of 'swinging' – taking me to meet a married middle-aged couple (two of his clients) with whom he took part in fun and games. While I knew their intentions and thought it all very interesting, I was turned off by the wife, who looked like Beverley from *Abigail's Party*, and the man was too letchy and leery, resembling Bob from the film *Rita, Sue and Bob Too*. On that occasion Philip just cut their hair and we left.

I couldn't actually imagine camp Philip doing anything other than their hair with either of them. But he told me he also participated in threesomes with gay couples, and once I let curiosity get the better of me and I accompanied Philip to meet a couple. Needless to say it was a disaster. Again, I just didn't fancy any of them. That Philip was a friend also put me off – as did the suspicion that he'd relay all the sordid details to others later on. Even after all these years I've never been one for threesomes, the politics of them too complex for my liking – inevitably someone ends up making the tea, and knowing my luck it would be me. On another occasion Philip took me to a gay club in Preston. This was the first time I'd ever visited a real one, but I felt totally underwhelmed by the whole thing. Philip seemed to be queen of the ball, but I just felt like a wallflower – it wasn't my scene at all.

Another of my close friends during my first art-college year was Roger Cocker. Roger was one of the best looking guys in the college, the archetypal sports-jock type. He was straight, but for a while we were inseparable. We made a strange couple: Roger with his hunky porn-star looks, flirting with Sue Halliwell; me with a Southport version of the seventies 'look'. One day I had gone into a hairdresser's near the college on the spur of the moment and had my hair cut off. The hairdresser who undertook this task was Michael – the campest, most outrageous person I had yet met. (Philip did have a masculine side to his nature, albeit somewhat limited. But Michael completely flaunted his being 'different' with a red wedge haircut, and dressed head to foot in Yves Saint-Laurent.) He chopped off my locks and replaced them with a severe wedge cut, dyed blonde: I became an androgynous soul boy. I loved recreating and reinventing myself. This was the first time I'd ever properly dyed my hair, and from that day on it was never to know its natural colour again. I walked into the college and stunned everyone.

The wedge itself proved to be just a little outré for me to carry off, so my sister – a budding hairdresser herself – cut it back to a blond crop, making me look fourteen once again. Michael was livid the next time I saw him – I'd destroyed his art – and it was not until I visited him at home that he forgave me. He lived with his mother, who made tea while he showed off the contents of his designer wardrobe. It was the first time I realized there was importance attached to designer names in fashion, and that they could up your status. Soon the hippy clothes were replaced by more toned-down jeans, tank tops and trainers. I got myself a Saturday job in His 'n' Hers: though not as fashionable a boutique as Clobber, it still sold some trendy clothes by 'well-known manufacturers', plus the odd embroidered kaftan. The owner was a formidable elderly Jewish woman called Sylvia, with rock-hard lacquered hair. She constantly smoked a cigar, and as a result the clothes stank of smoke, but she puffed away regardless, never smiling, making sure that I didn't let anyone leave the shop without buying something – she virtually held the customers at gunpoint. She had no sense of humour whatsoever, and at lunchtimes munched constantly on cream-cheese bagels.

Actually, she must have liked me, because she took me (during the college break) to work in her Blackpool shop. I loved it, because at lunchtimes I could try all the rides at the Pleasure Beach, going time after time on the roller coaster. I must admit I hated the car journey each day, when I tried desperately to make conversation, but I endured it, mainly because I was making extra money under the counter. Looking back, I can't believe she didn't have an inkling that I had a neat sideline in fiddling, yet she said nothing. She had so many piles of clothes that she didn't miss the odd pair of jeans that were sold with no receipt, so I would pocket the money, or slip another odd item of clothing into my bag. Once when she left me on my own I didn't hand out a receipt all day! I was terrified that someone might bring something back. I soothed my conscience by citing to myself the strain involved in working with Sylvia, and for such low pay; but eventually the whole set-up got to me and I left.

I found another job at Southport Fairground. When Roger found himself a café job, I managed to get a job nearby, first on the bingo stall, then even nearer, on the Hook-a-Duck. I loved the fairground's gaudy awnings, candyfloss smell, rickety old rides and colourful characters, who were always very kind to me even though I was hopeless with the bingo. It felt good to earn my own money to spend on the latest records, or to enable me to hang out in the evening at one of the coffee bars at Southport Art Centre. The crowd from art college would meet at the El Cabala (known as the Elk), Mellors or the Covered Wagon. The Covered Wagon was the most popular, because it had a jukebox with the latest selection of records. When we weren't in a coffee bar, it was the pub – the Scaresbrick Hotel bar – or else any of a number of student parties, all an excuse to drink cheap alcohol, take cheap drugs and try to have sex with someone. Some things never change.

*

Mercifully I made it to the second year, and I hoped that this would pave the way for a BA course. But I was realistic. I knew I didn't have the required qualifications, and Barry Cox, one of my main tutors, gave me no illusion about getting them. In fact, it seemed to me that he didn't like me one bit, and felt I was there by some sort of default. In a way, his coolness was a good thing: I was able to prepare for the consequences of not being accepted. I considered drama school instead, and prepared myself despite my stammer, by learning a speech from the play *Marat/Sade*. I had seen the film version by Peter Brook, starring Glenda Jackson, and loved the form of theatre it embraced. Luckily for the world, I was never going to have to recite it.

Even though I was learning all the basic skills for going off the rails (of course I thought I was fine), I still managed to do some interesting work, thanks to the guidance of Sue Halliwell, Max Eden and my ceramics teacher, Carol Wyndam. I liked exploring organic shapes, but I also started to be interested in performance art, working on a number of strange pieces – one of which Max Eden was to comment on years later in that Granada TV documentary. I was apparently trapped in an invisible box and struggling to escape, but the box wouldn't let me out; it kept shrinking, suffocating me. It was a crude and clichéd mime performance, but Max remembered it and thought it was definitely an allegory for something that was happening in my life. In some ways the box was me, and I was my anger and rage, bursting to escape. All right, no need to comment, for those of you who didn't skip Chapter 1.

I made twisted ceramics of root people and organic cages that my mother, bless her, still proudly displays. I compiled a scrapbook full of pictures of clowns and pale models with Biba lips and eyes, vampy film stars, androgynous boys, and the performance artist Lindsey Kemp (who was canonized by David Bowie, and later Kate Bush). I loved Lindsey Kemp's interpretation of Jean Genet's *Our Lady of the Flowers* and his collaborations with Ballet Rambert. He has a lot to answer for in encouraging dreadful mime artists in leotards like me, but I adored him.

The London shop Biba was still all the rage, and Huw and I longed to visit London so we could go to it. I had read that the New York Dolls, whom I loved, had even played there. It sounded like a hallowed shrine to Bohemian glam, glitter and decadence. Then my chance came.

The college organized a trip to London to see the galleries and the theatres. Huw and I put Biba high on our list of these cultural venues – Huw was keen to collect as much Biba memorabilia as possible, as we had just read that it was about to move from its site in Kensington. It was closed the day we went. So we went to see *The Rocky Horror Show*, at its regular venue on the Kings Road, and it became our latest obsession: genuinely new, alternative and outrageous. Its

leather-jacketed transsexual cartoon style seemed to epitomize a gay
subculture. Now, of course, Jerry Springer brings transsexuals bound-
ing into our living rooms, and all forms of transgenders have become
part of the media mainstream. But at that time transexuality and
transvestism were still mystical terms.

Now *The Rocky Horror Show* itself is fodder for tourists who
want to throw on some suspenders for an evening – it all seems so
much sadder when no longer outrageous. But there wasn't much
access to transgenders and drag in Southport. We had read with
fascination about the Warhol films, but most of us hadn't seen them.
I had also read about a fat American drag star called Divine (who
apparently ate dog shit). To me, all these people were on the fringes
of society, as I felt I was. The issue wasn't just about transgenderism
or violence or eating dog shit – it was about shocking society, people,
our parents: shocking them into hearing that we had voices, that,
whoever we were, we were people who should be listened to. Quite
what we wanted to say we hadn't yet worked out, but that was beside
the point.

During the London trip we were staying in a seedy hotel in Earls
Court, and one night went out to explore. It all seemed pleasantly
seedy. Huw and I entered a dark, smoky bar. It had dim red lighting,
and all around stood rough-looking men in denim and leather jackets.
I remember commenting that it looked too rough – that it must be a
bikers' pub – and we turned and left. Little did we know that it was
London's oldest and most famous gay leather pub. At seventeen my
innocence was akin to vulnerability, and the sooner it was gone the
better. Years later when I lived in Earls Court in a cramped flat I
rediscovered the Coleherne for a second time, but saw it through
much more jaded eyes.

*

Back in Southport, I was not getting on with my mother at all. She
had remarried and moved to a more pleasant house, where she had
given birth to a baby girl, my sister Sarah. Though I liked my new
stepfather, Richard – a complete contrast to my own father – as an
eighteen-year-old I resented anyone telling me what to do. I felt my
mother tried to control my life, and I would argue and fight against
her at every opportunity. The more she interfered, the more I resented
it. Looking back, I don't blame her – she was, after all, just trying to
be a mother, trying to make a new life for herself, and I was
troublesome and unappreciative. My sister had also become wayward
to say the least, and, though better adjusted than me, she too had her

moments and problems. To my mother I was also no doubt showing all the signs of becoming an unpleasant reminder of my father. I answered her back at every opportunity, and she in turn nagged me. I had stepped into my father's shoes, and strangely found that they fitted.

I had inherited my father's temperament. I had a rage, an anger, that would boil up inside me. It was a form of self-protection, and once ignited I was unable to control it. One incident remains particularly clear. A fellow student on the foundation course, Steve Battershill, started a drama group, which I duly joined. We were to put on a play at Southport Art Centre, *The Sport of My Mad Mother* by Anne Jellicoe. The play – a strong, confrontational piece – centres around a group of disillusioned teenagers in the fifties. I didn't have a big speaking part: my character was a troubled rocker. But part of what I had to do was supply a live soundtrack to the play. Along with Roger, I built a percussion set, made up of pieces of metal, wood and battered instruments which we would use to punctuate scenes and actions. As the play progressed the sounds became more aggressive, until eventually my character exploded in a violent rage, smashing up the percussion and the stage set. When I worked myself up to this I felt myself losing control, becoming so explosive and extreme in my violence and my smashing up the stage that the audience were stunned into silence. Afterwards my mother and my dear grandmother, who must have been baffled by the performance, were visibly shocked and said very little – obviously feeling more than a little uncomfortable that my public display of rage went just a touch further than acting.

Other problems were beginning to manifest themselves, too. At this time I'd begun to get a taste for spending way above my means. I'd already started to flirt with alcohol and drugs, and I was learning that sex (already confused with love in my mind) could fill my emotional void for short periods, giving a false feeling of high esteem. But now I discovered that, momentarily at least, another sort of fulfilment and euphoria was created, by shopping. New clothes would do the job for a couple of days; I would also have to buy at least two or three new albums every week to stem the craving. Nothing gave me a buzz more than buying new records – music that I could lock myself away with for hours on end in my tiny bedroom. But there was never enough money to fill my shopping needs, so I began to borrow. Then I began to steal. Soon I found myself in a deep well from which I could find no way out.

Steve Battershill also set up a students' union at the college and, in a moment of utter madness I still cannot fathom, made me treasurer. Of all the people he could have chosen! I was to take charge of all the subscriptions, which were kept in a biscuit tin. When money was needed to pay for a band at the college party, for example, Steve would call upon me and ask for it. Unfortunately, by the time he came to need the money (by then about £300) it had all gone. I had spent it. It had started innocently enough, borrowing a little for the occasional packet of cigarettes or a few drinks. Then a bit more (I was smoking about thirty a day at this point). Then just enough for a couple of new albums, and maybe a night out at a club or a visit to the cinema. I had every intention of paying it back, but soon I passed the point of no return. Every day I was racked with guilt and worry, knowing that eventually Steve would ask for the money.

The anxiety made me ill. I couldn't sleep, and lost weight. So I decided to sign on and claim unemployment benefit in an attempt to pay the money back out of my Giro. I had to pretend to the authorities that I wasn't a student at all but a recent school leaver looking for work. I filled in all the forms, undertook the interview, and waited for the cheque. When it came I was in a state of bliss. How could it have been so easy? But, instead of using the money to put towards the depleted union fund, I went out and spent that too. Every Tuesday, when the Giro was due, I lingered around home, intercepting the postman before he got to the door, to prevent my prying mother finding out. Then one Tuesday morning the postman was late. My mother caught me as he handed me the brown envelope at the gate; she demanded to know what it was. All hell broke loose. I shouted into the face of my stepfather, eventually provoking him into giving me a black eye. I ran away in tears, vowing never to return, and stayed on Steve Battershill's floor for a week. I told him about the money and he was very understanding, promising not to tell anyone and giving me the chance to pay it back. I was terrified of the shame if anyone found out. I eventually returned home and apologized, but there remained a tense and frosty air.

Then one day at college something happened that made me finally snap, causing unpleasant and serious consequences which far over-shadowed the student-union-fund embezzlement. I had by now become unhealthily attached to Roger (the college hunk), and hated the thought of him having other friends. Roger was very understand-ing – he was such a pleasant guy – but I'm sure it all got too much for him. I had also become friendly with an American girl called Colony, spending evenings around at her house, laughing and drink-ing, playing music and watching television. One day in college, Roger told me that he'd been seeing Colony on the side, and that every evening, after I'd gone home, they had been intimate. I felt betrayed by my friends, made into a fool, the idiot once more. The fuse was lit, and all the troubles of the past ten years flashed through my mind – the moves, the rows, the schools, the times I'd cried, felt isolated, been ridiculed, the struggle with learning, the name-calling – all flying around and around like a tornado, clouding my mind, my reason, and all ignited by absurd jealousy. Of course it was not Roger's fault – in fact it really had little to do with him at all. This was about me – the writhing trouble inside. I felt that I had no one to turn to, that I was alone, and it was my fault. A blackness descended over me.

Shortly after Roger left, I became rooted to the spot, my fists clenched, my face drained, unable to see or hear anything. Then I walked towards the wall and began to bang my head against it, faster and harder, again and again. I saw my head as an egg, and all I wanted was to crack it open and let all the troubles spill out over the floor. I felt my skin break and a welt forming, then I turned and walked towards the balcony overlooking the stairs and climbed over. I felt numb, my body on automatic. I didn't look down; I just started to go limp, ready to fall to the marble floor below. The voice in my head was telling me to jump.

Suddenly arms grabbed me and pulled me back to safety. I crumpled up and started crying, first quietly and then hysterically, louder and louder, shrieking. I was sat down and given a cup of tea. The police had been called – the head of the college was obliged to call them after a suicide attempt. In confusion, I was driven home to my waiting family.

My mother immediately made an appointment to visit a doctor, as I psychotically paced up and down insisting that I was fine. Eventually I was driven to the surgery, where a pale-faced elderly man quietly pulled a curtain around me. What happened next still remains very unclear. I remember that two large men came into the room and held me down on the bed while the doctor injected me with a sedative. The next thing I remember was being taken in an ambulance to a hospital in Ormskirk, terrified, feeling I had been duped. All the while I was screaming and fighting, shouting at my mother, whom I felt had betrayed me – she was helpless, I know now. I had broken the law by attempting suicide, and was deemed a threat to myself and others (I can't quite work that one out). Now the law had taken over. I was sectioned. On arrival my trousers were pulled down and I was injected once again, then everything went black.

The next day I was awakened by a nurse, who handed me a plastic tumbler and some vile-tasting tablets, standing over me to ensure that I swallowed them. The medication had the effect of keeping me awake, yet making me unable to function constructively (or destructively). I felt in a numbed, agitated state. The pills made it difficult to concentrate, or even to watch TV or listen to the radio for long – but in this environment it was also impossible to sit in a corner and keep yourself to yourself. I wandered in an aimless circle round and round the ward. It dawned on me that I was in a high-security hospital and my companions were manic depressives, schizophrenics and even psychopaths, as one girl from the next wing proudly proclaimed (we mixed at mealtimes) as she showed me her badly scarred wrists. The pills were administered twice a day to maintain the blanket of grey fog.

I was eventually taken to see the visiting psychiatrist, who informed me that I had had a nervous breakdown and that I was depressed. Hey, you don't say! I told him that I felt fine now and wanted to go home.

'Of course you do,' he said in a calm, patronizing voice. 'But I'm afraid you are not well enough yet. Let's see how you are next week.'

'No,' I explained, 'you don't understand. I shouldn't be here. I'm fine now, and I want to go home.'

'Of course you do,' he cooed, his face devoid of emotion. 'We'll see how you are in a week or two.'

'No, no, please.' I began to panic.

'You see how easily you are getting agitated,' he explained. 'That proves you're ill.'

I was led back towards the ward, getting increasingly irate as release seemed further away than ever. Maybe, I thought, I might never get out. I knew that I had to prove to them that I could be a good machine. A calm, obedient, good machine.

It turned out that I would remain there for four more weeks. The longest weeks imaginable – hours that seemed like days that seemed to never end. Friends came to visit, but I was usually too out to respond, dosed up on tranquillizers, incapable of holding up a conversation. I couldn't even hold up a cigarette! Nevertheless, Huw and the others who came to see me cheered me up immensely, even though many of them were embarrassed that I'd flipped out and ended up in there. I suspected that they had found out about the money and blamed that for my suicide attempt. The worst of it was when the family visited, maintaining the pretence that nothing happened, and everything was normal! Mother talking about the weather, the house, the garden, all the while arranging and rearranging the flowers she'd brought, unable to relax, commenting on how nice the nurses seemed, or how young the doctors were.

Yet there were also whispers, accusations that Roger was the catalyst that had caused this disaster, accusations that *he* was responsible for me being in Ormskirk Mental Hospital. My family obviously blamed him. But he was the innocent party in all this. Blame anyone or anything so long as you don't have to look inwards.

My incarceration meant I missed my audition for drama school – the one where I was to perform the piece from *Marat/Sade*: a play set in a lunatic asylum. It was too ironic. One day I was allowed to shuffle around the garden in my slippers. Then another day I was allowed to go to the shop. Eventually I was allowed to go home. My family and I left the hospital in silence. It must have been hard for my grandparents. I don't know if they understood things clearly – or was it that they understood too much?

Upon arriving home I immediately threw away all the pills I had been given, and then the same evening suffered an anxiety attack. It took me a few weeks to settle back into college. Roger had been warned to stay away from me, but I told him it wasn't his fault. It transpired of course that things could never be as they once were, which perhaps was for the best.

*

I threw myself into work. I wanted to go more in a performance-art direction, and I went to see as much theatre and performance as I could. Southport Art Centre played host to many dance and theatre companies, and I saw them all. One of the companies was called Clown Cavalcade – a troupe of clowns putting on an old-style *commedia dell'arte* show called *Harlequinade*. I met them after the performance and spent all the time I could in their company, listening to their stories and anecdotes, learning about the history of clowning. I became friends with the troupe, though I had ulterior motives in befriending Chris, a tall, blond young man who played the white-faced sad clown. But other members of the troupe had ulterior motives too: myself, a seventeen-year-old blond youth. There were many hints and suggestions as they attempted to draw me into their coterie; I liked their attention. I suppose I encouraged them.

From as early as my first viewings of *Batman* on TV, I'd been fascinated by the idea of masks and assumed identities which seemed to carry special meaning. *Batman* thrilled me. Too young to appreciate it as a triumph in camp, I was transfixed by its clown-like villains – the Riddler and the Joker. But for me theatrical clowns, as opposed to circus clowns, were always preferable. I loved the white-faced, beautiful Harlequins, the Augustes with their spangly outfits that never seemed to be comical at all. I wished I could hide behind a face of white pan-stick make-up and wear glittering outfits.

Years later, I became one such clown, as I stood on stage or in a television show in the spotlight, my clothes sparkling and my make-up just a little too pale – a ghost of all those past yearnings, fearful of revealing who I really was. It's a great tradition, and there is something decadent and perverse in the face of a clown. Fellini tapped into this sensibility, as does Joel Grey's character in *Cabaret*, leering into camera, as lewd and fearsome as those early images in *Batman*. The face as a mask, a complicit cloak to disguise our vulnerability.

Huw and I made ourselves up as clowns for a series of photos – me in white face and Huw as a tramp. We even dared to make an appearance at a charity event, where we worked a little performance: any excuse to dress up and be exhibitionists. I loved the fact I could use make-up, take on a new character. Make-up, disguises, distortions, lies.

I also found myself a new part-time job at Southport Theatre. It was a chance to pay back some of the money I'd taken from the union, but it was also an opportunity to work backstage in the theatre, to see the workings and the secrets, to mix with theatrical people. I loved the way it all functioned like a well-oiled machine – if you were late with one of the cues, everything fell apart and the rhythm of the show was lost. The theatre was starting its season with the pantomime *Jack and the Beanstalk*, and was looking for stage-hands to fetch, carry, climb ropes and put up props. All right, it was only a pantomime, but it taught me a type of discipline. There were so many colourful characters in the show. An old northern comedian played the dame; he kept his teeth in a glass in the dressing room, wore drag on stage and occasionally off, and molested the young male stagehands whenever possible. Many of the cast were gay, and of the type that indulged in debauchery whenever and wherever possible.

Once, at an after-show party, it was my turn to be harassed. A northern panto impresario slobbered all over me, cornering me in the toilets. On that occasion I didn't succumb. There was also a duo variety act who claimed to be brothers but were obviously boyfriends; it was rumoured they liked to lure young boys to their caravan and smother them with baked beans. Don't ask! One of the cast who definitely wasn't gay was the Irish comedian Tom O'Connor, the show's star. When it quickly became obvious that I was no good at lifting and climbing ropes, I was promoted (or demoted) to fetch and carry for Mr O'Connor. I was to get his drinks and fags for the interval. Tom was charming and funny, seeming a little bemused by the queer goings-on.

Eventually I was promoted to follow spot, and started working the odd afternoon as well as evenings, even though it meant occasionally missing college. In all honesty I never really improved my theatre work, unable as I was to tell my left hand from my right, missing cues, lighting the wrong entrances and causing the actors to flounce around, miss their cues or dramatically trip over a prop.

It was during this time that I met someone rather special. Ken Barrow, a six foot five actor in his late thirties, played the Giant, bedecked in stackheels. Ken first noticed me reading Jean Genet's *Our Lady of the Flowers*, and decided then and there to take me under his tutelage. To me he seemed to know everything about literature, theatre and films – it was the classic scenario of the older intellectual adopting the impressionable youth. He was very handsome, with a fur coat and moustache, and seemed to me to be so worldly. I loved to spend time with him: he six foot five and me five foot six – what a pair we must have made! You couldn't have made it up. When Ken told me *it* wouldn't hurt, he lied; it did. That was the first time, with anyone – and damn near the last.

A little later I went to visit him at his small flat in Hampstead, where he showed me his scrapbook and photo albums. He took me to see a beautiful film, *Les Enfants du Paradis* – the cinema classic featuring a mime artist played by the handsome Jean-Louis Barrault. This was the first time I had sat down and watched a three-hour black-and-white foreign film (albeit with subtitles), let alone one with such staged stylization. It thrilled me. I became increasingly interested in films, and yearned to see more like *Les Enfants du Paradis*. But I lost contact with Ken soon afterwards.

Almost ten years later, in the London club Heaven, I heard a familiar voice say, 'Marc, is that you?' I turned round, and there was an elderly-looking man with grey hair and beard looking down at me. He stood out from the crowd in a pair of leather chaps and nothing but a black G-string underneath, his bare bottom hanging out and a red handkerchief protruding from his belt. I barely recognized Ken – he had changed so dramatically – but it was extraordinary to see him. He told me how special I had been, and in turn I told him what an important influence he had been on my life. A couple of years after that occasion I met him on a gay march; by this time his appearance had been ravaged by AIDS, the signs of his suffering quite plain. Gone was the elegant, handsome panto giant, although I knew he was still there somewhere. The next time I heard of Ken was in 1985, when I learnt he had died, and that he would have loved to have had me sing at his funeral. In all honesty I don't think I would have been able to sing for him, as the sadness of it would have been too difficult to bear.

*

When the theatre season ended, the job came to a close and I was brought back from my circus world of white-faced clowns and panto giants to the hard work of my final term. I also started to listen to music away from pop and rock. I started to collect Jacques Brel and French *chanson*, film and show soundtracks. I became curious about a development I was reading about in the music papers – a new music movement heralded by the Sex Pistols. The movement was punk. It was 1976, and I was nineteen years old. This new movement was about to change all our lives, to blow musical tastes apart, and make me throw out much of my old record collection. It was also time to move away and start a life of my own. I applied to Leeds Polytechnic's art department, which had a BA Fine Arts course that had a reputation as the country's best for performance art – the avenue I wanted to pursue. In addition to this, Leeds had positive memories as a place where I had done a great deal of growing up. It seemed like a home already.

However, I didn't feel I had a hope in hell of getting a place on the course: standards were high, and there were few places to be had. Taking my interview were Jeff Nuttall, a performance artist of reputation and author of a book in the sixties called *Bomb Culture*, and Jeff Teasdale, a northern painter who revelled in bad language and equally bad behaviour. These were two individuals who would have little patience with time-wasters. God only knows how I got through the interview – they casually skimmed through my portfolio of paintings and drawings, dismissing them, even laughing a little. Thankfully it was me as a performance artist they were interested in. They asked me to mime some situations for them, so, red-faced and sweating, I obliged. Of course they wanted to see how fearless I was and how I could face up to the cynical scrutiny of two successful artists who had done it all. I talked my way through the interview like my life depended on it. My life *did* depend on it – all my hopes were resting on this place, and if I'd known then just how it would change my life I probably wouldn't have made it through.

I returned to Southport unsure of my performance. I knew I didn't have the qualifications normally required, so I knew how much rested on the interview. But a couple of long weeks later I received the letter I had been waiting for.

I was stunned.

I had been accepted. I could finally be me and do what I wanted to do, what I loved doing. Everything was mapped out for me for three years. Little did I know I was to be catapulted to a far higher stratosphere – one that even I could never have dared imagine.

3

'I left my home with a pain in my heart'

On my first day at Leeds Polytechnic I collected my grant cheque and hit the shops. It was the normal thing, to spend your grant cheque in the first week and live the remainder of the term on a bank overdraft. I bought a couple of flamenco posters, a can of flame-orange paint, several red light bulbs, some packs of joss sticks, a second-hand full-length fur coat (animal type undetermined), an assortment of clothes, shoes, scarves, and a copy of David Bowie's *Low* album.

The joss sticks were necessary to mask the unpleasant smell of the basement flat I'd just moved into. I remember my family's reaction when they found the flat with me, situated as it was in the grim red-light area of Chapeltown Harehills in Leeds. My family had driven me up from Southport for the day the week before term began, to find something. We searched the small ads in the papers and went to a couple of agencies, but each time were unlucky, beaten to the door by someone else. Then we found this basement room in Bayswater Mount, opposite Chapeltown's Gaiety Strip Club and the notorious Spencer Place, where the prostitutes walked up and down, day and night, or frequented a small greasy café on the corner where truckers and lorry drivers parked outside for egg and chips, or blow jobs and hand shandies in their vehicles.

I had turned the key in the lock and pushed open the door. Tentatively, my mother had followed, a mixture of revulsion and bewilderment on her face as I told her it was perfect.

The bedsit was no more than a hole in the wall. Some small steps led down to a single door in which was the only window. Outside the door was a second door that led to an outside toilet, next to an overflow drain which frequently blocked, filling the flat with a pungent smell. In the room there was one electric point, which, as I discovered, fused frequently, leaving me without electricity for days on end in the freezing northern winters. There was no hot water; it all had to be boiled in the kettle. In an alcove were a cheap, battered dressing table with a cracked mirror, an old double bed with broken springs, and a cheap wardrobe. A Dralon armchair completed this picture of Bohemian elegance. It was the kind of room you would find in a brothel, rented out by the hour, but not a place to live in. I later discovered the remainder of the house *was* in fact a well-known brothel; the local Asian shopkeeper told me that it had on several occasions been raided. I used to wonder, as I lay in bed during those first nights, why I could hear the continual clunking of platform shoes up and down the stairs. I had thought perhaps it was nurses journeying to and from their night shifts at the local hospital. There were other delights in store too. The only other resident of the block, who lived directly above me, used his sink as a urinal – I knew this because the outflow ran down my wall from a broken pipe. He was also the pimp. I could occasionally hear him violently throwing girls around the room or against the wardrobe, which more often than not fell crashing over. Or maybe it was the girls falling. It disturbed me a great deal; it was a sound that was all too familiar.

With a certain reluctance my mother had paid the Asian landlord his £32 for the month, and the following week dropped me off, despair and worry written across her face. But, even though the room was a filthy hell-hole, it seemed like heaven to me. I splashed on the orange paint, put up the posters, fixed in the red light bulbs, lit the incense, and put Bowie's album on the small plastic portable Dansette. The fur coat was to keep me extra warm on those upcoming winter nights.

Chapeltown was a grey and sooty place, always damp, the evenings filled with an etherized fog that lingered in the streets, curled about the houses, and fell asleep there. The days were brightened only by shops selling glittering saris, scarves and brightly coloured Indian sweets. I loved these shops, the sounds of Indian music that wafted from them. To me it all seemed so exotic.

But a particular darkness descended over Chapeltown in the winter of 1976. It was the time of the Yorkshire Ripper, and a mood of insidious disquiet hung in the air. You could almost feel its chill, hear it muttering through deserted streets. Two prostitutes had been murdered near Spencer Place, and now the remaining girls had fear on their faces as they walked the streets, restless, always in twos or threes. At night Leeds turned into a ghost town, the city genuinely ill at ease, waiting for morning to come to consciousness. Those who lived there at the time of the Ripper will understand what I am talking about. The intensity was made still greater by the brutality of the murders, the media hysteria, the 'who next?', combined with the fact that the police knew that he must have an ordinary life to be able to continue doing it – that he was among us. He might be anyone – someone known to us. All you talked about, or heard of, was the Ripper. When would he strike again? Where will it be? Who is he? Everybody had a theory, but no one had an answer. I will never forget the night I was in a Leeds nightclub and the police came in, stopped the music, and played a tape they believed was from him. The disco fell silent as the police made their appeal. 'Hi, this is Jack' was how the tape began. It ended with the song 'Thank You for Being a Friend' by Andrew Gold. Everyone listened in utter disbelief, and afterwards no one felt much like dancing. It later transpired that the tape was a hoax and set back the police investigation considerably.

Each night as I walked back from college I felt uneasy, nervous at the sound of footsteps behind me, and relieved when I reached the sanctuary of my basement flat. But, despite it all, I personally never felt happier than during the time I stayed there. And this was the place in my mind when years later I wrote a song called 'The Room Below' for the *Mother Fist* album, and of course it was in my thoughts when I wrote 'Bedsitter'.

*

On that first day at college I was so nervous. I arrived with a grown-out seventies perm (an experiment that had gone horribly wrong), looking like Leo Sayer. I'd broken out in nervous hives, and I posed for my college photograph feeling sweaty with prickly heat. After the introductory talk, we were shown around the vast fine-art studios, split into small compartments, intricate and maze-like. Each student was given a small area to temporarily call their own. We were told we could do what we wanted at this stage, to be self-motivated. No one was going to force us to work, but we would be assessed each term, and if we had failed to produce work of a certain standard we would be out. I was like the proverbial kid in a candy shop. There were a film department, a ceramics studio, performance areas, materials available for painting and sculpture. And I had three years to find myself and my direction.

In those first few weeks I was confused, wandering aimlessly, trying a bit of this and a bit of that. I eventually took up residence in the performance area, where I started to make a large cave out of chicken wire and papier mâché. I didn't know quite why or what for, but if nothing else I could always crawl inside and hide. It was while working on this abstract structure that I caught the eye of a young man working nearby. His name was also Mark, and he was a talented painter, creating sensitive still lifes in shades of greys and yellows in large daubs of oil paint. He had the sweetest smile and a twinkle in his eyes, and in him I made my first close friend there. We were to spend most of that first term together, and he remained one of the kindest and most considerate people I was to meet. When it snowed that winter we spent evenings drinking wine and talking into the early hours. *Low* became the perfect soundtrack to those Chapeltown days. We also played tapes given to me by a German girl called Ulrika, *chansons* by a rich variety of artists, German music hall, as well as Piaf and Mistinguette. It all seemed too perfect. I felt like I was in an Isherwood novel, touched by Sally Bowles in her divine decadence.

*

When I finally moved out from my basement flat, it was to an utter madhouse, and Mark moved with me. The house was dingy, dark, riddled with mice and always freezing, even in the midst of summer. We lived at first in the attic room. I painted it black, to match the void inside me, and at first everything was good. Then it all started to go wrong. Mark was *too* nice to me, so my self-destructive side started to show once more. I assumed that it was only a matter of time before Mark would be mean to me, so I felt the need to strike first. Next thing I knew he had moved to his own room. We rapidly became strangers. If the Chapeltown bedsit was the flat in 'The Room Below', Mark was the person I sang about.

As for the madhouse: apart from myself and Mark, the other occupants were Grade A oddities. There was a strange, feline girl who stared wildly from behind large, thick glasses; her name was Sue Swift. She painted minutely detailed canvasses of costume balls and medieval scenes, but all the faces were those of famous people. It took her so long to do these paintings that I think she painted only one each year in the whole three-year-course; but they were very beautiful. Sue would chain-smoke cigarettes and eat nothing but chip butties. In those first months we would spend a great deal of time together, intensely chatting and fagging.

Another inhabitant was Big John, a well-built part-time transvestite, who painted his eyes in wildly exotic colours of green and yellow, which came eventually to match his teeth, which he never cleaned. He wore miniature dolls hanging from his ears, and floral dresses over his jeans. He too was a brilliant artist, and painted his dysfunctional family – a favourite of mine was a painting of his Auntie Jean and her dog, which he had framed in carrier bags from the supermarket chain of Morrisons. He ended up sharing his room with Sue, and the pair of them locked themselves away for days – much to my annoyance, as I hated to be excluded from their relationship.

The last inhabitant was a heroin addict called Meg, who staggered around from room to room like a zombie, almost always topless and with bruised track marks on her arms. Her complexion was wan and pale, as much from her strict vegan diet as from her chronic heroin use.

On the top floor was me in my black, oppressive room. My disastrous Afro was now chopped off, in its place a blonde, spiky crop – I'd left the bleach on for too long and had burned the top layer off my scalp.

Punk was taking over the music scene rapidly, and its effect was felt throughout the art department. Recently I'd watched the Sex Pistols, accompanied by a blonde Siouxsie Sioux, guesting on the Bill Grundy television show. Coaxed and goaded to be as outrageous as possible, they delivered. 'Fuck off, you dirty old man!' said Siouxsie. 'Fuck, fuck, piss, fuck!' said Johnny Rotten, on live television, and in so doing created television history. The public were outraged, and the tabloids went predictably hysterical the next day, catapulting the group overnight into the realms of superstardom. So our look was changed in accordance with this new fashion. Shortly there was to be little else in our lives but punk.

I remember the night we held a housewarming party, and everyone had to be in fancy dress. I wore a full bondage outfit, and Big John dressed as Salome, greeting the guests with a belly dance until he eventually collapsed drunk on the floor. The house party spilled out on to the road, with drunk, pot-smoking, debauched art students in bizarre costumes jumping around to the sounds of the Damned, the Clash and the Sex Pistols; later on this music blended into the heavy dub reggae sounds of Tapper Szukie and the Abyssinians. Punk and reggae seemed inextricably linked, and Leeds record shops were selling the pitted white-label records of the latest dub sounds as well as punk. Punk was our soundtrack to that first year at college, to the parties and gatherings – Leeds was swept away by it. The polytechnic played host to the Anarchy Tour with the Pistols, the Damned, the Clash and the American band Johnny Thunders' Heartbreakers. The ex-New York Dolls star was now hailed as one of punk's forerunners, and this new band's classic single 'Chinese Rocks' – an ode to smack – was the punk anthem. It was always doubtful whether Johnny Thunders could remain standing for his entire set, as he was an infamous junkie. Years later, on a concert tour, I bumped into him a couple of times backstage at festivals. The only words he ever uttered to me even then were 'Hey man, got any drugs?' Well, what else would you have wanted him to say? Many years after that, when he died, I was given his favourite waistcoat as a gift. It still smelt of Johnny's patchouli oil.

*

So my long hair was chopped off and dyed black or blond, or both. My jeans were tightened, paint-splattered designs were emblazoned across my T-shirts, and an old leather jacket completed the new look. My favourite T-shirt was one made by two students on the fine-art course, Michelle and Tony. It had a photo of the Queen greeting a group of Teddy boys, the image splattered with red and blue ink. This was very provocative, for gangs of Teds often roamed around Leeds at that time, looking for punks to beat up. The National Front also had a heavy presence in Leeds in 1977: swastika graffiti was daubed everywhere. There was always a march taking place, and all the leaders were well-known faces. There was a heavy NF presence at the punk clubs too, and even throughout the polytechnic. This sort of nationalism was fuelled by the fact that this was the year that the Queen's Silver Jubilee was celebrated, which disgusted dissatisfied, disadvantaged youths in a Britain that was rife with dissent, frustration and social deprivation.

Michelle and Tony were two of the coolest college students. They came from London, and had a typically snooty attitude towards us comparatively uncool northerners: they knew all the newest records and trends. But they took me under their wings (for a while), improving my image with a few style hints. If you were *in* with those two you were part of the coolest clique in college.

My favourite band at this time sprang from the punk movement – Siouxsie and the Banshees. I had read their first interview in *Sounds*, by Jane Suck. They had a following around the north of England before they even had a record deal, such was their mystique, and we wouldn't have thought twice about travelling to Huddersfield or Bradford to catch them in concert. Often we'd travel to see them and they wouldn't even turn up; naturally we thought that was *totally* cool. I loved some of their early songs: 'Make up to Break Up', 'Suburban Relapse', 'Love in a Void' and 'Carcass' were definitely on my wavelength.

Some of the lyrics from 'Carcass' found their way into an assemblage in my first exhibition at Leeds Polytechnic in November 1977. The exhibition was entitled 'Limbless', and featured car crashes, punks in bondage outfits garbed with swastikas, and truncated limbless clowns with erections, all made out of gaudily painted ceramics and covered in chains. The collages, framed in pink plastic, were about Jayne Mansfield and Anton LaVey. Across one of them was the Banshees' lyric 'Be a car crash, / Be a carcass, / Be limblessly in love, / Limblessly in love.' A bit of J. G. Ballard I suppose. The ceramic figures were inspired by the current punk scene, by the Leeds National Front presence, while the others were just freaks and hermaphrodites without arms or legs. The idea of the 'freak' was a preoccupation – and in many ways still is. Anyhow, this is how the programme for my exhibition read, to give you an idea of the extent of the fixation:

1. Three Dead Pierrots
2. Three Freak Shows
3. Three figures for Hans Hanowitz and Carl Meyer's Circus
4. Figure in Bondage
5. For Anton Le Vey – Five Seconds as Jayne Mansfield's Head Smashes through the Windscreen
6. Nazi's/Schmazi's – What's the difference?
7. About Glass & Points

Besides my own observations, the figures owed as much to the drawings of Jean Cocteau, the German expressionist paintings of Georg Grosz, and Tod Browning's 1932 film *Freaks* as to anything else. I was attracted to the dark shadows and jagged edges of black-and-white expressionist cinema – films like *The Cabinet of Doctor Caligari, Doctor Mabuse* and *M.* And the pre-Nazi nightclub figures of Georg Grosz had made me think of some of those bizarre carica-tures I'd met when working at the Southport panto – those debauched after-show parties, the theatrical half-world figures encountered in the twilight side of Southport.

To me things could be both ugly and beautiful – the paradox of beautiful ugliness. Ugliness was simply inverted beauty: individuals' flaws and scars are their unique features, their identity: that beauty is my preference – the broken nose, the twisted mouth, the missing teeth. I identified with struggle. This kind of beauty also translated into sexuality, with its idiosyncrasies and conundrums. The freaks in my work were equally special, and I knew too that their missing limbs were sexually stimulating to some people. Their freakishness was the essence of their specialness, and offered validation of the something special in all of us. Personally I have always found conventional beauty boring, aesthetic conventions bland, perfection sexless. I love the broken parts of our bodies and souls, the misshapes, the flaws, the ugly traits of a personality, and so am drawn to the damaged, the displaced, the socially lost. It's what I was, and what I could so easily have remained (as to some people I have).

In an old junk shop I had picked up a battered copy of Anton LaVey's *Satanic Bible*. I read it with a thrill as I recognized and acknowledged many truths about myself. Anton LaVey was, until his recent death, the founder and leader of the Church of Satan. To some he is a dangerous idealist, the enemy of Christianity; to some he is no more than a carnival showman: to others he is an artist and philosopher with a set of ideas and theories about the Satanic nature of man. It was the latter view that I subscribed to. The belief that man's *real* nature is dark and melancholic, inherently romantic, was what I found and acknowledged in the text. I know it's a dangerous thing to say, even today, and leaves yourself open to be misconstrued. The tabloids still brandish the word 'Satanic' around, often whipping themselves into a frenzy of ignorance and hysteria, applying it to the words 'worship', 'murder' or 'abuse'. This is of course hyperbole and nonsense. Do we ever see these words preceded by the word 'Christian', even though many of the atrocities of our society are perpetrated by those who call themselves followers of Christ? Of course I am not so naive as to assume that so-called 'Satanic' ritual is not being undertaken in some remote place or other – but why call it 'Satanic'? Abuse, torture and murder need no prefix: they are simply terrible crimes. Calling them 'Satanic' may help to sell newspapers or enhance viewing figures, but ultimately this serves to disguise the need to examine the real issues.

The works of Anton LaVey are not concerned with these things. I read them with the macabre interest young people have in such subjects, as part of my growing interest in all religions, and in mysticism. I got the measure of Christianity, but had more trouble with Christians. The intolerance of the Christians I encountered seemed to me to be at total odds with Christianity itself. The Bible is a fascinating collection of stories, wildly elaborate and fantastical, full of contradictions and complexities: it is not something for people to extract elements from to suit their own personal needs, then claim that to be the word of God. And I remain sceptical.

At the same time I was fascinated with the actress Jayne Mansfield, and her image kept recurring in my work. Beautiful, amorous glamour goddess, she died in a horrific car accident, her head severed from her body, allegedly after Anton LaVey had put a curse on her brutal lover. (Quite why Jayne had to die from the curse is not entirely clear.)

The reality, of course, was that much of my plundering of this imagery was no more than a juvenile attempt to shock and be outrageous – the result of watching *Cabaret* and Visconti's *The Damned* too many times. Swastikas, for instance, were always the most misguided and offensive images of punk, dangerously attractive in their immediacy, but should have been consigned to history where they belonged. The paintings and sculptures that made up my collages were – how can I put it? – not really very good. I didn't feel my talent lay in visual art, anyway. When I looked around at the work of my peers, I saw people who could use paint to express their feelings in a way I never knew how to. Jeff Teasdale loved to take the piss – one day literally, when he and Jeff Nuttall held me down whilst Teasdale urinated in front of me. His intentions were good, though – it was all part of a hardening process, the preparation needed to send students out into a hostile (meaning cynical) world. After all, the majority of the public didn't care about art in general, never mind performance art, about suffering and the creative process, the baring of the soul. The public bought the art that matched the sofa.

Despite his bullying and intimidation, I liked Jeff a great deal: his humour reinforced my armour. But it was Jeff Nuttall who was the strongest influence on me. Like Max Eden before him at Southport, he was a milestone figure in my learning. He revelled in being a slob – large and overweight, unkempt and slovenly. He wore a checked flat cap, and constantly tried to shock us by exposing his small, rather walnut-like penis. His passion was performance art, and he was himself infamous for his work. The more extreme, shocking, visceral and disturbing a performance was, the more he applauded and enthused. It was he that steered me back in this direction – to the reason I'd been given a place on the course at all. There were others putting on performances too. One of them was Frank Tovey, who went on to become Fad Gadget, and made a number of albums for Mute Records. Frank's one-man shows were mime-influenced (having studied with Lindsey Kemp), suitably dark (underlit usually) and disturbing (nudity, sexual swear words, simulated sex – you know the sort of thing). There was also a student called Green Gartside who went on to form Scritti Politti. He was extremely aloof, and frighteningly intellectual. Years later when I met him in a New York bar and really chatted, he turned out to be a friendly, sincere guy.

Leeds Polytechnic had a notorious reputation. The performance art was getting increasingly extreme, often involving blood-letting, experiments with raw meat and offal (always useful in performance), students trying to outdo each other in their attempts to shock. On one particular occasion two students locked the audience into the black-painted performance room, took out air pistols and began firing at live budgies and goldfish bowls, stapling live mice to wooden boards, and blowing up television screens, while all the time the tune of 'Camptown Races' ('Doodah, Doodah') played on the sound system. The desired effect was achieved, and much more. As the budgies died, all hell broke loose in the audience. The lights were then turned off, and sheer panic ensued, while the artists continued to fire the air pistols at random. People rushed to the exits, stumbling over each other in the chaos. Later on that week the two students in question were severely beaten up, by people who had been sickened by the cruelty to animals. The police were duly called in, and for a while the tutors feared that the tabloids might get involved. We were all instructed to keep quiet about the whole incident. Eventually the two students ended up in court facing charges of cruelty, but managed to evade prosecution in the name of art. It seemed to me the result of their performance piece had far exceeded their expectations, and when they emerged from court labelled 'art terrorists' it was Tony and Michelle who posed with them – always the hippest people. Art terrorism was cool.

I had also started to enjoy writing, even though I found it a struggle. I think that's why I eventually started to write songs and poems: short lines, compactness and directness appealed to me (and my dyslexia). I also began to write scripts and notes for performance shows, endlessly filling notebooks with ideas and plans, and drawings for stage sets. Thankfully most of them stayed as ideas and didn't see the light of day, but some went through development into perform-ance. A few ambitious ideas even involved Super-8 films, costumes and projections, which I made myself. I can look back and laugh now at some of the shameless displays I undertook, designed to scandalize and offend. Yet occasionally something interesting emerged and magic was created – a moment or two, a stunning visual image, a theatrical spark of ingenuity which eventually developed into a style. And, though my artistic intentions were serious and I worked hard, I had learned not to take myself too seriously. I used the blackest humour.

One early performance was *Icebox*. I sat at a mirror and shaved half my body. I covered half my face in stylized garish make-up, naked except for black boots and a strategically placed swastika. I then smashed a small mirror and with a shard cut myself, drawing blood. For the climax I lay face down on a large mirror and simulated sex, bathed in cold white light. I remember most of all how cold the mirror was! All right, I know what you're thinking, because I'm thinking it too, but you do have to start somewhere.

Another show was entitled *The Vampire Cat* – part dreamlike ritual, part camp cabaret, all in pink, grey, black and white. It was based on an anonymous poem called 'The Vampire Cat of Nebash-ima', a twisted fairy tale. The performance featured a great deal of blood, strange surreal masks and swastikas (yes, again). Huw Feather had travelled up from his design course in Nottingham to play Anton Le Vey (yes, him too); dressed in a skullcap and sporting a black beard and a long cloak, he recited the Satanic Laws. In the interval I performed a punk number called 'The Pussycat Song', accompanied by a thrashy guitar and tape loops I'd recorded myself. I was dressed in a pink pussycat hat. For the climax I smeared cat food all over my naked body. Art students, honestly! Well, it was 1977; I assume I was imagining this constituted some kind of punk expression.

There were a couple of my performances that I am still quite proud of though. *Zazou* in 1978, my second college year, dealt with an androgynous nightclub singer in a club called Blue Heaven. The character lives for the night, has a nihilistic relationship with a rent boy called Johnny, and lives out his/her life through a series of clichés, eventually slipping into madness and turning into an imaginary narcissus flower. Anyone we know? Well, I did base the piece on my personal experiences, and on various people I'd met. The club where Zazou sang was based on a seedy gay Leeds nightclub of the time called Charlies. Naturally enough, I played Zazou, the lead, and my college friend Anne Tilbey played the destructive Johnny. It was the beginning of a working relationship with Anne, and we went on to work on several performances together. Anne was one of the most prolific workers at the college; she later went on to be a set designer for Ken Russell, and has worked on many Channel 4 commissions. She loved to make bizarre sculptures on people's heads out of food. Together we once staged a highly blasphemous nativity play in which I played the Virgin Mary. It involved giant masks, elaborate costumes and one ton of goose feathers, which needless to say took months to clear up afterwards.

It was the performance of *Zazou* that I remember most clearly though. It took place at a space called the White Elephant Gallery – I knew it was important to do as much as possible outside the safe confines of the college – and I charged a 50p entrance fee to cover some costs. It involved projections and a whole musical soundtrack. I sang, while another college friend, Ed King, played guitar, and a third student was credited with synthesizer, stylophone and electronic wizardry. In one part of the show I performed a bizarre electro disco version of 'I am Sixteen Going on Seventeen', naturally with alternative lyrics about incest, frigidity and existing in a mental home. This recording was later to plague me when it turned up on various early Soft Cell bootlegs; taken out of context, it sounded extremely juvenile. You really did have to be there. The *Yorkshire Evening Post* came to review it, and called it 'one of the most nihilistic depressing pieces that I have ever had the misfortune to see'. So it was a success then.

I had no problem with nudity in performance – in fact I revelled in the exhibitionism, which to this day is strangely at odds with my other, more personal side, which is private and reclusive. These two extreme sides of my personality have battled against each other for years; yet total privacy and uninhibited exhibitionism are linked together in their extremes. The extrovert side of my personality urges me to be on stage in the spotlight, to lay bare my soul and give the performances all I can. I can do this because it is a performance; afterwards I can retreat back into my private personal world.

For as long as I can remember there have always been two Marc Almonds.

First is the side of me that is private – the side that the public do not know. The protection of my feelings, all that I intrinsically value personally, requires that the private side of me is sheltered as much as is feasible. When I sit in a dressing room preparing to go on stage or to do a performance on television – even an interview – I, like many other singers and actors, have to undergo a transformation in my mind. If this involves the props of make-up or a glittering stage outfit, so be it. I call it putting on my Marc Almond face. So the public Marc Almond is flamboyant and stagy, over the top and some might say feminine. Well, that is part of the pretence that protects the personal side of me. Misconceptions arise because the public see only this side of me that is flamboyant and stagy (which is in part my own doing), and then assume that this is all there is to me. This belief is reinforced by prejudiced journalists and bigoted individuals who refuse to examine the nature of my performances, or consider their subtexts. They categorize me as effeminate and fey; they read the signals I send out as being literally the person I am.

Of all the singers in my genre, I am probably the most theatrical – in the sense that what you see and what you think you see do not correspond. I pile on the make-up, the eyeliner, the glitter in an attempt to create the ultimate mask. I am not saying that this is not part of who I am: I am saying that this is simply one element of who I am. Yet this one element – the public side – is perceived by so many to be one-dimensional, and therefore weak. Which is simply not the case. A great many men do not fit exactly into society's nonsensical criteria of masculinity; as part of an attempt to overturn these criteria my public side has compelled me to be as outrageous, shocking and downright in your face as possible. If the public don't like it, that's tough.

The love of film I'd discovered with Ken was fully indulged and satisfied at art college. Every week you could see a choice of two or three films in the lecture theatres. In addition, the Leeds Playhouse had an ever-changing programme of art or cult movies. I was introduced to the visual orgies of the Italian film director Fellini, my favourite being *Satyricon*, with its surreal Roman decadence and gay subtext; Pasolini, Visconti, the bleakness of Bergman, the stylized tableaux of Syberberg and his *Ludwig – Requiem for a Virgin King* were favourites too. The cult trash of John Waters' *Pink Flamingos*, Jack Smith's *Flaming Creatures* and the excesses of Ken Russell amazed me. I watched and digested them all, storing images in my mind for future reference. I borrowed, then bought, a Super-8 camera and kept it with me right up until 1983, documenting whatever I could. (Unfortunately in 1983 it was stolen, along with many films; somewhere perhaps there is still a document of that life.)

I made a number of Super-8 epics of my own to accompany my performances, and later to play at early Soft Cell gigs. My first half-hour epic, entitled *Glamour in Squalor*, featured drag queens and punks committing acts of violence in filthy bedsits. *Teenage Vice* featured a girl and boy – both punks – observed through a crack in the door as she provoked him into an argument. Eventually he killed her with a red silk cord and scrawled the words 'Teenage Vice' across her naked back in red lipstick. No marks from the feminists for that one! Another was about a shadowy figure living in a squalid bedsit. The camera explored the room, the ornaments and the objects contained within, eventually alighting on a figure dressed in grey and sitting on an old sofa. The figure was eating a can of cat food, then picked up a book and started to thumb through it, looking at photos of yesteryear. The photos flickered to life, and bizarre-costumed people danced across the pages.

I also appeared in a couple of films directed by other students. Once, as Caligula, dancing in a toga and bedecked in laurels, I pranced across a hillside. Another time I was a bondage-attired androgynous villain in a film entitled *Glamarama* (a homage to spy movies, sixties kitsch and *Barbarella*), the music-video style of which now seems almost ahead of its time. It was made by one of my best friends at the college, Sally Bairstow. She was later to marry the man of her dreams (and star of *Glamarama*), Ed King, becoming Sally King – a name fit for one of the Avengers. Indeed, when I first met Sally she was dressed in leather biker gear from head to foot, and her whole life was styled around *The Avengers, The Man from UNCLE* and their like. We hit it off immediately. Together we would sit in her pink-fur bedroom, decorated with disco balls and lava lamps, and co-occupied by her cat, Puddles. Sally would lie on the pink-satin bed, smoking the longest joints imaginable.

It was with Sally that I lodged after leaving the 'madhouse', due to an incident that proved to be the final straw. The house was by this time entirely infested with mice, which forced me to get a cat of my own. Naturally I bought it a diamante-studded collar, and named it Johnny Johnny (from a line in a Clash song). I stupidly thought that I would overcome my allergy to cats and build up a tolerance if I actually lived with one. I also thought that the asthma would be preferable to the mice. But it was not – one day I collapsed in a wheezing fit and an ambulance was called. A severe chest infection ensued, which took me a fortnight to recover from. So Johnny Johnny had to go, and Huw and his girlfriend Liz took him. A short while after the cat had gone, I awoke suddenly in the night and discovered an old man dressed in white leaning over me, poking me in the chest. I jumped out of bed, every hair on my body standing up, and ran for the door. It seemed to me to be so real, though I thought it might be the insomnia which still plagued me that had invoked the image. The next morning I came down to breakfast, much the worse for wear after my sleepless night, but said nothing of the incident. When Meg joined me for breakfast, even her pallor looked worse than usual. 'God, I had such a fright last night,' she said. 'I was sitting on the toilet having a fix when the door opened and there was this old man dressed in white standing there, just looking at me. I thought I'd taken too much smack – I was in such a state I was going to wake you all up.'

I was horrified, and after that I couldn't remain in the house. I moved in with Sally. The small bedroom in a cramped house in Marlborough Gardens was an ideal escape, and I was to stay there until I finally finished my course. I decorated the room in crimson and blue, with sari scarves and painted dummy torsos, and covered the walls with paintings and faded Victorian photographs of dead people.

Sally was to prove one of the closest friends at college, but in later life friendship and work proved to be difficult to mix. Some years later, Sally wanted to direct videos, and naturally enough asked me to put in a word for her at my record company, which I did. But nothing came of it. Record companies very rarely have any interest in the suggestions of the artist (although thankfully this has changed). More particularly, my record company had their own ideas. Further, there was already an influx of young video directors in London, trained at film school and artful at wooing record companies themselves. Sally didn't believe that I'd spoken to the record company about her when nothing happened, so was annoyed. However, I felt more aggrieved, as it seemed she had sent out copies of *Glamarama* without asking me first, and it had ended up being bootlegged. I felt I was losing control of my image and quality of work for public consumption; she felt I wasn't making much of an effort to get her a break. So the rift widened, engulfing our friendship.

Among the people who made a great impression on me at art

school I mustn't forget Alan Selka. Attired in cloaks and with a cane and monocle, he was Salvador Dali and Noël Coward in one. Alan knew everything about Dali and Dietrich, and was obsessed with the mad King Ludwig of Bavaria. Alan made these people come to life for me, and it was hard not to be swept along by his enthusiasm and stories. Alan liked to surround himself with strange and wonderful people, human oddities: dotty old ladies in veils and heavy, leaden make-up; colourful eccentrics. One such companion, named Majesty, in fact claimed to be a direct descendant of Ludwig, would dress in German military uniforms, and kept a clod of earth from Hitler's Berchtesgarten in a jar. Another, a grocer by trade, actually believed he was Hitler, and later was to appear as the Führer in Alan's film *Malice* (in which I appeared as Caligula). In his BA show, Alan created a surrealist's tearoom set piece in which I played a singing waiter. On display was a length of his own intestine (removed after an illness) in a glass jar of formaldehyde. Years later Alan went on to become a much sought-after British butler in New York. He had found his forte.

I joined Alan's circle of friends, and he would pick me up in his car along with a friend called Charles (the gay black sheep of a wealthy business family), and the three of us would go to Charlies. This was the sort of place you had to *know* about. Situated in a dark part of Leeds, behind the Corn Exchange, you scaled the steep steps and knocked hard. A latch slid back and you were quizzed suspiciously before being allowed entry by a burly broken-nosed bouncer. Inside, Charlies was all red flock and chicken in a basket. It boasted a chequered seventies dance floor (as in *Saturday Night Fever*, only with fewer squares) and was frequented by transsexuals, drag queens and rent boys. No elegant escorts here – these were the roughest Leeds could offer. The drag queens sported the ugliest stubble through their pan stick, and were of the variety who would glass you if you looked at them for too long. Hard crop-headed lesbians in donkey jackets completed this picture of late-night gay elegance. One evening a woman cornered me and pulled up her top to reveal large sagging breasts. On one was tattooed the word 'mild', and on the other, 'bitter'. 'Guess where the lager is?' she howled, spilling her pint all over me.

Though Charlies was reminiscent more of a gin house than of a nightclub, Alan, Charles and I loved it, revelling in the air of sleaze. Together we took over the dance floor to the new sounds of the Bee Gees' 'Night Fever' and 'Staying Alive', as well a new record by a black American singer called Donna Summer. This had an electronic pulse rhythm to a machine beat with spaced-out, other-worldly vocals that sounded cold yet sensual at the same time. It was the entrancing, ground-breaking 'I Feel Love', and was to herald a new age of music, an electronic dance phenomenon: disco. It bridged the gap between Kraftwerk and David Bowie in the past, and the new nearer-to-home sounds of the Human League's 'Being Boiled' and 'Reproduction', and Cabaret Voltaire, and it would sweep us all away.

I had in many ways become bored with punk – I had seen every band and bought every record. For me it had climaxed the day I was recruited as a go-go dancer for the girl band Cheap 'n' Nasty. We supported the Vibrators (always the fag end of punk), and I'd left the stage covered in slimy spit and pints of beer – traditional at punk concerts. By this time every band around was cashing in by bashing out a three-chord song. Leeds still had a rather good scene – with Gang Of Four and the brilliant Mekons – but it did feel like it was time for something new. I was tired of all that anger; I wanted songs about good times, songs to dance to, get drunk to, get high to. And disco created them for me. A dark cloud may have descended on Britain in the form of Margaret Thatcher, but a transvestite singer called Sylvester danced into our living rooms, waving a gold fan and urging us to feel 'Mighty Real'. Donna Summer was to take us even higher as she worked with the producer Giorgio Moroder on songs including the incredible 'Once Upon a Time' and the enthralling 'MacArthur Park'.

On one visit to Charlies, I met Paul. He had that certain some-thing, whatever it is – 'that beautiful light of madness'. I was to meet quite a few people with this strange aura, and trouble and disaster accompanied them always. Irresistibly attractive, a darkly compelling presence, yet with a troubled edge that usually proves to be the picture of disturbed madness. So it was with Paul. Schizophrenic Paul. Paul had that strange light in his eyes: ambitious, unfulfilled, angry at the world. When I talked to him one night, he told me he was a rent boy. I was immediately captivated. I'd never met a real, in-the-flesh, rent boy before. I'd seen documentaries on television, but here was an actual one, and I had so many questions. And so I befriended him – a move I was to regret. Paul had told me how he liked to make regular trips to London to make extra money, and I decided to accompany him on one of these.

In London, Paul introduced me to a secret twilight world. But it was to hold a few unpleasant experiences for me. The first came while we were waiting for a so-called contact of his, Ginger John. We were arrested behind Piccadilly Circus, just outside Cecconi's Restaurant. We were dragged, protesting, into a police van while the police discussed openly how they were going to beat us up. Fortunately, on this occasion, they let us go a few hours later. Though Paul found it all very amusing, it shocked me. Another incident was when Paul took me to a sleazy photographer's flat in Earls Court. He was having his photo taken. I sat patiently waiting while the photographer flounced around in a silk kimono, swigging from a bottle of vodka. Fat old men entered the studio and hovered by me suggestively; I sat there fascinated but uncomfortable of how stupid I was to be in such a vulnerable situation. I quickly left. Finally, one day while sitting around in Leicester Square, I was given the eye by a middle-aged man. Paul was nowhere to be found, so I decided to follow this stranger and ended up at his hotel in Kensington. Once there I was filled with trepidation and immediately tried to leave. But he had locked the door. What followed can only be the truth because it is too insane to make it up. He put on a tape of Boney M full blast – 'Brown Girl in the Ring' – pulled out a map of Germany, and in a thick German accent began to inform me that Hitler wasn't all bad. I spent a terrifying night in the clutches of a Nazi fruitcake!

But the last straw came when, on returning to our friend Mary's squat in Covent Garden, I discovered that Paul had stolen a huge piece of hash from her private stash. Mary was an ex-art student from Leeds and was kindly putting us up. I was furious with Paul, and told him to return the hash before Mary found out. Paul just thought it hilarious. By now I'd had enough of Paul and his life, so I returned to Leeds on the next coach. The following day Paul turned up at the house, and I slammed the door in his face. I hoped I'd seen the last of him.

I'd managed to get a part-time job behind the bar at the Leeds Playhouse. I was well liked, and had a good reputation (which was surprising, since I usually mixed up the orders and couldn't work the till). I got on especially well with Lawrie, the bar manager. Then one day there was a thunderous crash, followed by shouting and swearing. We ran to see what had caused the commotion. It was Paul, drunk and shouting obscenities. He had thrown a bin through the Playhouse's plate-glass window! 'I think that is your friend,' whispered Lawrie, a little less than happy. Sent to the manager's office, I was warned that the Playhouse would not tolerate the behaviour of my strange friends. I was humiliated, and my relationship with the bar was never quite the same. But that was the last time I saw Paul. I'd believed that it would be easy to step into the sleazy underworld and then back into my safe art-student life, just as I thought years later I could cross between that underworld and my pop-star life. On both counts I was wrong. You delude yourself; you believe that because you're not inherently part of that world you're immune to its dangers. But, as I was to discover, if you swim with the fish you get mistaken for a fish, and when you swim with the sharks, you're meat!

*

Towards the end of my course I found a book called *City of Night* by the American writer John Rechy, and was greatly inspired by it. It is a personal journey through the gay half world of New York and Los Angeles. John Rechy was a hustler who writes, and a writer who hustles. Hustling – the American slang term for male prostitution – gave him the inspiration for his writing. I believe that the greatest art comes from personal experience. You have to partake in as much as you can, sample all kinds of life, explore and sensualize, and turn even the most negative experiences into positive creativity. Many of the songs I have written come from such personal experiences. You've got to live the life you sing, and sing the life you live.

The final year went too quickly. All those nights spent drinking with the other students, partying through the evenings – gone. Now the real world loomed ever closer. Trying to squeeze in as much as possible, I took part in a couple of plays, once as a dancer in the university production of *Cabaret*, and another time as a jack-booted Mussolini in a production of a surreal play entitled *Him*. Don't ask what it was about, but I had to stamp around the stage, barking orders, while a chorus of toga-attired screaming queens grovelled and fawned at my every word. No change there then. Sally made me a gold-lamé Nazi cap with a diamanté swastika and Alan Selka, in the poorest taste, called it 'concentration camp'.

It was my experience with Paul the rent boy that inspired a new show I wrote myself, entitled *Dilly Boys*, a collection of songs, poems and dialogue. The guy who'd helped with the music for *Zazou* helped me again. Again, I performed at the White Elephant Gallery.

I used this venue one further time, for my diploma show, *Twilights and Lowlifes* – a kind of 'greatest hits' compilation. Judging the shows were the columnist and novelist Molly Parkin and her husband Patrick Hughes, the artist. I was star-struck by the stylish Molly in her black frock coat and wild hats, and we were to become good friends for a while. I had never met such a strong and fascinating woman, with such Bohemian style. She swore like a trooper, held a diploma in put-downs, and was an expert in wry, dry commentary. Apart from my performance piece, I showed her my sculptures, drawings and Super-8 epics. Finally I was awarded a 2.1, which I was assured was the next best thing to a first. Jeff Nuttall and Jeff Teasdale said they considered me to be very self-sufficient as an artist, and felt that they couldn't award me a first as I wasn't going on to a master's degree. Despite their assurances, I felt cheated. If they honestly felt my work was worthy of a first then I felt they should have given me one.

*

It was now the summer of 1979 and I was twenty-two. I, like the times, had experienced so many changes. In ten years we had lived through three quite separate musical genres – glam rock, punk and disco. I had worn all the clothes, sported the hairstyles and lived each of the lifestyles fiercely. But much as music remained a passion, there were also other realities to consider. I was soon reminded how hard the outside world can be. I found myself with no money, and took to living on a diet of Complan and potatoes. I strove to repay the huge overdraft I'd accumulated, and that, combined with general living costs, constantly swallowed up any money I earned at the Playhouse. I found myself constantly returning home to stay for short periods.

On one of my visits home a gang of forty or so football supporters entered the railway carriage where I'd been sitting alone. At first I went unnoticed and slowly tried to edge out of the carriage. Suddenly, all attention turned towards me, and the chase began. I ran down the length of the train pursued by the gang, until I eventually found myself in the driver's compartment. I used my foot to stop the sliding door from opening, and every ounce of my strength to stop them bursting in to attack me or the driver. I remember their faces, twisted in hate, pressed up against the glass as they tried to prise open the door. The equally terrified driver phoned the police, who we were told would be waiting at Wigan station. When the train finally pulled into the platform, the thugs leaped out and over the barriers, the police in hot pursuit. I went to the police station to give a statement. The real world, I realized, was a hostile place.

Art college had been a kind of drug, and now I was having severe withdrawals. For a while I hung around the departments like a ghost. Many of my friends still had a year to complete, and I felt a need to remain part of it all. But it didn't seem to work. I eventually came to the conclusion that I needed a complete break, a new environment, so I made a decision that would prove to be one of the worst so far. I called up my old friend Huw Feather in Nottingham, where he had just finished his theatre-design course. I told him that I fancied coming to Nottingham to live. He promptly told me that his girlfriend, Liz Pugh, had a spare room in her house. Now, Liz was a student on the fashion course in Nottingham: she shared my sense of humour, and was a great girl. So I took the room. Packing my things into Alan Selka's car I said goodbye to Leeds and set out for another new life.

Almost as soon as I arrived I regretted it. First I had to sign on, trying to justify my situation to a bunch of hard-faced individuals sat behind steel grilles. Second, the house where Liz lived was in a dark and dismal red-light area. My mattress was infested with bedbugs. I effectively had no friends: Huw and Liz had their own life and circle of friends I just wasn't part of. I spent many long, lonely days and nights sitting making plans that would never be carried out, and living for the next Giro. The only times my spirits lifted were when Liz and I spent an evening at home drinking canned cocktails, singing along to *West Side Story*.

One week, after collecting my Giro, I just took a bus to London. Drawn to the lights of the West End and Soho, I was able to get a job on the door of a clip joint just off Walker's Court. The place was basically an office where unsuspecting punters would come in, lured by the promise of a sexual liaison, and be sold a ticket to a strip show or a porno cinema just around the corner. Of course, it was a rip-off: when they got there, they would be charged a second time. The person in charge of the office – a young black guy called Maurice – also gave advice (perhaps not quite the right word) to girls who came in off the street looking for work; he would give them the number of a pimp or a blue-movie company looking for fresh young talent. The place also had a number of porno movies for sale. This was still the sleazy, over-the-top Soho, as yet untouched by the Thatcherite clean-up. Porno cinemas showed hard-core films, both gay and straight. Every other doorway advertised models for hire (second floor), red lamps shone in windows, and flashing neons promised your fantasies realized – though they never were. A direct consequence of the sex exploitation was of course a great deal of misery and disillusionment, not to mention drug-addiction. The 'glamour' was really squalor. Yet to those people who frequented the dark doorways looking for that illicit thrill, that touch of sleaze – to them, the squalor was the glamour.

I wasn't hard enough, or physically large enough, for my job on the clip-joint door. I didn't have it in me to rip people off; I felt guilty conning people out of their money. Besides, this was for real, and the consequences of my job I knew would sooner or later be dangerous. Often punters didn't take kindly to being made fools of and returned for their money back, pulling knives (one even pulled a gun), and threatening me. This, with the visible side effects – drugged-up girls and boys staggering around, irretrievably lost – was too much for me at twenty-two. I returned to Nottingham, broke, miserable and at my lowest ebb. I couldn't even afford to take drugs or drink myself into a stupor. The life of the rent boy and a life of crime both seemed to be dead-end roads too. At least I had the common sense to know that much. The final straw came when I invited a 'street' friend up from London. He stole my treasured record collection, and left me a present in the form of an infestation of crab lice. I spent an afternoon tentatively picking off the crabs with a pair of tweezers, sealed them in an envelope, and sent them back to him.

That was it. I telephoned Sally and Ed in Leeds, and they came to rescue me. A short while later I found myself in their little spare room. I knew then that I should never have left. I was to be so glad that I'd decided to return.

4

'A man could get lost'

When Dave Ball had walked into Leeds Polytechnic in the autumn of 1977, the first person he had bumped into was me. We couldn't have been more contrasting: Dave in a denim jacket, jeans and desert wellies, tall and stocky with black curly hair; me in gold-lamé trousers, a leopard-skin T-shirt on a small skinny frame with a blonde crop. He asked me the way to the art department, and I pointed him down the corridor. Neither of us then could have imagined the strange adventure we would be embarking on in less than three years' time, nor even that this encounter would have any significance at all.

Despite our contrasting appearances we had more in common than we at first realized. Both of us hailed from north-west coastal towns – Dave was from Blackpool, a town you could see from Southport beach on a clear day. We both shared a love of the bizarre, the kitsch and the seedy. But most importantly we both loved electronic music, and between two poles of musical tastes we met in a shared love of Kraftwerk and the New Industrial sounds that were emerging. Throbbing Gristle, Cabaret Voltaire and the early Human League had evolved from the three-chord thrash of punk, and came to inspire us equally. Dave also loved their American counterparts, such as Devo and the sounds of Père Ubu. Both of us were crazy for a hardcore New York duo called Suicide – Alan Vega on vocals and Martin Rev on instruments. Suicide used a minimal sound arrangement drawing from fifties rockabilly, yet with psychotic vocals, set against an electronic keyboard drone and a basic beat box. Their sound was totally original, ahead of its time, paradoxically tender and aggressive, erotic and paranoid, and totally fucked up. An ex-Northern Soul boy who used to back-flip on the Wigan Casino dance floor, Dave also avidly collected sixties soul records and early seventies disco. All these influences, together with my ensemble of Jacques Brel, torch crooners and punk, were to come together in the melting pot that we would later call Soft Cell.

I noticed Dave a great deal around the art department doing bizarre collages (it was what he described as his 'pink and green period'), and I heard him, too. In one corner of the art department was a small studio run by a technician called John Darling. It was filled with equipment, including tape recorders used for making soundtracks and sound projects required by the students. It was here that Dave could be most often found, recording songs on a Korg synthesizer keyboard.

Up until then I had never actually seen a synthesizer. It was still a new and exotic instrument, normally confined to those groups with flash keyboard wizards experimenting in progressive sounds. But by now it was beginning to make its way into teenagers' bedrooms – becoming another means of expression. Perhaps it was Brian Eno who took it from being a pompous instrument (exclusively for the likes of Keith Emerson) to one used for all kinds of pop experimentation, and he did this through his early Roxy Music incarnation. The advent of the microchip was changing the world for ever, making all sorts of technology compact and affordable.

The squelches, squeaks and swoops I overheard fascinated and excited me. I felt they were just what I needed for my performances. I approached Dave and asked him to work with me on some music, and he proved more than happy to be involved. I suppose that's how it all started.

Dave called my performances 'Industrial Cabaret', and the sounds we made involved tape loops, guitar thrashes, pulsing electronics, sound effects, and even one or two rudimentary songs. It all owed a lot to Throbbing Gristle, the group led by the art terrorist Genesis P. Orridge, an individual who caused tabloid sensations by sending pornographic postcards and organizing an exhibition called 'Prostitution' at the ICA. Other members of Trobbing Gristle included Peter 'Sleazy' Christopherson, a designer and film-maker who experimented with tapes and effects; Chris Carter on electronics; and Cossi Fanni Tuttii, a female guitarist who also moonlighted as a stripper. Extreme and uncompromising, their songs or soundscapes were resourcefully entitled 'Hamburger Lady', 'Zyklon B. Zombie' and, ironically, '20 Jazz Funk Greats'. Techno pioneers, they were our heroes.

When I presented my 'performance pieces', Dave would be present, along with a group of like-minded friends. These included an androgynous colleague of Dave's from Blackpool called Paul Banham, who resembled a prettier version of Gary Numan (think of the *Down in the Park* cover). He worked on the sound and generally helped out. And it was Dave who played such a significant musical role in *Zazou* and my degree show, *Twilights and Lowlifes*.

Leeds was full of ex-students killing time, looking for employment and drinking their lives away in snakebites. It's bad enough being an ex-student, but being an ex-art student, used to life in a licensed playground for lunatics and coming down after a three-year, govern-ment-funded high, seemed unimaginably worse. Without focus, social and creative stagnation beckoned. I began to write letters, under the heading LOWLIFE PRODUCTIONS, applying for grants, begging colleges to let me perform, even lecture. Surprisingly, a few responded, and I was invited to perform at York, Manchester and Reading. I also made tapes of the soundtracks to my shows and advertised them through sympathetic fanzines under the name Peter Mayhem, and actually sold quite a few. Gentle reader, I know you think by now you're used to my performances, but, believe me, for the one at York University you are still quite unprepared.

I called the piece *Deterioration*. To a tape loop of the car crash from the record 'Terry' by Twinkle ('Don't do it, Don't do it, Don't do it / CRASH', repeating over and over) I smashed glass photo frames on to the floor, swallowed a bottle of pills (on this rare occasion not real), donned a flowing white wedding dress, and broke a blood capsule in my mouth while thrashing chords out on a white electric guitar. The performance climaxed with Barbra Streisand's 'Memories' playing while I crawled among the debris of broken glass and discarded photos. When the performance ended there was silence. That feeling of 'Well, there's something you don't see every day' filtered from the audience. And yet for my troubles I was paid. Paid £100. So in fact I was the most surprised of all.

Circumstances forced me to consider all kinds of other things to do; at one desperately low point I even (briefly) entertained the idea of becoming a professional singing telegram. But the people I per-formed birthday greetings to were more likely to punch me than applaud me. No, I needed to be something far more sane and reasonable – like a pop star, for instance. Why not, I thought. Why not indeed?

Dave had been busy writing a number of songs, and played them to me. I thought they were great – catchy, with good hooks. To me they *sounded* like pop songs, they sounded like success, and they sounded like an escape. In those very early days Dave wrote the lyrics himself – 'A Man Could Get Lost', 'Metro Mr X', 'Potential', 'Facility Girl': these were all early Dave Ball compositions, both lyrics and music. The songs were simple, each lasting two or three minutes, with an electronic beat that Dave bashed out on his Korg. The beat was no more than the keyboard percussion sound repeated over and over, almost that repetitive disco sound. We sat and talked about the possibility of becoming a song-writing partnership – Dave with endless brilliant pop ideas, I with my lyrics and poetry. We envisaged naively that we would become Britain's first electro duo. Inspired though we were by Suicide's economical look, we'd be more pop and dance orientated.

I visited Dave's house with a borrowed Revox tape recorder and microphone, and together we put together about twenty songs that were to become the early Soft Cell repertoire. *Non-Stop Erotic Cabaret* may have been the world's introduction to Soft Cell, but we had a whole album's worth of songs much earlier, and played them at our first gigs. Our first few compositions were like suburban pocket operas, dealing with the mundanity of life, featuring housewives hooked on tranquillizers having nervous breakdowns, the banality of factory work, Penthouse Pets and the general detritus of modern urban living, accompanied by a machine-like repetitive beat over a galloping electro pulse. Sadly, they can still be found today, circulated as bootlegs called *Science Fiction Stories*. They're only bedroom demos, and were never even meant to be heard in that form. We used vocoders or distortions on my voice; listened to now, they seem so simplistic and minimal – both juvenile and ingenuous. Many still retain the intended feeling of claustrophobia and paranoia, and are slightly disturbing, but others are toe-curling. Yet in some way I'd like to think they all have an originality that still shines through. My voice is monotonous and flat – hence the heavy use of effects – but the music had hooks and riffs and the ideas that were to become Dave's trademark sounds were clearly there. These were later to be imitated and plagiarized by many that followed in electronic music.

Dave also had a discerning sense of the cinema soundtrack, a vision of music that probably came from his love of the composer John Barry (perhaps best known for his James Bond music). Barry has scored countless films and remains a major influence on a wide variety of musicians, but Dave was the first to acknowledge his influence. Years later we were to meet him at Trident Studios in London when he was recording one of the Bond songs.

Dave Ball is an incredibly underrated, intensely talented musician and producer – and, above all, a techno pioneer. It's partly his own fault that the press and public have always been slow to acknowledge him; always quiet and modest made him invisible at times. He was never one for getting out there and proclaiming his brilliance – and yet there are so many less talented people who readily do that for themselves, and take credit for a second-hand thought or idea, to be admired by the music press. Being arrogant and self-opinionated is all that Dave is not. But you do have to tell people your worth, whatever little it is, and keep telling them over and over or they don't believe it.

Perhaps we sold ourselves a bit short in the early years, Dave in his silence and me in my self-deprecation. When paid a compliment I would throw it back, apologetically. Disbelieving or embarrassed by it. Neither Dave nor I used the press to proclaim ourselves; not once did I say I was a great singer or Dave that he was an excellent musician. Never hearing it, the public never particularly thought about it, I suppose. Well, I am a bloody brilliant singer, so fuck them all! And if you had any doubts, well then, I've now ironed them out. But the real misconception was that *I* was Soft Cell because I was the front man, the singer, the lyricist. I took the interviews (even though it strained me to do so) so I was the most visible. But Dave was probably more Soft Cell than I could ever be. He was the *sound* of Soft Cell. He took my post-punk, off-key crooning, rooted it down, and made it commercial.

All the early songs were recorded in Dave's bedroom and the polytechnic sound studio, where we built up our repertoire. Sat around idling in the art department one day, we tossed around suggestions for a name. 'Here's Health', 'Hard Sell', 'Soft Soap'. On and on it went. Then Dave came up with 'Soft Cell'. It seemed to fit – the play on words embodied our themes of consumerist nightmares and suburban insanity. It also sounded modern – dare I say high-tech? – and seemed to incorporate both a warmth and a coldness. It summed us up.

So there it was. We were a band, if you can call two people a band. A duo – Britain's first electro duo. Having a name created a sense of relief, for it seemed to affirm a sense of direction, an aim for the future. Our ideas could now be focused, applied to this one idea, Soft Cell. Dave would soon stop writing lyrics to concentrate fully on the rhythm and musical arrangements, and my poems and dialogue would became shorter, simpler – in other words, pop lyrics. What a relief to discover that a three-minute song can communicate a feeling or idea. Goodbye to self-indulgent, decadent, hour-long exhibitionistic performances. Hello to self-indulgent, decadent, three-minute-long exhibitionistic performances.

*

But Soft Cell was still embryonic, particularly as Dave still had a year to do at art college, not due to collect his BA until the summer of 1980. I still had to think about making a living. Any kind of living. The Arts Council wasn't bombarding me with cheques, and colleges and performance spaces ceased replying to my resumé. I asked Leeds Playhouse for my old job again, and Lawrie took me back on. Lawrie was in his sixties, and we must have made a strange couple behind that bar. Despite my lack of ability with arithmetic, I managed to get by. Lawrie and I shared quite a few laughs at the expense of some of the self-obsessed thespians who patronized the place. Who was sleeping with whom? Who was a bitch? Who was gay? We would line up their interval St Clement'ses and tear them apart. Lawrie had such a dry sense of humour – well observed and wickedly bitchy. The Playhouse liked having me around, as I must have added that art-school punk colour, and besides all my friends came in to drink copious amounts. (The bin-through-the-window incident had long been forgotten, along with psychotic Paul.)

After I'd finished work, Alan Selka or some other friends would come to collect me to go on to a new 'super-disco' that had recently opened, the Warehouse. It was run by a tall man who looked a little like Kris Kristofferson (complete with a Texan stetson), called Mike Wyen. Together with his formidable mother, Blanche (who sat on the door), they owned and ran the place. It boasted the best sound and lights in the north of England – a mean feat if ever there was one. An American DJ called Greg played the latest American disco imports, mixing them in and out of each other while smoke and strobes flooded the dance floor, sending you higher and higher into blissed-out euphoria. Of course the music wasn't the only thing that elevated you to new heights. As the glitter fell, champagne flowed – and cocaine snowed.

This was my first brush with cocaine. The Warehouse was visited by the north of England's glitterati, who came from far and wide to experience its soon-to-be-legendary hedonism. Immersed in fog on the dance floor, you were virtually lifted up and down by the pounding bass bins, while rich Leeds debutantes in sequined boob tubes, sparkling eye make-up running down their faces, draped themselves around you, sticking spoons up your nose. I got quite a taste for coke, but it was way beyond my financial means to buy my own.

To me the club was nirvana, disco heaven, and when I was there I felt I hadn't a care in the world. I was seduced by the newness of it all, the 4/4 beat; the repetitive bass lines took me over. For the next two years the soundtrack of my life would be such records as 'Love and Desire' by Arpeggio, 'Pistolero' by Galaxy, 'I Need You' by Donna Summer, 'In the Pocket' by African Suite, 'Funkytown' by Lipps Inc., 'E = MC^2' by Giorgio Moroder and 'No More Tears/ (Enough is Enough)' by Donna Summer and Barbra Streisand. It's difficult to describe how exciting it was without sounding merely nostalgic.

I asked Mike, the owner, for a job – anything at all – and straight away he put me on the cloakroom. I wasn't the only one from the art

college with a job at the Warehouse; Kris Neate, who had left the
year previously, also worked there, in the restaurant. I'd always liked
Kris, cool and laconic in his black T-shirts and jeans, with a biting
sense of humour and a contemptuous frown. Constantly smoking
cigarettes, alternated with puffs on an asthma inhaler, he treated
everyone with a suspicious eye and had a great line in verbal put-
downs. Naturally, we gravitated towards each other; Kris leaning
over the cloakroom door with fag in hand, we'd gossip like Gladys
and Ada on the street corner about the characters and creatures of
the night who inhabited this disco hell. While for a punter this was
heaven, to work there was an entirely different story. I suppose it was
a fun hell, though – the type of place you constantly complain about
but wouldn't much mind going to when you inevitably didn't make it
to the *other* place. Every night there was a drama, an episode in the
soap opera of too much disco, drugs and drink. There would always
be somebody passing out, or freaking out from excess; glasses or
punches would be thrown, women would scratch and fight; lovers
previously kissing (or occasionally having sex) ended up slapping
each other about. Hedonism can be hard work.

Behind the half-door of the cloakroom I was often the recipient of
drunken kisses, occasional punches from a jealous boyfriend (theirs,
not mine), or unwelcome attention from drunk guys who had started
to discover awakenings in another side of their sexuality. That could
be tricky – first they'd try to kiss you, and then they'd try to hit you.
Kiss or hit? They couldn't decide. On one occasion I was sexually
assaulted by an army cadet who pushed and locked me inside a toilet
cubicle with him. When I wouldn't perform to his bidding, he began
to get offended – 'What the fuck's wrong with me? Eh?' he shouted.
He tried to push my head downwards, unsuccessfully, then punched
me in the stomach, winding me, and hit me in the face, causing a
black eye.

All the staff at the Warehouse were encouraged to dress up in the
most outlandish outfits. Needless to say, I needed very little encour-
agement in this – sometimes wearing little more than a dab of disco
glitter. Then there were the money scams. Mike, like most club
owners, paid his staff meagrely, and so forced us to be inventive. My
personal scam is relatively well known in coat-check circles. By simply
placing two coats (or 'items', as they are known in the trade) on to
one hanger, but charging the unsuspecting punter for both, you can
successfully pocket the difference. One for you, one for me. On busy
nights there would be hundreds of coats, and my pockets would be
stuffed with cash. Me being me, of course, it would all go horribly
wrong – coats lost, tickets misplaced, jackets muddled and mixed up.

I once stood on a woman's handbag and crushed the entire contents. When she came to collect it and noticed its condition, she leaped over the counter, put her hands around my throat, and tried to strangle me. The bouncers had to prise her off. It turned out she was a well-known local prostitute. 'Don't talk to me, bitch, until you get tits,' she screamed at me as she was hauled off. Just a typical night. The bouncers were actually a godsend, and saved my neck more than once. In particular, a half-Russian man named Uri looked out for me, and I looked out for him.

As I was working lunchtimes and evenings at the Playhouse and nights at the Warehouse, my sleep suffered drastically. I would stagger home in the early hours, usually wired and/or drunk. I was exhausted most of the day, and acquired an ashen pallor to go with my seven-and-a-half-stone frame. Cocaine was not something we could rely on to keep us awake – still no more than an occasional treat that came our way – but Kris and I had discovered something else that kept us going: cheap sulphate speed. There were also Dodos – cough tablets sold over the counter in chemists – which induced a speedy effect. Unfortunately, when consumed in considerable amounts they made you extremely irritable and short-tempered, and prone to crying fits when they wore off. And wear off they always did, leaving you vulnerable, tired, oversensitive and deeply emotional. There was more than one scene at the Warehouse with me storming out in tears thanks to the Dodos. We never learned though, never could. Every day we'd be back at Boots, feigning a cough, requesting Dodos from a suspicious assistant.

So began a pattern that I was to continue right through until the mid-eighties – speeding all day on amphetamine (of some sort or other), crashing the next day and then speeding all evening, crashing the next day and speeding all evening again. Is it any wonder I became prone to periods of insane behaviour? I stood behind that cloakroom half-door banging my knees in time to the disco beat until my jeans wore through. I ground my teeth until my jaws ached, and wound up tense, wired and on edge, a drama waiting around every corner.

Time passed in the coat check. In my head I wrote hundreds of little songs, one or two becoming early Soft Cell numbers, including one called 'Mix', which we performed in our early set. To a galloping beat and syndrum sound, I would sing, 'Mix your drink, / Mix and match, / Mix with people, / Mix and watch, / Watch them mix, / Mix and meet, / To the disco mix they're mixing feet.' Hardly a candidate for an Ivor Novello Award. But it passed the time and livened up the nights as they became monotonous, the beat of the records still pounding in my head as I tried unsuccessfully to sleep.

Months passed.

After a while it became clear that the glittering star that was the Warehouse was beginning to fade. The fashionable and trendy began to tire of it and moved on, despite it being still the best club around. During my sentence in the coat check the disco boom had peaked and all the best records seemed to have been made and played. The glitterati decided that it was time to chill out and entertain at home: dinner parties became all the rage. At the Warehouse, all those people who had queued so devotedly only to be refused admission months earlier were now let in. It became rougher, down at heel, more volatile – and a more perilous place to work. The crowd were less tolerant, and it became a nightly ordeal to face up to drunken louts who wouldn't tolerate any poofs around. Having now travelled the world, I can firmly say that there is nothing scarier than a rough, straight, northern nightclub on a Saturday night.

People began to be laid off, fewer bouncers were employed, fewer staff. We grew worried for our jobs. On the early nights of the week the club was empty, the boredom intolerable. Our wages were cut, and we were given fewer nights to work. It's a well-known pattern. A new club opens, and, if it takes off, it has a boom period. Everyone wants to be seen there, all the right faces, the beautiful people, the place is electric with the buzz. The DJs are the hottest, money flows through the door, everyone is on a high. But then one day, whether after a few months or a few years, it inevitably happens. There are suddenly less people than expected. Excuses are made: 'it's raining', 'it's a holiday', 'ah well, it *is* just after Christmas'. But the trend continues, and, before you know it, the word is out. It's over. It's yesterday. It's spent. And just as abruptly there is somewhere new to go, something new to do. There are few things sadder than a club, once hip and vibrant, in its death throes. It's like arriving at the party too late; the drink and drugs are gone, the good times all been had.

Things came to a head at the Warehouse when Greg, the American DJ, had a nervous breakdown. Suddenly the music stopped and he began to throw glasses down on to the wooden dance floor. Everyone stopped and looked up in shock as he let fly, screaming abuse across the dazed silence. Then, as a grand gesture, a noble finale, he began to rip out the expensive equipment and turntables, throwing them down on to the dance floor too. Aside from creating untold damage, he nearly injured several customers. The security staff ran upstairs and dragged him protesting and shouting from the club, throwing him into the street. It was a terrible sight – Greg had been the heart of the club. He had brought in the customers, even though later he had contributed to the reason they were staying away – tastes had changed. Maybe someone had indiscreetly pointed this out to him and he'd taken the news very badly; maybe he'd been told to change his music policy or leave. More likely he'd just been sacked. Whatever the reason, the music was over.

*

Soft Cell made its debut at the 1979 art-college Christmas party. We recruited a college friend as a technician – Steve Griffith, a tall, good-looking, easy-going guy, was to be the third, invisible, member of the band, looking after the effects and our back-projection set-ups. One side of the stage was to show Super-8 films and the other side slides and projections, a device adapted from Throbbing Gristle, Human League and Cabaret Voltaire, who all used projections of some sort in their shows. We also wanted to use films that Dave and I had made ourselves – industrial landscapes, the neon lights of Soho, city buildings, motorways, smashed and demolished radios, shop dummies, words and colours that flickered across the stage and on to a white screen behind us. Dave prepared all the bass and percussion on backing tracks which would be played on a visible battered Revox placed behind the Korg synthesizer and syndrum set-up. It looked simple, stark and minimal, and, principally, postmodern: an industrial futuristic seaside cabaret act. (Or the Little and Large of electro, as someone once joked.) We were to be the first one of half a dozen acts from the polytechnic and the university. We knew the other groups would all be taking themselves very seriously, with grey raincoats, pallid complexions and suicidal demeanours, and would all have a political agenda. Soft Cell remained non-political, sparse and electronic, but also an antidote to this melancholy. We intended to be humorous, however ironic and black.

When we took to the stage that night we opened with an industrial song called 'Bleak is My Favourite Cliché' – a swipe at all the over-privileged miseries who traipse their way through university, professing poverty and claiming to be hard done by, yet relying on their parents' support. 'I had my back teeth taken out, / My eyes stare far away . . . / I like to dress myself in waste disposal grey. / I'll tell you bleak, / My favourite cliché' went the words, and I spat them out with all the middle-class, hard-done-by venom I could muster. We followed with 'Factory Fun'. 'Factory fun, / Live your life on the line', I sang in a robotic, stilted voice, images of mass-consumerism flickering on the screen behind. 'Pyrex My Cuisine' and 'Tupperware Party' followed. Dave pounded electronic sounds, echo effects and violent percussive rhythms out of the keyboard, his eyes staring blankly ahead in that psychotic fashion that he was so terrific at. One side of Dave was a gentle pussycat, but here was the darker, edgier side. The other songs in that first set were 'A Man Could Get Lost', 'Mix', 'Penthouse Pet' (about gold-digging Page 3 girls), 'Science Fiction Stories' and a fast-paced 'Living for Today' – 'There's always tomorrow, / That's what they say, / But seeing is believing / I live for today.' The penultimate song was 'Facility Girls', aping fifties teen-ballad kitsch.

The show was shambolic, to say the least. I yelped rather than sang, inspired by very early Siouxsie and the Banshees if anyone – we certainly saw some of our own songs as inhabiting that same dark world. But we ended our set with a song more akin to Throbbing Gristle and Suicide's 'Frankie Teardrop'. It was called 'Persuasion', and was based on a device we had read about – a small black box allegedly employed in supermarkets to transmit subliminal messages. It supposedly urged people to spend money – 'Buy more! Buy more now!' The track also drew on the early George Lucas film *THX113*, in which the inhabitants of a post-nuclear world are placated with soothing messages, and urged to buy products that maintain them in a state of tranquil calm. To a throbbing, pulsating beat, I recited the story of a housewife suffering a nervous breakdown while in a supermarket – the tape loop repeating 'Buy our product.' Unnerving, it was extremely draining to perform. As the strobe lights flashed, the screen images flickered to a climax, and me screaming through echo effects until the sound became ear-piercing. Then . . . silence. I'd heard that silence before – after the performance at York University.

As we left the stage there was a mixed and confused reaction from the audience. Most of the students were there to see friends in other bands and received us with at best lukewarm clapping, at worst laughter. Some were just stunned, standing with beer glass in hand, staring in bewilderment. Others – our friends from the college – cheered wildly and seemed genuinely excited by the performance. Certainly, no one had seen anything quite like us, and our debut had made an impression. And anyone following our performance that evening would have seemed deadly dull and conventional. The reaction was one we got used to: either adoration or derision, glory or disdain. Some would buy into Soft Cell, get it, and never quite get over it; others just never got it. Even to this day some people still feel an intense passion about Soft Cell, and every time the albums are reissued rush out to buy them all over again. Many consistently stayed the course, but others who claim now to have loved us all along, even to have discovered us, and who say that we were to them a seminal inspiration, were hardly allies. Back then college friends, close friends, and a couple of music journalists were our only champions.

Nevertheless, after the Christmas gig Dave and I were exhilarated and wanted to do more. We suspected we might be on to something very special and so we were all the more desperate to get out, fine tune, and write more songs. With things at the Warehouse having gone from bad to worse, Kris Neate and I put our heads together and had an idea. We had been reading about clubs down in London, run by people such as Rusty Egan and Steve Strange. These new clubs were playing an alternative, electronic dance music, and people were buying into it. Clubs like Blitz, Hell and Le Beate Route were all the rage, with people dressing outlandishly in make-up and bizarre outfits. There was a new movement afoot, with its own music, entrepreneurs, designers – and bands like Spandau Ballet, Visage and Landscape. This scene had its own faces and stars, made up largely of hard-core clubbers who lived for hedonism, creating new and more outrageous looks at every public appearance. Colour supplements and pop magazines featured them, with photographs of the scene's leading lights in their exotic finery: Steve Strange; George O'Dowd (before the 'Boy'); Julia (now known as Princess Julia), who ran a shop called PX which catered for the new fashion; Chris O'Sullivan, a fashion designer who later had his own band, Blue Rondo à la Turk; milliner Steve Jones; and Philip Sallon. We heard about the queues at Blitz, and how Steve Strange would turn people like Mick Jagger away.

This New Romantic Movement had the edge of punk but the glamour and glitter of disco. With hindsight, perhaps it wasn't the best cocktail of ideas, but it was the first fashion movement of the eighties, and for a while eclipsed the influence of punk. Kris went down to London to see things for himself, and when he returned we'd talk into the night as I interrogated him about every aspect of what he'd seen. It was only a matter of time before we approached Mike with a bid to save the Warehouse.

Kris and I pitched the idea that we would start our own electronic alternative music night, with an emphasis on new electronic dance sounds mixed in with alternative funk, industrial, post-punk and disco. We would encourage all the Leeds alternative freaks to come out of the woodwork and dress up – the better (meaning weirder) they looked, the greater their chances of free admission (only at first, of course). It would be a young, hedonistic crowd, we explained. We knew that Leeds had a strong Bowie constituency – the north of England always had – and the Bowie clones who years earlier had taken over the dance floors in soul suits and orange hair, who had walked along invisible walls against invisible panes of glass miming wildly to *Station to Station*, were still around. We knew there were loads of fashionable punks, too. Leeds and Sheffield have always been a glam stronghold; with all that industry, there was a need for glitter and lippy. With the Warehouse's legendary sound system and lights, we hoped they would come from far and wide to hear the new sounds they were reading about. We would also showcase the best of local electronic bands – after all, I had a vested interest in doing that. Everyone knew the Warehouse. Now it was time for them to learn it had entered a new era.

Mike sat back in his chair, pondering our proposition for a while, admitting he was a little sceptical. After all, it was a crowd he didn't know. But what choice did he really have? The place desperately needed a kick start. He agreed to give us a share of the door money on Monday nights for a trial period. We would also have an expense allowance for new records, even though we both had a substantial record collection already. Thus overnight Kris and I became hosts – entrepreneurs if you're feeling generous – and, not least, DJs. It felt like nothing on earth for me, being behind the decks of the most famous club in the north of England, playing music I loved. And no more hellish nights of taking coats and handbags.

*

Sally and Ed decided to leave Marlborough Gardens for a larger flat of their own, so I had to give up my grace and favour room. Along with Dave, I found a room in a house in Leicester Grove, overlooking an unkempt square in a run-down area of Leeds. Kris Neate was already living in the house, as was Cirus, a moody singer from another Leeds band. The house, having several rooms, underwent many changes of occupants over the two years I was to live there. Often it resembled a squat, with people coming and going, and just staying over. You never knew most of the people, and personal possessions would often go missing. Other occupants included a young rockabilly called Tim Taylor, who played bass in the Leeds band Pink Peg Slacks (who later covered the Soft Cell track 'Bedsitter', and even played on one of my early Mambas records), and a young DJ who played around various Leeds clubs, called Annie Hogan. The house was constantly filthy and in need of repair, and at one point was entirely overrun by mice. I remember one morning when Dave suddenly picked up a carving knife and beheaded a mouse as it scurried in full flight across the draining board.

I think this is a suitable time to clear up the first of many popular fallacies. Dave and I had separate rooms. It was assumed by many when we became famous that Dave and I must be sleeping together. This was not the first assumption of its kind – it was commonly thought years earlier that Marc Bolan was sleeping with his percussion player Mickey Finn. Sorry to disappoint, but Dave and I were not intimate in any way. Dave is as heterosexual as they come, and the thought never crossed our minds. But Dave certainly had no problem with my sexuality; he'd been through five years at art college, after all, and an upbringing in Blackpool. He'd seen it all. And it's often the case that straight men who are completely at ease with their own sexuality have no problem with accepting a differing sexuality.

During our time at the house Dave was rarely seen, disappearing for days on end into his tiny room piled high with keyboard equipment and Revoxes. We were now starting to gig locally around Leeds, Bradford and York, occasionally even as far afield as Manchester. We began to get a reputation and a small following, with the same faces turning up again and again. The concerts became more and more chaotic as people began to invade the stage and to dance with me, often causing the show to grind to a halt as equipment was sent crashing to the floor in a mayhem of pushing and shoving. New numbers began to make their way into the set, including one particular song entitled 'Martin'. I'd seen a film by George Romero called *Martin*; set in the bleak post-industrial landscape of Pittsburgh, USA, it is about a teenage vampire who drains the blood from his victims. I thought it highly original. The story was a metaphor for alienation (though the AIDS crisis has since given it a new layer of meaning) – an early recurrent Soft Cell theme. Dave and I imagined we were writing our own theme song to that movie. It typifies the way we would work.

The live set was becoming more dance orientated in its beats and grooves, and a quite different type of audience evolved through Dave's love of Northern Soul finding its way into our music. We couldn't exactly call ourselves mainstream, though: not everyone was seduced by the Soft Cell beat – far from it. A great many people took offence at my behaviour and appearance; in the rough pubs and clubs where we often played, I had to deal with many incidents of homophobia. At one gig in Bradford, in a venue called Splash, I was dressed in a Captain Scarlet outfit. We played on the dance floor (there was no stage), and a girl decided to dance right in front of my face, toying with me. Her boyfriend took great offence, walked up to me, and smacked me hard in the mouth. This is where I was thankful to have Dave and Steve Griffith around. Nobody messed twice with those two – especially when Dave went into his psycho mode. A fight ensued and punches were thrown, but we made it out unharmed. However, it didn't help matters that I was unable to keep my mouth shut in such delicate situations.

Our first paid gig was at the Warehouse, on one of the first Monday club nights we held. We earned the bank-busting sum of £40. Everything before that had been for expenses only, and more often than not we had to break into our own money to cover costs. But soon we were to get a bigger break.

John Keenan was at that time a Leeds promoter who had built a reputation running the F Club in Leeds. From punk to post-punk, New Romantic through to Gothic, everybody who was anybody had played the F Club. It was a great venue to see all the new and hip bands. Every year John put on a three-day event at the Leeds Queen's Hall (a huge hangar of a space) called the Futurama Festival. It was a showcase not only for all the biggest bands of the moment but also for the cream of local talent. Naturally I felt we fitted into the latter category, and I begged John to give us a spot on the bill. At first he was reluctant. I pestered him and gave him a tape, hoping he would change his mind. I'd already personally handed tapes to people like Tony Wilson from Factory – and even John Peel – but had heard nothing back. When I listen now to the quality of those early tapes, it's not surprising. John Keenan eventually relented and gave us a spot extremely low down on the bill – actually, while the hall was filling up. Years later John, disgruntled in an interview, complained that he'd discovered us and hadn't been given due credit. Strange, but I don't remember him being that keen to even give us a chance! But it was a spot nevertheless, and John must be given credit for single-handedly creating and enlivening a Leeds music scene with the F Club and Futurama.

Our set that day at Futurama was very poor. I was as nervous as hell. Exposed on the giant stage, the two of us felt dwarfed, our scant equipment leaving acres of space unfilled. Our sound was tinny, we had no soundcheck – nor even our own sound crew. The sunlight streamed through the glass roof and there was no place for our projections, films and strobes to be effective. So we limped through our set (as one press report put it), my voice faltering, unable to project. The mood lifted only when we burst into a frantic rendition of Black Sabbath's 'Paranoid'. The gig was also being filmed, so huge lights shone in my face, making me feel even more anxious. However, after a few numbers I found my feet and put everything into what I was doing, I shook nervously and paced wildly through-out each song, trying to occupy as much of the stage as possible, even running in circles and falling to the floor. At the end of forty minutes I looked down to see about five thousand faces staring back at me. Suddenly they burst into applause. Despite all the drawbacks, they seemed to like us! I was surprised but elated. It was to be a turning point.

But Dave and I also felt disappointed. A couple of months earlier we had made our first record with a loan of £2,000 from Dave's mum. It was a four-track EP called *Mutant Moments*, in a limited edition of 2,000. The EP featured four scratchy tracks: 'Frustration', 'Potential', 'Metro Mr X' and a tongue-in-cheek song 'L.O.V.E. Feelings' (complete with me breaking down into laughter). The record was supposed to be available for the Futurama Festival, but pressing problems meant it had been delayed. We knew we could have sold every copy that day. This misfortune was a pattern which was to repeat itself over the next few years.

There were one or two mixed press reports about our appearance, but word of mouth created a 'buzz', and talk reached the ears of a young London DJ and music-paper contributor who compiled a weekly chart for *Sounds*. His chart – somewhat embarrassingly called 'The Futurist Chart' – was made up of demos and debut recordings by electronic and industrial bands, most of which were unknown to the general public but part of a thriving underground scene. Quite unexpectedly one day the payphone rang at the house in Leicester Grove. A rough cockney voice on the other end said, 'A'wight? It's Stevo 'ere. I've 'eard about your Futurama gig and I've got a copy of your EP. I wanna put you in my Futurist Chart.' At first I thought this was someone playing a joke, but I listened and, excited and intrigued, realized that this was *the* actual Stevo. We talked for a while, and he invited me down to London for a meeting. I was curious as hell about this rough-sounding London lad and what he would actually be like.

Meanwhile, the Monday nights at the Warehouse were proving a resounding success. Once again the wild and creative, the colourful and loud were piling through the doors. It was a younger crowd than the disco coke glitterati, but they excelled themselves in the wildest costumes, excessive make-up and all kinds of finery. One person, who called himself Roxy, came every week, each time in a wilder outfit, which he must have spent all week working on. His outfits became an event in themselves, eagerly looked forward to by all. Kris and I held court spinning the records – Human League, Giorgio Moroder, Kraftwerk, Adam and the Ants, Gary Numan, Siouxsie, as well as

Frank Sinatra and early Goth groups such as the Cramps and Bauhaus. Glam fans were kept happy with lots of retro Bowie, Roxy and Bolan. Kris and I were like cats who had got the cream as we took our percentage of the door. In turn our drink and drug intake increased too, and our behaviour became more and more unruly and outrageous – along with our outfits, which of course had to be different every Monday night. We must have been extremely obnoxious, lording it over everyone and giving attitude left, right and centre. We played whatever music we liked (no requests, please), and if we didn't like anyone in the club (meaning if they didn't grovel enough) we would have them thrown out.

We had two camps of people. On the one hand were our best friends; on the other were those who were jealous and wanted to let us know what they thought. The latter didn't stick around for too long. Kris and I went to exhausting lengths to create our looks for the night – one night I favoured an Indian-prince appearance with turban and pearls, while Kris loved the Goth look of crosses and white make-up. One time we spied a pile of cassocks through a church window and later broke into the vestry and stole them. Black cassocks became our regular wear – on a Saturday night in Leeds, skinheads would follow us shouting, Where's the bloody funeral? Another time we travelled down to London to visit a theatrical costumiers, and came back laden with velvet jackets and embroidered tunics.

Our youthful desire for attention became insatiable. The local newspaper came and wrote about the club and printed photos of the strangest customers. I was pictured with two girls above the heading 'One Big Happy Family'. The piece ran as follows: 'Trendsetter Marc Almond, leader of Leeds electronic band Soft Cell, is a dedicated follower of fashion – he helped to start the New Romantic trend in Leeds. Polytechnic student Marc used to get funny looks as he walked through the streets in his self-designed clothes and heavy make-up, but here at the Warehouse they're just one big happy family.' 'It's a gentle and stylish movement, which means we don't cause trouble for anybody,' I said.

Local TV news show *Calendar* sent a TV crew down to film a piece. The interviewer was a nervous young man dressed inappropriately in a bow tie and tuxedo. 'Why am I dressed like this?' he enquired to camera. 'Because something special is happening at Leeds Warehouse. They're called New Romantics – let's go and meet them.' I was interviewed wearing half a ton of make-up, with strange plaits hanging over my face; and later, while he interviewed other people, Soft Cell performed in the background. It was our first television appearance. It was also one of the first TV assignments for a young Richard Madeley.

*

With money in my pocket I began to make trips to London. I'd become friendly with the beautiful and stylish Sophie Parkin, Molly's daughter. Sophie was doing a course in fine art, and I loved spending time with her. One of our most memorable soirées was at Molly's New Year's Eve party to herald 1981. It was an occasion that heightened my resolve to be successful, to be part of something better. I wanted to meet interesting people, despite feeling uncomfortable in the company of strangers. And to be a person others wanted to meet – especially artists.

Molly's house was beautiful, oak-panelled throughout, and once belonged to Anita Pallenburg and Keith Richard. It was still imbued with a Bohemian spirit from the decadent sixties. The party was a wild affair with celebrities, artists, designers, photographers and countless beautiful young vivacious things. George Melly performed, later cornering me and slipping his hands deftly into my pockets for a grope. I sat and talked to him as he held court with blue jokes and jazz anecdotes. Later still I found myself sandwiched between actors Hywel Bennett and Jill Bennett. By this time, I was extremely drunk and stoned, and I ended up arguing with Hywel by telling him that his finest performance was in the film *There's Something Nasty in the Woodshed* – especially the naked full-length shot of him in a mirror. He disagreed. I ended up angrily telling him, 'Fuck off, you old queen!' 'Oh I love it, I love it,' Hywel replied glibly.

Things went from bad to worse, to much worse. I found myself upstairs, barely conscious, in a room with a rotating mirror ball while a woman performed a barefoot Isadora Duncan number for me. The room itself had been Jimi Hendrix's favourite, where he loved to lie on the floor stoned and play his guitar – it was full of those sorts of vibe. Across the hall there was a man in a Hamlet costume performing oral sex on a lesser member of the cast, while a woman in body paint straddled a naked half-caste boy. I felt like I was in a scene from *Blow-Up*, expecting David Hemmings to appear any moment.

As dawn dredged itself up, Sophie ended up in a fight with the club entrepreneur Philip Sallon, who slapped her face for some reason. Shortly thereafter the music stopped. Allegedly Boy George (still not yet a pop star) had stolen the ghetto blaster. I ended up disgracing myself by being sick everywhere, lying in the corner, a mass of make-up and vomit.

I stayed with Molly Parkin for a few days, helping her clean up the house, while George Melly continued unabated with his anecdotes from his 'rum, bum and concertina' days. The following weeks saw Molly and me running around town, visiting various nightclubs (me still dressed in a floor-length cassock) with a friend of hers, Roy, who worked for the Rolling Stones and actually looked like a cross between Keith Richard and Ronnie Wood. At one point we had dinner at Langan's with a stranger called Terry, who was apparently an escaped IRA prisoner who, so the story went, had just blown up a gasworks. I'd been insulting him all evening, but this revelation shut me up. After dinner we ended up at Tramp with the model Minah Bird and boxer John Conteh (whom I attempted to snog), and with Roy paralytically drunk and smashing glasses. Molly and I finally had to crash at Roy's because she had lost her keys to the Cheyne Walk house. A typical night out with Molly!

Molly also sent me to meet various friends of hers she thought I would find influential or interesting. One afternoon I found myself in a large warehouse in Bermondsey – the extravagant studio of artist and designer Andrew Logan. We sat and took tea, chatted, and afterwards he showed me his glittering collection of art, mythological sculptures covered in broken mirror, that dominated the room. Andrew hosted every year the Alternative Miss World competition – that wonderful a anti-beauty pageant of the freakish, bizarre and beautifully weird. Some years later I performed a special show at one of these events on the theme of fire.

Later in the year I stayed with Molly again when I was in London recording 'Memorabilia' but I lost contact when new-found fame swept me off on a fresh wave of destructive madness. She soon moved to another address, and we lost contact. I bumped into Sophie years later. She'd become a younger version of her mother, with her own wild hats and flamboyant outfits. 'Mother would love to hear from you,' she said. I did so want to call her, but by that time drugs were making me a nervous wreck – withdrawn and reclusive – and I just never managed to pick up the phone. Molly had given me a major impetus, for which I'm eternally grateful. More practically, she gave me a bed. I see her now, free from the demon drink, and looking as radiant as ever. As much as anyone, she discovered me.

*

Back at the Warehouse, things had been going so well that Kris and I were due for a fall. And one day it came. We were victims of our own success. Mike's wife had persuaded him that we were getting far too much from the door money, and he put us on a wage. We were told we ought to be grateful; we felt quite the opposite. Kris and I – highly strung, constantly soaring on alcohol and speed – grabbed our things and dramatically stormed out.

Of course there was someone else to step into our shoes. (Isn't there always?) At first the crowd promised to support us and boycott the place, but memories are short in clubland, and soon the place was as full as if we'd never been there. I suspect there were quite a few that felt secretly pleased that we were out in the street, clubless and humiliated. We started a couple of other nights – including the Curfew Club at a sleazy dive, the name of which I've forgotten – but I eventually ended up DJing at Phonographique. However, the music I was playing proved too strange and eclectic (punk and obscure funk, electro and rockabilly mixed with Sinatra, Minnelli and Peggy Lee, with a large helping of trash), and after a huge argument, and being punched in the face by a bouncer I was fired. A year later, when the New Romantic star had faded, Kris and I did go back to work at the Warehouse, for a funk and Northern Soul night called White Savage Dance. Mike welcomed us back. Maybe it had something to do with Soft Cell's raised profile after 'Memorabilia'.

I tried promoting at other venues too, but it never worked, just like the DJing. I even started a club in Manchester, at Devilles, but they had their own scene and we were outsiders. Anyway, by this time Soft Cell was starting to take up more and more of my time, and soon I didn't want anything more to do with hosting nightclubs or DJing for as long as I lived. I had had my time, and had loved it – well, most of it – but it did become tedious dealing with those nightclub owners. I have on many occasions over the years been asked to DJ again, and have always refused. When I was young, DJing offered an opening for me, as it does for so many young people I've met. It's a way of expressing yourself through music, without needing to be a musician. You just need to love the music, and be able to create moods and atmosphere for people to dance or chill out to. It's really something for the young still in search of something to dream about or aspire to; it's a lamentable sight to see a mature celebrity listening to more Kiss FM than his antiquated consciousness can safely assimilate, spinning the decks with youthful tunes. It kind of reminds me of those overweight rich businessmen who drive around in open-top Ferraris, raging impotently against the dying of their golden youth.

5

'Trying to please all these people around me'

If you've just turned to this chapter from page 1 then let me bring you up to date. Born in Southport; alcoholic father; younger sister; miserable schooling; confused sexuality; great college years; dabbled with drugs; met Dave Ball; formed Soft Cell; groped by George Melly; about to meet guy in London who thinks the music has potential.

*

As I sat in the offices of *Record Mirror* one late July afternoon in 1980, it was with trepidation that I considered what kind of person I might be about to meet. I imagined him to be some painted Steve Strange London trendy, dressed in the latest PX outfit and with matching attitude. But he did run a successful electronic music night in Hammersmith (well, it was at least London); he did contribute to *Sounds*. He must, I thought, be a *somebody*. But nothing could have prepared me for the person who came into my room.

''Ello! Stevo!' he said, sounding like a gruff cockney barrow boy, reaching out to shake my hand. Stood before me was a stocky (dare I say chubby?) young lad. His hair was badly cut in a kind of grown-out Phil Oakey of the Human League style, slightly long on one side. He was dressed in black, with a loose-fitting overcoat and large black boots. Across his jumper was a diagonal glue mark where once had been stuck a piece of tape, I suspect to give the garment a Gary Numanesque make-over. On his face were the remains of blusher and make-up, totally at odds with his demeanour, and looking as if they had been applied several nights earlier. They gave his whole face a decidedly grey complexion. As it had been raining heavily, the whole ensemble had a bedraggled and damp appearance. This was Stevo.

It turned out he didn't even work in the building; it just seemed a convenient place to meet since he was dropping by in search of a free ticket for a gig that night. He bragged to me about how many bands wanted him to manage them (he couldn't decide between Soft Cell – not that we'd asked him – and a London band called Naked Lunch) and how successful his club nights were. He had the gift of the gab,

and was immensely likeable. It worked. I was impressed. He told me
he was putting together an album of London underground electronic
and 'futuristic' bands; everyone wanted to be on it, he said, but he
was only interested in bands who 'broke down barriers'. His personal
favourites were undiscovered bands. He was going to start his own
record label, called Some Bizarre, and license his artists' recordings to
the major labels. He wanted Soft Cell to contribute a track, and he
wanted to be our manager.

I returned to Leeds and told Dave all about the eccentric character.
Between us, we made the fateful decision to go with him. After all, it
wasn't like we were being inundated with offers, and at least Stevo
might be able to bring us to a London crowd. We did have a couple
of other offers of management, though – one from Warehouse owner,
Mike Wyen. One night he wined and dined Dave and me at his home
in an attempt to woo us. I thought it curious; I still felt resentful
about having created a successful night and then having been double-
crossed over it. Mike was furious when we went with Stevo. Our
decision especially angered his wife, who convinced herself that
Mike had discovered me. Yet Mike still let me DJ at the club – and
I still accepted the work; he was, after all was said and done, a
businessman.

Dave was as intrigued by Stevo as I was. It was hard to believe
that Stevo was only seventeen years old. He came from Dagenham –
a rough, deprived area of east London, well known to be a National
Front stronghold. His brother was the infamous Joe Pierce, a member
of the National Front who was later jailed, and whose name became
graffitied across the area – 'FREE JOE PIERCE.' It was remarkable
that Stevo, growing up in this environment and exposed to such
intolerant attitudes, was able to remain fairly liberal and break free
from it. Stevo and Joe were total opposites. One newspaper article
described them as 'The Saint and the Devil', and, while I wouldn't
describe Stevo as a saint, he certainly wasn't a bigot. It's true that he
had in his time run with gangs and found himself in trouble, leaving
school at sixteen with no qualifications. After a number of labouring
jobs, he had gone on a work-training placement which just so
happened to be within the record company Phonogram, as a general
run-around – this was to be his introduction to the music business.
He slaved and saved, bought himself a small disco unit, and began a
series of nights that were to gain a reputation as weird happenings.
He became an attention-seeking showman, often performing in
bizarre outfits or even naked while he spun the discs of some of the
new underground or experimental electronic bands.

When he had left school Stevo could barely read or write, and suffered from a chronic speech impediment. By the time I met him, he was still working on improving his literary skills, often writing down long or impressive-sounding words in a notebook. He drew upon these at what he believed to be appropriate moments, more often than not committing malapropisms. He practised the longer words at every opportunity. He was never afraid to learn openly, yet remained sensitive about his shortcomings. But he knew he was as good as anyone else, and in that he was right, and he was determined to learn – 'savvy' and uncanny in his ability to carve himself a life of his own, to rise above his roots and ultimately free himself of the restraints of his upbringing.

One of his favourite pastimes was to annoy his family – especially Joe. Stevo would take home black musicians for afternoon tea. Zeke Manyika from the band Orange Juice was a regular visitor, which would cause his father and brother to seethe with anger. Yet Stevo never blamed his parents for their attitude; it was their own background which had instilled this in them, and he knew it. They had had no way to escape it; they simply became part of it. Nevertheless, Stevo took every opportunity to rub their faces in it, to hold up a mirror to their intolerances. Once, he meticulously researched his family background, and unearthed evidence that his ancestry was in part Jewish. You can imagine his relish when he confronted his bigoted father with that!

Sexism was also rife at Stevo's home. Mother did what father said: that's how it was. Once, Dave and I offered to make Stevo's aunt a cup of tea. She stood there looking confused, and then began to cry. It turned out that no one, let alone a man, had ever made her tea before. She was so overcome by this gesture of kindness that she found it impossible to contain her emotions. But where women were concerned Stevo was slower, and still had a lot to learn.

It was this complex, roguish, unique personality who was to become such a major part of my life, my career and my history. Of all the people I have worked with he was to remain with me the longest. We were to stay together for seventeen years; a love/hate relationship that many artists have with their managers. While it survived good and bad times, it was a working relationship that was to outlive its productive life, to become grotesquely symbiotic and destructively dependent. Finally as I felt unable to cope without him around, he became complacent about me. If I was impossibly difficult he probably drove me to it – but then he allowed me to get away with it. Yet as many times as I wanted to strangle him, for just as many I would be eternally thankful. So to add to the other paradoxes in my life, I now had this charismatic amalgamation of W. C. Fields, Max Clifford and Robert Maxwell – a selfish generous maverick, a considerate pain in the ass, a stupid genius. There were always two sides to Stevo: manifestly sensitive and yet wholly inconsiderate.

Stevo seemed genuinely to love Soft Cell and to have faith in us. He never suggested we have a management contract at that time, and our relationship was built on mutual trust.

*

We recorded 'The Girl with the Patent Leather Face' at John Darling's small studio. It was tinny-sounding, a trashy synthesizer song that owed much to 'Warm Leatherette', an innovative early electro track by the Normal. This group was really Daniel Miller – a pioneer of British electronic music who later went on to own Mute Records, which was to sign such bands and artists as Depeche Mode, Nick Cave, Erasure, Diamanda Galas and many more. At one time Mute Records and Some Bizarre had between them the cream of electronic and experimental bands. The song was inspired in part by the J. G. Ballard book *Crash* – a book that inspired Siouxsie and Throbbing Gristle through to John Foxx and Gary Numan: a story of sexual fetishists turned on by car accidents, a perfect bleak scenario for so much post-punk industrial electronic music. The track cost £20 to make and was almost erased at one point, quite by accident; half the song went missing, but no one noticed. 'You can laugh, point at me, / They do it all the time, / But how would you like it / If you had a face like mine – Kiss me shiny baby.'

The *Some Bizarre* album was Stevo's vision. It was always the *music* he believed in, as opposed to the style and fashion aspects. Apart from Soft Cell, the album featured notable acts who were to go on to bigger things, namely Depeche Mode, The The and Blanc-mange. But when the record was released it was received with derision by most of the music press, who sneered at Stevo and his 'poor little album'. Some chose to ridicule electronic music in general – 'a collection of robotic bands with no feelings, bloody synthesizers, total nonsense, cold and soulless'.

Only *Sounds* journalist Betty Page (who had named herself after an exotic fifties glamour model) was to champion Soft Cell in the early days, writing a glowing review of *Some Bizarre*, singling out Soft Cell's track, and topping the review with a large photo of me. 'What a Little Pervert' read the piece – an early indication of how the public would come to perceive me in the future. It's thrilling to see your first mention in print, a glow of recognition, however small. Nothing can be more exciting in an artist's career than the first time people write about you or play your music on the radio. Then to witness a nightclub crowd dancing to your track, riding that first thrilling wave of excitement when people discover you, and you encounter the feedback. It is what the music business unimaginatively calls 'the buzz', mouth to mouth – 'Oh God, have you heard of . . .' Everybody starts talking about you, everybody is interested, everybody wants you – everywhere. Hype. Exaggeration. Overstatement. Embellishment. Ballyhoo. Hoopla. Call it what you will.

Hype had a great deal to do with our first flush of success. The truth was that nobody was really *that* interested in us, even though 'The Girl with the Patent Leather Face' was singled out as one of the more interesting tracks on the album. But an enigma was being conjured up around us, and we began to feel a response. Nevertheless, the major record companies were still not very interested. They thought we were just a strange, oddball northern couple. People advised Stevo to drop us, convinced that we'd never get anywhere. But this made him all the more determined. Eventually, through the constant badgering and bullying technique he was developing, though had not yet perfected, he secured us a licensing deal with Phonogram Records. Our A & R man was Roger Aimes. We suspected we were really signed only because Phonogram wanted another of Stevo's acts, the Manchester group B-Movie – a pleasant enough group of guys who were better looking than us and, more importantly, thought the record company, played proper instruments. We were what you would call part of a job lot, a favour granted, and very soon felt unwanted.

We were grudgingly given £1,000 and told to buy some instruments. I recall that Dave spent the money on a new drum machine and a few effects. I didn't give up my day job in Leeds. Then Stevo brought us down to London to record four new tracks. It was an exciting time for us, and an honour that we were working with Daniel Miller (as we had requested). How we secretly yearned to be on his label! He had recently signed Depeche Mode, who were to be the perfect electro pop band. He had himself been releasing bubblegum electronic records under the auspicious name of the Silicone Teens – now Depeche Mode were to be his Silicone Teens for real. But Daniel had also been involved in some of the darker and weirder electronic pop of the late seventies and early eighties, and it was with this in mind that we'd wondered if he'd work with us to produce our first proper record.

We chose a handful of songs from our live set – the Ball compositions 'Metro Mr X' and 'A Man Could Get Lost', and the paranoid, pulsing 'Persuasion'. The night before recording we came up with a new, hypnotic, repetitive bass riff based on a James Brown funk track, added a disco beat and sound effects, while I improvised and rapped a list of kitsch and trashy objects ('key chains and snowstorms'), mentioning souvenirs of places and people ('pieces of people to help me to remember'). I was imagining a serial killer surrounded by trophies, sat in a plastic-decorated bedroom – almost conjuring up images for a 'Blackpool Chainsaw Massacre'. During the recording session we timed the track to one of our favourite Donna Summer records, and used Roland space-echo effects on the voice. The song was 'Memorabilia'. It was to become one of the most talked about dance records of the year, and the first acid-house techno record ever.

'Memorabilia' instantly expanded our following. People sat up and took notice. It also made us more dance-conscious and changed our direction. The track made its presence felt in the lower reaches of the national charts, but more importantly it became a huge club hit, even as far away as New York. Years later, black guys would come up to me on the street (for some reason, even today, I am recognized the most by black people) and say, 'Hey – Marc Almond, Soft Cell, "Memorabilia", great track.' Soon, of course, almost no recognition would pass without another song title being mentioned. 'Memorabilia' is a track that has inspired countless techno records; DJs still approach me or my management requesting to remix it. It also inspired various American artists – not least Trent Reznor of Nine Inch Nails, who deconstructed it on one of his own albums in the early nineties. Needless to say, when he'd finished I barely recognized it!

But it was not all plain sailing. Dave felt a friction developing while working with Daniel, who wanted to turn us into another of his perfect pop creations. Dave wanted us to be dirtier, grittier. Nor was the situation helped by Stevo, who in a celebrating mood one evening in the studio, insulted everyone, drank an entire bottle of gin, fell down the stairs, and finally vomited all over the equipment. Dave was understandably furious, and from then on became wary of him. Yet Stevo seemed to disregard any bad impression his behaviour might have caused, and would continue to do so.

Working with Daniel Miller was a rich experience for me. He was such an imporant part of our story as a band, and I am proud that I had a chance to collaborate with him. He is one of the most congenial and honest people in the music business to this day; doubtless as a result, Mute became a lasting home to some of the most innovative, unique and challenging bands and singers of our time.

Straight after the recording session we were whisked to Phonogram and given a cheque for £3,000, which was quickly snatched by Stevo for safe keeping. The next day it was our first interview with Betty Page. Betty, who wrote for *Sounds*, along with her boyfriend, Tony Mitchell, championed Soft Cell from the word go. How quickly is all this happening for you, dear reader? Well, it was all happening that instantaneously for us.

Soon it was our first photo session, with a photographer called Peter Ashworth. I couldn't believe the results – I looked a complete prat. I'd for some inexplicable reason chosen to wear sub-Adam Ant garb, plaits in my hair and full make-up. A remarkably youthful-looking Dave, relatively subdued and normal-looking by contrast, is clapping his hands, wearing a bow tie and a white shirt. In all honesty, I should have been arrested by the fashion police and charged there and then with fashion felony. Thankfully the photos were not widely seen. Soon afterwards we had better ones taken.

*

I was still DJing in Leeds to make ends meet. What was odd was that I was gaining a celebrity status, and I suspect this was the only reason I kept my job; my choice of music had become totally far-out. People didn't know whether to dance, cry or commit murder.

Soft Cell were starting to get more work on the live front, and as Dave had taken the opportunity to improve and adjust our backing tapes while working in the studio, people could now actually hear us – which wasn't necessarily a good thing. Things had to improve, I thought, after we'd played our worst gig ever, a headline show at the pseudo-glamorous Crocs Nightclub in Rayleigh, Essex. Supporting us were Depeche Mode, on their home turf. It would have been like us supporting Depeche Mode in Leeds. The crowd had come to see Depeche Mode, who played their set with all new equipment, improved tapes and sequences, dressed immaculately in glittering New Romantic outfits, complete with blusher and coiffured hair – Daniel Miller's vision realized: the perfect, pristine, professional pop band. Not only did they play well, you could hear every word Dave Gahan sang. They went down a storm, the audience shouting and baying for more. Then there was us.

I shambled on, dressed in black, dishevelled, drunk, and staggering around on too much cheap speed. The set seemed to start well enough, but then it all turned to disaster. I suddenly couldn't hear myself, and the backing tapes sounded distorted – like hoovers and washing machines competing with a hydraulic drill. I couldn't hear the monitors, and the microphone kept cutting out. Still I staggered through the motions. Then, through the dry ice, I saw them, slowly coming into focus – a line of the Who's Who of British electronic pop music. Members of Ultravox, Spandau Ballet and Visage were watching. I couldn't concentrate. All I could see were their faces, chatting inattentively, sneering – and then laughing. Louder and louder. And then the crowd started throwing coins. To add insult to injury, they only threw pennies. One hit me and I completely lost it. My voice faltered and gave in, which didn't matter anyway because I'd forgotten all the words. Everything ground to an excruciating halt. Well, it didn't stop exactly, just everything seemed to get slower and slower – like an old gramophone running down. I left the stage and Dave followed, both of us downcast and defeated, feeling like poor northern cousins from the sticks.

Afterwards Tony Mayo from Naked Lunch came up to me and laughed in my face. 'You couldn't make a decent dance record if you tried,' he said. I hoped his bitterness stemmed at least in part from the fact that Stevo had turned him down in favour of us. I hoped he was wrong. I learned afterwards that Rusty Egan, club promoter and drummer with Visage, had advised Stevo to drop us. Ironically, less than six months later Rusty would become one of our biggest fans, playing thirty-minute mixes of 'Memorabilia' when DJing at his club nights. As perfectly charming today as he was then, he was also part of the publishing team that we would sign to in our early deal. However, I had to admit that we were bad that night, and I would have advised Stevo to drop us had I been him.

After that disastrous experience we buckled down. With better backing tapes our live set sounded more polished, and it looked it too. My art-college friend Huw Feather designed a padded-cell stage set, complete with neon bars that flashed. We already featured a large 'Soft Cell' neon in front of Dave's keyboard. Huw's girlfriend Liz was establishing herself as a clothes designer, and started to design and make my stage outfits – simple black trousers and tops. Dave meanwhile favoured a jacket and bow tie, resembling a cross between a game-show host and a member of an East End firm. We had wanted to disassociate ourselves from the New Romantic movement as quickly as possible – it had suited us for a while, but it didn't reflect what we were about. Dave's Northern Soul influences were now making themselves felt in our music. He had turned me on to many obscure sixties soul gems; I loved the beats, the way the songs were so short and compact and the lyrics were always poignant – about lost love and heartache, yet always with a touch of hope, smiling through the tears.

When Kris Neate and I visited an all-day New Romantic Festival at the Rainbow in London's Finsbury Park, I discovered that what had been a fun scene in Leeds – somewhat tongue in cheek, and not to be taken too seriously – was in London both highly competitive and bitchy. The first thing I noticed when I entered the foyer was Steve Strange tearing down posters for the *Some Bizarre* album, screaming, 'I hate that fat cunt Stevo'. (His imaginative use of language has never ceased to astound me.) Rusty Egan was collecting the money while making cynical comments about the stupidity of his punters. To me it all seemed sad, cynical and foolish – a parade of pretentious, posing clowns. Then, to top it all, Jasper Conran arrived with a painted crone on his arm. 'I don't know what I'd do without my little Jasper,' she squawked. I felt just a little queasy. 'Where are we?' said a friend. 'At the St Valentine's Day massacre?' When Daniel Miller arrived with a sheepish Depeche Mode in tow, all dressed in their new designer outfits, I knew it was time to make my exit.

Back at home, I threw away my outrageous outfits and swore to wear simple black from then on. (OK, so I've had an occasional relapse.) Black represented purity and drama. It could be a soul look, a rock 'n' roll look or a *chanson* balladeer look – Piaf, Greco, Jim Morrison and Johnny Cash all chose black. Black can accentuate a face or disguise a multitude of sins. Besides, it goes with everything.

*

To promote 'Memorabilia' we did a series of gigs around small clubs: the Venue and Cabaret Futura in London, the Zoo in Birmingham, and Rock City in Nottingham. It was in Nottingham that our stage set was destroyed. It all came crashing to the floor after a stage invasion by fans; the padded-cell walls collapsed and the neon bars shattered. The gigs had been getting increasingly chaotic and were ending up as free-for-alls; we had never taken things too seriously, allowing people up on stage and generally messing about instead of concentrating on the quality of the music and the performance. In hindsight it was actually insulting to those who had come to see a show but who were instead made to witness what amounted to a private party on stage. This was reflected in the reviews: thick and fast they came, inevitably focusing on me as the culprit, the epitome of bad taste and talentlessness:

   'Soft Cell would be OK if it wasn't for Marc Almond' (I had a bit
     of trouble working that one out).

'*Marc Almond has no charisma*' (short and to the point, I
   suppose).

'*The problem with Soft Cell is a very big one: Marc Almond. He
   just can't sing.*'

'*Soft Cell have flaccid little dirges, laughably pointless.*'

Steve Sutherland, a *Melody Maker* writer, described us as 'Tommy
Cooper supported by a bad Shirley Bassey . . .' No guessing who
was who. I think you get the picture. All the critics seemed to be
writing us off! Even now I'd like to justify our behaviour, but, as
Kenneth Williams said in his last diary entry, 'What's the bloody
point?'

I felt bitterly hurt. I was right back in the school playground,
facing childish name-calling. I was unprepared for the attacks; no
one had warned me or explained how to deal with the blows. It was
years before I learned to mellow out, to take it all in my stride and
let the criticism wash over me. Life also gets much easier when you
have a team of brilliant libel lawyers on hand to help you cope with
these annoyances – inaccuracies, as the lawyers would say!

I feared reading reviews, but read them I had to, compelled by
some inner curiosity I was unable to resist – but the thing I was to
hate and despise above all else, the thing that was to cause me the
most misery and heartache, the greatest embarrassment and mistrust,
the one thing that contributed more than anything else to my drinking, drug-taking and sexual promiscuity, the one thing that I hate as
much today as I did back then, was THE INTERVIEW. I *hated*
interviews. I *still* hate them. Each interviewer is desperately trying to
find that new twist, that different angle, and yet each of them,
however unique they might believe their approach is, ends up just like
all the rest. The questions are always the same.

'Who are you? No, but who are you really?' Now there's a
question: did the public really want to see into my dark, worthless,
guilt-ridden and shamed soul? However much I tried to deflect the
interviewers' line of questions away from personal issues, relentlessly
they returned, as though they would betray their vocation if they let
such issues pass by. To me it was as though they were mining my
most personal thoughts, my most private moments, desperate for
nuggets from which to construct an interesting article.

'Why are you like you are? No, but really?' All the while expecting
a short reply, a few well-chosen words to a question that a team of
psychiatrists would need years to unravel.

'Why do you do what you do?' OK, so justify yourself, and your
three-minute songs. 'What are they about?' 'What are you trying to

say?' 'Why did you do it?' 'Is it true that such and such?' 'So, who are you?'

Always the same questions. And of course they were all leading to the 'G' question – 'Are you gay?' I didn't like that question, and I would duck and dive, avoid answering it. Why? Well, first, I didn't think it was really anyone's business, and, second, I was in denial – wary of all the baggage and consequences that would accompany an admission. I just wasn't ready at that time to embark on such a commitment. So I spluttered and gabbled, giggled in a coy, girly manner, and said anything that came into my head, just so I could keep the interview moving on in an attempt to get the whole nightmare over with. My answers were at best naive, and at worst stupid or inflammatory. I tried hard to say as much as possible without saying anything at all, to give enough copy without committing to anything substantial. Even when I am interviewed today I often come over as fey, my speech punctuated with nervous laughter, every answer a 'kind of' or 'sort of', dodging and squirming in my seat, trying to be witty or anecdotal but just sounding confused, contradictory and baffling. If I try to camp it up I end up just sounding flippant and femme because I don't – and I didn't – feel comfortable with my campness. Even now I still don't feel entirely at ease with my sexuality, nor satisfied with myself.

An early embarrassing interview was with Jon Savage. He asked me directly if I was gay. 'I'm experimental, I'm theatrical. I'm kind of bisexual,' I replied. How vague is that? I should probably have turned to him, looked him in the eye with a steely gaze, and said 'Mind your own fucking business!' But I didn't, or I couldn't, or the record company warned me I shouldn't.

But in many ways I always thought the question was a bit redundant. If they wanted a sworn affidavit about my sexuality they were never going to get it, yet my sexuality was undeniably obvious to all. People just had to look at me! What further confirmation was really needed? I mean, did anyone ask Stevie Wonder if he was black? More often than not the gay question would come from gay journalists, eager to ease you out of whatever closet they thought you'd created for yourself, eager to have you join their ranks. Usually armed with an air of superiority or contempt (now it was their turn to be the school bully), they were annoyed like hell when I wouldn't roll over and play gay. With their agenda of gayness, these journalists want you to admit that your life revolves, like theirs, solely around your sexuality. They seek to justify their constant badgering with political or social ends, but their motives are often questionable. I refuse to be defined simply in sexual terms, nor do I think anyone has

the right to intrude into anyone else's private life. Our sexuality
should be protected from judgement, and it surprised me that gay
journalists above all didn't recognize and respect that.

Self-consciousness was – and is – the other prime interview
obstacle. When I try to sound intellectual, I just come across as
pompous. Not that I consider myself one, yet so many people seem
to look for an intellectual interpretation of my work from me. I end
up out of my depth. After all, I'm someone who left school with two
'O' levels, who couldn't write or speak properly, suffer from dyslexia,
and have a related inability to concentrate. I have tried to educate
myself since leaving school, but put me up against any intellectual
journalist, eager to promote his or her own wittiness and esteem, and
I lose hands down. It's a self-fulfilling prophecy. My defence mech-
anism is primed from the moment the interview starts; because of my
aversion to interviews I go in assuming it's the interviewer against
me.

Interviews would begin with me stammering and flustered, a
pained expression on my face, and end with sweat running down my
back. A sleepless night would follow as I turned the events of the day
over and over in my head. To add to this, I would often smoke a
joint or take several lines of cocaine before an interview, which only
served to intensify my paranoia. The result was either a meltdown or
a short circuit. I would end up ranting ten to the dozen about any
spaced-out nonsense, or close myself off entirely. Recalling this afterwards led to still deeper depression.

Don't think I'm anti-journalist. I've met some who were actually
people at one time in their lives. I've even met several that I've
genuinely liked, and a couple that I've admired as writers. But as far
as befriending journalists goes, in my experience any journalists worth
their pay cheque write the truth, and one day they inevitably write it
about you. My worst experiences were with the ones who were there
at the beginning, who were counted as friends. If as time passed you
had failed to keep in touch you would all of a sudden come across a
review written with all the bitterness that only old friends can conjure
up.

Of course occasionally they get it just right, and to those writers
who do I am eternally grateful. Looking through my crate of clippings
('friends come and go, but clippings stay for ever'), I see that I have
had tons of great press – it actually outweighs the bad. (Although I
can't really be sure about that, as I only keep the good stuff – bad
reviews ended up lining my parrot's cage, where Jacko deposits his
verdict on the quality of the writing.) I have a simple philosophy –
good reviews are well written, bad reviews are not. I find the good

reviews equally difficult to read and accept. Surely, I think, they can't be writing about me. I can't be worthy of this kindness or consideration. I can't live up to it. I'd better take another tranquillizer, I grew to think: one to build up confidence, one to maintain it, and finally several to quell it. When will I believe it could be true?

Over the years I have witnessed a change in the nature of journalism. Caustic, vicious, cruel now equals good copy. It seems that to write pleasant positive remarks is boring. This style of journalism even extends to television interviews, where hosts are often rude and irreverent to their guests. We seem to live in a culture of the unsympathetic, a culture of mean. As so many people have pointed out, in Britain fame and success must coexist precariously with the threat of ruin, injury and failure. To make it to the top means that your fall is then that much further, and the pain in your life can be revelled in by so many for whom it tastes that much sweeter. Public success seems to make you a fair target. I can testify to this because it happened to me. Let me quote you some of the examples of literary dexterity used to describe me over the decades ahead, as they make insightful reading. I have arbitrarily chosen words: 'slimy', 'creepy', 'sleazy', 'ugly', 'beady-eyed', 'wonky-mouthed' (don't ask), 'nasally challenged', 'pathetic', 'snivelling', 'miserable', 'mincing', 'filthy', 'dirty', 'perverted pipsqueak', 'midget', 'pigeon-chested', 'cunt'. It's interesting to note that these relate not to my singing or my music but to my appearance or attitude. So what did I do that provoked such responses? I made records and sang songs. I was called some of those names in the press just over a year ago, so nothing much has changed in journalistic standards. If you add the sentiment in which many of these pieces are written, but which words dare not state, then a clearer picture of what is behind these tirades of hatred emerges. What fascinates me today is that much of what I have described is not about me personally; it is about the prevalent attitudes of homophobia in our society. I represented, and to many still do represent, a real opportunity for journalists to vent their homophobic feelings. Add to this our new culture of laddishness, where sexism and homophobia are applauded, and you wonder what hope is there. The school bullies are no longer confined to the school: now they can legitimately ply their anger, hostility and frustration as part of their jobs.

It's taken a long time to be more stoic about criticism. Before, how many times had I thought of revenge againt journalists? How many ill-thought-out letters had I sent, fuelled by cocaine and amphetamine (which always added that required dash of paranoia)? How many times had I even contemplated suicide? (In the early eighties that bastion of intellectuality Gary Bushell actually wrote he couldn't wait for my suicide attempt. Here was a man I had never even met who wanted me dead!) Even if you try to meet a critic halfway it doesn't work if they already have it in for you. Paul Morley (famous for his Frankie Goes to Hollywood slogans – you know, the 'Frankie Says' ones) wrote a damning review of Stevo's *Some Bizarre* album – 'All the groups seem to be rejects, futureless. It's a sad LP, all the rejects finding a home, chuffed to be lifted by the wind of a trend.' Later he begged Stevo for an interview with Soft Cell. Originally Stevo told him to fuck off, but he was eventually swayed by Morley's influence as a writer with the *New Musical Express*. Stevo allowed him to come up to Leeds to interview us. We went out of our way to accommodate him. But the piece he wrote was a complete swipe at us, an utter put-down, using 'soft sell' as a play on words to illustrate our irrelevance. Sometime later I bumped into Paul at Rusty Egan's club, with Steve Severin from the Banshees. I bit my tongue (for once) and smiled at him. We had had three hit singles by then, so what did I care? He looked decidedly shifty and uncomfortable. I knew he regarded Soft Cell as trite and shallow. Later, he became Trevor Horn's PR puppet.

But his piece had hurt me very much. It created a dilemma, a question I went over and over in my head. Did I really want to be in a 'successful' band? Could I handle it? I wrote in my diary at the time, 'I don't want Soft Cell. I just want to be an obscure performance artist, just doing my own thing.'

If there was an upside to the early criticism, fair or unfair, it was that it triggered a long learning process of self-discovery. I became aware of my shortcomings as a performer, and looked at the impact of my natural shyness and introversion as an individual on what I was really doing on stage. I turned the magnifying glass on myself, determined to *learn*. To learn how to play an audience, how to use *them*, and how to project. How to discipline my voice. How to breathe. It's an ongoing learning process, and perhaps one that never ends. I'm not the same person as I was back then, and if we are lucky – or sensible – none of us is.

*

Together, we were learning more about the mechanics of the music business, and in particular how the relationship with the A & R department worked. I assume that many of you know nothing of the music business (which may actually qualify you for A & R), and so I'll try to explain what A & R people do. A & R stands for Artist and

Repertoire. The A & R man (or occasionally woman) within a record company is responsible for discovering and signing bands and artists, then cajoling, pushing or forcing, manipulating, blackmailing or bribing them into making the records the A & R person wants, while at the same time convincing the artists that they are recording the music they themselves really wanted all along. It is an advantage if A & R persons are themselves failed artists, thereby having just the right mix of resentment and ambition. If a record is subsequently a complete flop, then the artist can be blamed and either be made to compromise their artistry even further, or be dropped from the label. On the other hand, if the record is a resounding success then the A & R person can take all the credit and thereby justify their high salary and a copious amount of cocaine consumption. Artists count for very little in the minds of the record company – they are those annoying people who stand in the way of corporates doing what they want. If only artists could be dispensed with altogether, everything would be that much easier!

If and when an A & R person is successful, another record company will lure them away with the promise of higher pay, and/or better drugs. Off they go, leaving the artists they signed isolated on a label where the rest of the company usually doesn't want them because they're all too busy looking for their own personal projects to sign. It's high stakes, a game of high-risk musical chairs (when the music stops, the one left standing takes the blame) where the artists are not given their dues or chances. As cleverer people than me have pointed out, its show business, not art business.

One song in our set had grabbed the attention of our A & R man, Roger Aimes. The number in question was an obscure old Northern Soul track, originally sung by Gloria Jones (incidentally, Marc Bolan's wife). It was called 'Tainted Love'. Wanting to feature a couple of cover songs in our set to show our roots, as it were, we had picked this three-minute piece of twisted pop perfection. But it nearly hadn't been 'Tainted Love' at all – it was a toss-up between that and another Northern Soul song, 'The Night' by Frankie Valli. But 'Tainted Love' won out, and we began to feature it in our shows. We gave it quite a different arrangement to the original, which features a frantic guitar motif and Gloria's wailing soul voice. Our version was stripped down, cold, with slinky electronics and just a hint of passion and yearning. The song took on a certain sleaziness just because it was us doing it. Roger wanted us to go into the studio with a producer called Mike Thorne to record it as our next single. So it was that in the spring of 1981 we went to Advision Studios and recorded what would be for all of us a life-changing track. Mike Thorne was Phonogram's in-house producer and had an impressive history of producing minimal, original-sounding pop. He had produced a few of the early electronic bands, but had more notably produced artists I had admired, including John Cale, Marianne Faithfull and the innovative punk band Wire.

(Before I continue, please don't expect me to give you endless rundowns of technical equipment and recording techniques – if those are what you crave, then this book is not for you. I've always thought one synthesizer is much like any other. Dave Ball was the one with the technical knowledge – I was just the bloody singer.)

Mike Thorne was gentle-mannered, frail-looking and even slightly androgynous, with a neat line in tight jeans and striped glitter jumpers. In the studio he became a bit of a boffin and loved the science of it all, although I sometimes thought him too methodical and perfectionist, a bit prone to sulking. But then I hated all the technical side of things, was tirelessly impatient and desperate for instant gratification. Looking back, when it came to vocals I wish that I'd had a little more guidance from Mike. I was giving it from my heart, which was always good enough for Mike, but technically I was all over the place. Most producers would have packed me off to a few singing lessons, or at least sampled my voice through a barrage of effects to disguise my lack of technical ability, but Mike did neither. He accepted the vocals after only a couple of takes, which encouraged me, but left them up front and bare on the track, flaws and all.

We recorded 'Tainted Love' as a twelve-inch single first, sequencing it into a version of the Tamla Motown classic 'Where Did Our Love Go'. This was at the time meant only to be a camp afterthought. Later we realized it was a decision which had cost us dearly. When the seven-inch single was cut and issued the record company put it on the B-side. We thus forfeited any publishing royalty we might have had if the B-side had contained a composition of our own. On the sale of a single, the publishing was split equally between the A and B side. And we were putting out two cover versions! Hindsight is an annoying gift. What naive fools we were! All we thought was that this weird little record could be a minor hit, a flash in the proverbial pan, then disappear to leave us to get on with being the dark, disturbing, alternative band we really were.

We loved the track, and were over the moon with Mike's production and recording. We were particularly pleased with the twelve-inch bridge that slows down and runs into the next song. And it had all seemed so professional, Dave and I bashing away on the syndrums in a recording studio. I played a small flying-saucer syndrum which gave the opening sound of 'Tainted Love' – the inimitable and instantly recognizable 'da dink dink' at the beginning of the track. How that sound would soon haunt me, and for the remainder of my career! I'd hear it in my sleep, in my imagination, everywhere I went. It would eventually put icy fear in my veins when I'd hear it in a disco (and a thousand handbags would be grabbed as teenage girls ran to the dance floor), on the radio, in a restaurant, taxi or shop, or on a building site. I'd like to be able to tell you that during the recording of 'Tainted Love' something quasi-religious happened, but it didn't. It was just three people making a record and having a good time. When Dave and I went back to our run-down hotel with no air conditioning in Bayswater after the sessions, we knew we had recorded something special, but we didn't pin our hopes on it. And when we played it to Phonogram they didn't seem excited, suggesting we put more real bass and real drums on it.

*

I was beginning to enjoy myself – the gigs, the recording, a general feeling of excitement that we were building up for ourselves. But I wasn't that star-struck about the music industry itself – I hated it. It was all so fake, contrived and patronizing. It seemed no one was interested in what we had to say, where we wanted to go, or what we wanted to do. I've since grown to like the business much more – and I have to confess that it's been good to me, as I am not the easiest or most deserving of performers. It must be the most bizarre, senseless, business there is – a corporate circus, cheap and selfish, tacky and wasteful. But it can be a hell of a lot of fun too; and ultimately, when it goes the way you want, it can be very rewarding. If you work in it, you have to learn to love it; you certainly eventually learn that you can't fight it. You have to give in and let the madness wash over you. I've not exactly been a player, though; I've not had the awards or accolades so many of my peers have received, and I probably never will. I don't particularly attend functions or go to industry parties. I don't socialize with the 'right' people – I still prefer remaining on the outside.

We carried on with our promotional gigs and our life in Leeds. It was fun, with constant clubbing and parties. I had a great group of friends, and one or two lovers, including a girl who was known as Janet Sleaze – famous with her friend Angela as the Sleaze Sisters. I genuinely liked Janet, but nothing much had happened between us until one day after a drunken pub session I ended up with her and another friend, Steve, in an inebriated threesome. Afterwards, in the cold light of sobriety, things were a little uncomfortable. Besides, I had just met Dillon, a fiery handsome young half-Spanish guy from York. We'd become friends after a gig. Dillon was one minute up, the next minute down – a punk with a stormy Latin temperament that matched his moods. He was also one of the sweetest, kindest people in the world to me (on a good day), and one of the few people from then who have remained a friend to this day, even through pretty tempestuous times.

We played a major Leeds show at the Amnesia Club. It turned out to be a homecoming party, with over a thousand people turning out to see us. This time we recruited two backing singers, the Vicious Pink Phenomena: Brian, an angular, blond-haired guy who moved in an android fashion, and Josie, a long-legged, mini-skirted, dark-haired beauty with the strongest Yorkshire accent. Josie had been known around the Leeds club scene from as far back as 1977, often turning up for the latest punk gig dressed in nothing but a black bin liner. It was really her we wanted on stage, to supply glamour and for the guys to ogle. As backing singers, all that was required of them was to 'oooh' and 'aaah' and generally act sexy. Josie brought a new following to the show – lads would stand and gawp at her, tongues lolling out (well, it definitely wasn't at me). The whole performance resembled a bizarre cabaret. Looking back at a video of it, Dave and I can hardly be seen among the dancing crowd, who constantly invaded the stage. My head bobs up and down as the crowd swarm all over, the volume cranked up so loud that all you can hear is a throbbing bass line. My hair was black and spiky, my face white, with thick black eyeliner (a developing trademark) around my eyes. Even when the equipment breaks down and the DJ puts on 'Memorabilia', I still keep on singing, leading the crowd, lost in the music. Looking back at it, I seem so young. I'd forgotten I was ever that young. I seem almost happy, to have not a care in the world. There I danced on the edge of that stage, on the edge of fame . . .

6

'Sometimes I feel I want to run away . . .'

It started that July in 1981, around my twenty-fourth birthday. A slow-dawning realization, a whispered threat, promising something fearful. Or something extraordinary. Something that would change my life for ever, turn it upside down and mangle it in the wringer. At twenty-four years old I should have been ready for success – after all, I was no teenager. But I was used to having my life all to myself – a small circle of friends, and my music, and the possibility of success a safe distance away. Used to having a life where I could keep on being creatively satisfied, make just enough to pay the rent.

But that wasn't enough. The problem with wanting something badly enough is that you might just get it. And I did want success, didn't I? Isn't that what everyone wants? I did want recognition, didn't I? I did want to be someone, count for something, didn't I? If I didn't, then why the hell had I started this band with Dave? But I was very young for my age, I had always been emotionally immature, had never really grown out of my teens, was constantly hoping to find them again, relive them, correct all those mistakes. I was still physically small – underweight, and, as so many reviewers were to note, puny. I was emotionally unprepared for what was about to happen.

'Tainted Love' was released to an uncaring, uninterested public. It was packaged in a pale yellow sleeve featuring two delicate drawings by Kris Neate of Northern Soul dancers doing backflips and sporting wedge haircuts. The press reactions were lukewarm – Linden Barber in *Melody Maker* said, 'It is one of the limpest pathetic pop records of all time' (no holding back there then, Linden). Other writers, such as Jon Savage, saw it as having a twisted sexuality – ' "Tainted Love" goes beyond camp to be sexually ambiguous in a direct way.' Writers twisted themselves in knots over this simple three-minute pop track. As for Dave and me, we naively thought the twist was simply that we were a so-called 'cold, soulless electronic band' who had made a passionate soul record. At first it didn't occur to me that my writhing about in leather and eyeliner gave the song a more subversive connotation, but once I did tap into this I took it all the way.

We first sensed something might be happening when one day Phonogram were actually pleasant to us, even smiling and being friendly, though they eyed my smudged eyeliner and studded bracelets with unease. Then suddenly everyone wanted to talk to us as radio began to play the song – no longer tucked away on the night-time shows but in that sacred place called 'daytime'. That 'da dink dink' sound began to echo throughout the land like a portent of doom.

Dave came off the phone one day a little paler than usual, announcing, 'It's number twenty-six in the chart.' I felt unease in my stomach, not unlike the onset of flu. Surely this wouldn't continue. Stevo was by now swaggering around – the words 'cat' and 'cream' came to mind. Soon, very soon, he was to be the manager of a hugely successful band, and, like me, he could anticipate the sweet flavour of revenge this would mean.

The excitement was reflected in our live shows too – we played a London gig at a club called Maximus, in Leicester Square, and people queued around the block to see us: many were turned away. The show itself was the usual mayhem. I should point out that Soft Cell shows weren't concerts: they were events, happenings. The set, based mostly around a long improvisation of 'Memorabilia', took place on the dance floor as we tried to break down that divide between audience and artist – we and the club, the disco, the audience would become as one. In this particular show I couldn't really be seen or heard, and eventually climbed on to a table to perform. The music press had not experienced anything quite like it, and found the whole affair *amateurish*. To be honest, it was. But what did we care then?

'Tainted Love' continued to climb the chart. In the Phonogram offices one afternoon we celebrated its continuing success. Stevo poured quantities of champagne into small plastic bags, each containing the drug MDA (used medically as a pre-med, principally for cancer patients). The champagne masked the foul taste of the drug, which gave a euphoric high and from which we didn't come down for quite some time. In moments like this I felt my life as I had known it beginning to slip away; I was afraid to let go, yet at the same time I was up in the clouds with anticipation.

*

Back in Leeds I got a telephone call. 'You're number two in the charts and they want you on *Top of the Pops*.' The legendary *Top of the*

Pops, where I had watched my childhood pop idols while growing up! The programme I had wished so many times to be on but had never thought I could be – not in a million years. Something like *Top of the Pops* seemed so far away, so dreamlike and unreal – a land of starburst lights, chrome sets, luminescent pink smoke, and dancers wearing fringes and Lycra sprinkling glittering handfuls of bad taste everywhere; the land where it was always the seventies. I was to stand on the stage of the most famous show in Britain, the marker of having *made it*. Everyone who had ever known me would see me, and all those who had dismissed me, laughed at me or been mean would, with luck, be sick to their stomachs. Me from Southport and Dave from Blackpool – it was happening to us. The dream would be complete. As for the nightmare, that was only just beginning. If events from now on appear to resemble those of a cheap soap-opera movie of the week, please forgive me. All I can say is that that is just how it was.

I was dazed as I arrived at the BBC that day and was shown to the studio. It was disappointingly small. Roger Aimes hovered around with other members of Phonogram's staff, concerned that we say the right things at the right time to the right people. It has always amused me to see powerful record-company executives kowtow to the *Top of the Pops* producers – nothing was as important as *Top of the Pops*, and Michael Hurll, its producer, put the fear of God into them all.

Roger grew increasingly concerned with what I had chosen to wear, especially my bracelets and thick eyeliner – 'Tone it down, Marc, would you? Tone it down.' He feared that I was going to blow it with a major display of campness. Those little demons on my shoulder encouraged me, and I decided that I should do just what I wanted and be me.

Sandwiched in between an artist called Aneka singing 'Japanese Boy' and Shakin' Stevens' 'Green Door', I frugged onto the TV screen and a nation's jaws dropped open. Immediately and from then on, it seemed girls wanted to marry me, mothers wanted to mother me, grandparents wanted to have me arrested, lads wanted to smash my face in, fathers buried their heads in their papers, and many young gay teenage sons blushed and made an excuse to leave the room so they could go upstairs and write love notes to me. Just as with Bowie and Bolan in the seventies, war was declared in school playgrounds the day after, when a growing army of Marc Almond fans stood up to be counted. I had been here before, except that now I was on the other side of the screen, looking out. It was now me who suddenly revealed to the lonely teenager in some remote place that there was someone out there who might understand how he or she felt.

But support was to come from the most unlikely quarters. I was to find out that a great number of my fans were heterosexuals who cared little about my sexuality because they loved 'Tainted Love' so much. I even got letters from self-professed straight guys who wanted me to be their one experience on the other side! I could have kicked myself for having so little time to spare.

This was still a couple of years before Boy George, before Holly Johnson and Jimmy Somerville. Though they too did their fair share of breaking down barriers, I certainly prepared the way. I took the flak then, and still am taking it today, never quite forgiven for turning many a teenage son into a studded-wrist-band-wearing, eye-liner-sporting individual. I had that loathsome thing the public hated – I had a sexuality. Boy George was to later succeed principally in the tradition of good old British pantomime, sexless and emasculated, reassuringly preferring a cup of tea to sex. He was to remain in the closet well until Culture Club was over and he had himself been through heroin addiction and the self-confession of rehab. By then he could be as vocal as he liked – he had already shocked his public. Frankie Goes to Hollywood's sexuality was equally blurred, with Holly and Paul's sexuality firmly upstaged by the rampant heterosexuality of the rest of the group. By the time Pete Burns and the likes of Marilyn were on TV screens, Boy George had already paved the way, and even they both claimed to be bisexual. Only Jimmy Somerville stands out, for he was upfront from the very outset. He told everyone he was gay not in metaphors or multi-layered rhetoric but quite plainly, and in doing so he created a climate for change. The nation responded to his clean-cut political voice, his angelic tones, his small built vulnerability – perhaps because what you saw was what you got. He was never out to fool anyone.

It was me who was to be labelled the *closet case*. After that first *Top of the Pops* appearance I was spat at in the street, punched in the face by strangers, insulted and ridiculed both in public places and on radio, on television and in the press, and it was all done in the most homophobic way imaginable. Yet I was still meant to be *in the closet*. All pop stars before me and most after have fudged their sexuality (in fact Jimmy Somerville is the only exception I can think of, with perhaps Tom Robinson in the seventies, though even he ended up getting married), and yet *me* the gay press accused of hiding something! 'Come out,' I was urged by them. But everyone seemed to know what I am: 'Why do I need to say it?' I thought.

I wasn't that naive; I knew that to actually come out and say 'I'm gay' could damage my career, and I was afraid. I went as far as I

Right: Aged five. The cute kid with the cheeky grin. What the hell happened?

Below left: At Southport zoo.

Below right: Aged two. In the garden with Papa.

As Merry Hump in the infant school play.

Left: Aged thirteen. Awkward teenager with acne and a seventies feather cut.

Bottom: Just a typical night in with Sally King.

Opposite page: Look, it's performance art, what can I tell you? Now, where's that cat food?!

1975

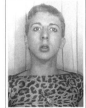

1977

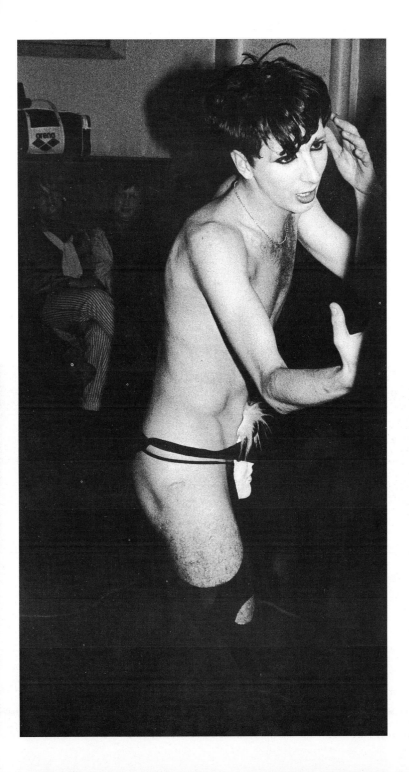

Opposite page: Early press shot – Sinatra in studded wristbands.

Stevo letting us know what he thinks of the music business.

Soft Cell – two clean-cut boys. *(Peter Ashworth)*

Top right: My first tattoo was designed by Genesis P. Orridge of Psychic TV. *(Eugene Abedari)*

Right: New Romantics with Roxy at the Leeds Warehouse Club.

Below: Happy. Happy. Happy. Nick Cave and me in a jovial mood. *(Anton Corbijn)*

Left: Taking a ride with Vanessa at the Baghdad Club in Barcelona. Vanessa ensures strategically placed rubber dildo is not in view.

Above: Me and Andy Warhol – 'I just loved your record, Marc – what was it called again?'

Below: Dashing! *(Nick Timms)*

Above: 1986. *Mother Fist* album photo shoot in New York. Somebody turn the sun off. *(Mark Langthorne)*

Right: Sulking. Who took all the coke? *(Nick Timms)*

Below: The Mambas in Israel.

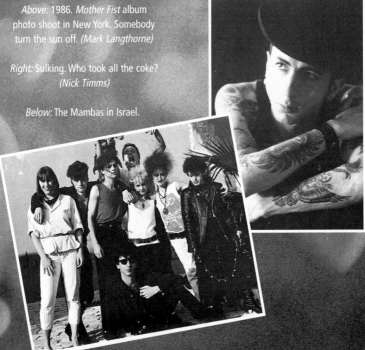

thought I could at that time without actually saying it. People cite other stars who have come out without it damaging their career – Elton John, for example. Elton has been around for so long he is a national institution, but for how many years was he 'bisexual'? He even married. It wasn't until the late eighties – when his career was at its lowest point, and he dumped all his camp outfits, recorded songs for the family-values company Disney and undertook his charity work – that he really came out. Nobody cares that he is gay now, because he comes across as a non-sexual figure, complete with boyfriend and happy relationship and therefore adhering to the terms of how homosexuality can be acceptable to the masses. And of course, brilliant as an artist, too. Now he is so establishment that he can even advertise Citibank.

When circumstances forced George Michael to come out (one wonders whether he ever would have had he not been caught out), his new image was that of an apologetic figure, remorseful to his boyfriend, foolish but otherwise monogamous – the behaviour that society prefers from the homosexual. But when Neil Tennant came out, something of the mystique he had contrived seemed to vanish. When you read interviews with these people about their homosexuality – *how openly out and proud* they are now (especially George Michael) – one would think they had single-handedly pioneered gay rights, rather than found themselves reluctantly conscripted into its ranks. The far more tolerant society in which we live today is a safer climate for the dubious star to take the plunge.

Even today, however, coming out as gay is still a luxury of the privileged, the emotionally secure or physically protected. It is in many ways a possibility only for those who live in large conurbations, surrounded by a support network of some kind, and a tolerant environment. The public will still only accept homosexuality up to a point.

When I began, in the early eighties, it was a very homophobic time – especially in the music business. I was continually told by Phonogram to tone it down, change my outfits, use less make-up, keep quiet and invent girlfriends, or else my career would be over. And remember, it wasn't just my career: it was Dave's too. Also, there was an aspect of what they said that appealed to me. For me, sexual ambiguity was always more interesting than being obviously straight or gay. Hadn't all the stars that I'd ever loved been sexually ambiguous, mysterious, enigmatic? I wanted to be like them. I couldn't see why gay journalists urged me to come out. The public seemed to have no doubts what I was, nor, presumably, did the gay

journalists who were asking me to 'join the gay community'. So I
refused.

I didn't owe anything to this imaginary thing called a 'gay
community', whose media treated me with as much, if not more,
hostility than the rest. As the tabloid controversy raged – was I or
wasn't I? straight or gay? – I encouraged it, trying to be as enigmatic
as possible, neither denying or confirming anything.

However, I was eventually 'outed', as if anyone needed telling, by
the late Kris Kirk. He came to my home to do an interview for
Melody Maker, and while I was making him a cup of tea he must
have rifled through my record collection. Upon my return, I found
him brandishing albums by Yma Sumac and Judy Garland.

'Oh, have it your way then, Kris, I am a raving faggot,' I said,
putting down the tea and holding up my hands in defeat. 'You've
caught me out.' But when this admission appeared afterwards in
print, it suddenly seemed to give everyone the right to refer to me for
ever after as 'gay artist Marc Almond'. It was enough to make me
spend the next ten years trying to climb back into that closet.

I take great offence at being labelled a 'gay' artist. I dislike that
pigeon-hole that enables people to marginalize your work and reduce
its importance, implying that it won't be of any interest to anyone
who isn't gay. And of course it's also a label that suits the homophobe. I do not want to be judged by my sexuality: it is not all I am.
I like to think of myself as a multifaceted individual. They don't say,
'And here's straight Mick Hucknall' or 'Let's have a warm welcome
for heterosexual Rod Stewart.' In my lyrics I often write from a
genderless perspective about human emotions that either a boy or a
girl can relate to. Pop stars, singers and actors are in many ways
peddlers of dreams or fantasies, and their followers take what they
want from their work to fit their own personal requirements or
desires. Some just like my voice and my music; others like my style,
my presentation or my look. Whatever attracts them, it is me as a
performer and entertainer I want them to admire.

*

That first *Top of the Pops* appearance changed my life, and many
others', too. If the first impression you make on the public is strong
enough, it remains for ever the way they see you, seared into their
memory. It is the way impersonators will for ever impersonate you,
always in the outfit you wore on that occasion – in my case, all black
with a studded neck band, dancing too hard, skinny and a little fey. I
watch that performance now and I see someone who just wanted to

get through it as quickly as possible; I was putting as much as I could into it, which was of course too much. It screams, 'Please like me!' I hardly looked at the camera, having not yet learned any technique, not been told to follow the lights for a cue. We had to do it twice that day, because my friend Dillon jumped up in front of the camera in a desperate attempt to get himself on TV; neither the producers nor Phonogram were pleased, as you can imagine. After the show Roger Aimes took me aside and suggested that I should have a little choreography if next week the record should reach number one. But no, I thought, that couldn't happen to us. This had to be it, didn't it?

Straight after that appearance, leaving the studio, people stopped me and asked for my autograph. No one had done that before. I remember how weird it felt, signing my name on a piece of paper for a complete stranger. Did this mean I was famous? Did this mean the clock was ticking down on my fifteen minutes?

We returned to Leeds.

One night I went out to the off-licence. Standing in the queue waiting to pay, I suddenly became aware of people staring at me like they never had before. I heard whispering voices ('It's 'im'), saw people nudging each other, others turning back to look at me, and then this girl came up and asked that one question, the first time I was asked it, that one question that I would hear more than any other – 'Are you him?' When you think about it, it's a bloody odd question.

*

A few days later it happened. I got a call on the payphone in the Leicester Grove house. 'You're number one!' shouted a jubilant Stevo. 'Congratulations!' I fell back against the wall, dropping my tea on the floor. I rushed upstairs to tell Dave, who was still sleeping. I burst into his room. 'Dave, Dave!' I screamed. 'We're number fucking one!' Dave burst into hysterical laughter and stayed that way all day. But strange feelings went through my head at the news. Number one is not at all the same as number two. Of course there were initial feelings of elation and disbelief – who wouldn't have those? But then my mind became crowded with negative thoughts. That old feeling of revenge returned – that feeling I knew Stevo was having too. That all those people who had ever put me down could now eat shit.

Then came the feelings of guilt and unworthiness. I mean, what had I done to deserve this? I'd made a trashy pop single – and hadn't the press already condemned it as crap? I thought what was happening to me must be a trick, or a dream. What was the catch? Then it occurred to me: 'The catch is', said that devil's voice at my shoulder, 'that you've sold your soul for a worthless piece of vinyl.'

How great the build-up to it all had been – the planning, the writing, the preparation, the rehearsals, our first gig at the art college, our first bedroom record, *Mutant Moments*, those first flickers of recognition as artists, the first good reviews, the press. But now what was going to happen? In my mind I suspected it was all going to turn bad. I kept thinking of all the horrible things people were going to say about me now. My mind kept turning to a scene in Brian de Palma's film *Carrie*, where her mother warns her, 'They're all gonna laugh at you, they're all gonna laugh at you.' And then I saw the giant face of Paul Morley floating above my head, distorted, sneering and laughing. In my mind, what had moments earlier been cause for celebration was now cause for anxiety and fear.

Was it going to be a case of too much too soon? Had we peaked before our first album was even recorded? Peaked with a song that I knew wasn't a true representation of what Dave and I wanted to do or be? I imagined the shadow of an albatross with a noose in its beak (I really did). We were number one, but what did that mean? I didn't have a clue – not really – but I sensed that the best was over. And we'd been number one for less than an hour! Then I thought of the Peggy Lee record 'Is That All There Is?' Is that all there is to getting to number one? We'd not had a chance to develop or grow into artists. I focused again and again on the negatives. And as it turned out, perhaps in part a self-fulfilling prophecy, they came true. From then on began the slow death of the band. It was goodbye to Soft Cell the dark little electro duo, with our twisted ambitions, songs about housewives on Valium, isolation and paranoia, and hello to Soft Cell the *Smash Hits* teeny-pop puppets for a million young misguided girls.

I remember that same day looking in the mirror and imagining I was turning a shade of green, ears growing pointed, and fangs breaking through my gums. My eyes narrowed and my nostrils flared as the demon of self-destruction (safely kept at bay over the last few years) began to reemerge, my new-found success provoking what was to be a terrible metamorphosis in me.

*

If my first appearance on *Tops of the Pops* had caused a nation to divide, that was nothing compared to my second appearance – my first at the number-one slot. Remember what I said: number one is not the same as number two. Number one on *Tops of the Pops* is a different thing altogether – they want you.

Taken aside and strictly coached the day before the show by a neurotic Phonogram staff, I was told how to react and move and when to look at the camera. It was to be a bizarre performance, made all the more camp because it was so manipulated and contrived. I was made to wear an ill-fitting suit over a gold and black shirt, and dark glasses. The glasses pleased the Phonogram people until I took them off during the performance, on a close-up, to reveal the thickest black eyeliner ever. Roger Aimes almost fainted in horror and disbelief.

My simple gesture caused the switchboards at the BBC to jam with one of the largest numbers of complaints the show had ever received. Viewers were shocked and outraged (as only British viewers can be) that at 7.55 on an ordinary Thursday night such an apparition, such a flagrant flouting of sexual barriers, should intrude into decent licence-payers' living rooms. I wanted kids throughout the land to squirm and blush in the way I had in my youth; I wanted to change their lives. I wanted to shock their parents. To all those watching families I was not a John Inman or Larry Grayson stereotype: I was something else – something insidious, dangerous, corrupting and sexual. I thought of Alice Cooper with his snake entwined around his neck, twirling a sword and hugging a girl in the audience. I felt like a Pied Piper for all the outsiders, for the unconventional, for the rejected and misunderstood, for the unattractive. And I succeeded. I received tens of thousands of letters telling me that that was exactly what I was – a window had opened in bedrooms and bedsits across the land, and a ray of light had shone down upon lonely beds full of fearful adolescent dreamers.

I wanted to reach out to the boys and girls who felt the way I had at school, to tell them I knew how they were feeling. When I had felt down in despair, a song and a singer had offered me some hope, saved my life; now I wanted to be a singer with a song for somebody else. I remember feeling a responsibility bearing down on me – which is a terrifying thing for an irresponsible person to feel. But in all honesty I also liked this new platform to shock. The jammed switchboards, the endless letters, the public reactions told me that I could be disturbing. In 1981 it was still possible to shock the public, whereas now it's almost impossible. Since then we've had it all – from gender benders to transsexual Eurovision winners, from Oasis swearing and fighting to Madonna revealing her all in the book *Sex*, to the Prodigy's 'Twisted Fire Starter', to the in-your-face Satanism of Marilyn Manson, to pop stars caught in public toilets or flaunting cocaine habits, to Jerry Springer's guests marrying farmyard animals. With video, cable and satellite, the public are anaesthetized to the most revealing or disturbing images, but back at the beginning of the eighties – there were still walls to be broken down.

As well as my self-destructive demon whispering at my shoulder to be part of my new success, my old art-college swastika-brandishing catfood-smearing mirror-fucking demon wanted to make himself known too. It would be hard to suppress all these sides of me. Very hard.

The Phonogram press department grew increasingly concerned. Now, the press department in a record company consists of people whose aim is to secure press coverage for the group or artist – irrespective of whether it is suitable or not, productive or not, worthy or not, truthful or not. This task is achieved by sitting on the telephone all day, begging, blagging, bragging and bribing, going to long lunches and late suppers, drinking oneself senseless into the early hours on expenses, and generally using every means possible to gain enough contacts to then leave and set up a company of one's own.

Heading Phonogram's press department was Colin Bell, who would later become one of the heads of the highly successful London Records, and later still be recruited as a member of Elton John's management team. Working with him was Mariella Frostrup, now a part-time television celebrity and husky voice-over person for sanitary-towel adverts. It was these two who immediately set about trying to butch up my public image with a flurry of fictitious stories; but it was obvious they were going to have their work cut out.

Years later Colin Bell was to claim, rather ridiculously, that it was he who gave me my sleazy image. I often wondered what he could have meant by such a statement, as at the time he had tried to do quite the opposite. If he meant he suggested how I should look and act, then that is in part true; but he instructed me to be as unsleazy as was physically possible. I had already ignored Roger Aimes's advice to tone my image down. Both Dave and I had come from five years of art college; we had our own image, our own ideas of style, and no one was going to tell us how to look. Perhaps, more accurately, Colin Bell meant that he fed the press the kind of stories that perpetuated a sleazy image of me. Who knows? That must be why in my mind I come to think of the words 'sleaze' and 'Colin Bell' as synonymous.

Whatever, the stories that were fed to the press were to cause me a great deal of hurt, and created a public misconception of me that I would find hard to shake off. For that I am not thankful. Later on

Colin Bell evidently said he never knew I was gay until he found a tube of KY in my handbag. This kind of immature statement (from a person in a position of power!), reminds me of the childish talk one hears in a school playground, not from a member of a major corporation. Colin Bell was in fact one of the first openly gay people I had met in the music business. He believed himself amusing with his camp asides and licentious comments, but he made me feel extremely uncomfortable at the time. I found it ironic that a gay man was to all intents and purposes trying to force me back into the closet. After press meetings Dave and I had a standing joke about whom Colin fancied and whom he was out to get. His openness, combined with his position in the company, translated for me as predatory and salacious.

Mariella Frostrup, on the other hand, was pleasant enough, and I felt more comfortable with her. She reminded me of some of the girls I'd been to school with – pretty, flirtatious and fun to be around. However, beneath her pleasantries, I felt a steely streak of ambition. I always suspected she never particularly liked me – especially towards the end of the Phonogram era. To me she represented the enemy. But by that time everyone at Phonogram represented the enemy, so what did it matter?

Anyway, the press department began to move into overdrive: Puerile stories prevailed, almost entirely fabricated and making us look at best like fluff and at worst like liars.

'DARK MARC' read the *Daily Star* headline:

Marc Almond always dresses in black from head to foot. The sultry singer from chart topping band Soft Cell even dyes his hair to match his clothes. 'Black is the sexiest colour there is,' said Marc – 'when I wear colours I just feel confused.' There is no steady girlfriend in Marc's life – 'they would soon get fed up, I'm so busy,' said Marc. Marc, who stands 5' 6" in his black socks, thinks girls should be taller than him.

All this drivel I allegedly said to Rick Sky. Mariella insisted that I meet all the tabloid columnists at a variety of parties, and be nice to them. So at party after party after endless fucking party, with cheap white wine and stale, fingered canapés, I acted like a whore, pimped out on command. Toe the line. Be nice. Smile. Shake hands. Toe the line. Kiss ass. I realized very soon that kissing ass, figuratively, was the axis on which all press departments turn. Journalistic asses were placed before me, Mariella shoved me forward and I kissed them.

The more journalists I met, the more repugnant the ass-kissing became. It soon became clear to me that this was just not going to work.

Then, Mariella came up with one of her ideas. (Mariella's ideas, I discovered, would always be a worry.) She had this *brilliant* idea that she would contact Bebe Buell in Los Angeles and set up a fake relationship for me with her. Bebe Buell was a famous rock stars' girlfriend – a professional groupie, a glamorous and fanciful access-ory, and the perfect beard for a sexually dubious star who felt in need of a little mutually beneficial, positive publicity. Needless to say this idea was soon forgotten, though I must admit I was prepared to go along with some blurring of reality about my sexuality, because I was afraid of the alternatives. 'If I didn't, I would be destroyed; Soft Cell would be finished,' I was reminded again and again. Stevo agreed with the press department that I should do as I was told (and this was my manager!). He was uncomfortable around gays, and very wary of Colin Bell. He was never homophobic as such, but felt out of his depth with what he considered the 'better than you attitudes, long words and arty concepts' of gay people. To Stevo, homosexuality was a secret club: he didn't really want to get into it, but it annoyed the hell out of him that he couldn't anyway. But for the most part Stevo was preoccupied. He had begun to celebrate Soft Cell having a number one record, and he didn't stop celebrating until sometime in the late eighties.

*

'Tainted Love' remained at number one, and Dave and I were like two spoilt, overgrown children, our arrogant attitudes growing worse by the day. Still with chips on our shoulders, we could have used a parent type to sit us down, protect us, and read us the riot act. Instead we had Stevo steering our career, and he had an even bigger chip on his shoulder and was still younger (for which read more immature) and worse behaved. It is at such times that management has to be strong and visionary for its artists, but Stevo, as inexperi-enced as us, began to find it all too much to handle. He was steering our career, storms were brewing ahead, and we were going to hit the rocks sooner rather than later.

I suppose, though, considering that Stevo himself was only nine-teen years old, he was doing admirably under the circumstances. After all, we were no ordinary band – we were sulky Dave and tempera-mental Marc. Both of us were forever undermining him, humiliating him and occasionally being downright cruel in the way that only two art-school prats can be when they think they're superior. In part this was because we couldn't respect him or take him seriously. The incident when he vomited all over Daniel Miller's synthesizer was only the first example of his unprofessional behaviour, which closed as many doors to us as he opened. He was probably behaving like any nineteen-year-old managing a band with a number-one record. Dave and I had discussed replacing him with someone who could cope better, but by this time things were happening too fast – and after all he had helped us get to number one. What more could we have expected from another manager? Also, Stevo seemed popular with Phonogram. People were intrigued and fascinated by him; he seemed to them a breath of fresh air in an industry bored with itself.

So we were number one. Big deal. Actually it was a *really* big deal. I decided to celebrate, and how better than to spend money? I bought a small terraced house in Leeds off an art-college friend for a few thousand pounds, and moved in with the moody young DJ and keyboard player I knew called Annie Hogan. I'd met her when she was a DJ at the Leeds club Amnesia, and she had become part of the entourage of friends who'd come to our early gigs. For a time she had lived at Leicester Grove, and she seemed the perfect person to share my little house and to look after it when I was in London on Soft Cell work. We had the same musical tastes, and planned at some point to work on a side project together. But she had a temperament to match mine, and we had many sulky rows. Annie too had grown up in a dysfunctional family and seemed always to be arguing with her mother, who in turn played guilt games with her. At such times I naturally felt protective towards her, and once I even grabbed the phone while she was involved in an argument with her mother, to whom I gave a piece of my mind. I was always happiest sorting out someone else's business, not having to look at my own personal turmoil. To complete a trio of temperaments, Dillon, my half-Spanish friend, also moved in and the three of us were to storm and stamp, shout and fight for the next three years.

It all became much worse when we all discovered that endless supplies of speed and acid were now available to us (I could afford them). Opening the fridge would reveal a cache of different drugs – all kinds of acid, MDA, speed, cocaine and later, after trips back from New York, pure Ecstasy. No wonder we had so many visitors, so many new best friends who would pop in and not pop out until two days later. We even had friends we didn't know we had, and they had friends they'd never met. Still, what the hell, we had a number-one record.

But people in Leeds began to behave very strangely towards me.

There was an element of jealousy and resentment, which I could feel when I walked around – first from friends, then from acquaintances and eventually from strangers. At the same time there were those who seemed proud for us and of us, and just wanted us to know it. They would follow me, watch and wait for me, call to me, sit near me, want to be part of our success. For a while I would acknowledge their friendliness, but eventually it would become tiresome and I'd say to them, 'Thanks for your attentions, but I just need some time to myself now.' And then they'd turn on me. 'Oh, he thinks he's too good for us now he's famous!' But I hadn't known these people when I wasn't famous. I was to get this all the time: such people either own you or hate you. I believe this has much to do with how fame changes people. Perhaps it is a cliché, but I found that those genuinely close to you remain as they were, and complete strangers are relatively easy to deal with; it's the people who were previously on the periphery of your life who change. Unable to ingratiate themselves with you and your newly found fame, they turn against you. By contrast, some people I considered close friends – people I'd known for years – began to avoid me, or made excuses not to see or talk to me. Their dismissal of me brought the feelings you have when you walk into a room and everything becomes hushed, or stops. But I always felt that it was not me who had changed that much, but other people's attitudes.

The week we got to the top of the chart, the *Yorkshire Post* splashed us across the front cover – 'NUMBER ONE FOR LEEDS DUO' – and duly printed our address. The local TV show *Calendar* wanted a feature every week, complete with the old clip of Richard Madeley interviewing me in my New Romantic days. Going out in Leeds became really difficult – I was instantly recognizable.

The meaning of having a number-one record would change its form over the years, but it would never go away. 'Hey, Marc ... "Tainted Love", "Tainted Love."' The looks of recognition, the murmurs, the head turning back for a second take: it would never stop. Countless times each day, strangers in the street still sing my own song into my face. *Why do they do that?*

I remember the first time it turned into something else. I was sat in the Warehouse having a drink with a couple of friends. A girl came up to me and rudely thrust a piece of paper and a pen in my face. 'Sign this!' she said. I refused. I'd had enough. I was having a quiet drink and just wanted to be left alone, not be hassled and poked. 'You fucking slag! You queer! You queer cunt!' she screamed, and slapped me hard across the face. Angry and confused, I turned and slapped her back – not hard, but in a gesture of defiance. But this shocked me, and I instantly regretted it. I was truly sorry that I couldn't control my anger, that I had hit a girl – after all, where had I seen the ugliness before?

The next day I opened my front door to a tabloid reporter and a photographer. 'Have you any comment to make about hitting your number one fan?' 'Yes. Go fuck yourself. Quote that.' I slammed the door shut, and the next day, sure enough, there it was: 'MARC ALMOND ATTACKS HIS NUMBER-ONE FAN. When asked about it by our journalists he replied with a tirade of four-letter words.' You can imagine the rest. It amuses me that whenever a star or a celebrity loses it with a member of the public, it always seems to involve 'their number-one fan'. Odd that. Soon whenever I visited the Warehouse or Phonographique, even when I was DJing, there would be some incident or drama, usually involving 'a number-one fan'.

Fans. More often than not it has been those who claimed to love me who have caused me the greatest fears and misgivings. I seem to inspire extraordinary loyalty and misguided affection in some people, to the point where I have had my life turned upside down. I have been stalked, had my life threatened, and had the lives of other fans threatened. I have had to move addresses, involve the police, employ protection, and even had the threat of being killed while performing on stage. One example typifies too many. A teenage girl stalked me for ten years. Always accompanied by her mother, the pair of them would follow me everywhere they could and wait outside my house or outside clubs or restaurants. After months of harassment I was forced to move house. In their frustration, they would write every kind of letter, moving from feelings of love to feelings of hate in one paragraph. They would talk of the plans they had made for me, and our future together. Then they would threaten to go to the tabloids with concocted stories. At one point they resorted to abusing and threatening other people close to me, or other fans. A couple of years later, after the album *The Art of Falling Apart* came out, the mother wrote me a long letter. 'My daughter has just redecorated the whole house for you,' she wrote. 'It is now painted in black and gold in dedication to you.' (I believe she was referring to a line in the song 'Sex Dwarf'.) 'As you know she is an excellent cook, and a virgin – she is saving herself for you.' (Well, she would be saving herself for quite a while.) The letter went into minute detail about their daily lives and tasks – page after page, forty-four in all, handwritten in tiny scrawl.

Around that time the girl came up to me and explained that her Jack Russell dog had just had puppies. She explained that they were named after song titles. 'There is Youth, Bedsitter and Numbers.'

Then, with a pained expression on her face, she continued, 'Unfortunately, Non-Stop Erotic Cabaret was knocked over last week by a car and we buried him on Tuesday.' It was becoming obvious to me, even at the beginning of my fame, that I was attracting a special kind of following.

Meanwhile my relationship with several of my old friends was being tested. Kris Neate accused us of ripping him off because he was not getting a royalty for his sleeve design for the 'Tainted Love' single. I explained that he had done the job and been paid for it: there's no ongoing royalty for sleeve artwork. I explained that he could do some more for us and would then be paid a fee relative to a band who were now successful; but he was having none of it, and threw a fit. It saddened me a great deal, because we had been through so much together. Over the years I should have learned, but never did, that work and friends seldom mix – it ends in tears.

Dave was having his own problems. His relationship with his long-time girlfriend had begun to crumble under the pressures of a number one. All his time was taken up with Soft Cell. They broke up. There seemed to be no room for Soft Cell and a relationship, as I was to discover in my own love life, too. I drew my small circle of friends around me and spent much of the time staying in Graham Avenue in Leeds with Annie and Dillon, playing music and watching videos. On the rare occasions we ventured out we would start the evening with a gram of speed and end it with a tab of acid.

I began to sink into a deep depression.

*

The record stayed at number one for week after week, and soon began to take off in Europe. We began to make day trips to the Continent to do bizarre television shows in Holland, Belgium or Germany, escorted by Phonogram staff. On one I was made to perform 'Tainted Love' in front of a Venus de Milo statue and a blue screen. Afterwards a dancer's arms were added growing out of the Venus and enveloping me just as I sing (mime, actually) 'Touch me with your tainted love.' On another occasion, on a Belgian show, the set was decorated with piles of shopping trolleys while mannequin-type models pushed more trolleys frantically round and round. Dave and I took one look, dropped a tab of acid right before the show and danced trippily through sheets of polythene reflecting coloured lights. Shopping trolleys, polythene and LSD – well, that says 'Tainted Love' to me. Doesn't it to you?

On and on these shows went, one after the other, each one

cheaper and tackier than the previous. It became a standing joke with Dave and me that the producer's inevitable coming over and saying 'The director's got an idea . . .' would be our cue to take acid. Most of the time we behaved, lost in our hallucinations, but sometimes we would be as difficult as possible. We both hated this side of the music business, the utter nonsense. We tried to laugh about it, but most of the time it irritated us intensely.

Then there were the European magazine interviews, which were banal in the extreme. Endless versions of each country's *Smash Hits*, all asking the same questions, all totally puerile, all the time wanting us to be cute. Dave and I, cute? Dave sitting snarling, dressed in his leathers, nursing a hangover, and me in last night's mascara and a five o'clock shadow, both of us with a drug comedown and feeling mean? We both felt mean – mean and stupid.

'Hey, tell me what's in your suitcase? The fans want to know.'

'Why do you like black?'

'What's "Tainted Love" about?'

'Why the name "Soft Cell"?'

'Say a silly joke?'

'Why do you like Belgium?'

'Can you stand on your head?'

'If you were a type of food, what would you be and why? Answer please.'

'What colour is your toothbrush? Answer please. Answer.'

Down went the drinks and up went the drugs. We sank into our own world and switched to autopilot.

'Hey, Marc! "Tainted Love"! Da dink dink. "Tainted Love"!'

'Da dink dink.'

'Da dink dink.'

'Da dink dink.'

Had I died and gone to hell?

Then one day I found myself on a show in Britain called *Tiswas* – a *zany* show dedicated to the stupid. People look back on *Tiswas* with a chortle and remember it as innovative and wacky. Well I'm not one of those people. It was crap. I remember being placed in front of a large pool of foaming soapy water, then I was immersed in it, swallowing the filthy foul-tasting stuff while three men sat on me. I felt as though I'd swallowed eight pints that day as I wretched and heaved in the dressing room, my clothes ruined and my face broken into hives from the reaction of the detergent. I was seething while the record-company lackey cajoled me – 'Hey, Marc, it's all to keep the record in the charts!' The demon at my shoulder was getting restless.

Then something exciting, thrilling, happened. Phonograph naturally needed a follow up to 'Tainted Love' and an album. How did we fancy recording it in New York? Were they kidding me?

We were indeed to record it in New York, with Mike Thorne. Dave and I loved the idea – not that we had any say in the matter. We had a large repertoire of songs, and it was up to us and Mike to choose just ten. Dave had already been to New York, and he made it sound like the most exciting place in the world, which I was to discover was true. It would become Soft Cell's spiritual home. We knew it was a city of clubs and night life, with a great dance-music scene, and we wanted to hear it, dance to it and take its influences into our own music.

We met with Mike Thorne at the Leeds Dragonara Hotel in the middle of September 1981. We had dicussed the track listing and made a selection. Mike already had ideas concerning certain songs which he felt stood out and would contribute to making a great album. We already had a title: *Non-Stop Erotic Cabaret*, after one of our favourite neon signs in Soho. It seemed to summarize what we were about at this stage: we wanted the album to be a peep-show of sounds, a glimpse into a seedy world, a soundtrack to a striptease clip joint, a well-thumbed diary of glimpses through a red-lit doorway. We sat and agreed on the tracks.

We chose 'Frustration' – a song about Mr Ordinary in suburbia and his fantasies. Of course there was 'Tainted Love', and then 'Bedsitter', a song I'd written on my bed in Leeds, about my life at that time. 'Seedy Films' was a song about porno movies, and the confusion between what happens on screen and in real life. 'Secret Life' is about kiss and tell. 'Youth' deals with lost innocence and getting old. 'Entertain Me' is a parody of a showbiz-style number about boredom and jadedness – 'I've seen it all before.' 'Chips on My Shoulder' was written with many of the university students I'd met in mind, about their political and social hypocrisies, but in time it was to become very appropriate to my own life. Then there was 'Sex Dwarf', a song about tabloid trash: the title was actually lifted directly from a *News of the World* headline – 'Isn't it nice, / Sugar and spice, / Luring disco dollies to a life of vice, / Sex Dwarf' – art imitating art imitating life. Finally there was 'Say Hello, Wave Goodbye', a ballad about a prostitute rejected by a lover who thinks he's too good for her, the song's atmosphere drenched in pink neon and tears.

*

We left for New York in that autumn of 1981 – travelling first class for the first time. And I didn't ever want to go back, ever, to economy. We took our two backing singers, Brian and Josie, the Vicious Pink Phenomena, to add some erotic-cabaret backing with their bizarre vocals and breathy noises. And then there was Stevo.

On the flight we all laughed and drank too much champagne, excited that at last we would be recording an album. We arrived much the worse for wear, tired and jet-lagged. Waiting for us was the longest stretch limousine I had ever seen. In that moment all the nonsense seemed suddenly worthwhile. First class, New York, champagne and limousine – me, Marc from Southport. Who'd have ever thought it?

The place I wanted to see immediately was Spanish Harlem, and it was a nervous limo driver who reluctantly agreed to drive us that particular route from the airport into the city. I didn't care about the Empire State or Madison Avenue – it was the poverty and danger I wanted to witness, to immerse myself in, and so it was that in a black-windowed stretch limousine we cruised through Spanish Harlem while I looked out of my rose-tinted spectacles of immaturity for guns and shot bodies on the sidewalk. That night I was unlucky and someone else very lucky, for I saw no bullet-ridden corpses.

I remember Dave and I smiling at each other, as though to acknowledge that this really was happening – that we were here in New York. I leaned back and turned on the radio. 'Six men have now died of a mysterious gay cancer which seems to attack the immune system. As yet no one has a name for it. No one knows what it is,' said the voice on the radio. It was not until much later that I was to remember where I first heard of AIDS, that I would recall that first limo ride into Manhattan.

'I'd love to see all the heavy S & M and leather clubs like the Mineshaft while we're here,' I announced to my fellow passengers. Much later the irony of that would return to haunt me. Much later.

We were taken to an apartment on Eighty-sixth Street that belonged to Media Sound. The studio itself was situated on Fifty-seventh Street, and was the place where Jimi Hendrix had recorded *Electric Ladyland*; it was also frequently used by the Rolling Stones. This and our apartment were to be our homes for the next few weeks. Phonogram had allowed us one month for recording and mixing – from 22 September to 22 October. If I'd known any better I would have felt the pressure, but I was too distracted. From the first instant, I fell in love with New York – with the streets that go on into for ever, the buildings a myriad of twinkling lights, the industrial steel bridges, the steam issuing from the sidewalks, the chaos among the order, the intensity and extremes, the passion and the cold sadness. Not to mention all the other clichés!

New York envelops you totally, like no other place on earth, and it's no wonder writers get swamped down in rhetorical attempts to describe it. I felt that New York was mine and that I belonged to it. I would return year in, year out, often two or three times a year because it is addictive; it is my drug of choice and I regularly need a fix. I could dance on its dance floors or hide in its shadows. I could explore the peep shows, the cinemas, the strip clubs and the drug dens, meeting characters who would stay in my mind and reappear in my songs and poems. I could be as visible or invisible as I chose. And most of all I could be free.

It is also a city that indulges an addict. New York is the best codependent I've ever had – always there to satiate and placate every neediness imaginable.

If you were a British band at that time, it seemed that everyone who was anyone knew you were in town, and wanted to share you, throw a party for you, take drugs with you. Since Soft Cell at that point had a major club hit with 'Memorabilia', and a British number one, we were the hippest people to know. We didn't know it yet but plans were being made for us all over the city.

I unpacked, and the next thing I wanted to do was stand in Times Square, to see all the neon lights and take in the atmosphere of the most famous city crossroads in the world. I jumped in a taxi and within minutes I was there, in one of the burnt-umber dusks that only New York provides. As I stood, gawping upwards, looking like the newly arrived tourist that I was, scrutinizing the billboards and neons, suddenly I was surrounded by a group of black teenagers who pushed and shoved me between them, their hands darting through my pockets, removing my money and wallet. And then they were gone, melting into the crowd. I stood there shaking. I'd been in New York less than an hour and already I'd been mugged. I loved this place!

That first night I received a call from a club promoter called Jim Fouratt, who wanted to take us to Studio 54. Though I felt dead on my feet and wanted to sleep, I couldn't resist. A couple of hours later there I was, on the hallowed dance floor of a thousand cocaine nights. Although Studio 54 wasn't what it had been in the seventies, the giant silver spoon suspended above the dance floor still shovelled invisible coke into the moon's nose, and the sound system was unlike anything I had ever heard. I couldn't wait to hear 'Memorabilia' or 'Tainted Love' through it. And I didn't have to wait long.

As 'Tainted Love' came on, I was leaning on the bar talking to a tall Puerto Rican topless dancer called Elise, who produced a small box. 'Here, honey,' passing me pills – 'these are for up, and these are for down. Try one of these and maybe one of these.' I gulped down the pills, and then snorted a spoonful of the clearest, most sparkling cocaine I'd ever had. 'Da dink dink' went the music. My head went up and my body went down. I staggered into the lights, which all of a sudden were spinning round at an ever-increasing speed. I felt I was turning to jelly. I laughed and sank on to the dance floor, and lay there until a beautiful girl helped me up and led me out into the street, into the night air. I collapsed on to the sidewalk, then managed to stand and stagger into the road – cars screeching to a halt. I found myself unable to focus – the traffic blurred past me, headlights and tail lights bewildering my senses. Then my feet seemed heavy, to be sinking into oozing, sticky sidewalk. All the sounds stopped, except for the single screaming sound of tyres skidding, and then I collapsed again.

I didn't know where I was, but I felt the arms of several girls around me, carrying me along. I soon found myself in an after-hours bar, slowly regaining my senses, and tiredness and emotion took over. I sat and cried into the girl's bosom for an hour. It suddenly all seemed too much. Jet lag and culture shock claimed me. It was all too fantastic.

A few nights later I was to find myself in an after-hours club called Berlin. There I met the girl who had saved me at Studio 54 and who was to have a major part in changing my life. In fact she would change both my life and Dave's profoundly, and our work in Soft Cell from then on.

I remember that night at Berlin very well, because after I left the club and staggered into the street – drunk and on cocaine again – I flagged a taxi. A some point on my journey the taxi driver passed out unconscious over the steering wheel and the taxi careered off the road and crashed into a wall, smoke pouring from the bonnet. I crawled out of the car, dazed and confused, and tried to flag another taxi or car to help. Nobody would stop – perhaps assuming that I'd mugged or shot the driver. Eventually a police car pulled over and I explained what had happened. When I eventually made it back to the apartment I suddenly remembered the pretty young girl with the thick Brooklyn accent I had met at the club. Her name was Cindy.

The following evening Cindy called me up at the Media Sound apartment. 'I want you to come over. We're going to do something special, and I want you to try it. You'll love it – I know you will,' said Cindy in that soft, purring voice that sounded like temptation. I took a cab to her apartment overlooking Brooklyn Bridge. There

were a couple of other people there, including a writer from the
NME. Cindy's apartment was warm and friendly, and modestly
furnished. On the record player was the album *Faith* by the Cure –
it's psychedelic Gothic sounds seemed just right for that moment in
the low red lights with the muted conversation.

'We're going to take a drug called Ecstasy,' said Cindy.

'What's that?' I'd never heard of it. Ecstasy – the drug that would
many years later influence a whole culture and whose name would be
on people's lips every weekend across Britain.

'Hardly anyone knows about it. I'm one of the only dealers, and
there is only one supplier – it all comes through just one person, and
it's like nothing you'll ever have had before, and it will change your
life for ever. In fact it's called Ecstasy because it is,' she explained.

'How do I take it?' I asked, intrigued, feelings of anticipation at
trying a new drug already forming. 'Is it like MDA?'

'Oh, it's much much better than MDA – much better. You'll love
everybody and everything here.' (I wasn't sure I wanted to love the
NME journalist.) She handed me a small, white gelatin capsule filled
with white powder. 'You have to take it with coffee, that's the best –
it lifts you right up.'

I swallowed the capsule, washed it down with coffee, and waited
for whatever effect it was going to have. I felt nothing for about ten
minutes, but then, ever so slowly, a warm feeling began to course
through my body. And then I wanted to talk, even to strangers (even
to the *NME* journalist). Soon all my inhibitions were forgotten and
an uncontrollable desire to tense and relax my muscles began, like a
muscular yawning. And then a grin spread across my face – a big,
shit-eating grin.

'That's the Ecstasy grin,' announced Cindy. 'You can't help it –
you want to grin all the time.'

We laughed and talked and laughed at each other's talk, at each
other, feeling so much intimacy, all giving shit-eating grins. And then
we all wanted to draw closer. I didn't know whether to give myself
over entirely to this new feeling or to hold back, it was so very
strange, cocooned in a warm glow that was both physical and
emotional, and getting stronger and stronger. Sounds were muted yet
enhanced, partly underwater, partly distanced and yet crystal clear.
Eventually I felt that I needed some air, as it was all getting too
intense. I staggered and almost fell at one point as Cindy walked me
to the elevator and took me out on to the front step, into the balmy
Brooklyn air. The lights of Manhattan and the surrounding windows
had shiny haloes of green tint, and the street lamps were encircled in
blurring colours, warm oranges and starbursts.

This was the best drug experience I had ever had. Cindy held my hand and talked me through an overpowering moment when I couldn't get my breath, and it wasn't long before I was telling her things I had never told anyone else – intimate things, private feelings. I wanted to tell her everything. Cindy had become the most wonderful person I had ever met.

Eventually we went back upstairs and joined the others. I was so pleased to see them again, and they me. I felt I had known them for ever, and we all hugged and squeezed each other, just held each other, and grinned inanely. On the record player the *Faith* album was playing again for the tenth time. The track 'All Cats are Grey' sounded to me like the best song I'd ever heard; I wanted to rush out and buy it. I felt sexy, but somehow sex didn't seem important. My new best friends were important. They were the most important people in the world. I wanted to talk. I wanted to dance. Yes, I wanted to dance. We all piled into a cab and went to Studio 54, where we spent the rest of the night losing ourselves in the music and lights.

After that night I wanted to do Ecstasy again and again, and I couldn't wait for Dave to try it. It wasn't long before both of us would come into the studio mildly buzzing from a previous night's hit. And soon after that it wasn't long before we were even taking it in the studio, especially in the mixing stage. How great it all sounded on Ecstasy! It sounded like the best album ever; my singing sounded like the best singing I'd ever sung. The reality, of course, was all very different. Josie and Brian, our backing singers, loved the drug too, and many of Josie's giggles and sighs on the album were the results. It was all so fantastic that we almost forgot that we were there to do an album. Mike Thorne, forever the professional, was bemused to see New York starting to eat us both alive, as we would come into work with shadows under our glazed eyes and dry mouths.

*

Most of the music was left to Dave, and he enjoyed himself doing what he loved the most. He became a little frustrated at times with Mike, who preoccupied himself with his Synclavier set-up. Things began to take longer than anticipated, which I found terminally boring. I spent my time in the studio lounge watching trashy television and eating perpetual deli takeaways. Or else I'd shop around, buying endless pieces of kitschy nonsense, or sit in the darkness of a nearby movie house. I was particularly delighted to discover that hard-core porn of all persuasions was showing in glorious 35 mm. All the time

I'd carry round my mini Super-8 camera and my microcassette recorder, filming and recording anything vaguely interesting.

Listening now to *Non-Stop Erotic Cabaret*, I feel very proud of it. It was recorded and mixed so quickly – within one month – that it has managed to remain fresh and contemporary. It is in many ways a classic album, rounded and complete and unlike anything else at the time. Most eighties bands were singing about boy meets girl and boy loses girl, or else boy meets girl and lives happily ever after. We were singing about boy meets girl and lures her into a life of drugs and prostitution. We celebrated the seamier side of life which we felt was part of Britain in the early eighties. Mike Thorne's importance in the early days should never be underestimated, and he and mixer Harvey Goldberg gave the album a warm, sexy sound. The New York influence combined with our Britishness which made the album sound unlike any other synthesizer-based music around. Mike's Synclavier system was at the time state of the art, and even today it sounds good, if perhaps a little dated in some of the approaches. Top New York session player Dave Tofani's woodwind and sax gave the music an extra twist, though perhaps just a little too polished for what we were about. I think there was also too much Vicious Pink Phenomena on the album, often detracting from the songs.

But my only real wish is that Mike had been more disciplined with my vocals, shouted at me a little more and told me when I was sharp or flat. I desperately needed someone to help me shape my singing, and what's more I have an inner-ear problem which has caused me difficulty throughout my career. My hearing in my right ear is slightly impaired due to a hereditary affliction called Menier's disease, which also affects the balance. I learned a long time ago to sing with my headphones off that ear and on low volume, so I can actually hear myself live in the room. But back then I wanted the sound blasting in my ears to the point of distortion, and I was so keen to sing that you couldn't hold me back. As with 'Tainted Love', Mike believed that my vocal was honest and impassioned, that the flawed moments contributed to its unique sound. And in part he was right. But it didn't stop the barrage of criticism of my voice hurting me. A good case in point is 'Say Hello, Wave Goodbye'. I gave it my all, yet it still sounded curiously flat. After the record went into the top three, I was mocked on a daily basis by Steve Wright on Radio 1, who affectionately imitated that final note that tries so hard and falls so flat.

Until the mid eighties I was never a very good singer at all, with no technique to speak of, just giving it all from the heart and reflecting the moods I felt at the time. Frank Sinatra once pointed out that singing isn't about singing at all. It's not even about technique. It's about telling a story and convincing the listener of the truth of the story you are telling. The most masterful storytellers in song – people like Jacques Brel or Nina Simone – were not great technicians but undoubtedly were great singers in their ability to convey the narrative. There are millions of technically perfect singers out there, from session singers through to amateur performers, but perfection is not what singing is about for me. A lead voice must be unique and distinctive, and as an instrument should be unlike any other; it is the individual sound combined with strength of personality that makes a star vocal. Barry Gibb, Phil Oakey, Billie Holiday and John Lydon have voices that are unmistakably theirs – and that uniqueness is what makes a great voice.

In the early nineties, when Phonogram released my *Greatest Hits* album, I saw an opportunity to revocal a couple of songs, including 'Say Hello, Wave Goodbye' – to prove to people that I could sing 'properly' and in tune. But of course this was complete folly. The sound of the voice, I now understand, was for better or worse synonymous with the song; it *was* the song, and people wanted the original, bad notes and all. In surveys made by the record company (marketing people are obsessed with surveys) before the release of *Greatest Hits*, 'Say Hello, Wave Goodbye', not 'Tainted Love', came out as Soft Cell's most popular song. Make what you like of that.

*

The New York parties continued. And continued. I very quickly gathered a small group of friends around me. Apart from Cindy Ecstasy (as she was now known), there were Janet, a Marilyn Monroe lookalike; Elise, the Puerto Rican topless dancer; and Skipper, a photographer. Skipper lived in a triangular building above the Hellfire Club, a famous S & M venue where the rich and famous mixed with freaks and lowlife, or in fact were one and the same. It was legendary for its extreme depravity, and of course I was eager to go there.

Every night became an Ecstasy night, and off we would go to clubs like Interferon, where the top-floor VIP room would be popu-lated by various visiting eighties bands, with their own groupies and sycophants. We had our own table in the corner, where we would huddle together in our Ecstasy friendships.

High on drugs, the whole group of us jumped in and out of taxis, from club to party, from party to after-hours bars, always a new opening as another club closed. More often than not we ended up at the Empire Diner, coming down, trying to eat chocolate fudge brownies or avocado melts. One night we descended on the Red Parrot Club, which mixed disco with big-band sounds; when the records stopped, the orchestra would take over. On this particular night Sylvester was playing, backed by a Glenn Miller-style horn section. He set the place alight with his stage presence, and afterwards joined us at our table. I talked with him particularly about the impact he had made on me (and on Britain) when his video for the song 'Mighty Real' was shown on *Top of the Pops* – his tranvestism shocking and confusing many.

A few nights later I found myself with another famous, though quite different transvestite performer: Divine, the star of John Waters' films. Divine hadn't yet crossed into the mainstream he later would with movies like *Hairspray*, even scoring several dance hits, but to me he was always a star. We chatted and laughed. I could never have dared imagine when watching his movies years before that I would get to meet him – that person who had made me laugh and shocked me with his performance of eating dog shit in the film *Pink Flamingos*. We went to see him whenever he performed in New York, and I would go backstage and gush over him in the way people on Ecstasy do. I later used a photo of both of us together as part of a montage on the back of the *Untitled* album. He was a lovely, sweet man, despite his overpowering appearance, and always made me feel welcome. Several years later he died of heart failure, and John Waters' movies would never be the same.

And that is how it was for us in New York then: always fascinating people to meet, always a new place to visit, always a new happening to encounter. I was like a baby bird, my mouth wide open, waiting to be fed a new experience. In many ways both Dave and I were wide-eyed innocents just waiting to be corrupted, to take in as much as possible.

The phone rang in the studio while we were recording one day. It was Jim Fouratt.

'Hi, Marc. Do you want to meet Andy?'

'Andy?' I asked. 'Andy who?'

'Andy Warhol, of course. He's over at The Factory and wants to meet you.'

Of course we did. Both Dave and I couldn't wait to meet the living legend who had meant so much to us in our art-college years – and *he* wanted to meet *us*.

Jim came to collect us and took us over to the tall building at the corner of Union Square which housed Andy's studio and the offices of his magazine *Interview*. My heart was pounding: I've always been terrified and uncomfortable about meeting famous people, especially ones I've admired, finding myself tongue-tied and star-struck. I remember thinking that day I wished I was on drugs to give me the confidence I normally lacked; instead I felt flat and depressed from the drugs I'd taken the night before. We were taken up in the elevator, through the studio and into what resembled a boardroom, with a long table down the centre and about twenty chairs around it. At the far end, alone, sat a small, frail-looking man, dressed in denim and a check shirt, his head topped with that famous mop of white hair. He looked incredibly old, his skin rust-blotched and pale, his famous glasses slipping down his nose. He held out a hand, and in turn we shook it. His grip was limp and fleshy.

'Hi, I'm Andy,' he said, his voice nasal and whining.

We introduced ourselves and sat next to him at the table. The talk between us was the smallest talk you could imagine – apparently Andy's favourite kind. We talked about our visit to New York and about going to see Sylvester a few days earlier, which led on to talk about transvestites, which led on to Andy's films and our saying how much they had meant to us. Andy nodded and his eyes glazed over. 'I see, I see,' he said. How many countless times had he had these conversations?

I had my little camera with me and, thinking 'What the hell', shot some footage of Andy. He in turn shot some of me. Wow – filmed by Andy Warhol! I then took a series of Polaroids, and he took Polaroids of Dave and me. It was Polaroids and Super-8s at fifty paces – a strange stand-off.

In trying so hard not to gush we ended up being so reserved as to really say nothing at all. Then we said our goodbyes and wished each other luck. Just one of millions of people Andy met: filed in, filed out, forgotten. Next. We didn't even make it into the diaries, though writer and columnist Michael Musto put it brilliantly in a piece he wrote for the *Village Voice*: 'You were damned if you were in Andy's diaries, and you were damned if you weren't.' I don't know if I was disappointed or relieved. I could well imagine what it might have read: 'Met English band Soft Cell today. I hear they're quite hip at the moment. I quite like their little record "Tainted Love". They didn't have much to say. The big one's quite handsome in a Lou Readish leathery kind of way, but the small camp one thinks he's Edie Sedgwick – so provincial it scared me!'

The day after meeting Andy, Jim Fouratt called again. 'Andy just loved meeting you both, and he wants you to be on his TV show.' Oh yes, Andy had a TV show on a 'local television channel' and Jim was his interviewer, talking to various celebrities on a couch in the top room of the Interferon Club. I agreed to do it. Then a friend

warned me, 'Jim wants to *out you* on television.' I panicked, told
Cindy, and the both of us decided to spoil his plan and announce our
engagement on the show. At this time Cindy and I almost believed
our engagement was for real, and seriously talked about going
through with it – we had taken that much Ecstasy. I almost began to
believe that I was in love with her.

Oh Christ, how many Ecstasy love affairs have I had over the
years? You meet someone, take Ecstasy, and fall in love – for a while
at least – and it's so intense that you believe it. The trick is to keep
taking the pills. But that becomes impossible after a while, and the
love rapidly fades. Relationships have to be built on something a bit
more substantial than drug-induced euphoria I was to learn later. But
in many ways then I felt I needed drugs to love, drugs to talk, drugs
to live, just to get through the day.

I created a false world around me, mainly fuelled by the drug. If
only I'd known where that warm Brooklyn night at Cindy's was to
lead me – to fifteen years of taking Ecstasy sometimes three or four
times each week, sometimes six or seven at a time in the course of a
night. At a conservative guess, of the money spent on Ecstasy,
cocaine, speed and hash (which would comfortably have bought a
penthouse apartment outright) I must have spent £250,000 on Ecstasy
alone – because of course you can't take Ecstasy alone: you have to
buy it for everybody. How many times had I risked my career
bringing those tablets through customs, long before it became the
most available drug in Britain? How many false friends, how many
bad bouts of health would I suffer – the liver damage, the blackouts,
the mood changes, the insanity? Unable to communicate, love, live
life itself without an Ecstasy. And now, eighteen years later, could the
panic attacks and short-term memory losses I suffer, and the aching
joints, be its legacy? I recently read in the paper that a report had
confirmed that even short-term Ecstasy use irreparably damages the
brain. So where does that leave me? Of course there wasn't just the
Ecstasy and other illegal drugs: through Harley Street, I was soon to
discover the great cache of legal drugs publicly available – and the
long-term effects of addiction to Benzodiazapine (sleeping pills), to
which I was a slave for over twelve years. As a result of all these, I
shall never know what awaits for me around the corner healthwise.

So we're back in the upstairs lounge of the Interferon club. As
planned, we announced our engagement to a shocked and disappointed Jim Fouratt, though I don't believe he bought it for one
minute. It killed the interview stone dead. Jim wasn't eager to be our
friend after that. Actually I became a little scared when somebody
later told me that Jim was a practising warlock and that things might

happen if you made a fool of him. Sure enough they did: 'Tainted Love' entered every Top Ten in Europe.

While we recorded the album, Phonogram requested that we take time off to do an important TV show in Germany, which would ensure the record went to number one. Dave didn't want to tear himself away from recording, and I too felt strongly about stopping the flow of the album. Besides, we had taken so many drugs we had fallen behind and now had only two weeks left to complete it. Still, the record company cared little about such things: it didn't seem to matter if the quality suffered, as long as you were available to sell it. Then I had an idea. I called my friend Dillon and, being tall enough, he agreed to stand in the shadows behind the keyboard and pretend to be Dave. So I just popped over to Germany (from New York) for the show, and was so busy hogging the camera during the performance that all that was seen of Dillon was a fleeting shadowy figure and a couple of hands on the keyboard. If anyone noticed the deception, they didn't say. Then I got the plane and just popped back to New York. The record went to number one in Germany the following week.

*

After a final week in New York mixing the record, we returned to England with heavy hearts and pockets full of Ecstasy – I couldn't wait for a select few friends to try it with me, to feel what I'd felt. Our new single, 'Bedsitter', was ready for release. The record company had wanted something else for a single, but we were adamant. Recorded as a twelve-inch track, as many of the early songs were, it had been edited down to become a perfect seven-inch. This was the first time that we were to make a promo video to accompany a song, and we met with a young director, Tim Pope. Tim wore a flowery loose shirt, his hair fell over his face, and he had a drugged-out hippy manner about him. He would go on to make many of the most inventive videos of the eighties, for he would also work with Siouxsie and the Banshees and the Cure, among many others. His videos always had eccentric twists and bright colours, and I loved the video for 'Bedsitter', as the swirling cheesy wallpaper matches my outfits and spins with crude effects. The video for 'Bedsitter' alludes to LSD, and Dave and I are supposed to be hallucinating, triggering the room to revolve and the wallpaper to dissolve. Actually, looking back, I think we may have been on acid for real.

Making videos was exciting for us – it was a relatively new idea, and a great way to be subversive. We wanted to see how much we could get away with, to push the boundaries, and wait for TV shows to react with lists of rules or of images they considered unacceptable or inappropriate. Their conditions soon became more and more ludicrous – an example was that you couldn't show fire, because it might lead small children to play with matches or commit arson attacks – and I suspect that is why so many of the videos from the early eighties have a zany, lightweight comedy element to them, in order to fit into the children's shows popular at the time. We wondered why Phonogram even wanted us to be aiming at these shows. We didn't want an audience of children; we felt our music was for an older record-buyer. But no, it was not to be – Phonogram had seen the results of 'Tainted Love', seen the *Smash Hits* features convert into sales, and were determined we should be a clean-cut pleasant little pop band. So Dave, Tim and I tried to create a subtext in our videos. The restrictions in part forced us to be more inventive. Now, without such restrictions, the underground is overground. Of course I would still get problems just by being me, though, and people would look for all kinds of sexual connotations even if they weren't there.

'Bedsitter' did well in the charts, getting to number four. I'd appeared on *Top of the Pops*, sitting on a stool, wearing a leatherman's Muir cap. I do cringe a bit looking at it now. Our set was the padded cell, which I think made quite a striking presentation for what was then a family pop show. The charting of 'Bedsitter' also showed that we might not be a one-hit group.

Non-Stop Erotic Cabaret was released late in 1981, rushed out by Phonogram for the Christmas market, eager to capitalize on the success of 'Tainted Love'. The record company were making it clear to us they didn't believe we would last for long. The sleeve of the album – a photograph by Peter Ashworth – depicts a strange fluffy-haired couple, Dave looking handsome, while I hide tired eyes behind more cheap sunglasses. At the last minute in the photo session I picked up a copy of *Vogue*, wrapped it in a brown-paper bag as if it were porn I was trying to conceal, and drew it surreptitiously from my jacket for a touch of sleaze. In fact both Dave and I preferred another photo, in which I am exposing my shoulder while a psychotic-looking Dave is about to plunge a switchblade into me. Needless to say the safe picture was chosen, complete with pink neon, looking cheap and cheesy – a perfect cover for the record some would say.

The album received fair to good reviews. Most of the major music papers ran double-page features by respected writers such as Chris Bohn, an early champion of ours. He saw in us a lot more than just a throwaway pop group, and was one of the first to write about us in depth. Tony Mitchell and Simon Tebbutt both wrote pieces that saw us from a more interesting angle too. However, Dave and I still came across badly in interviews – guarded and unsure of ourselves, mistrusting people, and often saying the first trite or pretentious thing we could think of. It would have been better to have been mysterious and aloof – perhaps not to have undertaken interviews at all – but Phonogram wouldn't have it. Everybody wanted to talk to us, and Dave and I were again pulled this way and that. We grew tired of the insensitive way we were treated, and often retreated into our shells. Then we began to refuse to do interviews, and on one occasion in Spain just sat with brown-paper bags over our heads. Interviewer after interviewer then refused to have us back, and it was only the fact that we continued having hits that allowed us that one more chance, despite being obnoxious or impossible.

And where was our manager – where was Stevo? He was around somewhere, but his behaviour was worse than either Dave's or mine. The three of us were making enemies. We were becoming Britain's most obnoxious trio.

We completed a hat-trick of hits when our third single, 'Say Hello, Wave Goodbye', got to number three. It was accompanied by one of the campest videos so far – set in an imaginary pink Parisienne jazz cellar, complete with existentialists and apache dancers – in some ways a sterilized version of Soft Cell's world. In it, my old friend Huw Feather appears as the club host, complete with pointy beard and moustache. I sit on a stool at the bar, clad in black like a Garlandesque torch singer. At one hilarious point in the video I attempt an apache dance with an extremely busty young woman (actually Tim Pope's then girlfriend, Eileen); this had to be filmed several times, owing to Eileen's large breasts getting in my face and knocking off my false eyelashes (which I flicker at the camera at every opportunity). When it was first shown on *Top of the Pops* the switchboard was once more jammed with complaining callers. Exactly what they found offensive was never clear to me. Was it me? My unashamed campness that translated as a type of sexuality? Most likely, because without an interpretation in sexual terms there would have literally been nothing to complain about. At the end of the video I throw my arms into the air and give that famous last note all I've got. It could for me have been the last note in the world ever!

7

'Sex dwarf, isn't it nice, luring disco dollies to a life of vice'

If 1981 had been a year of major changes in my life, brought about by a number-one record, then events didn't look like letting up in 1982. In fact it was to be a year never to be forgotten – if only I'd been in a fit state to remember it at all. In a surreal, often nightmarish, blur, events, places and faces were distorted by the endless amounts of drugs and our ever-expanding entourage.

There had been a New York launch party of *Non-Stop Erotic Cabaret*, with journalists flown over for the event. It was held at the Interferon club, recently revamped and relaunched as Danceteria, and was hosted by a tall, flamboyant German called Rudolph and his beautiful, voluptuous wife, Diane Brill. Diane's piled-up blonde hair, tiny waist and swinging hips made her resemble a cartoon Jayne Mansfield who had poured herself into a rubber dress and forgotten to say when.

The club was decorated with red lights, peepshow booths and pink neons, and had a Who's Who of New York downtown glitterati. In addition there were strippers, real hookers, dominatrices, leather boys, pimps, go-go boys, exotic dancers and exhibitionist freaks, mostly hired for the evening to add colour. Many of the dominatrices staged scenes or tableaux with their slaves. The strippers danced and stripped to tracks from the album until fully naked, and then stayed that way for the rest of the evening. Blue movies flickered on screens as the best of New York drag queens performed in sequins and feathers, lip-synching flamboyantly. Legendary downtown performers like the late John Sexx sang bump-and-grind numbers specially for the occasion. The cocaine was 'flowing and snowing', virtually everyone on Ecstasy or acid, and everything swirling into a kaleidoscope of erotica.

The hostess for the evening was Paula Yates, flown in especially for the occasion to write about it in her 'Paula's People' tabloid column:

> Soft Cell's New York Party was anything but a flop – all the
> strippers except one had busts of at least 68 inches and the odd

one out was a fella – still he was no slacker and stripped off at least fourteen times during the evening. With all the female naked flesh flying about the Danceteria club was packed out at least from the waist up. Blue movies were shown on TV screens and the only folks with their clothes on were record company executives. Guests seemed to be attempting to act out the title of Soft Cell's album.

It was the most talked about party for years, but I nearly didn't go at all. At the last minute I had an attack of nerves at the prospect of meeting and greeting so many people. I've never been a party person. I find crowds difficult to deal with, especially when I have to be host. I would always rather hide in a corner. But it had also occurred to me that it might just be cooler to be conspicuous by my absence. However, after taking an Ecstasy I decided to rise to the challenge.

As I became more nervous, I found myself taking more Ecstasy, cocaine and even half a Quaalude to help me cope with being the centre of attention. Then I felt totally out of it. I staggered on to centre stage halfway through the proceedings, stammered a few words, and promptly fell off. Fortunately I was so relaxed I didn't hurt myself or even care.

*

I returned to England and discovered that things were getting stranger and stranger for me. A prime example came one evening when I was sat watching television. The comedy show *Not the Nine O'Clock News* was on, and I was horror-struck when Rowan Atkinson did a cruel and (naturally) inaccurate impression of me. Dressed in a black polo neck and thick eyeliner, he did an interview in which he (I) mimed to a tape recorder which kept speeding up and slowing down. To this day I don't understand what he was trying to say, or why it was supposed to be funny. It portrayed me as weird and rather stupid. Was this how the British public perceived me?

Of course I later laughed it off, insisting how flattering it was to be acknowledged at all, to be that famous at last. But while watching it I felt embarrassed, and neither my friends nor I laughed. I felt wounded. In time, when I came to realize how unfunny Rowan Atkinson actually is, it stopped bothering me. But then I began to realize that this is what being famous is about – being fair game for ridicule, or for satire, if this were that.

Within a short time Russ Abbot too was impersonating me, a

portrayal I found marginally funnier than Rowan Atkinson's. I can be the first person to laugh at myself, but I always seem to have been portrayed in sketches that have no comic merit.

But fame at least brought me wealth. Money was flying into my bank account – and just as quickly out again, into a black hole. I never knew where it came from or where it went; it just seemed to appear, and then was just as quickly gone. In fact my lack of concern for money was due to hardly a day of 1982 passing when I wasn't on acid. Of course I took other drugs, but my memories of that year are recalled through a haze of hallucination. I was assigned accountants who despaired at my lack of concern. The brilliant Ronnie Harris at Harris & Trotter tried every means he could to curtail my excessive spending, devising investment schemes to try to prevent me getting my hands on money. Some of them worked, and I was grateful to him later. But I put Viv Nicholson to shame.

Naturally, spending and shopping became just another addiction. I would buy presents for people, lend money and never remember to ask for it back, and always paid for dinners, holidays, clothes, anything. If someone wanted something, they could have it. I thought they might cease to be my friend, might not like me, if I said no. And then of course there was the guilt. The guilt of all that money made me want to get rid of it even faster. Then one day came the terrifying realization that the money was quite simply coming in faster than I could spend it. So I bought houses and sold them to friends for next to nothing. I deliberately made a loss to alleviate the guilt of having so much. I had no business having this much money I thought; I had no business sense whatsoever.

This carefree generosity was ultimately to lead to one of life's biggest disappointments – some so-called friends exploiting the situation. I was a meal ticket, and this was the feeding of the five thousand. There was also the joy of being generous. I wanted the friends I had to share everything with me; but of course they couldn't. They had their own lives to build for themselves, and it must have been difficult for them to see me wasting so much money.

Then there were the drugs – one means of siphoning off money with phenomenal speed and regularity. You can only have so many material things before they start to clutter up your life and become a nuisance. But with drugs that never happens. The drugs consumed the money faster than I could consume the drugs. I always paid for drugs for everyone, anyone. I wanted to share my addiction, as addicts do. I know that I must have spent over half a million pounds on them in all, and that is an outrageous and pathetic truth that I have to live with. With most addicts their addiction destroys their life, when they steal money or sell valuables, threaten their family or lose their job. For many, such a crisis then forces them to acknowledge their disease and seek help. For me there was no such crisis. The addict with an endless supply of money can remain indefinitely in denial, in danger of never hitting rock bottom. My spending went unchecked, the money kept rolling in, and the drugs kept coming.

Today, I don't have a great deal to show for all the money that has passed through my hands. I remember never paying bills until I was cut off; I never bought essentials like cups or plates. Of course I did buy things, but what *I* considered essentials – like pieces of art or paintings. Necessity dictates that I am now a lot better than I used to be, but there was many an occasion when a court order arrived or the bell rung.

'Marc Almond? It's the bailiffs.'

'Oh, he's not here. I'm just a friend renting the flat off him,' I would say over the intercom.

*

Early in 1982 Soft Cell were nominated for Best Single at the BPI Awards. Dave and I snubbed the occasion. We felt uncomfortable about the whole thing – the fake smiles, the back-slapping and ass-kissing with people we either disliked or mistrusted, who would be against what we stood for (whatever that was). We thought if we went we would be turning into 'establishment', and we always wanted to be as 'anti' everything as possible. Even to this day I find such events absurd and farcically shallow. How can one artist's work be judged better or more worthy than another when everything is purely subjective? Inevitably, the results are entirely contrived. Sceptically, I suppose the record executives get together and decide between them whose turn it is to win. Who's had a massive recording and marketing spend and needs a boost? What reflects well on the industry? It's all about return on investment.

Stop me if my scepticism is turning into cynicism. It's not that I'm still trying to be anti-establishment – I'm just realistic. I know that any artist who's been around for a while automatically becomes establishment. Even the most rebellious artists are tamed with time, or else die. We all sell out in the end. Some of us may struggle and resist that bit longer, but it's ultimately futile. However anti-establishment you are at the beginning, that becomes just part of your marketability. Whether Germaine Greer or the Sex Pistols, the establishment absorbs you, and eventually you become seen as simply harmlessly eccentric, or emasculated.

Would I accept an award now? I'll answer you honestly and say I'd be tempted. There's a hypocrite in all of us just waiting to be praised. Back in my youth I could turn down awards because they were on offer. You tend to think a lot harder about your position when they're not so forthcoming.

That night of the BPI Awards we stayed sulking in the Columbia Hotel. Needless to say, Stevo went to receive our accolade – he couldn't resist any opportunity to rub people's noses in our success. When he finally returned he was brandishing the cheapest-looking perspex award imaginable. 'Best Single – Tainted Love.' I remember feeling a little regretful I never went; it might have made for a good story.

*

'Tainted Love' turned out to be a monster. It showed no sign of slowing down or going away. It sold over a million copies in Britain alone, and was number one all over Europe. We still travelled everywhere, promoting it again and again on terrible TV shows. The only appearance I can recall with affection was on *The Amanda Lear Show* in the south of France. I was a big Amanda Lear fan – she was the model on the cover of Roxy Music's *For Your Pleasure* album, had recorded some brilliantly trashy disco records, and of course was a close friend of Salvador Dali. Before the performance she flirted with me in her introduction: '. . . And now for that naughty duo Soft Cell.' As we talked at length, I couldn't take my eyes off her striking features, trying to believe she used to be a man. After the show we were introduced to the legendary French songwriter and mischief-maker Serge Gainsbourg. I was awe-struck at meeting him. We joined him for dinner, and everyone listened enraptured as he told stories about his exploits, a drink ever present in his hand, surrounded by fog from his chain-smoking.

*

America continued to express fascination in us, and Dave and I went for our first promotional visit to LA to perform the single on two top television shows – *Solid Gold* and *The Merv Griffin Show*.

At first I hated Los Angeles, as I was given no time to explore or to meet like-minded people. We were chaperoned at all times by the record-company reps, who had everything planned out. They had schedules to maintain, and couldn't risk us being late for the television shows. When a long, black Rolls-Royce limousine collected us from the Sunset Marquis Hotel, Dave, Stevo and I decided to liven things up.

We were to be given a guided tour of the Hollywood Hills by two obviously gay record-company executives who'd drawn the short straw, but we couldn't be late because we were due on *The Merv Griffin Show* later that day. I'd bought with me some Black & Gold Pyramid acid, the perfect accompaniment for such a ride. I thought of the lyrics to 'Sex Dwarf': 'In my Rolls-Royce, / Look it's so huge ... Knocking them cold with Black and Gold.' It seemed like it was meant to be. Dave, Stevo and I swallowed a tab each and sat in the back of the car, really enjoying the ride. The record executives humoured us, quite unaware of what we had taken, and endured joke after joke at their expense. As we glided through the scenery the acid began to work, the 'Hollywood' sign melting into the midday sun. We visited the observatory where Sal Mineo's character in *Rebel Without a Cause* is shot. On to the beautiful Ashram temple, where the flowers became blurred carpets of colour. Malibu Beach, where we walked along the sand, the Pacific glistening like a cloth of diamond.

I climbed back into the car and we set off again. By now the acid was so strong that I started to hallucinate. Figures became blurred shapes, sounds were muted, words slowed down to long-drawn-out syllables. My skin felt prickly and sweaty. I tried to keep looking out of the window, but instead found myself staring at the two record-company executives. Their faces became misshapen, distorted, twisted; the slightly effeminate one began to turn into Lucille Ball, smiling at me, telling me how she had put too much soap powder in the washing machine and flooded the kitchen. Then the other one turned into Desi Arnaz. Lucy reached across for a drink out of the cabinet, but her hands were now long claws, painted in stars and stripes. Desi was mumbling and scratching when suddenly his mouth seemed to get larger and larger, enveloping his whole face; then his lips rolled back and he began to eat his own head. Lucy was pouring herself a drink, but the liquid looked like oil, or blood, and then like chiffon. Then she took off her jacket and was covered in feathers, clucking sounds coming from her mouth. By this time Desi seemed to have eaten his own head and had grown the head of Liberace, by which time Lucy had changed into Tiny Tim. I tried to pull myself together, I looked at Dave, who oddly enough was still Dave, and he stared back at me fearfully. But where Stevo had been sitting he was no longer there but had turned into a corpulent, fleshy, lolling Buddha. I tried to pull myself together. Liberace, Tiny Tim and Buddha.

'Are you OK?' asked Liberace, leaning across to poke me.

'Yeah. Fine,' I said. For the rest of the journey I just stared out of the window, terrified.

We cruised along Hollywood Boulevard, past Grauman's Theatre, past people staring at the Rolls-Royce wondering who the inhabitants were. In LA, people expect you, if you're a star, to behave like one. Nothing can ever be too ostentatious. EVER! The trappings of wealth and success must be flaunted. It's all part of the American dream, because one day the onlookers may be able to have the same and behave that way too, and they want to be able to NOT FEEL GUILTY ABOUT IT.

The car stopped. I took a deep breath and looked at the other passengers. The record-company executives seemed to have resumed their normal appearances. We all sat there, no one speaking, the record executives smiling, when all of a sudden their faces began to dissolve, liquefy, then reshape, their skin peeling and leaving all the muscles exposed – just like those medical books in which you peel away the layers of a face page by page. Then they were just skulls, but somehow still smiling. Smiling, laughing skulls. Then one of them leaned over to me and spoke: 'What are we waiting for? It's time to do the TV show!'

We had been delivered to the studio, on time, which was all that mattered. We must not be late for one of the highest-rated television shows in America. Falling out of the car, trying to stand up and walk, I found myself unable to coordinate the steps as we were ushered into the building. I tried to pull myself together. I looked for my dark glasses to conceal my dilated pupils, but couldn't find them. 'Never mind, the camera will be moving about,' I thought – 'no one will be able to tell.'

I was taken to my dressing room. Left alone in the room, I looked in the mirror. Oh God! My skin was folding, melting, like wax. Blotching and flecking, huge spots bursting out of my nose and forehead. This was not good! I tried to apply make-up, but my skin was sweaty and greasy and the make-up wouldn't take. I applied more and more. I couldn't keep the eyeliner pencil straight and I smeared it all over my eyes; smudged, spidery lines seemed to grow all over my face when I looked in the mirror. This wasn't good at all. My hair was both dry and greasy at the same time, and was frizzing up when I combed it. It had turned into a very bad hair day. I tried to calm myself down, breathing deeply and regularly. Then I felt my hair was growing every which way, longer and longer, and turning into small black snakes, hissing and wriggling. I tied a coloured scarf around my head. I looked in the mirror, but with my black vest and large nose I couldn't see myself any longer: I could only see Al Pacino

as the Puerto Rican junkie from the film *The Panic in Needle Park*.
Hey, maybe this Puerto Rican junkie look wasn't that bad! It looked
a bit like Johnny Thunders too, I thought, and he looked cool. Didn't
he?

While I was trying to keep calm, and getting to like my new junkie
look in the mirror, a small man burst into the room without knocking. Startled, I turned around. He seemed to have a dyed black mat
of fuzzy felt on his head, an industrial orange complexion, and was
sporting a brightly coloured knitted sweater. The colours from the
sweater began psychedelically to swirl around, creating a vortex in
his midriff which I felt I was being sucked into. I held on to the
dressing table with all my strength, but the suction was overpowering.
Then, quite suddenly, it stopped.

He stared at me curiously, and I stared at him. His thick black
eyebrows arched, and a wide-eyed plastic-surgery expression made
him resemble a plastic troll. The longer he stood there, the more troll-
like he became.

'I just wanted to tell you why that "Tainted Love" record is so
successful,' he said in an affected whine. He moved closer and leaned
against the dressing table.

'Oh yes, please tell me,' I said, startled at how articulate I was.

'It's not the beat, or the music, or the vocals. It's that little run-
down sequence in the middle of the twelve-inch mix where "Tainted
Love" goes into "Where Did Our Love Go".'

I looked at this strange little orange man who was now, through
my acid-tinted vision, becoming a garden gnome, and then a monkey
– a stuffed monkey like the Jacko monkey I'd had as a child. Unable
to control myself, I spluttered and laughed out loud.

'Who the fuck are you, and what the hell are you talking about?
What do you know? Piss off out of my dressing room!'

His face contorted in anger or surprise or both, and then darkened
to an industrial rust colour. If the surgery had permitted him to, he
would have frowned angrily; as it was, he just stormed out.

The acid was still getting stronger. 'Who was that?' I asked a
horrified record representative who flustered in straight away.

'That was Casey Kasem – one of the most powerful figures in the
American music business. He is well respected. He can make or break
a record. Maybe you should have been a bit more pleasant to him.'

The name meant nothing to me, especially in my present condition. But years later I saw him on British television hosting the
American chart run-down, and the curious thing was that he looked
just the same as when I'd met him while hallucinating.

Still, I had more to worry about that day than offending one of

America's most powerful music-business moguls – I had a top-rated TV show to do. I had to pull myself together. Then the record-company rep dropped a bombshell. 'Merv wanted me to ask you,' he said nervously, 'if he can interview you just before you perform the song.'

I panicked. 'No!'

'Actually, Merv *insists*.'

Even in my state, I understood what that meant.

'He wants you to sit on the sofa with him and to ask you all about Soft Cell.'

Valium – I needed Valium.

In the commercial break, Dave and I were shown to the set. Bright lights shone in our faces as a glazed studio audience looked on. And then, there he was: *the* Merv Griffin, the household name and American institution, sitting on his beige sofa in a beige outfit with beige skin, waiting for us. As we were ushered over, he eyed us with suspicion and curiosity – I suppose, hoping that we were not going to sabotage his respectable high-rated clean-cut family show. We sat down next to him. His face was frozen into a large smile. Like Casey's, his skin too seemed taut, but his eyes were cold, glassy, wary.

My eyes just couldn't keep in one place. I felt myself dribbling, fidgeting, giggling. I tried to focus on Merv's smile, but his teeth kept flying out at me like clacking dentures. Occasionally I would twitch as I tried to avoid them. Around my head they flew, clacking and biting, while I tried to dodge them as discreetly as I could. I knew I had to compose myself. I was sure that Dave was trying to grapple with a similar problem. Oh my God, we were on American prime-time television on acid!

'Hey, welcome back. Here we have the English group . . . Soft Cell. Hey, but there's only two of you. Where's the others?' joked Merv. Boards were held up to the audience, who laughed on cue and then clapped at Merv's witticisms. Every time I opened my mouth I spluttered and stammered, coming out with something stupid as I tried to goof back to Merv. But Merv was having none of it – it was his show, and he was the funny man. Dave sat back and began laughing. Merv seemed to sense at one point that we might not be in full charge of our faculties.

'Hey, do you think you're gonna be as big as the Stones?' he said, and then turned to the audience laughing. 'Bigger – bigger than the Stones?'

I tried to reply, attempting to be sarcastic, but the irony was lost on the American audience. No one held up a laugh board for me, I noticed.

'Thank you . . . you've been just great . . . er . . .' said Merv. The autocue slowed down, and we all waited tensely on the edge of our seats. Once again Merv said, 'Thank you . . . you've been just great . . . er . . .' Still we waited for the autocue to roll up. An eternity passed. Then, there it was. 'Soft Cell!' said Merv as our name appeared. Applaud boards were held up on cue, and the audience of automatons clapped, barely enough life in them to coordinate their hands.

We were ushered to the stage to perform 'Tainted Love'. Still tripping, I stood behind the microphone trying to calm myself when suddenly, out of nowhere, a group of the cheesiest dancers appeared and performed a mincy routine around us, arms flailing, legs high-kicking, and massive white toothy smiles fixed in just-glad-to-be-working happiness. As I stood there aghast at this spectacle of naff nellies, I missed the opening line of the song.

After that ridiculous American television debut, anything might be bearable. The following day we appeared on *Solid Gold*, now with our own industrial-strength orange make-up. It went without a hitch. We insisted on no dancers, much to the chagrin of the record company, who were reluctant to confront *Solid Gold* (which was as sacred a cow as *Top of the Pops* in Britain). But no dancers it was, and Dave and I gave a good performance, both of us dressed in black with dark glasses. We must have done something right, for 'Tainted Love' went on to spend more time than any other single in the Top American 100 ever, and so gained a place in the *Guinness Book of Records*, replacing Bill Haley's 'Rock Around the Clock'. It even became number one on every black radio station. The record's success paved the way for the British invasion of eighties electronic music.

*

No doubt one person was extremely pleased with the success of 'Tainted Love' – the writer, Ed Cobb. We were told that Ed had written the song about Jackie Onassis, and she had been seen buying our version the day it was released. On a visit to London, Ed Cobb invited Dave and me to dinner, which we refused. 'Fuck dinner – a house would have been nice,' Dave said. It was sickening that we weren't getting any publishing royalties, despite having given the song the unique sound which had made it a huge hit. Most people believed we had written it. Many groups have tried to cover it since, and often people come up to me and ask what I think of so and so covering our song. I've never cared. No one else managed to have a major hit with it apart from Soft Cell. It is the combination of the hook, the electro sound, the arrangement and my impassioned slightly flat vocal that makes it special. We had unknowingly made a classic.

Ed Cobb expressed regret that we didn't promote and exploit it even more, and apparently blames me for not plugging the song for the remainder of my life. We stopped promoting it because it had done its job and we wanted to move on. The idea of singing it for ever terrified me. Besides, what incentive was there? I was bored with it.

Of course I am grateful for 'Tainted Love' – it made me world-famous and paid for a great many comforts in my life, and even now cheques come in for mechanical royalties. What makes me sad, I suppose, is the way that Phonogram and Polygram continued to exploit the track, constantly cheapening it by including it on every tacky compilation imaginable. I have no say in this, and it has been a constant thorn in my flesh.

The very sound of 'Tainted Love' tormented me for years. Even Soft Cell stopped playing it in live shows at the end. Now I've learned to love it again. There are times when I've been on stage in front of a hostile crowd and just an impromptu few bars of the song have been enough to get everyone eating out of my hands. After all, it holds so many happy memories for many people. That's all a part of what popular culture is, and what a lot of my work is about. Heard years later, the best pop songs can set off a chain of memories of those moments when we were younger, still full of hope, passion and recklessness, when our senses were at their keenest. A certain song can evoke astonishingly detailed memories of the past – a party, our first kiss, the school youth club, being away from home for the first time. 'Tainted Love' is one such record for a great many people.

*

Somebody came up to Dave and me with the idea of remixing some of the Soft Cell tracks for a mini-album. We were sent back to New York to work once more with Mike Thorne, both to rework half a dozen tracks, and also to record a new single. We thought we would be the first group to do a remixed mini-album, but were beaten to it by the Human League.

Our mini-album was called *Non-Stop Ecstatic Dancing*, and for me it was a wasted opportunity – another rushed-out album by a record company eager to cash in, regardless of quality. Martin Rushent, who remixed the Human League dance album, had a natural feel for electronic dance music, whereas Mike Thorne lacked that same dance knowledge and sense of timing. Dave and I both loved dance music and wanted the opportunity to work with different people on the project. We wanted to get New York's club culture to work with us, to utilize the local talent. We wanted to give our songs to young DJs and producers in the clubs to do as they wanted with. Nobody was doing that then, and it would have been a first. But a nervous record company refused to let us. In the end we went along with what they wanted. At least we would get to go back to New York and meet up with the friends we had dubbed The New York Cell.

Cindy Ecstasy was waiting for us when we arrived, and this time she had serious plans. Apart from wanting to stay with me in the Media sound apartment, she suggested we hire a black Lincoln Continental, on permanent call, to drive us around town. She suggested we fly to Florida to go to Disneyland, to meet her mother, to meet her family. 'Wait a minute,' I thought, 'I don't want everything organized for me.' Things were getting scary – me meet her mother?

We flew to Disneyland, and it was a disaster. I hated it. Mostly because Cindy had forgotten the top-class mescaline and brought only Ecstasy. I'd been looking forward to Space Mountain on mescaline; the thought of Ecstasy in the bright afternoon sunshine didn't appeal to me. Still, what can you do in such circumstances? I took it. Cindy had booked us into a double room at the hotel. A double room with a vibrating bed. I started to get worried. I started to miss New York. At Disneyland the two of us attracted more attention from Midwest tourists than any of the attractions. I hate fucking Disney, and particularly hate fucking Disneyland. The next day I felt flat and despondent. Still Cindy had more plans. We drove halfway across Florida to meet her parents. I'm not the best person for social situations, and on an Ecstasy comedown in the humid climate it was a particularly bad idea. Still, I went along and remained on my best behaviour. But that was the last straw. I flew straight back to New York.

It was good to be back. I spent time in the studio, taking more Ecstasy than ever while we recorded and mixed the mini-album. The remix of 'Memorabilia' is for me the only track that really stands out on it. We turned it into the first Ecstasy dance track, giving it a psychedelic drug edge. It features Cindy (by now a guest on various songs), who raps, 'Let's take a pill and shut our eyes and watch our love materialize . . . just look at me and you will see why they call me Cindy Ecstasy.' It was also the first British white rap record. The track 'Sex Dwarf' was also given a radical remix, complete with drugged-out chainsaw noises and screaming. The rest of the mini-album is average fare.

The new track we recorded for a single is to me Soft Cell's most feeble effort – another Northern Soul cover, entitled 'What', which was originally recorded by Judy Street. I can't remember for the life of me why we recorded another Northern Soul cover after becoming so fed up with 'Tainted Love'. Maybe it was a decision reached on drugs. Perhaps we thought it might be ironic – Dave and I delivering the poppiest song imaginable. But the irony was lost on the public, and it just sounds cheesy, tinny and kitsch. All right, I know cheesy, tinny and kitsch can be good – but not if its your career asociated with it. 'What' just didn't happen for me. I think it has a great deal to do with the high key I sang it in, with not a hope in hell of reaching the top notes. Still, the record company told me that high vocal equalled commercial equalled hit record. Is this what record companies conduct market research for? To me, 'What' is complete fluff.

On the release of 'What' that summer, back in England, I tried to counter its fluffiness by appearing on *Top of the Pops* dressed in a black hat, leather trousers and a necklace of chicken bones. Earlier that day, on the train down from Leeds, I nibbled on a piece of opium. Just as I took the stage for the performance, which that week was transmitted live, I felt as though I was going to vomit and fall over in front of a watching nation. The possible headline 'Almond in Live TV Drug Overdose' came into my mind, and I suppressed the urge to retch. Thank God the song was so short! I staggered through it, returned to the dressing room, and collapsed.

The opium had been part of a twenty-fifth birthday present in New York – the glorious centrepiece of a massive selection box of every kind of drug imaginable. All my friends had contributed to it. There were bags of all types of grass, packets of speed, uppers, downers, Quaaludes, a bag of Ecstasy, phials of cocaine, crystal meths, a vast selection of acid tabs and an envelope of MDA. More generous friends one couldn't have hoped for. I immediately tried a bit of this, a dab of that, a draw and snort of the other. It was amazing that I lived through my birthday party at the Roxy club. I sat with Cindy Ecstasy and Anita Sarko – New York's first and at the time only woman DJ, whom we had met on our previous visit – my head spinning, my eyes rolling into the back of my head.

Earlier that evening they had thrown a party for me at the legendary Tavern on the Green, a beautiful restaurant in Central Park, all covered in fairylights. By the time the starter arrived sick. I began to hallucinate, this time from the MDA and crystal meths. Or was it the Ecstasy? The prawns in the salad seemed to I felt scurry around the plate, jumping up and down among the rocket. When I eventually impaled one on my fork and brought it to my mouth, it looked at me and pleaded not to be eaten. I pushed it aside. But this was nothing compared to the arrival of the main course – an enormous pizza. As I tried to eat it, I noticed that it was growing, the centre beginning to bubble. I peered down at it, and saw the toppings flailing around in the cheese. I tried to tell my fellow eaters, but they just laughed, lost in their own drugged-out stupors. Drugs and Italian food are not a good idea. Really they're not. So I sat at the table barely conscious for half the night and for the other half vomiting in the toilet. Still, it was my birthday and all these people had made such an effort that I couldn't let them down.

At the Roxy I was presented with a birthday cake decorated with a naked man in leather bondage. Faces joined me at the table, strange and familiar, coming in and out of focus. One minute I was chatting with Billy Idol and the next with Tina La Hotsky, the talented down-town actress, performer and clairvoyant. She read my palm and warned me never to eat mayonnaise again. It seemed good advice. Maybe that's what had made me ill earlier. It was that kind of night.

The performer on stage for us was a young woman called Madonna. She performed with her dancers, singing her heart out, her first record still unreleased. A little later Cindy came to my rescue when I had somehow managed to become trapped in a toilet, jammed between the bowl and the cistern. It was time to take me home.

As we made our way out, I ran into Seymour Stein, head of Sire records, who Soft Cell were signed to in America. 'Hey, Marc!' shouted Seymour, helping me stand. Seymour is loud and flamboyant, and I like him a great deal. His behaviour is legendary in the music business, and he has a brilliantly sharp mind and an astute sense for business. 'Hey, Marc,' he said, 'I want you to meet a big fan of yours. This is Madonna.'

'Nice to meet you,' she said, taking my hand. 'Good luck with what you're doing.'

I smiled and took her hand, unable to utter a word as my legs began to give way. I was relieved to finally be in a taxi and on my way to the hotel.

I was now staying permanently at the legendary Algonquin Hotel, the site of Dorothy Parker's infamous Round Table. Cindy walked me around my $800 dollar a night suite, and spent the remainder of the night trying to stop me falling into a coma. I would occasionally make my way to the toilet to be sick, picking my way across the debris and mess strewn around the room. I rarely allowed the chambermaid in to make up the room or clear it, often for weeks on end. Tray upon tray of food lay around, no longer recognizable to me as anything I had ever ordered. Every inch of floor was covered in clothes, unpacked shopping, empty alcohol bottles or full ashtrays. All the lamps were covered in makeshift shades of my worn clothing, the furniture stacked in one corner, the television was permanently on in every room, blaring out American TV mediocrity all hours of the day, mirrors laid around with cocaine cut out on them. Drugged-out non-stop binges. Home from home.

Later that year I was to get a call from Martin Burgoyne, a talented young designer who worked on Madonna's early record sleeves. I'd become friends with him after meeting him at Danceteria, where he worked behind the bar.

'Madonna's coming over to England for a promotional tour. She's got her first record out, "Holiday", and I've designed the sleeve,' he said. 'She needs a place to stay, because the record company won't pay for a hotel. Any ideas?'

I told Martin about the disgusting little bedsit room I rented in Earls Court on Warwick Road, just above where my friend Jane Rollink lived. I didn't usually stay there – it was a secret place for clandestine meetings that I hoped might happen. The house was inhabited mainly by junkies and prostitutes. It was my attempt to pretend that, despite my pop-star status, I was still in touch with the bedsit world. The room was bare and depressingly furnished – the kitchen in the corner, a broken double bed covered in a cheap duvet, an old gas fire, a single lamp shaped like a naked black woman, and Indian dyed cloths hung on the walls.

'Madonna's welcome to stay there with you,' I told him. 'But I warn you, it's not very nice.'

Martin took up my offer, and for couple of weeks lived there with Madonna. For years she remembered that I'd given her a place to stay on that first visit. As time passed I have felt embarrassed and wished I'd given her somewhere better. I joked later that I should have saved the sheets, cut them into squares, and sold them to her fans. I thought of the imaginary headline 'MADONNA AND MARC ALMOND SHARE A BED.'

I saw her perform a few times in New York clubs in the early eighties, and never imagined just how famous she would become. Nor was I a fan of her early records. I was even bitchy about one of her recordings in a guest review spot I did. But what did I know? I was bitchy about everyone then – I thought it was clever or cool, when really it's just another symptom of my lack of self-worth. I regretted my lack of foresight when I watched her grow into a multi-talented and beautiful woman – one of my favourite stars. I even covered her song 'Like a Prayer' for a charity album years later.

On a sadder note, Martin was one of the first of many wonderful people I knew who died of AIDS. In his last few months, I visited him in his New York apartment. In those bleak days it was often not long between the onset of the disease and the inevitable end. Through it all he remained buoyant and determined. He often spoke of new consignments of pharmaceutical drugs smuggled in from Mexico which were thought could help him. Martin was a beautiful, popular boy with a promising career ahead of him, and Madonna stood by him and illuminated his life, as she did for so many.

I think of all the people I miss because of AIDS. The brilliant performer John Sexx, a regular at Danceteria's 'No Entiendes Cabarets', with his lamé jacket, high quiff and outrageous striptease numbers. The sweet-natured Howie Montague, club host and entrepreneur. With my friend Anita Sarko, Howie was the regular face on the door of any club worth going to. The unique and special performer Klaus Nomi, another regular face on the New York scene. I remember laughing and joking with him at Danceteria. Or Freddie Mercury, who would pick me up and carry me over his shoulder on to the dance floor at the nightclub Heaven, both of us screaming and laughing. Now sadly not with us – and the world has lost some of its magic, lost some of its glitter.

*

I left New York after my birthday binge in a semi-comatose state. I travelled back on Concorde. As it was my first time on it, I wanted it to be special. So before the flight I took a piece of opium, inserting it suppository fashion, as someone had recommended. Unfortunately, as the plane reached supersonic speed so did I. I spent the entire journey vomiting in the toilet. Flat and miserable as I disembarked, it was a testament to my addled state of mind that I walked through customs with my jacket pockets stuffed with every drug conceivable, the remains of my birthday selection box. The customs officer stopped me to comment on how much he liked 'Tainted Love'. I staggered on. Then he called me back. I froze. 'Could I get an autograph?' he asked. I quickly obliged. I pale when I think of my stupidity now.

However, I was back on British soil, and that could only mean one thing. Party time. Every night Jane Rollink and I would be down the Camden Palace at Steve Strange and Rusty Egan's new night, mingling with other prominent pop people of the eighties. I was also drinking heavily on top of taking cocaine and acid every single night.

Just like I did at college, I would suffer the next day, but do it all over again that evening.

I met an old college friend, Mark Manning, an illustrator and cartoonist, who now was working for a teeny-pop magazine called *Flexipop*. Mark had been made editor, and was out to subvert the magazine as much as possible. He wanted my help. I liked Mark a great deal. He was dry and cynical, very intelligent and great socially. He was also fantastic-looking, with blond spiky hair, tattoos and round dark glasses.

We made plans at the Columbia Hotel. Mark wanted me to pose nude for *Flexipop*, and I unhesitatingly agreed. At the photo session, I did a series of striptease poses – much to the shock of the photographer, who thought he was doing a pop pin-up. In the final photo I posed on a red velvet cloth with a stoned grin and a strategically placed bowl of fruit. It was the kind of photo normally taken in an Earls Court backroom for a couple of sweaty fivers. We thought the whole thing was hilarious – unlike Colin Bell from Phonogram, who couldn't see the amusing side at all. He was fuming with me, stunned that I would put my career on the line with such a stunt. He contacted the photographer, and Phonogram bought the entire session for £1,000 and immediately locked it away. To be honest, I was grateful to Colin later. Having seen the photographs since, they are far from flattering – the sort of thing that would have returned to haunt me for years, long after the joke had worn off.

Mark and I did manage another photo session, however, this time based on *Mad Max 2*, which had just opened at the cinema. This time I was dressed in full leather and covered in oil, applied ever so artistically, and then sat among twisted and broken metal. The results appeared on the cover of *Flexipop* and on a centrefold pull-out poster. Needless to say, Phonogram were not amused by those either.

Mark and I hung out together, even after *Flexipop* bit the dust – Mark having gone too far too often, and alienated all those pre-pubescent readers. He would come to my Brewer Street flat and hot-knife opium with me while we watched video nasties. Then he disappeared for a while. When I saw him again he had reinvented himself as Zodiac Mindwarp, and formed a band called the Love Reaction. He had finally become one of his own brilliant cartoon creations. He had some hit singles, and made an album called *Tattooed Beat Messiah*. Now he has reinvented himself as a writer. I will always have a fond spot for him.

*

Through 1982 and into 1983, when I wasn't at home in Leeds, I lived at the Columbia Hotel on London's Bayswater Road. At that time the Columbia was almost like London's equivalent of New York's Chelsea Hotel, in that bohemian-gathering-of-musicians-bands-and-hangers-on sort of way. It was certainly the place to see a Who's Who of the early eighties music scene. Over breakfast you'd find Phil Oakey and the two girls from Human League, Martin Fry from ABC, members of Talk Talk, Teardrop Explodes and Limahl and Nick Beggs of Kajagoogoo. Other pop stars passed through its doors depending on their promotion schedules. Every morning we all sat there, each trying to be more aloof than one another. Buttered toast and disdain.

By the time evening came around, everyone would be in the bar. As more alcohol was consumed, more guards were dropped. All-night parties and long drawn-out drinking sessions ensued. As a result, night after bloody night, week upon week, there'd also be new intrigue, gossip, fallings out. The sessions Soft Cell hosted became legendary in West London as we always had the best drugs, and after the Camden Palace or the Club For Heroes closed a huge entourage would gather in the hotel. There would be me, slumped in a corner, barely conscious, while Nick Beggs would desperately try to convert me to Christianity (barking up the wrong tree or what?), or Julian Cope would be talking me down from a bad acid trip. I'd return to my room, overcome with depression and anxiety and trash it, throwing the TV set against the wall, or run out into the road towards the oncoming traffic in a dramatic suicide attempt, only to be brought to my senses by a concerned Julian. Julian, who knows when someone's taken too many drugs, talked sense into me and saved my life.

After one such evening, late in the morning, Stevo passed out drunk in his bedroom and set fire to the bed with a cigarette. The alarm was raised and the fire brigade broke down the door to Stevo's room. He was barely conscious, even though the flesh on his leg had begun to smoulder in the heat. Refusing help, he simply crawled into another bed and passed out again.

Soon even the liberal Columbia Hotel, so used to rock and roll lifestyles, sickened of us and asked us to leave. When you consider everything else they had seen, and how few people were actually thrown out, I suppose this was quite an achievement. But since by this time I had money in the bank, I moved up-market and down the road to the Portobello Hotel in Notting Hill. I moved from one exotic theme room to another, finally settling on the Honeymoon Suite where I spent my days nibbling on tablets of orange sunshine acid and walking barefoot down to the bar.

*

With everything else that was going on in 1982, I am amazed that we found time to record a video special. I seemed to remember it had been Stevo's idea to film the whole of *Non-Stop Erotic Cabaret* and even some of *Non-Stop Ecstatic Dancing* as a surreal cabaret. No one had tried anything like this before, and I found the prospect very exciting. It was again to be directed by Tim Pope, who was to direct all Soft Cell's videos and even a few of my solo ones. It was another opportunity to be mischievous and subversive.

The whole thing was to be filmed over a week in April, and involved a great deal of planning. One or two of the numbers, such as 'Youth' and 'Secret Life', would be quite simple; 'Secret Life' was filmed in front of our padded cell and neon set. Others, such as 'Entertain Me' and 'Sex Dwarf', were more complex and featured a cast of performers. The whole thing was intended as a peep into Soft Cell's twisted world. The schedule was gruelling, so naturally we took copious amounts of sulphate speed to keep going.

Cindy Ecstasy was flown over for an appearance in 'Seedy Films', where we glide around London's Soho and West End in an open-topped car, both clearly on Ecstasy while I nibble on her earlobes. 'Memorabilia' includes home-movie clips, many filmed on our acid trip through LA. Cindy does her rap wearing a large hat, and when she looks down and up again I have through the magic of film become her, wearing the same hat and make-up. In 'Entertain Me' we featured circus performers and midgets (always good for a surreal moment). 'Frustration' was filmed in suburbia, complete with psychedelic washing line and me perched like an imp on top of a coffin.

'What' was a pop-art pastiche and featured a special guest star in the shape of singer Mari Wilson, complete with giant beehive hairstyle. I'd met Mari at one of her concerts, and I later stole her backing singers, a bunch of girls who later became my string players – the Venomettes with Marc and the Mambas. Mari and I got on like a house on fire, and I asked her to make a cameo appearance in the video. Phonogram were naturally delighted that I had a female friend – it was a further excuse for them to leak ridiculous press stories: 'SOFT CELL ALMOND GOES NUTS ON MARI.' Pop's most unlikely romance was allegedly blossoming. 'He's a real gentleman,' said Mari. 'We have a lot in common – I like to think we're good friends.' Mari and I thought it all harmless fun to keep them guessing at whatever it was they were guessing. Meanwhile press stories continued unabated about my relationship with Cindy Ecstasy and our plans to marry. The more confused the gay issue became, the more the record company rejoiced.

We finally got to film a video for 'Tainted Love' almost a year after the single was released. Dressed as Caligula – attired in toga and laurels, and with the skinniest limbs ever seen – I sit swinging back and forth on a swing and tempting a small girl to dangle her fingers in a tank of real piranhas. Meanwhile Dave is in the background dressed in a wicketkeeper's outfit, pretending to play cricket. What is it all about? Don't ask me – it was the result of a collective of warped minds.

One of the most enjoyable parts of making the video was recording the links between the songs, some of them featuring friends like Jane Rollink, who dressed as Mrs Mop in a spotted headscarf. Why? Why not?

We filmed one of the links at the Golden Girl Brothel in Meard Street in London. (Walking past many of the peep shows and strip joints in Soho at that time you could hear *Non-Stop Erotic Cabaret* playing – 'Seedy Films' being the most popular track. Life was imitating art imitating life.) On the morning of filming at the brothel, while the girls stood around, we managed to get extremely drunk on cheap sherry and couldn't keep from falling about and laughing. 'Pissed again and it's only eleven in the morning,' I say in one link, camping around like only a northerner can, and then in a cerebral moment beckoning to the lens and blowing a raspberry. Highbrow just wasn't the word. I find those clips embarrassing now – strangely voyeuristic, and far more revealing than ever intended. But people seemed to love it and shouts of 'Pissed again and it's only eleven o'clock' followed me for years afterwards.

Then there was 'Sex Dwarf'. The video for 'Sex Dwarf' has become legendary, though very few have actually seen it. We knew at the time we were making something outrageous, but no one realized how shocking it would be, or how people would respond to it. It is a tabloid-inspired video nasty – a cross between a cheap porno movie and the film *The Texas Chainsaw Massacre*. Tim Pope hired a selection of real-life Soho characters for extras – a muscled black guy, transsexuals and transvestites, and an actual rent boy. Oh, I nearly forget, and a dwarf. In a stark white room like an operating theatre, one of the transsexuals is tied to the bed. I explore her body, and then chase the dwarf around in bondage outfit and lead (he's in the bondage outfit; I'm just in a leather jockstrap). Meanwhile Dave, dressed in a butcher's apron, is brandishing a chainsaw and cutting open sides of beef hanging up abattoir-fashion. Pandemonium ensues as blood and flesh, viscera and naked bodies vie for the camera. At the climax Tim Pope rushed on to the set and threw a bucket of live maggots over everyone while filming their reactions of disgust and revulsion. In the final scene I have my hand down my jockstrap, which could be misconstrued as masturbating, though I was just trying to brush away the maggots.

Actually, Dave and I didn't think the 'Sex Dwarf' video was that unusual, having come from an art college where students executed budgerigars, smothered themselves in elephant dung, chewed razor blades and draped themselves in buckets of stinking offal as part of their end-of-year performances. But others were to disagree – strongly.

Before anyone had seen the video, the dwarf went into the video production company and requested a copy to take home for his private viewing. Stupidly, he was given one. Two days later I was awoken by a telephone call from the Phonogram press office. Phonogram hadn't seen the 'Sex Dwarf' video yet (we knew their reaction might be less than exuberant), but copies had arrived on the desks of every newspaper and music magazine that morning, wrapped quite imaginatively in brown-paper bags. The reaction was not favourable. People were stunned. The video was condemned as obscene, a video nasty, a piece of utter filth. (Fair enough.) Every newspaper in the country ran the story. Soft Cell were supposed to be a clean-cut chart-topping pop duo, albeit a little left of centre. What were they doing in this outrageous video?

I found myself on the telephone trying naively to justify it to inquisitorial journalists. 'This video is sexist filth and deeply insulting to women,' said one. 'Actually, there are no women in the video – only men,' I replied. The journalist was unable to answer that. 'It's meant to be a statement on the tasteless trash the tabloids feed us on a daily basis,' I continued. 'It's not meant to be taken too seriously. I mean, there are several tongues firmly placed in several cheeks.'

But it was too late. A police van pulled up outside Some Bizarre's Soho offices and raided them. The police took everything away.

It was ironic that the track and video had initially been inspired by a *News of the World* headline, and now the *News of the World* was running the story that I'd tied up and drugged girls in my hotel room, and the dwarf and I had whipped them into submission. The tabloids were eating their own fantasies and regurgitating them for public consumption.

Events went from farcical to whatever it is beyond that. It transpired that the dwarf had been managed by a well-known Scottish club promoter and group front man who was infamous for scams. Stevo and I had already come across him. Once, when we were visiting his club, Stevo had for one reason or another (stupidity or defiance – I can't decide which) decided to strip naked and sit cross-legged, pixie-like, on a stool. The whole incident had been videoed, and we were later told it had been circulated. The promoter had seen the opportunity for a scam, having never gotten over Malcolm McLaren's *The Great Rock 'n' Roll Swindle*, by which he was obviously influenced. Now the 'Sex Dwarf' video appeared boot-legged for sale in collectors' magazines, making someone a substantial amount. (No guessing who.)

On one occasion there was an unpleasant incident in the bar of the Columbia Hotel when I ignored this person I haven't named. He was angry at having the alleged finger allegedly pointed at him over the alleged distribution of the aforementioned video. He threatened to bring his gang over and break all our legs, and then without actually bringing anyone over he stormed out of the bar. Stevo followed him out and threatened him with his own East End gang. It was a stand-off. Eventually the situation calmed down and hands were grudgingly shaken. The whole incident was stupid and ugly and filled with macho posturing, and I just wanted it all to go away.

Needless to say the fuss over the 'Sex Dwarf' video took much longer to die down. The tabloids know how to milk a story. And needless to say the video did not appear on the compilation. Instead we filmed a spoof version, with some of the transsexuals from the original dressed in suits and glasses conducting a classical version of 'Sex Dwarf'. At one point a dwarf runs on and announces, 'Hey, I've been exploited.' Not the same thieving dwarf, I might add.

The original video remains locked in Phonogram's vaults, and that's where I now hope it stays. We have ensured that it is no longer licensed for broadcast, to prevent television companies from transmitting it in some bad-taste retrospective. At a time when eighties bands were making shiny-bright videos about glamour and high life, Soft Cell were celebrating the low life. Nothing as shocking as 'Sex Dwarf' has ever been done by a commercially successful pop band since. With its depictions of women as submissive bodies (the fact that the 'women' are transsexuals is really irrelevant), of violence perpetrated on them as objects, of the exploitation of physically challenged people as freaks, and of disfigurement as a suitable subject for derision, the video is deeply offensive to some people. But if you take what you see only literally, then you really do miss the point. I don't have to justify the video any more than any artist should have to justify their work. Perhaps it was ill thought out in many ways, but who really cares? Newspapers and broadcasters make their own decisions about what is permissible to show, what is morally acceptable, and try to trick us into complicity. The real purpose is to disguise the truth. In fact the truth might at first frighten, worry or disgust you, but you might just end up liking it.

When I now look at the video overall, I think it was way ahead of its time – innovative, exciting and funny – especially the selection of tops and trousers, the scary hair and the ever-expanding false eyelashes and Spock-like eyebrows, which threaten to take over the whole show. And in many ways it helped to make up for the lack of Soft Cell concerts.

We had tried to do a tour to promote *Non-Stop Erotic Cabaret*, but right from the word go it was mismanaged and badly promoted. We'd miscalculated, still trying to be the cult band, trying to be underground and feeling that we had to create a buzz by playing small clubs. Nobody told us how big we were at that time. We had had three top-three singles in succession, and a hit album – believe me, we were big – but we just didn't grasp what it meant, and we failed to capitalize on our success. By playing the small clubs, we were doing our fans a disservice and shooting ourselves in the foot. Club promoters, though, capitalized on our naivety. When a club was packed, they rigged up a video system outside the venue and then charged people to watch it. People rightly thought they were being ripped off, but none of the money was reaching Dave or me. It was years before I would make a penny from live dates – it was always expenses only, everybody coming away in pocket except the two of us. Years later I learned to toughen up, and now I rarely perform for free, other than for charities close to my heart. And I believe even charity is a luxury for an artist – having seen so much money go into the promoters' pockets for alleged expenses with very little reaching the good cause itself.

On the tour, those fans who could get to see us went crazy, invading the stage throughout and singing along to every song. As a result, nobody could see much of the set, which consisted of flashing neon lights and screens showing projections. Nor could they see Josie and me silhouetted on a giant screen as we did a striptease to 'Seedy Films'. The whole tour was another wasted opportunity in what was becoming a catalogue of missed chances. Despite this, writers like Tony Mitchell remained enthusiastic and generous in their praise; yet even he pointed out that it was chaotic. We had to grow up and start thinking. The shows on the tour were more like private parties for our friends, and in retrospect they were chipping away at our potential and stature as a major band. But, instead of reviewing the situation, what did we do? We stopped playing live altogether. From one extreme to the other.

*

But in June of 1982 we had a success that confirmed that Soft Cell really was more than just a flash in the pan. Our single 'Torch' was released, and went straight to number two in the charts – our fourth (or was it fifth?) top-five record. I was very proud of 'Torch', and it remains one of my favourite Soft Cell recordings. We had recorded it in New York, again with Mike Thorne, and it featured Cindy Ecstasy rapping as the voice of the torch singer in my head. The song is about a person in a bar who is moved by a singer and a song. That person was me and I wrote 'Torch' one night in New York after a bar-room blues singer had brought me to tears. As she had sung, I remember feeling so low, alone and loveless – an addict's self-pitying: 'Poor me, poor me, pour me a drink.'

Cindy came over to England for the video and a *Top of the Pops* appearance. But she hated the video. Somehow I'd convinced myself that the singer in my imagination should be bald, which we made Cindy up to be, imbuing her with a strange, androgynous look. She was none too pleased. The result was surreal and beautiful, in a mannequin sort of way, but she thought she had been made to look ugly and that I had done it on purpose. It was the beginning of the end of our friendship.

Cindy did a couple more raps on a few tracks on our album *The Art of Falling Apart*, but that was all – she had other interests by then. She had ambitions of moving to England, but when our marriage never came about she quickly moved on, and neither of us got our second citizenships. She wanted to make her own music and had met a keyboard player. One day the Ecstasy wore off and there wasn't a friendship of substance any longer, only one of substance abuse. I am grateful to Cindy for opening new doors and changing my life – mainly with a little white capsule. Things would never be the same again for me or for a huge percentage of Britain. It is strange to think that this was the girl I had cried to on the phone for hours, missing her so much, when I'd first come back to England from New York.

There was also an element of jealousy when Cindy started show-ing interest in other people, especially Dave. And Cindy being a friend of Anita Sarko, whom Dave was involved with at the time, added to the complications – she felt she had to phone Anita to explain the situation. As it turned out Dave wasn't interested in Cindy, and Anita just found the whole thing amusing. Cindy eventually ended up with David Balfe, the keyboard player from Teardrop Explodes. After a nasty case of venereal disease was passed around several people, she eventually came to rest with Rick, the keyboard player with B-Movie, with whom she started the group 6 Said Red. The rest, as they say is . . .

I soon convinced myself that perhaps she'd been interested in me only for what she could get. But I also had to question whether perhaps that was why I had been interested in her – those delights of Ecstasy, New York, the high life.

*

I can only suppose that it was being high on success from 'Torch' that made us foolishly accept an offer to make a personal appearance at a nightclub in Hickstead, Sussex, called Cinderella's. Stevo convinced us it would be good to do – excellent promotion and well paid. But I wasn't so sure – the idea of turning up at a club without performing a show, just playing a few records and waving to everyone, seemed facile. Even the name 'Cinderella's' filled me with foreboding – I remembered there had been a club of that name in Leeds, filled with straight drunken louts and chart music, and with a reputation for fighting. The people at that place would gladly have smashed our faces in for the hell of it.

'It'll be great. Give it a go,' said Stevo. 'They'll love you – you're number two in the charts. It's good to get out there and meet your fans.'

Did my fans go to places called Cinderella's? I questioned. Surely not. The group of fans all dressed in black I saw everyday outside the Some Bizarre offices looked like they wouldn't survive five minutes in a place called Cinderella's. But Stevo assured us it would be fine. And he was our manager. So we trusted him, and Dave and I reluctantly agreed.

Stevo himself was to make a DJ appearance, and armed himself with a selection of records by Throbbing Gristle and Cabaret Voltaire, as well as a couple of novelty records like 'The Laughing Policeman' and *Sooty and Sweep Sing Hits*. He also, stupidly, took along the 'Sex Dwarf' video to play on the club monitors. So it was that a small group of us – Dave, Stevo, Jane Rollink, Huw Feather and myself – set off for Hickstead.

We had hired a black Rolls-Royce for the evening, and decided to liven up the proceedings by each dropping tabs of mescaline. We arrived at the club staggering and giggling, piled into the upstairs dressing room, and immediately downed all the tequila that had been laid on for us. Then Stevo and I were led to the DJ box. I immediately felt uneasy, seeing the distorted faces of the crowd as the mescaline began to come on strong. I couldn't see anyone that looked even remotely like a Marc Almond fan. The crowd looked threatening, boisterous, rough and very, very straight.

Stevo started DJing, playing Cabaret Voltaire at the loudest volume. Everyone stopped dancing. Then he played the Sooty and Sweep record, speeding it up and slowing it down. The crowd stared at us. Then he played Throbbing Gristle. The crowd was getting very restless, not at all amused by our antics. But by this point it didn't matter, because the effects of the mescaline had made us feel invincible. I started to taunt the crowd, laughing at them. It was then that Stevo stopped DJing and put on the 'Sex Dwarf' video. After it finished there was stunned silence. Then the crowd turned, their faces twisted in shock, disgust and hate: a few even gave the Nazi salute. The security men clustered around and quickly escorted us through the hostile crowd and up into the sanctuary of our dressing room.

The crowd were not amused. They were out for a Saturday night of drinking and dancing, not to be the butt of some overprivileged jokesters. Once again we had been part of another debacle. Stevo thought he was being an art terrorist, but the people who lost in these situations were Soft Cell. I felt that old feeling of anger surging up inside me. Why the hell had we come here? I felt a fool.

Then all of a sudden the club DJ burst into the dressing room and started screaming at us. He called Stevo and me unprofessional, pathetic wankers – and, you know, he had a point. I screamed back at him, calling him every name imaginable. Then the DJ went for me and tried to punch me. Stevo and Dave jumped in, and a fight ensued. Bottles were smashed over heads; people screamed; broken glass was everywhere. The DJ staggered out, his head bleeding. Everybody was shaken and shocked.

What followed will always haunt me. The whole of the club security staff ran up the stairs to retaliate for a colleague having been hurt. All five of us barricaded the door with strength we didn't know we had, while the bouncers screamed from the other side, attempting to break the door down. 'We're going to kill you, Almond! You're dead when we get you!' they shouted. (Note again how *I* was always the focus of attention.) They heaved and we pushed, panic and fear charging us with adrenalin. Things died down for a moment as we heard the promoter outside the door trying to reason with the security. Inside the room we found a phone and tried to call the police, but the call was intercepted and a laughing voice said, 'You can't phone the police. We've got you trapped, and sooner or later we're going to kill you.' Then we heard noises from outside – club customers had climbed on to the roof and were banging on the small window, and tearing off tiles and throwing them down. The glass shattered, but the window was thankfully too small for them to climb through. All the time the mescaline was working on all of us. It had turned into a very bad trip indeed.

We stayed trapped in there for over five hours. Eventually the situation calmed down, thanks to our promoter, Paul Boswell, who talked to the club manager and arranged things. It transpired, naturally, that we weren't going to be paid. In fact I would have gladly paid them everything I had to get out of there. The gentle-mannered Huw Feather was white and shaken, and Jane just sat and cried. I did likewise. Dave and Stevo were pale and shook-up too. When we eventually made it to the Rolls-Royce, it had been scratched, smashed and dented, the tyres slashed and the wing mirrors torn off. It cost me several thousand pounds to repair. As dawn broke, we limped back to London in silence, none of us speaking until we reached the Columbia Hotel.

It took me a long time to recover from that incident. We cancelled all future public appearances, which angered Stevo. Jane was so upset and shocked that she never made it to work the next day and lost her job as a hotel cleaner. Yet something positive came out of it: Stevo employed her as his assistant and secretary at the Some Bizarre offices.

8

'I'm lost again and I'm on the run'

Back we went to New York. Back and forth. After several such trips, Dave set out to establish his independence. He was determined that our next album was going to be his record, done his way. He spent the journey listening to demos over and over again, checking tape preparation. He wanted it to be right. He had hated the lightweight sound of *Non-Stop Erotic Cabaret*; it drove him crazy, especially when he heard our tracks played in clubs and sounding so much smaller than all the others around at that time. Instead of Mike Thorne's usual production style, he wanted a grittier, much bigger-sounding album this time, orchestrated with John Barry-type strings.

He also decided that this time he needed to make his own apartment arrangements. On one of our previous visits he had met the DJ Anita Sarko, and they had started to have a passionate relationship; Dave disappeared into her downtown apartment for days on end.

With her beaded glittering dresses, wild hats and vivid vampish make-up, Anita Sarko resembled a character from a Tennessee Williams play. Born in Detroit, the daughter of a wealthy businessman, she had years earlier married a lawyer and then become one herself. For years she had her own radio show in Atlanta, and eventually she brought her vast knowledge of music and an equally extensive record collection to New York. She decided to become famous, on her own terms. You've heard the maxim 'If you can make it there . . .' She set about making it. Too intelligent for much of the transient night life she moved among, she was to prove a formidable friend or adversary, and soon she found that no door in New York was closed to her. Her outrageous dress sense and strong personality initially made me think she was a man (I hope she'll forgive me for saying it), which caused me to look at Dave in a new light. But she was a strong woman, competing in a male-dominated club scene where a woman saying she was a DJ was often met with a dismissive wave of the hand.

Dave and Anita had met one night at Danceteria. We were sitting with a small group around a table, all hugging, kissing, rubbing each other, and giving those Ecstasy grins – part contentment, part lock-jaw. Anita came over to our table.

'What are you all on? You look to be having such a great time.'

'We're on Ecstasy,' I replied, drawing her into the group.

'Ecstasy? What's that?' Anita asked.

I handed her a white pill, and she took it. The next thing I remember was that she had disappeared with Dave.

Anita had Dave under her spell; he was besotted. For a time he stayed at her apartment while we recorded *The Art of Falling Apart* album; but soon he wanted his independence back. He rented an apartment from the producer Phil Ramone and stayed there.

I actually felt jealous of Dave's friendship with Anita. Who was this exotic person, and why wasn't she *my* special friend? I soon made it my business to make her my special friend, while Dave was in the studio. It's one of the very few friendships that have sustained themselves over the years. I have a great deal to thank Anita for. As well as being a great friend, whom I can always call on at any time, she has also introduced me to many types of music and literature over the years. It was Anita who first introduced me to the French writers Baudelaire and Rimbaud, as well as J.-K. Huysmans, the author of *Là-bas* and of my favourite book of all time, *À rebours (Against Nature)* – the story of a decadent who longs for an elusive ideal and searches for meaning through aestheticism. As well as being one of those strong, dominant women – the type I have always been attracted to – Anita proved a great tutor for someone like me, who didn't begin my education until I left school. She is also one of those friends who you don't have to speak to for months but when you do the friendship simply resumes where it left off. I hate having to call people up every five minutes to indulge in meaningless small talk. To me the best friends are those that don't impose but are always there when you need or want to see them. I hope I am the same.

Dave's not staying at the Media Sound apartment upset me at first, but then I came to understand how he needed his space too. But it was the first time that I sensed a kind of friction between us. It was hardly surprising, as we were constantly thrust together in so many stressful situations, and with any band or working relationship there is always strain. But there were also times when I wanted to talk to him about the album, or even to talk together about the personal problems we were both going through, and it never happened. There was a wall between us. To talk would have meant having to say things that neither of us might want to hear, having to face realities or even just acknowledge them. We were both as close and as distant as two people sharing the same space, and fantastical experiences, could be.

I would ring up Anita like a jealous wife. 'Where's Dave? I want to speak to him.' Anita would say she hadn't seen him, and I would get angry, not believing her. The truth was she probably hadn't seen him either. Dave was always a dark horse.

When Dave moved out of Anita's apartment, she was stung, and it signalled a break in their relationship – or at least in Anita's eyes it did. Anita and I are too alike in that way – it must be all or nothing: no compromise; no middle ground. We are both obsessives, and the smallest chink of doubt in a relationship becomes catastrophic, cataclysmic, and we instinctively begin to destroy in order to prevent ourselves getting hurt. Even a lover's change of mood is construed as a rejection and dealt with unreasonably. In my case I become totally smothering, controlling and possessive – a result of feeling insecure.

Actually, I couldn't blame Dave for wanting to escape the Media Sound apartment. It had become an open house, and at different times there would be Jane, Liz, Huw, Cindy Ecstasy and Simon Tebbutt – a British journalist who was researching and writing a book about Soft Cell – staying there. I suspect it was the presence of a journalist that frightened Dave away. I personally liked and trusted Simon, despite his having outraged the Phonogram press department by reporting in his gossip column that I'd been 'Canoodling with a hunk' (actually my friend Dillon), which provoked an outpouring of letters from distressed female fans. A cartoon was published depicting me stood beside a bed where a fan was lying face down, crying; the caption read, 'Now look what you've done!' The magazine printed a letter (one of many, supposedly) from a fan exclaiming that her world had fallen apart because I was 'a queer'. Other fans replied angrily, damning the previous letter with 'So what if Marc is gay?' I suspected the letters were actually from Simon himself.

Another regular at the apartment was my new friend, a handsome British man called Peter, whom I'd met at Danceteria. It was a stormy friendship, and we were constantly falling out and making up, and falling out over making up – most of the arguments stemming from my insecure side. Peter had a job, and therefore had a life, so I never knew what he was doing or when he would show up, which fuelled my frustration and paranoia.

As our success continued, everybody wanted a 'Cell's Eye' view of New York. Betty Page and writer Tony Mitchell came to do pieces for *Noise* and *Sounds* respectively. When they arrived, we gave them both Ecstasy and toured the city in the stretch black limousine that I always had on call, visiting some of the notorious night spots and

S & M clubs. Betty thought she shocked everyone when she appeared dressed in a tight black-and-red rubber dress, black wig, stilettos and a Nazi cap. Later she stood on a table in Danceteria and posed for photos, bathing in the attention.

We visited the Hellfire Club, one of Soft Cell's favourite haunts. The first time I'd visited the place I'd been utterly stunned. It was a long way from the Faversham pub in Leeds, I can tell you. The air was pungent with the smell of rubber, leather: stale and musky. The music was muted, and the lighting low red. It all served to create a heady, depraved atmosphere – and the effects of the drugs I always took made it all the more unreal. In every corner there was a bizarre S & M ritual being enacted. Women and men tied to crosses, being whipped and tortured. Men having hot wax dripped over their chests and penises by nail-hard mistresses clad in harnesses and suspender belts. You could even buy your own candles and implements from a small stall by the bar if you felt like doing your own dripping and whipping. One very fat woman with pendulous breasts was a regular. She always sat naked on a small stool as eager men queued before her for blow jobs. After each participant had finished, she would wipe her mouth with alcohol clean-wipe tissues from her handbag and take a sip of wine before continuing. Groups of men stood around masturbating, while others watched middle-aged couples have sex as a third person shone a torch to illuminate the point of penetration for all to see clearly. Elsewhere a man in a full Nazi uniform led a gaunt-faced woman in a little girl's dress around on a leash, while she shouted about how her father, the Nazi commandant, had murdered hundreds of Jews. Just a regular night out with the folks. This last scene even I found distasteful – but fascinating. Voyeurs were encouraged, but the rule was that you could involve yourself only if verbally invited – strictly no shoving in.

There was no toilet as such – just a room with a large bath in which some happy punter had taken residence, waiting to be urinated on. Still, when you've got to go you don't mind obliging. Yet, despite all this, the club had a strangely calm and respectful atmosphere. With scenes reminiscent of Sodom and Gomorrah, it managed to remain quite polite and convivial, with no real heaviness. Actually, it felt more like group therapy.

That night we went with Betty Page, Tony Mitchell and Anita Sarko. Anita and I went and stood in an empty corner with our drinks, and within five minutes we had a group of men standing around us waiting for action. They soon became bored as Anita and I just stood laughing and staring. Anita and Betty were wearing spike high-heel shoes, which became the focus of several men who knelt before them and licked the heels. Anita played along, and aroused the man so much with her playful mistress talk that he ejaculated all over Betty's shoes – red patent leather splattered with pearls.

After Hellfire we went on to the Anvil club – a famous leather bar that was one of the first to be closed down as the AIDS epidemic took hold. We walked in just as the performance artist Zette was miming to 'Bedsitter', and then to 'Youth' – perfect timing that added to our journey through the night.

But this was only one night of many nights. Clubs, bars and parties all blended into one. At that time Soft Cell had the keys to New York. There was always a party being thrown for us at a club, whether we were there or not, an opening or an event we were invited to. 'Tainted Love' was being played everywhere – on every radio station; in clubs, shops, taxis, cafés; and even on street corners from beat boxes. It became a standing joke. Night after night we cruised the city in the stretch limo and soaked it all in. We were recognized constantly from our appearances on television – most notably the Merv Griffin show. Our faces were famous.

My favourite places at this time were the transsexual bars, like the Grapevine; this was no more than a brothel run by the large Madame Sherry, who informed us, 'This is a whorehouse where the men wear women's clothes. If you don't like it, fuck off!' No false pretences there. Then there was L'Esqualita, a Spanish/Puerto Rican drag club where the stunning divas performed for dollars. How good they were determined how much you chose to push down their cleavages. What I loved about L'Esqualita was that Spanish families went there for a night out, clapping and cheering the impersonators.

One of the city's premier dominatrices, Terence Sellars, invited me for a personal tour of her house of domination. The rooms were tastefully decorated in red and black, with four-poster beds, racks, stocks and neatly ordered accoutrements. From a cupboard, she pulled out a little pink dress to show me. 'This is a favourite with the businessmen,' she explained.

Yet there was one door that was closed to me. It was New York's heaviest gay S & M club, the Mineshaft. We turned up at the door, Cindy disguised as a man. Yet it was me the stubbled, tattooed door man singled out. 'He can't come in,' he said – 'I can see eyeliner round his eyes. He's too femme.' I feigned disgust at the accusation of wearing make-up, but to no avail.

The Mineshaft was closed down within a year, like so many other sex-led venues. The AIDS crisis was leaving its mark, and the clubs and bathhouses were thought to be in some way responsible. Yet at the time various gay figures tried to prevent the closure of such places, suspicious that authority was again restricting the gay rights that many over the previous decades had fought so hard to win. How could anyone have known that such a terrible disease would come along and turn sex into something so cruelly fatal? I thought back to the words I'd heard on the radio on my first-ever visit to New York: the talk then of a mysterious gay cancer. It was now profoundly changing all our lives. There would never again be such uninhibited sexual freedom without the threat of illness or death. Maybe that eyeliner had saved my life that night.

I never actually participated in S & M, but simply remained a voyeur. The image of me being into lots of kinky sex and S & M is entirely false. Sorry to disappoint! I'm too afraid that I might just laugh, unable to buy into it. It just doesn't toss my salad. Of course, I've been to the clubs, and even worn the occasional leather – though as much for effect as anything else. For me the leather scene evolved from punk, from Lou Reed and Jim Morrison, but I've never found it sexually stimulating. In the clubs, I love the theatricality of it and the aesthetics – the strange, bizarre and beautiful people – though the practitioners of serious S & M are rarely that attractive. Someone once wrote that 'Marc Almond has all this kinky sex and writes about it in his songs.' I can't think of a single song I have written about my sexual exploits: not one. 'Numbers'? That's a cautionary tale inspired by the author John Rechy. 'Sex Dwarf'? That's a song about tabloid trash. I prefer to write about love. Although I've certainly experimented in the past I consider myself to be fairly vanilla (as in ordinary, not daring, plain) in sex terms these days. And anyway, I used to be of the opinion, Why have sex when you can have drugs?

And S & M is also not for me since I cannot stand pain, or be bothered with all that preparation and role-playing. Sex is something that you have to do to remind yourself that you still can. I much prefer passion, sensuality and emotion. If gay sex has any advantage over straight sex, the only one I can think of is that you don't have to take your clothes off. But the image the public have of me is one that I myself am as much to blame for as anyone. After all, I would dress up in leather and rubber, get photographed in baths of blood, appear submissive before a dominatrix, adopt a sleazy demeanour, wear eyeliner and make-up, make videos with hookers, chainsaws, scantily clad dwarves, animal carcasses and maggots. Yes I am guilty of all that, your honour – of theatre. I was, after all, a performance-art student. None of it was meant to be taken literally, but I didn't know then that that is the only way the majority of people take anything. It was theatre: nothing more, nothing less. Which I suppose leads me on to that rumour.

The Rumour. The most untrue urban myth of all time. The one according to which I am supposed have ingested between two and eight pints of semen, depending on your tabloid source, and as a consequence had to have my stomach pumped. You must have heard it. No? Then where have you been for the last twelve years or so? I have no idea how the rumour started (and my lawyers would love to know) but one day it was there – on everyone's lips (no pun intended, though believe me I've heard every single one). Like all urban myths, it became considered as true because how could so many people know of it if it wasn't?

In fact the rumour wasn't even exclusively mine, for two super-stars in the seventies had allegedly suffered the same smear too. But even today some journalists writing about me feel they have to allude to it, emphasizing carefully (for legal reasons rather than moral) how untrue it is. It lets them get in a cheap pun or double entendre, but in so doing they and I know they are willingly perpetuating the lie. Which is precisely why I won't name the two stars who suffered from the same lie as me. Both of them were rich and extremely famous – one known to sue easily, and the other consistently heterosexual. Then there was me. I wasn't the typical pop star – sang songs which were supposedly all about sleaze and debauchery, wore make-up, and acted outrageously. I was the perfect target for the homophobe. But the rumour cannot be shrugged off, because for me it hasn't gone away – and nor has the homophobia that perpetuates it. The image of a man as receptacle – compliant, passively down on his knees – is one of weakness and acquiescence. It is an ugly, vile image. It is an image homophobes at the same time applaud, though, because it is about control, mastery, superiority, dispensing humiliation. It con-trasts with their own supposed moral uprightness, and reaffirms their own sexuality, dispelling any doubts they might have about it.

It constantly surprises and disappoints me that intelligent and liberal people feel the need to perpetuate this rumour, without stopping to consider how deeply hurtful it might be. Because it has been around for so many years, many self-proclaimed liberally minded people accept it as a matter of fact, without having the intelligence or sensitivity to question it, or to consider how deplorable or contemptible reiterating it is. Even comedians Vic Reeves and Bob Mortimer have felt a need to incorporate it into their act. Celebrity presenter Mark Lamarr, who once spoke out against homophobia on the TV show *The Word*, now finds it irresistible to make childish references to it: 'Don't buy Marc Almond a pint!' Nudge, nudge! Perhaps all these people should bear in mind that their remarks fuel the aggression and violence that homophobes need to express themselves. Every time a reference to the rumour appears in print or on TV means another day that I get insulted, shouted at or threatened. Those who perpetuate such rumours are themselves more distasteful than anything of which I have spoken, written or sung.

*

If I had to associate each album with a different drug (*Non-Stop Erotic Cabaret* was the Ecstasy album), *The Art of Falling Apart* would be the acid. I don't mean that it was psychedelic; just that throughout recording Dave and I were sampling a wide variety of very strong acid. For example, one evening Peter and I went along to meet Anita and Dave with a view to seeing a film. Anita suggested that we all do some 'mild' acid she happened to have. I should have known better what 'mild' might mean. She went to her fridge, which was a veritable pharmacy of acids approved by Timothy Leary himself – certainly not the light, Mickey Mouse, giggling variety I often dropped at discos in later years. This was to be the 'Let's go on a twenty-four-hour trip into cosmic consciousness' type.

Or another evening while staying at the Gramercy Park Hotel we all dropped some of her so-called mild acid. We hired a video of the Kubrick film *The Shining*, and the drug began to work. As the drug got stronger, I was mystified as to why the entire film took place in a Japanese restaurant; I put it down to the way Shelley Duvall looks. I was still tripping the next day when I had to check out. Unbeknown to me, the hotel seemed to have put all the service charges run up by another musician staying there on my bill. I refused to pay, and was in such a destroyed state that the police were called. Just as I was to be led away in handcuffs, Anita arrived and bailed me out. The acid seemed to have hardly affected her – but then she is a strong Detroit girl. She saved me that time, but I was to discover that her mild acid was nothing compared to her mild mescaline.

We swallowed that in the darkness of the cinema, and waited for it to take effect. By the time the film had finished I'd discovered it was not only anything but mild; it was anything but mescaline. Anita rooted in her bag. 'Shit!' she said. 'I think we've taken the Purple Haze by mistake. But don't worry – it's the original stuff that Hendrix used. You're going to have a great trip.'

From the cinema we made our way to Danceteria, where thankfully the roof garden was open. As we came out of the elevator on to the roof, the song blasting out over the sound system was Hendrix's 'Purple Haze'. We looked at each other, or tried to, attempting to read some mystical significance into the coincidence. (A couple of days later Dave and I recorded the song as part of a Hendrix medley to be included on *The Art of Falling Apart*.) We made our way across the roof garden to the bar and clung to each other. As I looked upward, Indian magic carpets were flying across the night sky and glitter appeared to be falling in cascades around us; comets and stars exploded around the Empire State Building, which was slowly melting, dissolving into the hot New York night.

I spotted Alan Vega, the lead singer of Suicide, making his way towards me. I didn't know if he was going to be friendly or hostile. Alan is a really great guy, and I was always a fan, but he seemed to have a bee in his bonnet about Soft Cell, even though we always acknowledged Suicide as being the first synth duo. 'Hey, those Soft Cell guys ripped us off and stole our ideas,' he said in the press. At first I had felt angry over what he said, and once stormed past him in the Gramercy Park, ignoring him. But now we had reconciled our differences. Nevertheless, I knew I wouldn't be able to talk to him in my current state. I hoped he wouldn't come over. But he did. He waved. 'Hey, Marc!' he shouted, pushing towards me.

'Alan . . . I . . . I'm sorry, Alan, but I just can't talk to you now.' He looked at me quizzically. 'I'm tripping,' I said.

He stormed off. He thought I was snubbing him again, but the truth was I was struggling to keep it together. Everyone was turning into strange, exotic creatures – gazelles, ibises and zebra. Eventually Anita dragged me into a corner, where we ensconced ourselves to watch the parade pass by. It was the best psychedelic display I have ever seen.

*

Peter and I were spending a great deal of time together, but the arguments continued. I never thought Peter was always – what shall I say? – truthful. He seemed a bit of an unknown quantity. But, hey, isn't that what makes people interesting? One day I drunkenly dragged him away from a party that Mick Jones of the Clash was holding. Everybody was there, including Billy Idol, with whom I sat drinking copious amounts of tequila. I'd decided that I'd had enough of the party and wanted to go to see a movie in Times Square – which of course meant that Peter had to accompany me. Naturally, he wasn't too thrilled at being dragged away from such a happening party to watch a crummy film on Forty-second Street.

By the time we reached Times Square I was as drunk as hell. I toppled out of the taxi on to the street, shoeless and still clutching a plastic beaker of tequila and cranberry. I threw some money at the ticket attendant, and we both fell down the aisle to our seats. Peter was furious by now, and we began to row. Eventually we ended up fighting in front of the screen while people howled abuse at us and a large black guy threatened us with a walking stick. Peter stormed out and I staggered after him, shouting all the way until we were back out on the street. That, I suppose, was the turning point – our relationship went downhill from there, and we saw each other less and less over the years, occasionally happy, more often than not sad.

Once, when visiting the city, I went to see him where he was staying at the President Hotel, a run-down place off Times Square. He had hit rock bottom, and was suffering from hepatitis. He seemed so lost. Another time I went to visit him in an apartment building that was owned by a prominent drug dealer. We were sitting talking when suddenly a gang of Puerto Ricans burst into the room and started shouting and threatening him for some reason. I guessed it had to do with drugs and, deciding that this was not the place for me, slipped out quietly. However, Peter proved to be a survivor, bouncing back stronger after each fall. Our last meeting was in the mid-nineties in Hamburg. I was performing at the Tivoli Theatre, and Peter came backstage afterwards to say hello. Looking great, he was now the owner of a popular bar and had become a well-known local character. I'm glad he survived. 'Survived' is an odd expression to use, but it does sum up a lot of people I've met. The songs 'Barriers' and 'The Blond Boy' were both written with Peter in mind.

*

With all these things going on, it was amazing that we accomplished recording an album at all. Yet we were bursting with so many creative ideas. From the start we showed a new strength, and, though I was still oversinging, I was developing a deeper, more passionate style and an anger which expressed itself most intensely on songs like 'Heat', 'The Art of Falling Apart' and 'Baby Doll'. Some of the songs have too much vocal drama, overdoing it. The experiences in my personal life, especially the emotional pain, were starting to surface in my work. This pain and my self-loathing manifested themselves in songs like 'Numbers'. 'Numbers' is based on the book of the same title by John Rechy – one of my favourite writers, who penned my Bible *The City of Night*. 'Numbers' deals with the emptiness of anonymous sex. The body count at the end was originally a roll-call of sexual conquests, but the increase in AIDS mortalities in the eighties imbued it with a new meaning.

'Martin', an early work that became a favourite in Goth clubs, had originally been inspired by a film in which a young man drains blood from his victims, but had unintentionally also become a poignant metaphor of the climate we were living in.

'Where the Heart is' is a song about the problems faced by adolescents, as is 'Forever the Same', which deals with the hopelessness of a young person working on a factory assembly line, unhappy and unfulfilled.

My favourite song on the album is 'Heat'. It has a subtext based on Tennessee Williams motifs – addiction, despair, pent-up sexuality, brutal truth. The song contains one of my favourite lines: 'Do you use up bodies like cigarettes? Do you need them for ego? Do you need them for sex?' The questions remain unanswered.

The Art of Falling Apart was greeted with rave reviews and swept away any misconceptions about Soft Cell. It also managed to alienate a large part of our pop youth market – especially teenage girls, who found it all too unfamiliar or puzzling. To some extent, of course, this had been our intention: to stamp out 'Tainted Love', 'Where Did Our Love Go' and 'What'. With hindsight we were ill-advised to not include our hit single 'Torch' on the album, and the decision cost us dearly in terms of album sales; but we were bloody-minded, determined to be as unconventional as possible. Can you believe that one of our biggest hits was not actually on any album? Does the phrase 'shooting ourselves in the foot' sound familiar?

Barney Hoskyns of *NME* said of *The Art of Falling Apart*, 'It is a stunning display of the duo's range and diversity. They've now progressed so far beyond both post-Kraftwerk electrobeat and the tight compression repatternings of Motown Northern Soul that one scarcely recalls the skimpy "Memorabilia", the unwieldy "Where Did Our Love Go", the timid "What".'

Tony Mitchell in *Sounds* said, '*The Art of Falling Apart* is the magnificent product of a year in the life of two very troubled souls, evidence if more were needed that the best Art comes out of struggle and turmoil, be it within the Self or externally, and proof that Almond and Ball have overcome the foe to emerge victorious.'

Another journalist noted, 'Whilst Depeche Mode sweetly charm their way into the nation's hearts, Soft Cell prefer to crawl right up their back passage.'

Without wishing to disparage Mike Thorne, this album really belonged to Dave. His warm slabs of keyboards give it a fuller, more American sound, and his use of samples was one of the first ever.

Dave had battled with Mike's obsession with the Synclavier, and
what had emerged was a great compromise between the high-tech of
Mike's set-up and the dirt of Dave's analogue synthesizers.

The first single taken from the album was 'Where the Heart is'. It
did well in the chart, but was not a major hit; it was too downbeat
and serious. Phonogram, beginning to show their lack of commitment, restricted the budget for the video, which was a simple affair
with Dave and me performing to an overhead camera. This was
underselling as only record companies know how.

The following single was 'Numbers', which didn't have a video at
all; although it made a dent in the chart, it never achieved any
substantial sales. Many thought it was a brave decision to release it
at all; others simply viewed it as commercial suicide. People wrongly
thought the song was glorifying sexual promiscuity and – worse! –
was just plain depressing.

Phonogram were disheartened by the album; it wasn't the record
they had wanted, and eventually they lost enthusiasm altogether. The
third scheduled single, 'Loving You, Hating Me', never came out at
all. But we felt we were revealing our true colours and deliberately
being subversive, hopefully attracting a new audience. We felt that if
we were to survive or make a difference then we really had to take
risks. What we couldn't have known, of course, was that the writing
was already on the wall.

On returning from a trip abroad, I found out to my dismay that
Phonogram had had a new idea about how to promote the single
'Numbers'. With every copy purchased, record shops were giving
away a free copy of 'Tainted Love'. This struck me as a most insulting
piece of marketing. First stunned and then furious, both Stevo and I
leaped into a taxi and raced around to the Phonogram offices in New
Bond Street. By the time we arrived we were both frenzied.

We burst into the offices, Stevo handcuffing the secretary, Katrina
Barnes, to a chair and throwing a fire extinguisher through the glass
doors. We overturned tables and desks, smashed all the gold discs on
the walls and threw the waste baskets through the glass windows.
Stevo was shouting at lawyers and accountants who appeared, and
screaming, 'Get those fucking records out of the shops now!' And
then, Stevo being Stevo, he started throwing punches. We were
eventually dragged from the building by security guards as we continued to shout and swear.

Once again I had lost control of my temper, but, for me especially,
Phonogram couldn't have done anything more insulting or damaging
to our reputation than attempt to make 'Numbers' a hit on the back
of that albatross 'Tainted Love'. Talking about the incident years

later to Katrina Barnes, by then herself a highly successful manager, she told me that Phonogram had always believed in Soft Cell and were never the enemy we perceived them to be. 'They really wanted it to work for you, and they wanted to get right behind you, but you just didn't make it easy,' she said. She did have a point.

Stevo and I had behaved in an aggressive and undignified way. It was a side of me I was showing all too often – to be inevitably followed by guilt and severe depression. And Status Quo were none too happy with our office rampage, as it was their gold discs that we had smashed and they took it personally. Of course our action was not aimed at them. To us the discs were just sad trophies of an exploitative record company, and we didn't care whose name was on them.

*

Back and forth.

Only in New York did my spirits lift. When I returned to London so did my depression. Within a week of that incident at Phonogram I was involved in another violent attack. I was guesting on stage with Matt Johnson of The The at the Marquee, playing guitar and percussion, and singing a couple of songs. During the performance an idiot at the front hurled a can of lager at my head. Luckily it missed. Stunned and angry at his attack, I took my customized Red Rapier guitar with solid-gold machine heads and speared him in the chest with it. Though he had only bruises and a small cut, he threatened to sue and call the police. I had to apologize and eventually gave him some money to forget the incident. It made the papers: 'A Hard Hit from Soft Cell Marc' reported the *Evening Standard*. 'Soft Cell's increasingly petulant Marc Almond has been involved in his second violent incident within a week, leaving a member of the audience injured after fans started spitting and throwing beer cans.' Why is it always supposed that it's fans who are involved in these incidents? I'm actually surprised it wasn't my number-one fan.

I surprised myself by reacting the way I did towards this person in the audience, by trying to hit him. Mind you, he did use me for a target practice. How would you feel if someone threw half-full cans of lager at you? I felt the need to fight back at anyone and everyone that threatened me or disrespected me. Was I ever going to escape from that playground?

9

The Mambas and the Madness

'Don't you understand? You've got to help me.'

I sat in the Harley Street doctor's office on that wet, grey February morning, my head in my hands, my hair long, greasy and stringy, two days' stubble on my chin, the picture of misery. 'You've got to give me something to lift me out of my depression, to help me sleep. I can't sleep.'

What I didn't tell him was that I was taking abundant amounts of sulphate speed each day. It had become a vicious circle of sleepless nights and intense depressions.

'Perhaps you should see a psychiatrist to help you with your problems?'

'What?'

'A psychiatrist?'

'There is absolutely nothing wrong with me other than I can't sleep.'

The doctor eyed me quizzically.

'Perhaps,' he said tentatively, 'you have emotional problems. It really might help to see someone. I know just the person.'

'Absolutely not. No! I'm not mad. I don't need a psychiatrist. Do you understand? There's nothing wrong with me! I just need something to lift off my depression and help me sleep.' I sat flinching and twittering and twitching, averting my gaze from his concerned looks and staring at the floor. Then I became tearful.

Reluctantly the doctor wrote out the prescription, and the bill – 'Just this once.'

My spirits lifted. He was just one of many doctors writing out similar prescriptions for me – some less interested than others; all private, naturally.

I handed the piece of paper over the counter in exchange for a little bottle of joy – small orange pills that reassuringly reminded me of the Haliborange vitamin-C tablets I'd taken as a child. I took one and closed my eyes, and before long I was filled with sunshine.

As my collection of tablets grew in both size and variety, so did my confidence. There were tablets of all colours and shapes: ones like

tiny eggs, which reminded me of those children's sugar eggs received
as Easter treats; tiny blue ones called Ativan; ones with seductive
names like Rhohypnol and not so enticing names like Largactyl;
chunky white ones, like breath mints, called Mogadons. Not forgetting the housewife's reliable friend Valium – I had lots of those. I
loved to take these tablets on a dull afternoon and just lie in bed
listening to the Birthday Party's album, by Nick Cave's band, and
rolling myself long, elegant joints. I kept an endless supply of hash by
the bed for such occasions – in fact for any occasion. It was to help
me sleep – which it didn't at all, simply filled my head with a miasma
of ideas while physically making me lethargic.

After prolonged use of every type of prescription drug in the
candy shop known as Harley Street, I settled on a firm favourite:
a small, blue, innocuous-looking tablet called Halcion. It gave me a
deep sleep with hardly any hangover – nothing that a strong cup of
tea couldn't put right. Halcion and Valium became my best friends
for about twelve years, until they eventually ruled my life. But at this
time all they meant was that I could speed all day and sleep at night.
Eventually the doctor just sent me repeat prescriptions without me
even having to attend the surgery. When I ran out of tablets, I just
bought some more. Easy!

Elated from my successful doctors' visits I would make my way to
the Some Bizarre office, situated in St Anne's Court in Soho. It was
above the famous Trident Studio, where Bowie recorded much of his
early work and where John Lennon played 'Imagine' on the famous
piano. I was to use the very same piano on my own recordings.

It was easy to find the Some Bizarre offices at that time, for a small
crowd of fans clad in black waited loyally outside every day, regardless
of the weather. I would try to take the time to stop and chat, even
getting to know some of their faces, though their names escaped me.
They were a pleasant enough group of people, and on many occasion
their presence lifted my spirit. But at other times, when depression
hung over me like an ominous rain cloud, I just wanted to be left alone;
then the fans' presence would irritate me, and I'd try to ignore them.
There was never any intention to hurt their feelings; I was just unable
to keep up the façade of being Marc Almond the accessible pop star
day after day. On these bad days there would be trouble. I now know
that I was overfriendly most of the time. I would take on the fans'
problems and burden them with mine. Before long they considered
themselves friends, not fans. I even said in an interview that I considered my fans as friends, feeling that the word 'fan' was too dismissive, too derogatory. That was a mistake. But it was all part of my
guilt about fame, my compulsive need to help others.

I'd seen other stars push their fans aside, refusing autographs. In fact I had been one such fan at the Bolan concert years earlier. When I dismissed fans I felt guilty and remorseful. So I'd backtrack and talk to them, sign anything, invite them into the concert soundchecks, while all the time voices in my head screamed, 'Leave me alone!' This familiarity was to breed contempt and jealousy among a small group. Jealousy because I would spend more time with one than another; contempt from me for letting them take up so much of my time. And, over the years, I learned that such a fan's love can turn to hate in an instant.

I would receive sackfuls of letters, some from unhappy teenagers with emotional problems, even suicide threats. Letters that for page after page poured out the writers' every thought and fear, saying how much my music had changed their lives or saved them from suicide, how a word of recognition would mean so much. How could I ignore them? I began to write as many letters as I could. All day I would sit and write. I took on all these people's problems until they weighed on my shoulders like a mountain of despair. I felt helpless. And when I wrote, back would come more letters and more problems – begging me to write back just once more. But what use was I? I was as hopelessly lost as they were. Eventually I learned to be less accessible. I recalled how mystique is important, that people are not going to like you less because you don't stand and talk to them for two hours. And if they do, well that's tough.

Then I did something much worse – I broke the rule. I made the mistake of sleeping with fans. It's always been a disaster, inevitably ending in tears. It's actually an abuse of someone who'll do anything for you. Considering the baggage it brings, the sex is always bad: those nerves and expectations, the recriminations when the fan realizes that he or she has been merely a one-night stand. I suppose they were looking for something more meaningful and lasting than a half-cocked fumble after too many drinks.

The next morning, if you even manage to stay till then, you expect to get on with your life. But they don't. They pester you and wait around and become a nuisance. You're unresponsive and, more often than not, the lurid details of the brief encounter are spread around the fan network, and before you know it everyone knows the size of your dick and the decor of your bedroom. Thanks to the Internet such revelations are no longer confined to a select group, but can be flashed all around the world for those interested enough to look. Yes, I've made the mistake and lived to regret it – and felt guilty as hell about it too.

Then there are also those who pretend they have no idea who you are, which is always refreshing until afterwards, unable to contain themselves, they blurt out that they know everything you've ever done, ever sung, ever performed, as if this will ingratiate you to them. Or who half way through the act whip out their demo tape, explaining the finer details of their budding musical career. To me, I'm afraid that's a complete turn off. Say hello, wave goodbye. It became more and more difficult to find someone to have an uncomplicated good time with, but as someone once said, sleeping with fans is like dipping your fingers in the till.

So what, if anything, does an artist owe the fans? An artist like myself spends a year, or often much longer, putting together an album, putting heart and soul into it. It is then marketed and sold. Hopefully people like it enough to buy it. At best it may become part of the eclectic soundtracks we all have to our lives, making listeners laugh, cry, dance, make love, reminding them of a place, a time or a feeling. That is the transaction. It is that simple. The artist owes the public nothing – no more than the public owe him. In my case, if I am accused of giving too much artistically then that is my choice. It doesn't alter the price of the CD for the public. On quite a few occasions I have sacrificed commerciality in order to make a record I believe in, and ended up in debt to the record company. It is in some ways the same when I perform live – two-hour shows when others do barely an hour. Still I get complaints for not giving enough. And so I try harder, perform for longer, and once again it is never enough. Now I understand that there never is enough. I am grateful when someone buys my record, and when they offer it forward I will gladly sign it. But that is where it ends. I learned the painful lesson that less really does equal a great deal more.

*

There were other clues to the whereabouts of the Some Bizarre office once in the building – just follow the pieces of burnt foil and the occasional needle. Some Bizarre's office assistant, Stuart, had a severe heroin problem and it had begun to impact on the office. Stevo didn't see it, or if he did he turned a blind eye. Stuart was a kindly young man of sweet temperament, and a close friend of Jane Rollink, who also worked there full-time. We were all concerned for Stuart as we saw him sinking into the abyss. Stuart had a friend called Wayne, another young man of similar disposition. They were like lost souls heading for disaster. In fact the Some Bizarre office was a gathering of lost souls.

Heroin was the only drug I hadn't tried until then. I had tried opium, and loved it – especially the dreams I had when I would close the curtains and light candles, drifting away on the pile of velvet cushions in my apartment. I didn't know how different heroin would be. Of course I had to find out what it was like, so I bought a small packet from Stuart. He was terrified that Stevo would find out; I was alarmed that anyone would find out – such was the stigma attached to it.

Right. Here goes. I snorted a small brown line. I should say that I have a phobia about syringes and needles, for which I am grateful. Had I not, I no doubt would have become a hopeless heroin junkie in no time and someone else would be writing this book. So up my nose it went. It immediately gave me a mild sense of euphoria, followed by just a touch of nausea. It had the effect of drying my throat out and making my voice sound low and hoarse. It wasn't that great but, more importantly, it wasn't that bad either, so I began to take little snorts of it daily, eventually buying further packets from Stuart. But the thrill soon faded and I needed something more, so I tried smoking it. Now this made me feel really sick, sweaty and incapacitated, though it did give me great dreams. It was then that I began to wake the next day feeling cold, sick and empty – a strange, abstract emptiness like my insides were chilled. I shivered and shook, and felt deathly. I knew just what I needed. More.

One morning I was awoken by the doorbell ringing frantically. It was Stuart, who, having been unable to score from his dealer had come round to my flat because he knew that I had some. He'd only sold me it yesterday. He was crying and shaking, so I chopped him out a brown line and within minutes he was calm and smiling again. Here I was giving heroin to Stuart, who'd only just sold me it. What the hell was I doing and where was all this going?

I should say that around this time, in 1983, I had moved into a flat on Brewer Street in Soho. It had been a dream for me to live in London's West End. My flat overlooked the notorious Raymond Revue bar. I could actually watch the girls getting changed through a window above the bar, and at night the neon flashed and lit up my room as I lay on my bed. It was like something from a Hollywood movie, from a film-noir set piece. Across the road, on the corner of Brewer Street and Wardour Street, was a café called the Coffee Pot, which was frequented by transvestites, hookers and rent boys. Its jukebox blasted out until the early hours, and often a police van would arrive and bundle everyone away. I could look out of my window and feel such a voyeur. It was the perfect place for Marc Almond to live!

Before that I'd been living at Stevo's house in Hammersmith, sharing a room and a platonic bed with Jane Rollink for about six months. Of all the madhouses I have lived in, Stevo's was the worst. Every night there was a gathering of musicians, drinking, taking cocaine or Ecstasy and being entertained by Stevo. He would turn up the music – usually by a new Some Bizarre signing – until the neighbours threatened violence. Stevo really was the neighbour from hell. On a typical night there would be Mal or Chris from Cabaret Voltaire, Matt Johnson of The The, Jim Thirlwell (the genius musician and arranger behind the provocatively named 'You've Got Foetus on Your Breath'), members of the German industrial band Einsturzende Neubauten and the British industrial band Test Department, and Edwyn Collins and Zeke Manyika from Orange Juice. It was the place to be, and the drinks flowed all night from Stevo's overladen gold drinks trolley.

A typical night saw a group of us lying around watching videos while Stevo played an assortment of sounds – particularly by Nick Cave, himself a regular visitor. Or I would sit and talk into the night with the late Billy Mackenzie of the Associates.

Billy and I bumped into each other on many occasions over the years. We had a mutual respect, but were also a little wary – overly cautious of each other in the way that singers are who inhabit the same world. We had both been labelled 'torch singers' – usually a moniker bestowed on female singers who sing of lost love and longing, burning a passionate torch to light the lives of the miserable or downbeat. I felt Billy was the better singer, but I was more successful. We both wanted a little of what the other had. When we ran into each other at gay bars or clubs – which always surprised me, as I was never sure of his sexuality – we would greet each other like long-lost lovers and then not quite know what to say. Usually we would plan to work together on a record that Billy said would be the greatest dance torch number ever. The last time I saw him was at a show I performed in London in 1996, and once again we made the same plans – though this time they seemed more serious than before. A year later, while waiting for a flight to depart from Bangkok, I read of his suicide. I wasn't entirely surprised by it – he was such a fragile, tortured soul. I was even a little envious that he had made such a dramatic exit. I felt we had been kindred spirits. What a record we could have made together – though I know Billy would have stolen the moment.

Living at Stevo's was difficult but never dull. Often I would come down in the morning bleary-eyed, to find Stevo still partying, or on several occasions having a blazing row with his Dagenham girlfriend, Marion, who also worked in the Some Bizarre office. 'You're an alcoholic bastard, just like yer old man!' she'd yell. One time I taped her bawling her head off and intended to set it to a disco beat on the next Soft Cell album; fortunately for Stevo I lost the tape.

I even came downstairs once to find Stevo sprawled over a bean bag being given a blow job by a young lady who shall remain nameless. 'Hello, Perk!' said Stevo, barely missing a beat, using the nickname he called everyone, hoping he'd shocked me. But for someone like me, who'd been to New York's more colourful sex clubs, this was nothing – I'd already seen it all. However, my presence caused the young woman to stop, come through to the kitchen, wipe her hands on the dish towel, and offer to make me some toast. I politely declined, made my excuses, and left.

Eventually Stevo grew sick and tired of everyone using his house as a pub and squat and, rather than tell people directly, he resorted to all kinds of hostile antics to put everyone off coming. This went as far as taking an axe and chopping down all the doors – including the one to the toilet – while we all slept in bed one night. 'It's my fuckin' house and I don't see why anyone should have any privacy.' Nobody did after that. I'll never forget the sight of poor Edwyn Collins sitting on a doorless toilet.

Stevo's behaviour towards guests became increasingly threatening; he even left cryptic messages on his answerphone to dissuade callers. Eventually he did drive us all away – me included. Nobody went to see him any more. Then he would call up saying he was lonely and had no friends. But that was no one's fault but his own. Everyone had a bad story about Stevo throwing them out of the house. Then even he discovered the Camden Palace, and found that by waving money around and promising free drinks he could get himself new friends. In fact we all did.

*

Despite being in tranquillizer universe and smack heaven each night, I still found myself bursting with ideas for songs and records. The fact that the Some Bizarre offices were directly above a recording studio encouraged me to put my ideas down on tape. Between 1982 and 1983, in addition to my Soft Cell work, I managed to record two double albums, which I put out under the name Marc and the Mambas.

The Mambas first appeared after a fun one-off idea for a fan-club twelve-inch record – two badly recorded demo tracks: 'Fun City' and 'Sleaze'. 'Fun City' is one of the first real songs I wrote. It comes from my performance-art days, and is about a young guy running away from home to the lights of the city and becoming a rent boy. The second song is about the same character further down life's road. While 'Fun City' has a certain innocence, 'Sleaze' is purely jaded. Both are extremely flimsy-sounding, with a repetitive beat box and Annie Hogan playing a Fender Rhodes piano and synthesizer. Though they have some charm, they were never meant for the mass public, but they became a huge cult record as far as Los Angeles and New York. After 'Fun City' had been extensively bootlegged, we made it available as a Soft Cell B-side.

The first of the double albums under the banner Marc and the Mambas was *Untitled*, and is a good example of why drugs are bad for you. It is the deluded ramblings of self-indulgence fuelled by too much acid. By side two of the album I was so out of it that I couldn't even get myself together to write any proper songs at all, so I murdered other people's. I think they were intended to be tributes, but even I'm not entirely sure. There are, however, some interesting moments. The title track, 'Untitled', has a good song somewhere in it and I still think that with the right production and discipline it might have been a hit – if only I could have been together enough to think of a title. It was one of two songs I wrote with Matt Johnson of The The, the second being a psychedelic slab of paranoia called 'Angels' (about my experience of first visiting LA and driving around in a black Rolls-Royce). Though both these tracks lack something, they are perhaps the album's saving grace.

'Empty Eyes' could have been memorable, but instead goes on and on and on for far too long – like most of the songs do. I just didn't have the time to be brief. They would all have benefited from a strict producer. Oh yes, and an artist not totally dysfunctional on chemicals. You can actually hear the effect the acid is having on my throat, and to make things worse I insisted that I only needed to sing the songs once. The cover of Scott Walker's 'Big Louise' remains haunting due to the brilliant strings of Paul Buckmaster, who had worked on many of the early Bowie recordings. I remember that when I gave the backing track to Paul to arrange strings his face dropped as I hadn't recorded it to a click track. On the day of recording, the wary old session musicians kept walking out in protest, complaining no one could keep time. Paul had his work cut out trying to cover for my substandard work, but he coped admirably. A solo piano piece by Annie Hogan is also quite beautiful – I gave her a solo piece to keep her happy for doing so much work for next to no fee. But, inspired a piece as it is, it was also just another piece of self-indulgence – an instrumental track on a Marc Almond album? Yet Lou Reed himself rated my version highly.

'Caroline Says' is OK, but a strange song to choose to cover. 'If

You Go Away' is demolished in an excruciating fashion by me. Years later I tried to make up for it by reworking it – ironically, fans adored the original.

Filling up one side of this double album was a painfully long free jam called 'Twilights and Lowlifes', which may have had a trash appeal, but should have been left back at Leeds Polytechnic, where it belonged. There was also a drugged-out, silly, giggling version of Syd Barratt's 'Terrapin', with Cindy Ecstasy doing irritating backing vocals and me on Ecstasy. As if this were not enough, a whole side was dedicated to an instrumental dub mix of the aforementioned 'Twilight and Lowlifes' – enough already!

Believe me when I say I'm sorry if you hold this album dear; I don't want to rain on your parade, but I must tell it like it is. I am trying to be objective while reflective, and I must confess my surprise at how kind and generous the critics were – 'The explorations of a typically British eccentric pop star,' said one. At the time I looked on the record as a pointer towards my artistic future. If I'd stuck with that idea, what a grim place the future would have been!

I celebrated my new album with a concert at the Drury Lane Theatre. It became something of a special event, looking back. I invited Anita Sarko over to host it, and she added the essential glamour to the show, clad in a black taffeta dress and sparkling diamonds. In all honesty it was tactless and insensitive of me to invite her at all (how unlike me!), for relations between her and Dave had recently hit a rocky patch – a waste ground, actually. The evening was to prove awkward for both of them.

During the show I played most of the album, plus a version of Nico's 'Wrap Your Troubles in Dreams'. Then I broke into a ten-minute version of Iggy Pop's 'Dirt', and then 'Caroline Says'. They made little sense except as a nod to my roots and influences. At the end of the show Dave came on unrehearsed, and we performed 'Say Hello, Wave Goodbye'. The audience had given me an enthusiastic response, suffering my indulgences, but it was really that moment they wanted, and they showed their feelings accordingly. I hated being a pop star. I hated audiences. I hated myself. I loved being a pop star. I loved audiences. I hated myself.

*

And then there was the long-suffering record company, Phonogram. After delivering to them a double album away from Soft Cell, I started on another double album straight after. No wonder they despaired. All these recordings and not a single in sight! Even though

Torment and Toreros – that second double album – is flawed in many ways, it is still something I remain proud of. With hindsight, I can see it for what it really is – a nervous breakdown committed to vinyl. All my anger, my bitterness, my sadness in that period is on that recording. The addiction, the emptiness and thick black despair, the stormy relationships, the drugs and the alienation from the music business all seeped into the recordings. To me the album shows an artist crying out, lost, resentful, sticking two fingers up at everyone and everything. It is a twisted cabaret of my life up to and at that time. It is Grand Guignol.

The album was recorded in a matter of weeks – late into the night, into the next day, fuelled by speed and heroin. The engineer and co-producer was a young man called Flood. He was patient, quiet and tolerant. A top producer in the making, he went on to produce many high-profile bands such as U2, Depeche Mode and Nick Cave. On my album he worked himself almost into illness, sleeping on the sofa whenever he could. His face was so wan and ashen that I thought he was going to die. I came in with new ideas daily, and he tried to incorporate them into the tracks, sort out the mess of that Gothic opera.

The musicians, the Mambas, were an ad-hoc group. The album was always intended to be a loose amorphous project, with a sort of mini-orchestra in which musicians could come and go, appearing on a number of tracks or as special guests. I auditioned a few guitarists, and eventually decided on a young man with black hair and good looks. He was called Lee Jenkinson – and he could play too, which was always a bonus. Annie Hogan played piano and keyboards. A saxophonist and flautist who played interesting psychedelic effects was Steve Sherlock (recommended by Matt Johnson), and the string section was Anne Stevenson, Gini Hughes (later to be Gini Ball), Martin McCarrick and Billy McGee. Dubbed the Venomettes, Annie and Gini had come from Mari Wilson's backing band; while Billy and Martin were fresh out of college. When they weren't playing strings for me, they sometimes alternated as Soft Cell's backing singers. This was the first time since the sixties that a string section had been used extensively on such a body of work by a British pop artist, and it was an integral part of the Mambas' sound.

Adding drama were flourishes of Spanish flamenco and eastern exotica. I loved Spanish music and culture, from Lorca to Dali, from gypsy flamenco rhythms to the passionate, overwrought songs of Spanish divas such as Lola Flores, Carmen Amaya and Rocio Jurado. I was even fascinated by the horrible beauty of bullfighting – the colours of gold, red and black; the vibrancy of crimson in the cloak, and the raw sexuality of the fight itself, as the matador plunges the sword into the bull. All very heady stuff. But over the years I have become more enlightened and, although I accept the historical and cultural significance of bullfighting, I feel that it has no place in the late twentieth century. I abhor all forms of cruelty to animals, and believe that the cultural defence of the corrida is no longer valid.

In fact my flamenco touches on *Torment and Toreros* were simply naive colouration. How could I ever know the true soul of a gypsy? What I gleaned from Spanish music was its exuberance and passion, the fire and conflict that speaks of struggle, of tears and of the eventual strength of survival. That was something I did relate to. I have often wondered whether I carry ancestral genes that draw me to the Latin rhythms, or to the sliding scales of Middle Eastern music, for which I also have a passion. I have searched my family tree without success, but perhaps a distant Moorish relative hides in there somewhere.

Most of the songs on *Torment and Toreros* were written on the spot, with me scribbling lyrics as I went along, everyone else contributing their own creativity. I would sing the string parts as I heard them in my head, and also many of the other parts; this was the first time I was creating music as well as lyrics. The drum parts were simple machine rhythms. I was worried that using a real drummer might seem too rock, though the reality was that it would have held everything together.

The photographer Peter Ashworth, once the drummer with The The, came by and hammered on some timpani for the track 'Animal in You'; Jim Thirlwell added brilliant percussion for 'Million Manias' (a track he co-wrote), as well as producing 'Beat Out dat Rhythm on a Drum'. Jim, with his shock of red hair and sunken black eyes that gave him a skull-like appearance, worked under many pseudonyms. He also consumed more sulphate speed than anyone else, always washed down with huge amounts of whisky. He seemed to exist on it, but the more he took, the more his face resembled a manic skull. His insides must have been screaming for help. He would lay down his percussion parts with painstaking accuracy, using anything he could get his hands on for effects – table tops, glasses, fire extinguishers – always managing to make them sound fantastic.

I have a favourite story of Jim's. When he was on the verge of signing a major American deal, the record-company executive said, 'Hey, Jim, we have a little problem with the name "You've Got Foetus on Your Breath".'

'OK,' said Jim, 'I'll change it.'

And he did. From then on he was known as 'Scraping Foetus off the Wheel'.

It was people like him that made Some Bizarre such an innovative and vibrant label in the early eighties. With a roster that included The The, Soft Cell, Cabaret Voltaire, Test Department, Einsturzende Neubauten and Psychic TV, it was one of the most credible labels around. It was the time when Stevo actually believed in and loved music.

*

I was expending so much time, passion and energy on *Torment and Toreros* that I couldn't see I was making myself very ill, both physically and mentally. The sessions were overly intense and full on, and I was so wired on sulphate that tempers became frayed. There was much shouting and screaming, storming out and throwing tantrums – usually by me.

On any album worth making there is tension and disagreement on some level, but this all got out of hand. I wanted perfection, but I suspected that that was out of my reach: it seems in my nature to be flawed. Often, to sound honest, you have to go for the moment that isn't the most technically correct. If I do too many takes of a vocal, overconsidering the technique, I end up ignoring the words and leave out the heart. Usually today I will do three or four takes and if it isn't happening come back to it afresh a week later. In those days it was one take, take it or leave it – supposedly pure and impassioned, in the spirit of Jacques Brel or some Spanish gypsy. I conceded leaving all the flaws in, to expose my shortcomings, to be naked. Looking back, I can't believe quite how many flaws I left in. The consequence is that much of the material is hard listening. The drugs also played a major part in the way my voice sounded, the vocal cords pithy from heroin. You can hear the dryness in the vocal on songs like 'Untouchable One'.

I was still using heroin from time to time to try to level out, but one evening I went too far and took too much. My eyes rolled back into my head and I felt myself drifting away, back into myself. Not the comforting drifting normally associated with heroin, but an inner detachment. I was unable to stand, but Anne Stevenson, the jovial, earthy violinist from the Mambas, forced me to my feet and walked me round the room, talking to me continually. She eventually brought me back to myself, and probably saved my life. On another occasion, when recording at the country studio Jacobs, the co-producer Flood worked on mixing *Torment and Toreros* while I sat dribbling and nodding out, unable to string words together. Not a good look.

Every day I felt deathly and looked even worse. My hair was long and greasy, a mass of split ends. I looked like a stick insect in a wig. I spawned some very odd lookalikes among my fans – a case for the style police if ever there was one. It's very odd looking at people who are trying to look like you, when what you look like isn't something you're entirely at one with.

The whole heroin thing stopped when Stuart from the office was arrested. It came as a relief to Stevo, who'd finally had enough of people calling the office asking where they could get smack. Enough of the tell-tale needles in the toilet and the fact that at least one of his artists was flirting with death. Jane and I went to visit Stuart in Brixton Prison after he was convicted. He was full of remorse, lonely and tearful. Looking around the deathly dull surroundings, all my Jean Genet fantasies flew out of the grey barred window. Imagine the most depressing social-security office in the world and double it. It became clear to me that heroin led either here or to the grave – the latter being preferable. I never took it again after that, apart from one brief relapse during a visit to New York. Drugs really hurt the people around those that use them, when someone you care about ends up the way Stuart did. His friend Wayne was devastated, and sank into a deep melancholy. I never saw Stuart after that occasion. I don't know what happened to him, but I hope he is clean and happy.

*

Torment and Toreros was finally finished. It was a sprawling mess of an album, too long and lacking in real production values. It was, though, certainly unique. It was painful and passionate, and fitted well into the whole Goth music movement that was alive (if that's the right word for Goth) in 1983. An album for pale, black-clad lost youths to plan their suicides to in their purple-painted bedrooms. I should know – I was once one of them. Some people thought this album was all too clearly about suicide – the record company thought it was commercial suicide. But what did I care? It is a classic Marc Almond album, full of great songs heavy with self-pity and bitterness – 'Catch a Falling Star', the Spanish torch passion of 'Black Heart' and 'Torment', the retrospective yearning of 'First Time', the confessional 'Million Manias' and 'My Little Black Book of Sorrows', the self-confrontation of 'Once Was' and 'My Former Self'.

The cover songs seemed to fit well into the whole mayhem or triumph of the work (however you want to view it) – Peter Hammill's compelling 'Vision', a version which was to turn many people on to his work; Brel's 'The Bulls', caustic, biting and prophetic; the torch suicide of 'Gloomy Sunday'; and the final madness of Rogers and

Hammerstein's torrid 'Beat Out dat Rhythm on a Drum' from *Carmen Jones*. I wanted to end the album with something insane and upbeat, a kind of redemption. I'd been listening to the soundtrack of the updated version of the Bizet opera, and it just seemed to make sense in an insane kind of way.

Listening to the album now is painful for me. I barely know the person I was then. I cringe at how young and vulnerable I sound – I was laying myself open to all sorts of criticism, especially, as it turns out, from myself looking back. Perhaps I should have shut up and hidden myself away, instead of making an open invitation for people to get out the knives. And, on top of all that, what the hell did my mother make of it?

The troubles didn't stop with the end of recording. I had to convince Phonogram to release the album. They were much happier than with the previous record, *Untitled*, as they thought there was at least a single in 'Black Heart'. But then they became concerned. I wanted this album to be sold for the price of a single album, not a double one; and I wanted a double glossy cover by the artist Val Denham. Was I being unreasonable? Hey, Phonogram! Here is another uncommercial double album, expensively packaged with barely a single on it – an album that you didn't even ask for. And, by the way, could you release it at a special cheap price to make it affordable to the fans? What a petulant mad brat I had become! I had to accept a lower royalty rate to get my way, but get my way I did. I was becoming the Violet Elizabeth Bott of pop music – 'I'll scream and scream until I'm sick.' (Stomp foot.)

The week of the release of *Torment and Toreros* was one of the worst and the most insane of my whole life. Everything and everyone, I believed, was out to bring me down, and every little thing, no matter how insignificant, became a major drama. My whole life had become a battleground where everyone was out to destroy me. Me, paranoid? Surely not. As it turned out, I was having a nervous breakdown – and I'd only just got over my last one. It was actually all part of the same nervous breakdown I'd been having for the first three years of my career. I was shoving back tranquillizers like Judy Garland, just trying to get happy. I'd stopped taking heroin and speed – well, heroin anyway – and I just couldn't cope any more.

To top it all, I was even having problems with my Soho flat, which turned out not to be the romantic place I'd hoped for. It was a nightmare. One night, for example, I stepped out and suddenly found myself surrounded by football supporters. They had ventured down from some suburban hell or other for a night of boozing and birds, only to discover Soho had been cleaned up, or else some clip joint had fleeced them of their monthly salary in five minutes. Discontented and angered, they wanted to take out all their pent-up frustration on someone. Cue Marc Almond. I ran, my friend Dillon ran, the football fans pursued us. Dillon fought as bravely as he could, but he was outnumbered. We eventually saw an angel in uniform and begged him to helped us, me grabbing hold of his tunic and falling to my knees. 'For God's sake save me!' He radioed for assistance and the football fans fled. I was shaken. Soho had become a difficult place for me to live.

But worse than the football fans were my fans, who had discovered where I lived. Upstairs in the flat, paranoid, on drugs, strung out and neurotic, I would hear the doorbell ringing all the time, day and night, over and over and over. Then the police came to visit me. Kids were running away from home to come to London to look for me. I couldn't see that that was exactly my responsibility. But the police visiting my flat with drugs strewn all over was not a good idea. Day after day after day, the doorbell went or the police came. At least my neighbours were understanding – until my pet snake escaped and terrorized them, that is. Then they hated me. Everyone hated me.

Then one fan went further than most in tormenting me. She rang the doorbell again and again, day after day. Eventually, one morning she just kept the button pressed. I tried to sit it out, to see how long she could keep her finger on the buzzer. Fifteen minutes. I tried to rip out the bell, but couldn't. Eventually I ran out into the street and screamed a torrent of abuse as she held out a pen and a piece of paper for me to sign. Then the man from the nearby sandwich bar ran out, believing I was assaulting her, and hit me in the face. At that point I knew the sense in not allowing handguns in this country, because I would have shot the pair of them dead and they'd probably be making a mini-movie about my life as I speak.

You know when you just think things can't get any worse and they do?

In my paranoid state, I decided to go out to a party for Siouxsie and the Banshees at the Camden Palace. Siouxsie was holding court in the upstairs bar like the Black Queen from *Barbarella*, wearing a spike collar that threatened to rip into people's throats. As I moved in to chat, photographers moved in for a shot of us together. We both snarled and warned them to stay away – what might such a shot inspire the Phonogram press department to do? Mariella was probably on the phone to John Blake of the *Sun* already. Enough of that!

Then Steve Severin of the Banshees took me aside for a chat – the type of chat where someone tells you, as your friend, what your friend wouldn't tell you. He began to lecture me on how *Torment and Toreros* was substandard. He and Robert Smith had written the music for the track 'Torment', and he was upset at what I'd done to his tune. 'It really could be better,' he said. 'The album's been badly produced. Somewhere in there is a brilliant album, but . . .' 'Don't hold back, Steve,' I thought. On he went. 'You should disappear for a while, lie low, live some life. You're too accessible to arseholes. I have to tell you this, because no one else will.' 'Why does he have to tell me?' I thought. It was like a knife in the heart from someone I liked and admired. I felt tearful, and sank even further into a depression. I'd only come out for a drink!

That night I staggered around depressed, trying to avoid Mariella Frostrup. A journalist, Mike Nichols, had been talking to me, but owing to my sorry state I wasn't listening. After he walked away, Mariella slithered up to me saying, 'I hate him, he's such a creep!' Unfortunately for Mariella, Mike's wife overheard her and said in a loud voice, 'Mike, Mariella said she hates you.' Mariella could have sunk into the floor. No PR points there. But even that didn't cheer me up. Nothing could cheer me up. Severin was right, and the truth hurt – as truth does. And the truth wasn't what I needed to hear right at that moment.

The week seemed to get more and more bizarre. I started to act more irrationally, unable to cope with the slightest thing. I sat in my darkened room and started to feel an overwhelming anger. I phoned *Smash Hits* and screamed at them for putting my photo in between Claire Grogan's and Adam Ant's (well, wouldn't you?), for spelling my name wrong (a thing I detest), and for calling my album 'tongue in cheek'. I ask you!

I phoned up Phonogram and shouted and screamed, goaded on by Jane Rollink at my side. 'Go on – tell them what for,' she said.

'Is this the five-minute argument or the ten-minute one?' replied the Phonogram representative glibly.

'As long as I want it to be,' I said, 'to tell you what I think of you. In fact I don't think anything of you. You're scum on my shoe.' You get the picture of ugliness I was becoming.

On it went, a descent into madness and breakdown.

Critic John Gill wrote a review of the album, calling me the Mills & Boon of S & M, saying I'd always have an audience of camps and fag hags. I sent him a bag of raw liver and a note: 'A few things to help you with your sexual problems.' He replied by sending me a banana and a note: 'For the baboon who is your creative consultant.' Oh well, you have to laugh.

The final thing that made me snap was another review of *Torment and Toreros*. It was neither original nor imaginative, nor particularly unpleasant, but it proved to be the last straw. I suppose it could have been anything that broke me, but it was this review in *Record Mirror* by Jim Reid. As I recall, it went on about how the album was a florid musical mess. That it was for people who find studs and black leather outrageous, and that it all came down to the fact that I wore black – 'I find Marc Almond's doodling neither outrageous or daring, just tedious.' 'Really,' I thought. It was dismissively droll and throwaway, and aren't they the worst sort of reviews?

My pain and my art had been slighted by this prat working for a second-rate pop magazine. With Jane begging me not to go – 'Ignore the wanker,' she said – I dressed up in black leather, bullwhip in hand, and made my way as fast as I possibly could to the *Record Mirror* offices. By the time I climbed out of the taxi I'd worked myself up into such a frenzy that I felt ready to explode with anger. 'I'll show him about Marc Almond and his black leather S & M obsessions,' I thought to myself, all rationality long gone.

I forced my way into the office, where everyone stopped in disbelief and stunned silence. 'Where is Jim Reid?' I shouted. A woman pointed helpfully towards the corner, and I advanced on the stunned Reid. Lash. I whipped him across the chest. 'How dare you review my album, you pathetic . . .' Lash. 'You aren't qualified to . . .' Lash. (Spit sprayed out of my mouth as I was barely able to get the words out.)

'I'm just doing my job,' quivered Reid.

Lash.

'Where is that rag of a magazine?' I picked up a copy on his desk and slapped him across the face, screaming more abuse while stumbling for adjectives in my outpouring of anger. What an apparition I must have looked. 'If you say one more word about me, Reid, I will kill you . . . Kill you . . . KILL YOU!'

Silence.

'Anything else you'd like to add?' said Reid, remarkably keeping his composure.

'Yes there is. Eat shit and die,' I said as I turned and stormed out.

The next day the shit hit the fan. The story reached Fleet Street and, what was bizarre enough in itself, became even more twisted.

Another pop writer scribbled a suitably inaccurate piece, ending it with what she considered to be scathing or witty or something approximating to humour – 'Hit by the puny Almond is akin to being hit by a mascara brush.'

I sent her a telegram:

So you want to get personal Fatso. Thank God I'm small and lithe and not the gargantuan blancmange that everybody tells me you are – do yourself a favour and don't put your photo beside the drivel you write – it's all too horrible and hideous to take in. I can't wait until you feel the force of my mascara brush. Keep fighting the flab – love Marc.

I was losing it.
I'd lost it.
I felt the world was against me. It was getting ridiculous. Out of control. I felt hysterical all the time. I was having a psychotic episode, and everyone around me was dreading what I might do next.
What happened next was a letter of retirement, to every paper and magazine. The letter goes a long way to revealing my mental state at that time:

Finding myself increasingly confused and unhappy within the music business and with my position in the scheme of things (whatever that may be) today sees a new Marc Almond, whoever he may be (could somebody tell me please). This means firstly a gradual detachment from the recording side altogether. Firstly the new Soft Cell album currently being recorded (*This Last Night In Sodom*) will probably be my last. The Mambas no longer exist – I don't want to be involved in any more interviews. This is no disrespect or show of petty arrogance to those that have written constructively fairly and favourably of me. By talking about myself too much I have lost touch with the person I really am and feeling I'm losing my soul – next year's recordings will be extremely few (if any) which will come as a huge relief to those who insist my singing is painful to the ears. I'd appreciate it if no one writes about me any more or mentions me. I don't know at the moment about my future. The immediate future is putting my heart and soul into the new Soft Cell album for if I am to do no more I would like it to be a fitting epitaph. Maybe more writing, maybe working for Some Bizarre helping new bands on the other side of the fence so to speak. Maybe some live work under a different banner. Overdramatic, hysterical, obsessive, self-indulgent (though for good and positive reasons as opposed to flippant and greedy), flawed. I am all these things and I don't give a damn. I am grateful to those who have helped me and supported me. Marc Almond.

The papers ran the headlines 'Marc Quits', 'Say Hello, Wave Goodbye – Soft Cell Split', 'Moody Marc Quits' etc. Each story was of course accompanied by the usual distortions and colouration. It seemed as if I'd died. Fans gathered outside the Some Bizarre offices in tears, and the phone rang off the hook. 'Marc, don't leave us with Duran Duran,' pleaded some callers, while others charmingly said, 'Almond, you tosser, I'm going to kill you.'

I felt pulverized and dissected. I felt I'd given far too much of myself away, and *Torment and Toreros* had left me exposed and naked – which was not healthy for a person who is basically shy and private. I spoke to Jim Reid over the phone, feeling ashamed of my ridiculous outburst over such an unimportant review. Reid accused me of gross self-indulgence as though it was a misdemeanour. 'Isn't pop music of any creative kind indulgent?' I asked him. 'Hasn't it always been indulgent? I am my own person, writing my own words in my own style, so to a degree it has to be indulgent,' I continued in my own defence. 'And look at you. Surely there is nothing more indulgent than indulgently writing about the indulgences of others.'

For all I tried to rationalize and discuss with him what had happened, it was impossible. The conversation went round and round in circles.

'I think you ought to shake this black-leather fetish off,' he said.

'Are we down to superficial judgements like clothes now?' I asked him.

'Well, you're wearing black on the album cover.'

'Yeah – me and half of London.'

Pointless.

Retired at twenty-seven. And retirement felt good. For the first few days (about a day and a half, actually) I felt refreshed. The cloud had lifted from my shoulders and I felt free, unchained, ready to take on something new, imbued with a spirit of adventure. I spent the day scrubbing the flat throughout, cleaning away the old Marc Almond for the new, born-again version of myself.

The phone began to ring. I began to get offers of new projects from every quarter. Journalist Mike Nichols, working at *Penthouse*, offered me the strangest of them all: a job answering people's sexual problems – a kind of agony aunt. At first I thought it might be amusing, but on reflection I knew that it was I who needed to talk to someone about mine. I was either the most or the least well qualified for the job – I couldn't decide, which probably suggested least.

One of the journalists who patiently tried to make sense of my retirement announcement was *Melody Maker*'s Steve Sutherland. He wrote:

Around the middle of last year Marc Almond began to question
his every action and reaction. Was he really being himself or
playing a role ... He couldn't live with false business standards,
the hollow handshakes and the absurd adulation, but he couldn't
live without them. Crucially his dilemma became the source of his
art and he knowingly hurled himself into the spirit of sensation
that must eventually lead to damage or worse. He hurt himself
and revelled in saying. 'Look what you've made me do.' In short
he became that most dangerous of artists, a romantic celebrating
his agonies, burning himself out for the sake of his songs.

I couldn't have put it better myself.

It was hard to make sense of the nonsensical life I was living. I'd
fallen into a pattern of abuse: abusing myself with drugs and destructive relationships; in turn abusing others with my anger, self-loathing
and guilt. I was tired and burnt out. Steve Severin was right: I should
have taken time off, time to myself.

But after a couple of days of retirement, unrestrained and feeling
carefree, I began to regret my premature resignation and began to
back-pedal furiously. Of course I had never intended to actually
retire, not really, surely everyone must know that. My letter had been
a public cry for help, a metaphorical suicide attempt. I'd wanted to
hurt and punish everyone – my friends, my fans, especially my critics
– but instead, as usual, I'd hurt only myself. I then began to retract
my statement.

As I sat at home one night listening to the radio, DJ Kid Jensen
was playing, 'Say Hello, Wave Goodbye'. 'We shall miss Marc
Almond,' he said. I panicked. 'No, wait,' I thought, 'I'm still here,
I didn't really retire.' I phoned the radio station and told him that I
was back, stronger and louder than ever, and a bemused Kid Jensen
responded by playing 'Million Manias' from *Torment and Toreros*. It
felt good to be back, I think. It certainly felt good to hear that 'Fuck
you, baby' at the end of the song being played on the BBC. I was
determined not to let people beat me down. I was not going away
again. I was going to go on and make even better records. I was going
to sing loud.

The next day I went to the Some Bizarre offices, leaned out of the
window, and announced I was back, throwing black silk roses down
to the handful of waiting fans.

*

Actually, despite all my melodramas, *Torment and Toreros* had generally been received quite well, and 'Black Heart', the single, received a respectable amount of radio plays and made a dent in the chart. Kris Needs wrote a glowing piece calling the album

> a ninety-minute creep through the darkest recesses of the Almond world of broken lives, spiteful romances, black laughs and despair in dark bedrooms – you're left sprawled out and squeezed dry like an invading horde of dancing wildebeest. Demons have ravaged your body and brain with a live pageant of all the personal disasters you've ever experienced and hope you don't – it's pretty dark in there.

At least I think it was a glowing piece.

The album received a wonderful reaction in Europe, where there seemed to be a deeper respect and understanding for me as an artist. It developed into a huge cult in the United States, especially on the west coast, where it was the perfect soundtrack for American disaffected Goths.

The Mambas received an invitation to play in Tel Aviv and Jerusalem. We would be the first band to visit there after several years of turmoil and troubles, and off we went. I was treated like visiting royalty, given the red-carpet treatment at every turn. I was stunned when I realized just how successful the album was there, just how many fans I had in Israel.

High on life, I remember we went down to the Wailing Wall in Jerusalem, but caused concern when the visiting pilgrims refused to allow me near it, taking offence at my tattoos, long hair and unsuitable clothing. The shows themselves were deeply emotional, with the crowd (oddly, 90 per cent men) hailing me as a hero, lighting candles and matches, singing along, and crying openly at the songs. They also seemed moved and surprised to hear a live string section on stage – it was a long way from rock 'n' roll.

Throughout my extensive travels in that period, I was always surprised at how successful I was abroad – often much more so than I ever was in England.

*

Despite my retirement announcement and the subsequent withdrawal of it, 1983 remained an incredibly busy time. Aside from the Mambas, I played a handful of secret shows with Jim Thirwell. We were supporting Cabaret Voltaire under the pseudonym 'Bruise 'n' Chain'. Our short set totally mystified the audience, who didn't seem to know or even care who we were. Still, Jim and I were having fun. There was also a guest appearance at a night dedicated to the writer William Burroughs at the nightclub Heaven. I performed a couple of Mambas numbers and then a version of Throbbing Gristle's 'Discipline', which certainly tested the audience's endurance. Finally there was a guest spot with Psychic TV on their album *Force the Hand of Chance*.

What can I tell you about Psychic TV? It was a group that consisted of Genesis P. Orridge, Peter Christopherson and Jeff Rushton, all of whom I met one afternoon at the Some Bizarre office. They were the strangest bunch of men, with shaved heads, ponytails and dressed in army fatigues – like military Tibetan monks. All of them had piercings and tribal tattoos (long before either became fashionable). Though these three were the main members, there was also a group of fringe members, similarly attired: the writer David Tibet (who liked to collect human bones), John Gosling and Paula P. Orridge (who was Linda to Genesis's Paul). The only fringe member who didn't follow the style was talented songwriter Alex Ferguson, whom I always bumped into as he furtively scurried from strip club to peep show. All of them were part of a cult they dubbed the Temple of Psychic Youth – part Hippy mysticism, part Aleister Crowley and Anton Le Vey, and part tribal magic. To be a member, followers were encouraged to send samples of body fluids – either semen or blood – which were then used in rituals. All this naturally created a mystique around the group, and both the public and press became fascinated, though cautious.

Genesis was a performance artist, adept at manipulating the press, and one wonders if this wasn't just another performance-art piece. The group looked striking – almost threatening – but they were the friendliest people you could meet. Isn't that always the case?

I was made an honorary member of the temple, but I assure you I didn't have to submit a sample. Genesis and Peter tried to talk me into appearing in one or two of their ritual videos, but, though I was tempted, I felt that if I did it would backfire on me in some horrible way. I still remembered the *Flexipop* nude shots and the 'Sex Dwarf' video. The sight of Jeff Rushton hooded, tied up and thrashed in the video certainly had an aesthetic value, but was not for me. Years later these videos were to make headlines in the *News of the World*, though they were really harmless enough. If that's what consenting adults want to do with their time, it should be nobody's business but theirs.

I wrote some lyrics for, and sang on the track 'Guiltless' on *Force the Hand of Chance*. I was proud of the track, with its lush string arrangements, and even Paul Morley singled it out favourably in his review. The song was basically about the Psychic TV philosophy of being without shame or guilt. (More than a touch of irony there! It was wishful thinking for me.) It was about recognizing your goal and exploring and acknowledging your sexual power: 'SEE IT AND GO FOR IT.'

I got on very well with Jeff Rushton, a strikingly good-looking guy who had joined the group through writing a fan letter. I remember an incident when he invited me to accompany him and a friend to Highgate Cemetery. This was before the cemetery was open to the public, though the unkempt, overgrown Gothic labyrinth had in the previous decades been popular with film companies – especially Hammer Horror – for location shoots. Intrigued, I agreed to go with them. After all, this was the year of all things Gothic, so what better experience than breaking into a cemetery?

It was a sticky July evening when we collected Jeff's friend Richard from his home in Finchley. His house was decorated in black, with skulls and bones on all the shelves, and in the centre of a room was a large four-poster bed draped in black net, complete with black pillows and sheets. From the outset, Richard made it clear that he didn't just want to break into the cemetery to look. He wanted trophies. It turned out he was a regular visitor, and knew what might be available. Before we set out, he insisted on showing us his snapshot album. Instead of happy holiday photos, there were ghoulish snaps of exposed decaying bodies he'd photographed during past visits.

When the taxi stopped at the bottom of Swain's Lane in Highgate, we casually walked in the direction of the cemetery, then squeezed through a hole in the fence, through a tangle of bushes and barbed wire. In doing so, I tore my finger open, a gash of blood. Was this a warning? On we went, through a mushy swamp area and into the midst of the deserted graveyard. It began to rain and my scalp itched with nerves. Not only were we trespassing, but I feared breaking taboos. But, not wanting to appear afraid, and letting curiosity get the better of me, I tentatively followed the others.

We walked up a path towards a huge gate – a gateway to hell, I imagined. It was the entrance to a circle of sealed iron doors, stairs and statues surrounding small mausoleums, with broken guardian angels standing in attendance. My imagination was running wild – I expected all the clichéd images to appear at once and overpower me. It was clear that many of the doors had been forcibly opened before, vandalized. Moving closer, we could see shelves of coffins. My finger was bleeding still, and I tried to stem the flow of blood with my handkerchief.

Richard found an old pickaxe in a wheelbarrow left by a gardener, and began to bang on a door. The door gave way. Inside the vault was thick dust and a carpet of feathers and dead birds. Then, to my horror, Richard prised open a coffin and slowly lifted the lid back. Suddenly I was hit by the smell of formaldehyde. I felt nauseous. Inside, revealed in the glare of torchlight, was a body. Flesh and hair still on the skull. That image remains with me even today. My face contorted in disgust and fear. Richard lifted the shrouded arm and moved the jawbone. It was like a scene from *The Texas Chainsaw Massacre*.

Jeff and I had seen enough, spooked out of our heads, we retreated. As we hastily made our way out, Jeff fell backwards in the muddy swamp. 'Two down, one to go,' I said. When we finally reached the street it was with huge relief.

I always felt uncomfortable about that whole experience, and felt that a curse was placed on us afterwards. I'd already had one curse put on me by a practising witch for taking part in a pointless television programme deriding the bizarre objects sold in witchcraft shops. Now I felt I'd done something else that would bring me bad luck. We all suffered after that. My finger became septic, Jeff had his own addiction problems, and Richard tragically ended up hanging himself.

*

In was in 1983 that I also took part in an art piece with Psychic TV member John Gosling. I did a reading about a person destroying themselves with drugs (anyone we know?) while both Jeff and John undertook a ritual of bloodletting and scarification on stage beside me, culminating with Jeff urinating and John defecating. Even Nick Cave, who was at the performance, was disgusted.

As I've constantly mentioned, the fashion that year was Goth – black clothes, black lipstick, black lace, black hair – you name it so long as it was black. Pale faces, bone jewellery – anything deathly was the order of the day. The place to go was the Batcave, which was originally held in a small strip-club, Gossips, in Soho; later it took over the Subway Club in Leicester Square. It was run by Ollie, a member of the band Specimen, and was the place to see members of the Banshees, the Cure, Bauhaus, Zodiac Mindwarp, Specimen and the Mambas. I even did a couple of small shows there with the

Mambas. It was there on one such night that I met New York poet, singer, performer, film-maker, actress and all-round wicked woman Lydia Lunch.

Lydia, with her bands Teenage Jesus and the Jerks, Eight Eyed Spy and 13:13 Head, had helped invent Goth. Small, red-lipped and voluptuous in bosom-baring black lace, she was the kind of woman that has always both fascinated and terrified me. Writer Jessamy Calkin, Lydia's similarly attired partner in crime and my long-time Soft Cell friend, introduced us. Little did I know it, but Lydia had plans for me. In fact she had the next nine months of my life mapped out, whether I liked it or not. 'I want to do a cabaret in New York on Halloween, and I want you, Nick Cave and Jim Thirlwell to take part,' she told me. 'Call me, and let's make plans.'

So it was that I called round at her Barons Court flat. The decor was as I imagined it would be. Heavy, frayed curtains in deep red, closed – always closed. The whole room deep blood red. A single white light bulb swinging in the middle, creating living shadows in the musty gloom. Once I grew accustomed to the lack of light, Lydia's taste in ornaments began to grab my attention – a line of leering devil masks, a stuffed deer head, antlers, magic symbols, cushions of animal fur, animals' skulls, pieces of bone that held some mystical significance. In the corner on the table was a vase of dried flowers; on the floor was a pile of *Penthouse* magazines. A drape curtain divided off the bedroom, in which I saw everything laid out in ritualistic order. All around the rooms sat dolls – broken dolls, misfits, crippled orphans. Further inspection revealed stuffed lizards, rubber bats, spidery things, religious paraphernalia, and a gruesome collection of weapons – a spiked ball and chain, flick knives, cleavers and axes – all rusted and chipped from an unthinkable past. In the middle of the room was the seducer's bed – red and black – where no doubt wicked deeds were carried out. Jesus and the *Laughing Cavalier* stared down from the walls, and a leopard skin clung for dear life to the peeling wallpaper. Lydia sat me down and proudly showed me her extensive collection of pickled amphibians, condemned to float in clouded jam jars. Lovely!

It was then she began to tell me about her planned performance, in which she intended to be orally raped by an oil-stained greasy-haired iron-bar-wielding Nick Cave. I wondered if Nick knew about this. 'I'm sure he wants to do it,' she said, excited at the delicious thought.

She then went on to tell me how much it would cost to film. Ah, so that was it. She wanted a sponsor. But at that point I had no access to my money. My accountant, Ronnie Harris, had put me on a wage. Before the Mambas project I had put most of my money into a New York apartment on Twenty-first Street in midtown Manhattan, but the apartment was just a raw space and the builders I'd employed had run off with all the money. For the first time since my success, I found myself financially curtailed.

'I love your stuff, I really do,' said Lydia.

I emptily offered her my services: 'If I can help I will,' I told her – a sucker for a bit of flattery. I hoped she'd have forgotten the idea by tomorrow, as she seemed to have a new one every minute.

I spent a lot of time with Lydia and Jessamy that summer, and also with Nick Cave. Nick – a pale, skinny Australian with melancholic boyish looks and a turned-up nose, topped off with a spidery mound of jet-black hair, roughly resembling a rocker's quiff – had a neat line in suits that seemed on the small side but suited his lanky frame perfectly. At that time he was still the singer with the Birthday Party. I was a little in awe of him and a bit wary at first. He didn't seem to have a regular sense of humour, and I knew he was a serious, uncompromising artist. I felt I was a serious artist too, but I felt inferior for having commercial success. Nick wasn't easy to talk to, but I could be the same. He was just as shy and introverted as I was, and, despite our friendship, both of us remained guarded, fearful of ever being lightweight or frivolous. I have always admired him enormously as a writer and an artist; I have been flattered when I have been called by more than one journalist 'the Nick Cave of pop'. Years later, long after I'd lost touch with him, he sent me a book of his burnished verse inscribed 'From Your Forgotten Friend', and I felt just a little sad and very touched. I was never good at keeping in contact with people once distanced, always afraid of acknowledging any change in myself. Even writing this book has made me shudder more than once.

Lydia continued with her plans for me – including records, soundtracks, films, you name it. I sat listening, I took a deep breath on her hash pipe as she passed me some lyrics to a song called 'Misery Loves Company'. 'This is the A-side,' she said, 'and the B-side will be a song by LA band X, called "Our Love Passed out on the Couch".' I felt like passing out on the couch myself. As Lydia continued with her plans for Nick and me, Jessamy kept me fuelled with her lethal cocktails called Car Crashes – a mixture of wine and vodka. I nearly passed out on the floor. It was always an intoxicating time at Lydia's.

Eventually we got round to planning Lydia's ambitious Halloween show. We decided to call ourselves the Immaculate Consumptives, and we met on a number of occasions at Jim's flat, at the top of a high rise in Brixton, with a breathtaking panoramic view over London. Taking profuse amounts of speed and talking twenty to the dozen we made plans which would involve each of us singing with each other.

When we finally made it to New York – no mean feat in itself, considering the state of us all – I checked into the President Hotel in Times Square. It was a run-down establishment that rented many rooms by the hour. It seemed the perfect place for this particular visit. But I felt tired, strung out, and wanted to hide from everyone until the performance.

New Musical Express journalist Chris Bohn had come over to cover the event for a lead story, and interviewed each of us. Lydia told him that we were four like-minded souls brought together in search of beauty, filth and truth. I don't know about that. None of us really knew why we were there. I think it had something to do with the huge fee Lydia was getting from Danceteria for getting us together under one roof. We had our photos taken in Central Park, all looking suitably miserable.

One day I went to meet Nick and his beautiful red-headed girlfriend of the time, Anita Laine. They were staying in the Latin area of the Lower East Side. When I entered their room, all I could see was a huge bundle of clothes, which suddenly came to life as Anita and Nick emerged from it. Anita had a most wonderful sense of youthfulness – part innocent, part naughty and truly magical. I'd met her a few times previously at Jim's, and was always amazed by her consumption of drugs – she took more than anyone else I knew. A favourite pastime was to snort a huge line of MDA and then a line of speed and cartwheel around the flat. Her slow, childish speech might lead one to think she was dull, but this was as far from the truth as you could get. She contributed to many of the Birthday Party's lyrics, and was planning her own record. One night she looked at me with her huge saucer eyes and said quite seriously, 'You know, we could go out for dinner, but we're always on drugs!' I stole that line and used it in my song 'L'Esqualita' as it amused me so much.

That day, Nick, Anita and I went shopping around the Lower East Side. Nick bought a purple suit fit for a pimp, and we browsed the Santeria store, buying little statues and charms. That night at a party we scored a small packet of smack and snorted it in the toilets. This was the first time I'd done heroin since the *Torment and Toreros* recordings, and it made me feel low and sick. It was to be my last ever time with that drug.

The show, though chaotic, went quite well. Nick and I sang one of my songs, 'Body Unknown', and I sort of sang 'Misery Loves

Company' with Lydia. Nick came on at the end and stole the whole show with his rendition of 'In the Ghetto'. What the show lacked in substance it made up for later in legend. It was the kind of show that improves in the memory, and with the telling: by the time you had had heard about it third-hand, it sounded bloody brilliant. We performed another show in Washington, but it was even more uncontrolled. Then we all knew never again. It was for the best.

*

In December 1983 I showcased *Torment and Toreros* with a series of Christmas shows at the Duke of York's Theatre in London's West End. I wanted the show to have a vaudeville feel, and for my support I had a mixed collection of performers – cabaret duo 'Sugar and Yvette', a group of flamenco dancers from Streatham (more kitsch than gypsy), and the 3 Mustaphas Three, who played Balkan-style folk and dance.

Huw Feather designed a beautiful set with snakes and drapes, lit in reds, pinks, purple and blue. The show had an 'anything could happen' feel, with songs often improvised on the spot, the string section bravely trying to stay together in the more chaotic moments. The hardcore Almond fans – now dubbed the Gutterhearts by Lydia Lunch – threw roses, notes and jewellery on to the stage, and I toyed with the audience. This playing with the audience became a regular feature of the shows, until it eventually got out of hand, interfering with the music and becoming an excuse for people to disrupt and shout. Finally I stopped doing it altogether: I couldn't get a suitable mood for a heartfelt ballad when people were shouting, 'Hey, Marc, show us your willy.'

Of course, you already know much of what was to come with the album's release. A disaffected time for me – and one that was to touch the disaffected youth that followed me.

As a footnote, I was one day watching a TV news programme about the eventual arrest of a notorious serial killer in the north-east of England. The TV cameras had gained access to the murderer's flat, where he committed the actual crimes. They panned around the room, and there beside his record player, at the front of his record collection, was the album *Torment and Toreros*. Now that said something.

10

'Should I laugh, should I cry, should I live, should I die?'

Despite the Mambas and the madness, Soft Cell still managed to do a series of tours in Europe and America to promote *The Art of Falling Apart* and to preview the forthcoming album, *This Last Night in Sodom*. We had started recording the new album with a single, 'Soul Inside', which was co-produced with Flood. It was an uplifting 'don't give a fuck' tune, and should have heralded a brand-new future for us as a group. However, in our hearts we knew that this was the end, and, after my erratic announcement of retirement, we seemed to accept that it would be so.

Dave had insisted that the new album be produced by us – by which I mean Dave, who wanted the music his way after the friction with Mike Thorne on the last recording. He wanted to show that he could also be a talented producer as well as musician and arranger, and perhaps sensed that this was his last chance with Soft Cell. He had clear ideas on how the music and mood should be, and loved being in the studio rather than out performing live – especially as we could never get the onstage sound we wanted, which made him frustrated and angry.

I, on the other hand, found the studio side boring. I had a limited attention span and sought rapid gratification. I liked it when things were actually happening, but not the waiting around involved in recording. I realized that, though it made me sick with nervous worry and untold anxiety, I needed to perform live as much as possible – something to do with 'waves of love across the footlights' perhaps. Performing live, I could make the songs come alive, find a power in my voice that I couldn't seem to draw upon in the studio. As the years have passed I have now learned to enjoy my time in the studio too, but my short attention span remains. Almost as soon as one track is complete, I want to write and record another.

This Last Night in Sodom might well have been recorded with Mike Thorne had it not been for a conversation he had with Stevo over the phone. During an argument over money or points or whatever managers argue over, Mike had pointed out that he was 'the goose that lays the golden eggs, so don't kill it'. When Stevo recounted the conversation to us – undiplomatically, as ever – we were furious. Was Mike saying that the success of Soft Cell was due to him? We had never questioned his importance in the creative process, but it had been a team effort. In that conversation with Stevo he succeeded in slaughtering the goose himself. It was time to break away. All bands reach a point when they end a period with one particular producer and move on, do something new, prove they have a hand on their careers. So it was with Soft Cell. Dave was adamant that he would not work with Mike Thorne again. The new album was going to be his project – dirtier, and grittier. I was all for that too, feeling that the last album was perhaps still too lush-sounding. The new album would be a mix of dirty R & B, and a nod to our punk roots.

*

The live shows had improved immeasurably since our earlier calamities. We had a larger and better selection of songs in our repertoire to choose from, many of which came into their own live – especially the intense drama of 'Heat', 'Baby Doll' and 'Martin', which sounded powerful over a deafening PA, with Dave adding layer upon layer of keyboards, percussion and even guitar. The audiences threw themselves into a frenzy, and the shows became ritualistic celebrations of something or other – I never quite worked out what. Fans threw jewellery, toys, letters, toys, toys, bunches of flowers and more toys. Girls and boys routinely invaded the stage to kiss me, only to be prised off by security. I loved those moments, and would do anything to encourage them. I would come off stage covered in bruises, cuts and lipstick prints, drenched in sweat, and often collapse or vomit through sheer exhaustion. In fact I was tired both physically and emotionally all the time. I could get through the shows only when I had my speed before and my Valium for sleeping afterwards, along with hash to bring me down.

And something else was happening to me. I began to get memory lapses. This is a common symptom associated with dyslexia but worsened by benzodiazepines, and of course with hash – which I was smoking endlessly. At times my mind would go blank and I wouldn't be able to remember the words to songs. (It is a problem that remains with me even today, long after giving up drugs altogether.) Often I would work myself into a frenzy on stage, walking round and round in circles, feeling myself going higher and higher, until I would black out. Once in a while I would get so exhausted that I would find myself only going through the motions on stage and then hate myself for doing so. But usually the audience lifted me into the right state of euphoria – which I found no amount of drugs could do. The applause, the adulation and the love of an audience was the most potent drug of all.

We were still dogged by unprofessional tour promotion and tour management. There was always something left unorganized or not checked out. More often than not the hotels were cheap and dirty, or there were no facilities for eating properly. Nothing seemed what it should be for a group with our global success. The smallest seemingly petty thing can seem like the end of the world when, after a sold-out show, you need some privacy or comfort on tour. The film *Spinal Tap* brilliantly parodies the music business and has in it a scene in which the guitarist complains because his sandwich filling doesn't fit the bread; like the best parody, it is cruelly observant. When touring, routine and order are essential if you are to maintain your spirits, and the slightest break or annoyance in the regime throws you off balance.

Then of course, when you are touring you are also expected by the record company to do promotion and interviews – more often than not just before going on stage. No one considers how exhausted or nervous you might be. The need to generate press coverage is paramount, and the company insist you comply with it because they are financially supporting the tour. It was only when I discovered no evidence of tour support from the record company itself that I refused to do interviews altogether. My only concern was to give my all to the paying audience, and I didn't want some journalist winding me up with smart-arse remarks before a show.

One hassle after another weighed Dave and me down, and hastened us towards the inevitable conclusion. On one occasion in Amsterdam we found ourselves booked into a hostel, with a long dormitory with communal sleeping space and beds of the metal hospital type. I tried to see the irony of it: we had a sell-out show at a major venue and we were expected to stay in Cell Block H. It was the last show on a tour that had already seen Dave threaten to disappear, but on this particular night I beat him to it. I went to the airport – closely followed by Stevo, pleading with me to return – boarded a plane and returned to England. It was unprofessional to have let down so many people, and the fans subsequently rioted outside the venue. But, as you will have gathered from events so far, responsibility was not the order of the day and I had had it.

Everything that could go wrong did. I began to suspect there was a curse on us. I certainly thought it possible, with all the things that had happened. A curse perhaps from the cemetery incident, or from ridiculing witchcraft on television. My suspicions peaked when during a television appearance on *The Tube* someone neglected to tell us the backing tape had started before we were on stage, and then when I eventually was in place and ready the microphone refused to work. I threw it down and stormed off.

And then I discovered it wasn't witchcraft at all: it was called lack of money. Everything to do with Soft Cell appeared to be done on the cheap, with every possible corner cut. But where was all the money going? Dave and I never saw a penny from all the touring we were doing; all we ever received was shortfall bills for our trouble. It all became a stressful, never-ending nightmare.

Yet, despite all this shit, we still somehow managed to gain a reputation as a great live act. Saxophone player Gary Barnacle joined us in our later shows, and occasionally the Venomettes (becoming the Cell-ettes) also joined us to do backing singing. Gary added a great visual touch with his black leather and rocker looks, and made the songs sound positively filthy. During the eighties there was hardly a record without Gary on it somewhere. Once I tuned into *Top of the Pops* and saw him play with three different bands – rarely discerning in his choice, but always a welcome addition.

And there was romance too, which for a while many of us were unaware of. Dave had fallen for one of the backing singers, Gini, and touring together gave them a chance to cement the relationship.

In the live set we included a manic version of Suicide's 'Ghost Rider', despite (or maybe because of) Alan Vega's caustic remarks about us stealing his ideas. We included the song as a tribute, and it introduced many of our fans to Suicide for the first time. We even performed it on a television show, *The Switch*, with Jim Thirlwell guesting. We finished the song by rolling and screaming all over the floor – now, there's rock 'n' roll for you! We had hailed Suicide as innovators when nobody else was interested. Then, when they reformed in 1998, everyone came out of the woodwork claiming that they'd always loved them. Don't they always?

*

In the summer of 1983 we set off on a tour of Spain that was as insane as any we were to experience. This was the first time I was to see just how passionate a following we had there. There were black-clad fans looking like me on the cover of *Torment and Toreros* (which after all was inspired by Spain); hysterical Spanish girls threw roses and letters; countless men – many Latin macho types – openly cried and tried to pass me green capsules of Spanish mescaline, which at times the whole audience seemed to be under the influence of. We of course stocked up, and took as much as we could on our days off. This was post-Franco Spain, where drugs were not yet criminalized under the new legal system. It was as if the whole country was determined to indulge its new-found freedom, to shake rid of the dogmatic rule of Franco, as if it was a shaken bottle of champagne just uncorked.

I learned a word, a word that became synonymous with the new Spain, and that was *mañana* – tomorrow. Everything would be done tomorrow – except, of course, the shows themselves, which had to run on time. When the equipment wasn't set up on time, people would say, '*Mañana.*' It was madness. And all the time an air of heaviness was present from some of the local promoters, who seemed to be part of a collective – I think the word 'mafia' was uttered more than once.

The one drug that had remained illegal was cocaine, and it was in abundance – the best-quality type, which was chopped out at every venue after the concerts. Naturally cautious of not being able to get drugs, I'd brought with me from England a jar of black-bomber speed capsules to help me through the fatigue. Stevo had come along for the trip, and at the time was dating Anne Stevenson, the feisty violinist from the Mambas, now one of our backing singers. Anne was a fun person and an excellent violinist, and I have worked with her on many sessions, but she and Stevo brought out the worst in each other. We really didn't want to get into trouble in a country that at times seemed volatile. The people we were meeting, when not incapable on drugs, were passionate Spaniards and Italians who were not amused when Stevo and Anne would have sex in public, shout, swear and fight together. It couldn't have looked good. One day I, along with everyone else, had had enough. I blew up and sent her back to England. Afterwards I felt bad, but the situation with her and Stevo was driving everyone crazy. I felt that Anne had a talent and was wasting it, demeaning herself by these displays with Stevo, who cared little for her. I wanted to bring her to her senses. Later she and I made up. Meanwhile she was replaced on backing vocals by Stevo's ex-girlfriend Marion, which suitably tormented him.

Then I discovered a way of keeping Stevo quiet. In the morning, at breakfast, I would put a sleeping tablet in his coffee. He would then doze off on the tour bus, never able to figure out why he was so tired all the time.

One night after the show Dave announced that he and Gini were to be engaged. As we toasted them with cocaine and champagne, I couldn't help thinking how Anita Sarko would react to this news, as she still burnt a torch for Dave, and I knew it was going to be me who told her. I kept putting it off and off, however, until she eventually read about it in a gossip column – and that hurt her even more.

As the tour continued, one unfortunate incident after another happened, almost all threatening each of us in one way or another. It all culminated in a concert we were to play in Alicante for a new promotion company. On the day of the concert we received a message at the hotel warning us that the stage was not safe and that we could receive electric shocks from faulty equipment. In addition to this, the warning stated, the security were very unreliable (meaning heavy-handed I supposed). As a result we were advised to cancel the show, which we did without hesitation. I wasn't going to risk my life by playing on a hazardous stage. But it turned out I would be risking my life by not playing.

Assuming that there was no show to do, myself and the group downed several large jugs of sangria, and ended up being carried out of the bar and back to the hotel. There we were told of an urgent phone call from Mike Murphy, our tour manager. The police were on their way to the hotel to arrest us – or, more to the point, to arrest me – for cancelling the show. It turned out we had breached our contract; that, despite the safety problems, we were in the wrong. It was alleged that one of the Spanish promoters held a high position in the mafia and we – or I – had angered him. He certainly had no intention of losing face.

The British embassy were called, but they wanted no part in it, just reassuring us that we could expect to spend at least three days in jail. Then the tour manager called back. 'Just get here now and look like you're ready to do the concert,' he told us. I tried to sober up, downed coffee, and climbed into a taxi. During the drive, I tried to remember the words to the songs, but I just couldn't. I tried to practise singing, but sounded like a drunk Glaswegian on a Saturday night.

When we arrived at the venue, we were told to keep a low profile. But by this time the stage and all the equipment had been destroyed by fans, who had started to riot. Informed we wouldn't be playing, and refused refunds, they wanted to kill us. They were chanting, and furniture was being smashed. We were all shown into a room where we sat on orange boxes, afraid of what might ensue. Mike was handcuffed and led away into another room. Men came into the room and calmly informed us that we would be beaten with metal bars, and have our legs broken. This last piece of news had a sobering effect, as you can imagine.

It seemed like an eternity of waiting before Mike eventually returned and told us that he had struck a deal and we would be allowed to leave. We were shown to a van and told to lie flat on the floor in the back. As the van drove slowly away, there was pounding and banging on the sides, accompanied by hollering and shouting. The backing singers were crying and I was shaking, but at least we were out of there. Our tour manager had to give the promoter all of our tour money so far – in excess of £10,000 – to secure our safe release. Later the official line from the promoter was an apology, as he didn't want his reputation sullied – he wanted other bands to go there. The British embassy then appointed an official to look after us for the rest of the tour. But I think Alicante was the last straw for Dave, and made him realize that he was not cut out for touring.

On this tour that I would prefer to forget, there was one other incident that springs to mind. It was during a show in San Sebastian. As I was singing, a stockily built guy at the front constantly spat at me and made crude gestures. As his threatening behaviour increased, Dave suddenly leaped from the stage and swung his guitar at him like a maniac. Then a roadie joined Dave and head-butted the man. I felt my heart sink, as I sensed the audience might turn against us. Then suddenly the man exposed himself for all to see, and I responded with the small-finger gesture – indicating to the audience his lack of manhood – the ultimate insult to Latin machismo. Luckily they cheered, and from that moment were on our side.

Later, after the show, Dave put his arm around me and told me how much he admired me. I told him likewise. It was a rare moment of closeness between two people who had been through so much but found it hard to communicate any real feelings. If only we had talked more things through regarding Soft Cell, it might not have come to an end like it did.

*

After Spain, we set off on a tour of England – our last tour there – and it was then that I started keeping a notebook and diary.

Tuesday, 5 July 1983

Today is the first day of our 'tying off ends' *Falling Apart* tour. First stop Blackpool, Dave's home town. I'm sitting in bed. Hope that these dates are worth doing, because after tonight's show certain things are obvious to me. I hardly feel glowing or inspired.

The audience loved the show, but I'm worrying that their tastes aren't too discerning and anything with a Soft Cell or Marc Almond label will suffice. I'm bored by the material. It feels overfamiliar, I hate to feel like I'm going through the motions, but tonight I felt like a tired clockwork toy creaking out the same old movements to the same lines and lyrics. Oh, in this bit I fall to my knees, and in this bit I whip the floor with my mike lead; in this bit I go mad, in this bit I stay still. I feel false and a little plastic at moments, and at points of real low I feel like walking off and leaving the audience to it while I have a cup of tea. I know it's theatre, and maybe I expect too much of myself. Dave was angered by the sound, which was forever fluctuating and off-putting, and between the show and the encore I heard the crashing of movable objects in his dressing room.

I crave for new songs, new words, a new image and new music to feed off – to present myself fresh and full of surprises. I feel annoyed at the audience, that they accept us at our worst. But what's the alternative – booing? I think that would be too horrible to bear – the depression would be too much. I want this tour to be successful, to show the doubting Stevo. At the end, during 'Say Hello, Wave Goodbye', I threw myself into the crowd and they grabbed and tore at me, grasping at anything removable, trying to prise my rings from my fingers – they're bruised and swollen. Oh God, what am I doing? Sometimes they have teeth gritted in determination – just a little piece of you. A piece you leave behind sometimes means more than the memory of a good song – some proof to 'show you I've been there'!

After the show I was introduced to some mentally handicapped children and – though a little nervous at first as they clutch and cling to me giving me love – found them so much easier to be with than so many other fans, who want to own, tear, steal. As we left for the hotel more fingers clutched at my rings and a Liverpudlian voice shrieked, 'Oooh sexual – you're sexual!'

The hotel is like a real living-dead gathering – more like a twilight home for the terminally ill than a holiday hotel. Everywhere there are doddering elderlies chuntering and shuffling along the bland corridors in search of tea and fancies. It resembles a social-security office. Wheelchairs in every corner – a line of amputees by the pool – people coming to play out the last rites of holidaymaking before popping off to that Butlins in the sky. There's a cabaret going on in the ballroom (the stage has a silver strip curtain behind, a backcloth for a wheezing showband) – a sense of déjà vu. A tinny seaside Hammond organ provides a plodding backing as a loud horror-bag of a peroxide stormtrooper patronizingly helps old geriatrics to cough up a few recognizable bars of 'Hello Dolly', or ancient carcasses rattle out between loose dentures 'Danny Boy'. Has it come to this?

Earlier today, in the fairground, people started to recognize me. At first I was obliging and quite polite as I was asked for autographs, but continual badgering made my patience grow thin. People are so ignorant. They don't say please: they just expect, demand – often six or seven autographs at once. More often than not they don't really know or care who you are, but they've seen you on the almighty fucking television. I began to feel like a fairground exhibit myself – just another attraction you pose with for a holiday snap. Roll up! Roll up! One old bag grabbed my arm for a photo with her ghastly daughter. Photographs annoy me at the best of times, but touching? Thank God for that speedy rush of the bomber, which sweetened my mood and boosts the tolerance level. Murder crossed my mind several times today.

Thursday, 7 July 1983

We play at Bradford's Caesar's tonight. Our hotel is like a swingers' paradise – an indoor disco pool complete with kaleidoscope lights and oil wheels. The bedrooms are tasty shades of turquoise and purple, with baths big enough for six people. Everything is frayed around the edges – including me. Took a dip in the pool, which was icy, then a go on an exercise bike. My body doesn't know what hit it!

The concert hall is a tatty make-believe glamour disco, and when we arrive there are queues down the road. The atmosphere is fantastic, and it looks like being a good concert in comparison to Blackpool.

I love the shows that are steamy and sweaty down the front, with all those hands to play tug-of-war with, faces to see and play to. The reception is fantastic, and from the first moment gifts are thrown on to the stage – roses, rings, beads. I drape myself with beads and bracelets and parade about like a gin-sozzled whore and a staggering stripper. Someone hands me some sherry, and I take a huge swig then pass it to the open mouths. I'm soon drenched, and so are the battling dedicated fans at the front.

Couldn't sleep. Took four Halcion and a handful of Valium. Why is every fucking hotel in the world never finished? Builders working outside at seven!

Sunday, 10 July 1983

We have spent the last couple of days at Lumley Castle Hotel, just outside Durham. An Elizabethan majestic building surrounded by green and shielded from the nearby estates. A perfect (well, not really but . . .) place to spend my twenty-sixth birthday, which was yesterday.

We had been performing the previous night at Kirk Levington Country Club outside Darlington – a small club that we had played at in the early stages of our career, and where we had our first ecstatic reception outside of Leeds. It holds special fond memories for us. The concert was being kept secret, as only 400 were allowed in, and we played a short set with a small amount of equipment. The heat was unbearable, sweat dripping off the ceiling, off the walls, the audience, me, everywhere. Thought I was going to pass out on stage – just kept thinking, 'One more song . . . one more song . . .' It was a touching moment when the crowd sang 'Happy Birthday' to me at the stroke of midnight. Afterwards I signed autographs for those who made it past Reichsführer Murphy, our tour manager.

Later had a small party in the back lounge but was too tired to do much. Spare ribs, chocolate cake and cheap sweet champagne – lovely combination at three in the morning.

The actual day of my birthday was a day I won't forget. In the evening we all attend an Elizabethan banquet – various friends from Leeds come up to join in the grosseties. It's a sure recipe for wild behaviour – messy food, gallons of drink, a riotous road crew, and a birthday to celebrate.

We're called to our seats by a bearded fruitcake in medieval lurex. We're addressed and entertained by a local drama group – a motley gaggle of drama queens in a vile selection of rayon, lurex and matching curtains, singing wicked naughty songs such as 'Where's the Keys to my Chastity Belt?' 'Medieval porn – you can't beat it,' says Huw Feather. As the performers go on and on, they begin to become animated and embarrassingly bizarre with their captive audience, and like a bunch of schoolkids we snigger and laugh as they make fools of themselves. The crew give me a present of a beautiful silver sacrament box, and burst into a chorus of 'Happy Birthday', which makes me very happy.

The food is greasy spare ribs and chicken cooked in mead sauce, eaten with fingers and a dagger, which begins to travel between ourselves and the crew's table. Food fights quickly develop – glasses of wine and mead soaking everything – and I let fly with an apple crumble. The rest of the hall of guests are horrified. In real medieval times there would have been much more rabble-rousing and even the odd murder – we just wanted to add a touch of reality. One of the performers, a tubby old queen, is flapping around yelling, 'This is a disgrace! I've never seen anything like it!' I reply that he should get out more. Meanwhile the crew have visited a couple of rooms and have hung everything upside down. The armchair hanging from the beams, foam and sugar in the bed.

The next morning sees a few pasty faces, pink eyes and throbbing heads. We are due to set off for Glasgow.

Tuesday 12 July 1983

We are returning from Edinburgh after playing the last date of our *Falling Apart* tour. The previous night we played in Glasgow – the reaction was fantastic. The feeling was more like a football match, with people clambering on to the stage and throwing more bloody beads and bangles. I nearly dislocated my shoulder when I attempted to shake hands. One very cute boy wearing dark glasses sat on the edge of the stage and shook my hand, then held out his hand for members of the audience to touch.

The only incident to mar the Scottish tour was when the brother of [the Scottish club promoter involved in bootlegging the 'Sex Dwarf' video – see Chapter 7] arrived. His brother had told him that if he turned up he would be looked after and given a hotel room. He got nasty and threatened me, Mike Murphy and Dave with a knife. The police were called and were itching to give him a good kicking, but we felt that this would only cause more trouble, so he was taken across town and put in another hotel.

I'm awakened by the Scottish club promoter himself. His voice on the other end of the telephone gives me the creeps: 'Hello, it's me. Thanks for looking after my brother. He's coming up to see you at the hotel. Look after him, won't you.' What an alarm call!

I humoured him, horrified to hear him. How many other brothers has he got up here in Scotland?

The brother was waiting downstairs to badger us for a lift and hospitality. I was fuming: this was obviously a ploy to annoy us as much as possible. Earlier the brother had made his simple sidekick do impressions of me doing 'Tainted Love', telling me how he looked and sounded like me. (Was he deaf and blind as well as insane?) The simpleton gave an embarrassing rendition, followed by an exhibition of his dancing at the demand of the idiotic brother. I couldn't believe my eyes. Eventually enough was enough – threats or no threats, we had him thrown out. We set off to Edinburgh.

Edinburgh looked a beautiful city, but unfortunately there was not time to explore properly. That's the annoying thing on tour – you only get a slight sniff at some of the places of interest. The hotel was nicer than the Glaswegian hotel, which was another of those characterless social-security offices – everything in the right place, white Formica, a couple of Boots prints, and the inevitable club sandwich with crisps: the sort of place you can't even be bothered to steal the towels.

The venue is a tacky disco with no dressing-room facilities. We have to walk from the hall round to an upstairs club that smells of stale beer and fag ends. The concert was great, but a lot more reserved than Glasgow – more refined. Also, a line of bouncers along the front didn't help matters. Once again they yelled for an encore, which was our version of 'Ghost Rider', now a firm favourite. I dragged Marion down the front to scream her head off, while I demolished the set and tangled myself in the mike leads and pieces of wood. I've lost nearly a stone on this tour.

Later the brother turned up again, but he was escorted from the place with stern warnings. In the bar afterwards I sat and talked with Mike Murphy and Kevin Millens, who had put the tour together. I had so many grievances about the promotion of the shows – though the venues are packed to the hilt, why do they insist that we weren't sold out? They blame PR and us not having a single out, etc., etc. I make decision to try and work with Phonogram now.

Wednesday 13 July 1983

Back in London I met up with Mariella, Phonogram PR, for peace talks. Maybe it's best if Phonogram do our press from now on –

Previous page: Moscow, 1997.

Opposite: St Petersburg, 1992.
(Mark Langthorne)

This page, top to bottom:

Busking on the Reeperbahn in Hamburg
with Neal X. *(Stefan Mussigbrodt)*

With pianist Martin Watkins in Athens.

In Morocco.

Entertaining the urchins in front of
the burnt-out Hilton Hotel in Beirut –
look at the alien. *(Mark Langthorne)*

Above: As Caligula (who else?) in the rarely seen 'Tainted Love' video.

Left: With New York artist and friend Scott Ewalt.

Above: As the 'Absinthe Drinker Verlaine'. Photo session with friends Pierre et Gilles. *(Tomah)*

Two old glam tarts, 1996.
(Mike Owen)

...ith Tim Pope, Huw, Dave
Ball and Jane Rollink
...uring the filming of the
...n-Stop Erotic video, 1982.

Sally King, Alan Selka
and Dillon, 1982.

...o, 1988.

Dave Ball and Mike Thorne.

Anita Sarko
in typical pose.

Left: Performing the song 'Kept Boy' in Dublin with the legendary Agnes Burnelle.

Centre left: Performing 'The Flame' with Marie France.

Centre right: The illustrious Huw Feather.

Bottom left: Gene Pitney and me in Las Vegas.

Bottom right: Jane Rollink and Martin Watkins.

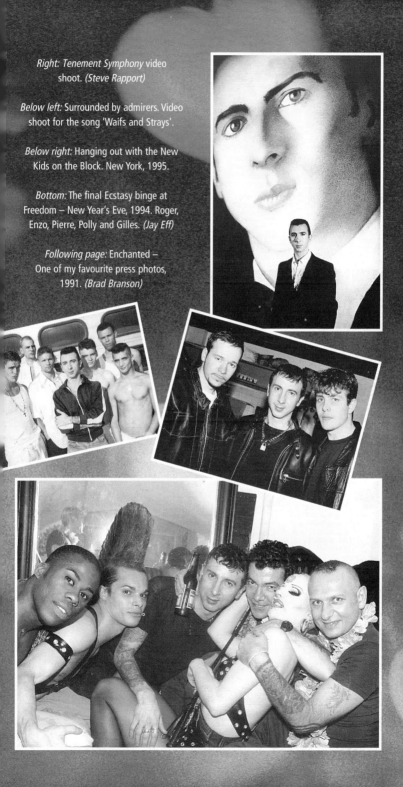

Right: Tenement Symphony video shoot. *(Steve Rapport)*

Below left: Surrounded by admirers. Video shoot for the song 'Waifs and Strays'.

Below right: Hanging out with the New Kids on the Block. New York, 1995.

Bottom: The final Ecstasy binge at Freedom — New Year's Eve, 1994. Roger, Enzo, Pierre, Polly and Gilles. *(Jay Eff)*

Following page: Enchanted — One of my favourite press photos, 1991. *(Brad Branson)*

maybe we were cutting our own throats. We sip cocktails in a trendy cupboard on South Molton Street. My mouth cracks at the sides, but peace is restored and I humour Mariella just as she humours me. There is a condescending review of the Blackpool show in *Melody Maker*: 'Marc's endearing . . . etc. . . . could get away with murder.' The fool just fancied a free day out in Blackpool. A three-page feature in *Record Mirror*: a good piece, but Simon – bless him – always writes the same things.

Late in 1983 I flew to Canada from New York, where I'd been doing the Immaculate Consumptives shows, to start the Soft Cell tour of Canada and the USA. Our first and last tour there – and our last tour anywhere as Soft Cell, despite its being deemed a huge success. We ought to have taken heart from this string of tours, especially the American side of things. We were as popular as ever, and the fans were increasingly supportive. If we had stayed together we would have been playing stadiums the next time round, even though we were still being bloody-minded and refusing to play 'Tainted Love'. Uncompromising actually amounted to mean-spirited really. After all, what did it matter if we played 'Tainted Love' – this was our last tour, wasn't it. Wasn't it?

In New York we played the beautiful Roseland Ballroom. A review said of the concert:

Lithe, graceful and radiantly sensual, the rather emaciated odd-looking Almond easily manages the stage presence of Bowie . . . members of both sexes reach out to touch him. Almond thrills on such exchanges. Occasionally he'll kneel dangerously close to the audience while continuing to sing flawlessly while dozens of fans caress every imaginable part of his body. Almond's love of being loved can get out of hand as it did this time when he permitted ten lovestruck females to tear off his shirt, cover him in kisses and finally hoist him into the crowd – a possible gang rape seemed imminent when saxophonist Gary Barnacle leapt off the stage to come to Marc's rescue.

After the show Anita Sarko came into the dressing room and everyone fell suddenly silent. I felt desperately bad for Anita; this was the first time I'd seen her since she learned of Dave's engagement plans. I'd spoken to her on the phone from London, when for ninety minutes she had turned the air blue across the Atlantic, cursing Dave into oblivion. 'I had to find out like a fucking fan from a fucking gossip column!' she had shouted. Dave had now married Gini, and a

little Ball was on the way – Dave was to be a family man. After
venting her anger over the phone Anita had broken down in tears. I
felt so very sorry that she had had to find out the way she did. She
deserved better than that. I don't know how strong Anita and Dave's
relationship had been, but it must have had some intense significance
for Anita to be so distressed. Now she stood in the dressing room,
looking stunning and braving the atmosphere. You could have cut
the air with a knife. We were all such milksops. Dave's name was
going to be shit now as far as Anita was concerned.

Neil Tennant, before his Pet Shop Boys success, was the editor of
Britain's premier pop magazine *Smash Hits*, and he came to New
York to do a piece on the Soft Cell show. If only I'd known then that
within a short time he would be fronting his own synthesizer duo,
who would go on to be bigger than Soft Cell. I've met Neil a number
of times over the years, along with his Pet Shop partner Chris Lowe.
They are two charming and respectful reprobates, and I have to admit
that I was just a little jealous of their early success.

In San Francisco a huge gay contingent turned out for the show
at the Kabuki Theatre, and we were lauded as 'conquering heroes'.

In Los Angeles we sold out our three nights at the Palace Theatre
– the place where Judy Garland had given her most infamous show.
This time round Los Angeles was a wonderful and rewarding experience compared to our earlier record-company-chaperoned visits. I
spent the day of the show being driven around in a huge red sports
car, sniffing ethyl chloride from a rag, laughing myself sick, and
visiting the Observatory, the Hollywood graveyard and voodoo
stores. Unfortunately the ethyl chloride tightened my vocal cords and
I had a few problems that night on stage, but I gave so much that at
one point I fell back over a monitor and knocked myself unconscious
for ten minutes. All the while, throughout the show, really distracting
me, a figure in a braided military outfit and dark glasses stood
watching transfixed in the wings at the side of the stage. It was
Michael Jackson, who had come to see us perform. I only wish I'd
agreed to meet him afterwards.

After the concert we were taken to meet one of Los Angeles's
premier cocaine dealers at his luxury house up in the Hollywood hills.
There we were greeted by the strange sight of an entire family of
three generations all completely wired on coke, chewing their jaws,
chopping out endless lines, and talking ten to the dozen. After being
cornered and talked at for several hours, it became apparent that this
was the daily routine of the household. It didn't bear thinking about.
At least the coke was top quality, and it further convinced me that,
hey, I didn't have a problem compared to these people.

All the reviews on the tour were ecstatic. It was only in America that Soft Cell made complete sense. Our dark themes and Goth references were understood, yet at the same time our sound was recognized as warmer and fuller than many of our synthesizer contemporaries who had started to break in America – owing to the success of 'Tainted Love'. This was what they labelled 'the Brit invasion'. Soft Cell paved the way for so many bands to break America in the early eighties, but that also bred jealousies. Gary Kemp of Spandau Ballet laughed and sneered at us, comparing us to the grocer's shop, while they were the chain store. I replied that it was the grocer's shops that sold the fresher specialist goods, while the chain stores had the mass-produced rubbish. In a country that has for so long been obsessed with drums and guitar, real rock 'n' roll, Soft Cell imbued the synthesizer with that same spirit. Dave used the keyboards like a guitar, and together we performed in an energetic rock 'n' roll fashion as no synthesizer band had done before.

*

We finished *This Last Night in Sodom* album back in England after the tour, completing it at Britannia Row in Islington in late '83/early '84. Of all the Soft Cell albums, it remains my favourite. It is a tough, gritty, uncompromising album, recorded in mono as Dave's tribute to Phil 'Back to Mono' Spector. If I had to link it to a drug, I would call it our amphetamine album – cheap sulphate speed and bad London coke. There are references on the track 'Mr Self Destruct' to 'shooting the A', and throughout the record is the edginess of all our sleepless nights.

'Meet Murder, My Angel' is the darkest Soft Cell song of all – about the lover who wants to murder his love as the ultimate expression of affinity. 'Surrender to a Stranger' is desperate and sensual, and self-explanatory. 'L'Esqualita' is about the famous Puerto Rican drag club in New York and its characters.

The punk-inspired 'Best Way to Kill' was inspired by a tabloid feature which described different types of execution methods – hanging, garrotting, guillotine, lethal injection – and asked readers to decide which was their preferred way to kill people. This to me summed up Thatcher's New Britain – flippant, uncaring, dangerously hard-hearted, and hypocritically moral. Much of the album reflected my feelings about those attitudes.

The album title was intended as an apocalyptic statement – to suggest that this was our final night of freedom before the impending catastrophe. God, in this case, was substituted by Thatcher. The cover artwork was a drawing by a psychotic schizophrenic girl whose work I'd found in a textbook about insanity. The album was a gob of phlegm spat in the face of whoever.

The reviews were mixed. Most people didn't get it and thought it was just more of our commercial suicide – no longer just a defiant two-fingered gesture, it now also showed contempt for Soft Cell's reputation. We didn't care. But we cared. We thought it was a masterpiece. Paul Morley smugly felt he had the last word and wrote in his review in *NME*, 'Piss off, Soft Cell.' Mirroring my sentiments about him. I always felt if it got up his nose we had succeeded.

The singles 'Soul Inside' and an R & B cover of a song about suicide by American beat poet Jack Hammer, 'Down in the Subway', made their marks on the chart, and we even did a *Top of the Pops* appearance for 'Soul Inside'. Number one that week were Culture Club with 'Karma Chameleon'. I read then that 'Boy George has stolen Marc Almond's crown.' I was not entirely sure what was meant by that – crown of 'camp homo of the year' or 'crown of pop'? Whichever it was, he was welcome to it. I'd never wanted the former, and the latter I was well and truly finished with.

Having said that, when Boy George wasn't commenting in the press about me with his usual candid eloquence – 'Marc Almond is for people who wear black and hate their parents' – he would be seen outside the Radio 1 building doing unfavourable impressions of me to groups of my fans. It was nice to know he cared. Years later, while he was reviewing a single of mine (favourably, I might add), he wondered why I didn't like him. The truth is, I admire him for being the person he is – bitchily indiscriminate. He's also talented, and a true survivor. He and I are as different as two people can be, but his achievements merit respect, and he'd be the first to agree that people should never assume that sexuality creates a common bond. Far from it!

This Last Night in Sodom was badly promoted and failed to make much of a mark commercially. There was no point doing interviews, and there was no point the record company spending money for promotion, because everyone knew it was over. Everyone knew we wanted to finish Soft Cell, at least it seemed to everyone that we did.

After my ridiculous and dramatic retirement announcement, it was just accepted. It seemed hard to go back on that retirement: I felt that I'd dug my hole and now all I could do was get down and lie in it. I'd finished the tours and the album, which had fizzled out before it was released. Perhaps if we had moved behind the album and promoted it to the maximum then it might have stood a chance, but we just accepted Soft Cell was over. Dave and I were burnt out and disillusioned, never having had a sensible break or a chance to really sit down and evaluate our careers. It could have been a good future for us if only we'd taken stock, made plans, thought things through. But that is all with hindsight. I asked Dave if he wanted to do a Japanese tour, but he wasn't interested in the live side any more, however lucrative it could be – he'd had too many bad live experiences. He was a family man now, with new responsibilities. I found myself saying the words 'It's over', and it scared the hell out of me.

'It's time to call it a day. I'm going to go solo,' I said to Dave, after he rejected the Japanese tour. Who could blame him really? Yet we should have seen from our American tour, from the final British dates, just what we had and precisely what we were capable of together. The two nights at London's Hammersmith Palais when we had played our final British dates in the previous year had been uplifting celebrations, even though so many tears had been shed earlier in the tour. 'Vive la Sleaze' said the press. 'Nutcracker suite.' 'Cabaret Futura.'

It should have been time for a crowning triumph, not for a sad farewell. We had both finally become the live act we had always aspired to be, and were at last making the records we wanted to. What we needed more than anything was for someone to make us see sense, to sit us down and explain to us from a bold business point of view just what we had. Someone should have explained that we could have had our own time away, our own solo projects, while convincing us that Soft Cell could carry on. I truly believe that after a period of rest we might have come back stronger than ever. No doubt we would have flitted in and out of fashion like all bands, made a duff album or two, but then come back with a great one. I think we would have survived into the nineties, avoiding the retro treadmill and becoming – dare I think it? – hip again. But we never had anyone to tell us this. There was no one capable of mediating – and certainly not Stevo, who Dave distrusted intensely by this point.

It may just be hypothesis, but it might all have turned out different; because I believe that neither Dave nor I really wanted to end it there. I so wanted Dave to shout at me, 'You bloody fool, think about it!' And I wanted to shout the same at him. Maybe a row would have cleared the air, but it never happened. We tiptoed around each other, carefully avoiding any real communication.

How many bands split and then regret it? I would say almost all – everyone regrets it in some way or other. How can you go through so much with people and not care? In America people still can't get enough of Soft Cell. I still hear the songs played, and there I will for ever be the former Soft Cell singer. Most taxi drivers still think I'm part of Soft Cell.

Had we remained together it might also have been harder for bands like the Pet Shop Boys or Erasure to find a vacancy for a synth duo and fill it. The Pet Shop Boys' first melancholy bedsit dance drama even opened with the words 'Zazou, what you gonna do?' Wasn't *Zazou* one of my performance pieces? Just coincidence. Erasure was perhaps a camp glam side of ourselves. And Depeche Mode, who had grown up alongside us – the nice boys of electro pop – after Soft Cell disbanded, didn't they suddenly change direction and go all dark and perverse with songs about 'Masters and Servants'? Interviewers constantly asked me what I thought about Dave Gahan transforming himself into me. I made no comment. So it was, and always is, that those who follow glean the accolades and success from those that went before. Didn't we from Suicide? Alan Vega thought so. But, before you accuse me of being bitter, let me tell you that bitterness is good – or at least a valid feeling for a person like myself who finds it difficult to locate any feelings at all. It is at least a reminder that you're alive, as my friend Anita reminded me. Use it, don't let it consume you.

There was no end-of-show party. No celebratory goodbyes. Not even handshakes that I can recall.

Five years of my life had been about Soft Cell – not a long time in the course of a life, but one in which I had lived an entire lifetime. I was sad. I was scared. I was foolish. I was regretful. I was bitter.

I was relieved.

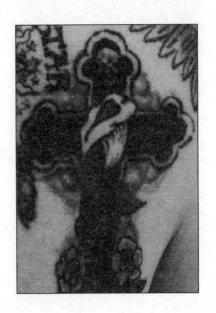

11

The End of the Beginning

It took a little time for the realization that Dave and I were no longer Soft Cell to sink in. But slowly it dawned on me, and I was filled with fear, confusion and, yes, regret. Fear for the future, and confusion over what I wanted to do next. I was to be a solo artist, with all that entailed – *freedom*! Freedom to do what I wanted musically, even to take surprise directions into other fields. Writing perhaps, films, film producing. The sky was my limit.

So why didn't I feel full of joy and enthusiasm about it?

I had destroyed something successful in my life. Everything good and successful had to be destroyed – it was all part of my unworthiness. I was bad and didn't deserve success, even though I yearned for it, and the love and affirmation that came with it.

Shortly, I thought, Dave and I would be on the phone to each other, laughing about our dramatics and planning our next album. We'd been through too much together. We just needed a break to re-energize our batteries. Each in our own way, we were both burnt out and needed to re-evaluate things. But it was unnecessary to finish Soft Cell. Did Dave really want it, or was he just going along with me, thinking I wanted it? Or was I finishing it because I thought that's what Dave wanted? With the passing of time, all the reasons have become blurred; most likely it was, as most things are, the result of the lack of communication and misread signs. As I've said, we never got round to really sitting down with a manager and discussing things.

Only recently I was watching the television show *This Morning*, hosted by Richard Madeley and Judy Finnegan. Richard was interviewing Kylie Minogue about her single, which had been written and produced by Dave Ball. Richard was very disparaging about Dave, and gave his own insight into the Soft Cell split. 'Oh yes,' said Richard, 'Dave left because he was tired of the whole gay thing. Sick of it!' Kylie looked surprised at his outburst. 'Yes,' continued Richard, 'that's a fact. It's true.' Facts usually are, Richard. I was grateful for finding out from Richard what I hadn't known. A thousand complex reasons had all boiled down to the fact that Dave was homophobic?

Or homo wary? I was also interested in what Richard meant by the 'gay thing'. Did he mean me? And I thought this rather insulting to Dave, who is the least homophobic person I know.

*

The days since I'd last seen Dave became weeks, and then months, then a year, and all too soon it seemed too late ever to go back. The phone call never came, and I just couldn't bring myself to make one to Dave. It's that thing called pride, I suppose – bloody pride. It always gets in the way and spoils so many things. 'I'm not going to be the one that calls. He can call *me*!' Maybe this would punish Dave for going and getting married, starting a family, putting me second. God, I hated being second – in anyone's life. I was to spend the next decade in interviews saying how happy I was to be a solo artist; how, no, I didn't miss Soft Cell or working with Dave . . . no, I love what I'm doing now.

The truth was that I regretted it like hell. I regretted it when our contemporaries went from strength to strength, still making records and now filling stadiums. I regretted it when struggling to write songs with temperamental, moderately talented musicians with whom I had no chemistry. I regretted it when I found myself playing in venues that resembled glorified toilets to a semi-interested audience baying for songs like 'Say Hello, Wave Goodbye'. I should add, though, that the latter situation came relatively seldom. I had so often wanted to pull a Soft Cell song out of the bag and make everyone happy. But I never did. Or never would. I was going to start again from scratch, not trade on past glories. Besides, I would have felt such a sense of guilt doing the songs without Dave. It would be over eight years before I sang a Soft Cell song again.

For the next decade I would be shunted around record companies who obtrusively hoped for another Soft Cell record and would become quickly disillusioned when they couldn't get one. In the end everyone was short-changed in some way – not least me.

Soft Cell was over. I was adrift, directionless and with no concrete plan. Besides, what would the press say if I said, 'Only joking – Soft Cell haven't split. We're going to make another album'? After the debacle of my resignation from music, then my return, I had a credibility problem. The fear was that, whatever I announced, there might just be a resounding 'Who cares?'

Why did I care? Because I still had that chip on my shoulder and I was going to show them all that I was an uncompromising, talented and multifaceted artist who didn't need anyone. Oh, but first I needed

Stevo to negotiate me a new record deal. Oh, and I needed some musicians to work and write with. And, oh yes, I needed a break. So it was that Stevo negotiated me a new deal with Phonogram, who were reluctant to let me go just yet. I was the face and and voice of Soft Cell, and they couldn't say goodbye to a possible asset until they were absolutely sure there was no mileage left. But they let Dave go. At the same time, he also parted company with Stevo. For him it had to be a complete break. He had never been an admirer of Stevo, and saw him as one of the reasons why it had all gone wrong.

So Stevo secured me a new record deal. In true Stevo fashion, instead of attending meetings himself to negotiate the deal, he sent along his toy teddy bear with a tape recorder attached to it, a recording setting out his demands, which included a yearly supply of sweets – forty-pence worth, delivered on a precise day each month to his office. And still the record company yielded to him. It was not the first time he had negotiated a deal this way. For Matt Johnson the deal had to be completed while all parties sat astride one of the lions in Trafalgar Square. Another deal had to be signed with each party sitting in a separate cubicle in the Waterloo Station toilets, passing the contracts under the stall doors to each other. Yet, despite the humiliation they had to endure, record companies loved to work with him; he was a likeable and colourful individual who reminded many of them of the legendary managers of the sixties and seventies, who imbued their lives with some interest – like Andrew Loog Oldham, who became almost as famous as the bands he represented. It was only after the deals were signed that the trouble would begin.

Stevo was a genius at deal-getting, but terrible at day-to-day management, and that failing would eventually cost him dearly as artists abandoned him. Artists signed for huge amounts of money would find themselves quickly left isolated at the mercy of a record company eager for a return on their overly generous investment. However, Stevo gave me one piece of advice that I always remember, because I never heeded it. It was something he emphasized over and over, and it was something I was to ignore again and again. 'Now you're a solo artist you can work with whoever you want, write and record with whoever you choose. Use that freedom. Experiment. Try writing with other well-known names, with different cutting-edge artists, musicians, photographers and video-makers. Always move on and leave the past behind you; never tie yourself to one group of people,' he told me.

But what did I do? I put together a group made up of old friends and remnants of the Mambas and called them the Willing Sinners –

the title of one of the fifties pulp novels I collected. I kept the same designer, Huw Feather, and the same photographer, Peter Ashworth; even the same video director, Tim Pope. I hadn't learned a thing.

It's not that I don't respect the talents of those people, but I'd been there before – it was all part of the Soft Cell story. But just as not having Soft Cell made me insecure and lacking in confidence, so having old friends around me made me feel safe – especially as my drug abuse was worsening. It would take me the rest of the eighties and into the nineties to have the sense to see that Stevo had been right. If I had, then perhaps today I could still count Huw Feather, someone I'd been at school with, as a close friend. Working together eventually drove us apart, and it was a friendship that was not worth losing. I also felt a kind of responsibility for the others too – especially for Annie Hogan. She was my house-mate and friend, and I felt I owed it to her, to them, to take them on to the next stage of this journey. But, as much as Annie and I tried, there was never a real songwriting chemistry between us, as there had been between Dave and me. I felt a constant pressure to keep everybody happy, but in the process I ended up just making myself miserable. And more misery meant more drugs, more pills and more alcohol.

Stevo was at his wits' ends with me. He hated my choice of musicians, frustrated that I'd chosen to think so small. He called them parasites and leeches, feeding off my talent, and said I was giving them careers they didn't deserve. I ignored him, but in my heart I felt there might be some truth in what he was saying. Yet I was terrified of meeting new people to work with. What if they could see right through me? What if they were more talented than me and made me look foolish? What if they recognized me for the pill-popping mess I'd become? I find it a strain to communicate with people at the best of times. Back then I needed familiarity – and we all know what that breeds.

*

Around that time in 1984 I made a couple of appearances on television. I was asked to perform two songs on *The Tube*. Instead of using the opportunity to debut a couple of new songs, I sang a song called 'Switchblade Operator', by Jack Hammer (who had also written 'Down in the Subway', covered by Soft Cell), and a country-blues song called 'Muleskinner'. I performed the latter as a duet with a small red-headed Scottish lady called Nancy Peppers. Nancy was the wife of our tour manager, Mike Murphy, but was also one of the best country-blues singers I'd ever heard. She had sung in Nashville, where she had recorded her own album, and been one of Elvis's backing singers. I owe Nancy a great deal, for she took me along to meet a well-known singing teacher called Ian Adams. Ian was constantly in demand as a voice coach by many major stars, as well as West End and Broadway musicals. It was hard to get to see him, but after one visit he was impressed by my singing and I was to see him regularly for years after. It was Ian who gave me the confidence to use my voice, and because of him it improved dramatically.

It was a strange TV appearance on *The Tube* – me in black eye make-up and my then trademark bandana; Nancy, all of five foot tall, with a belting voice, in a slim-fitting trouser suit. I was amused later to hear the singer John Lydon (a.k.a. Rotten) say in an interview that he had seen the performance on *The Tube*. 'I think Marc Almond is brilliant,' he said, 'but I couldn't understand what the hell he was doing with that old bird.'

I very nearly didn't make the appearance at all. As I was due to board the plane to Newcastle from London, I had in my bag a silver stiletto flick knife. It had been a present from Lydia Lunch, and I'd intended using it as a prop in my performance of 'Switchblade Operator'. I put my bag through the X-ray machine, and the knife showed up. The bag was searched and the offending article removed. I was taken aside to wait until the police arrived, then I was arrested and taken to the station. I was told that I was committing a serious offence by carrying an illegal implement. I explained that it was a present, and said how naive I had been in forgetting it was in my bag and that of course I'd never realized the seriousness of owning such a thing. I explained that I was on my way to do a television show. The word 'television' caught their attention, and the atmosphere changed. The officer said he was a fan, that he loved 'Tainted Love' (don't they always!), and agreed to release me with a caution. That song had saved me again – although I didn't get the knife back.

A few weeks later I made an appearance at the Bloomsbury Theatre in a night dedicated to the French erotic writer Georges Bataille. I was contacted about the event by the poet and novelist Paul Buck, who thought I would be perfect for it. Of course I was flattered. I'd heard of Bataille, but I must admit I'd never read him, so I thought I'd better brush up. Anita Sarko was well versed in his work and supplied me with the relevant material. I read *Blue of Noon* and *The Story of the Eye*, pretending to all concerned that I'd read them years earlier. I performed four songs on the theme of love and murder, including 'Body Unknown', which I'd performed with Nick Cave at the Immaculate Consumptives show in New York. The Bataille evening was a beautiful presentation. I sang the songs from a black leather sedan chair, while religious images were projected on to the back of the stage. Another performer that evening was the New York dominatrix Terence Sellars, who read from her new book *The Correct Sadist*.

*

During the tour of America and Canada, while sitting in my room between shows, I'd been writing lyrics and songs, filling notebooks with ideas. I always found so much inspiration in America: its extremes, its darkness and violence, its melting pot of cultures and forms. When visiting Los Angeles on the Soft Cell concert tour, we had been taken over the border to the Mexican town of Tijuana. Walking through the streets of little coloured shacks lit up by cheap neon and visiting the strip bars, I found the inspiration that – combined with the sounds of North Africa – was to influence my next works.

Aware that I needed a break before I began to record again, I considered a holiday, away from London, from England. I did what I always did throughout the eighties – I ran away abroad. But, as much as I tried to escape from myself, wherever I went, there I was!

'C'mon, Armi,' said Jane Rollink, in that broad Yorkshire accent that sounded so cheerfully reassuring, but invited recklessness. 'Let's go to Morocco. I went there a couple of years ago. It's lovely, and you can get a great salade niçoise.' So we threw our things into a couple of bags and flew off – to Agadir, to be precise. There we rented a small apartment and tried to relax. Personally I would have liked room service; but, no, Jane thought we should try to be sensible, economical (whatever that meant). Still, it turned out to be a good opportunity to get my head together, and I started to plan my next record, finding further inspiration in the run-down Moroccan streets, full of sounds and spirits, darkness and danger.

Every day Jane and I donned kaftans, djellabas and sandals and sat in the cafés or on the beach watching life pass by, and trying to avoid the endless stream of carpet salesman and rough young men who wanted me and Jane to milk their big cobras – whatever that meant. (They seemed fascinated by Jane's blonde hair.) I felt more like Kenneth Williams than Joe Orton. At times, as their hands grabbed at me, I thought of the film based on Tennessee Williams's *Suddenly Last Summer* when Sebastian is torn apart by a clamouring throng of native boys. It's tiring after a while, though, when the young hordes that follow you shout over and over, 'English! Fish and chips! English!' Jane, less patient even than I am, would scream, 'Fuck off, yer buggers!'

One day we took a rickety ride on a dilapidated bus across the mountains to Marrakesh. Halfway through the eight-hour journey we stopped at a squalid roadside café in the desert. As I attempted to use the toilet, squatting over a fly-infested hole, I suddenly understood why they wore djellabas which could be hoisted up. That day I had trousers on, and it was a nightmare. Meanwhile, outside, Jane had been petting and feeding a herd of goats and their kids. We went in for coffee, and when we returned outside I felt sick at the sight that greeted us. It seemed that Jane's attention to the goats had been misconstrued. Their decapitated heads had been laid out on a trestle table for us to purchase. The image of the heads, still warm, with flies around their eyes, haunts me still, and strengthened my resolve to be a vegetarian. We fled back to the bus and continued our journey.

I loved the colour and bustle, the hustle and excitement, of Marrakesh, the sound of Moroccan folk music from the restaurants and sidewalks filling the air. We were still followed everywhere by hordes of children, begging, stealing and selling. Only in the cafés would we find sanctuary, as we sat drinking mint tea overlooking the main square, where at the end of the day fire-eaters, jugglers, snake-charmers, storytellers and dancers congregate, creating an expressive cacophony of sensual enchantment. At other times we would explore the souks and the palaces, soaking up the atmosphere and the smells of exotic spices, sweets and cooking. I have to say that the nightlife was very disappointing as there is only so much couscous you can eat, and only so much pseudo-Bedouin folk dancing you can take – especially when the jaded performers are bored senseless, giggling and gossiping while going through the motions for the camera-clicking tourists. Oh well, nothing's perfect, and it was wonderful to be away from England and all the problems I knew I would soon have to face up to.

I fell in love with Morocco for a while, and whenever life was getting me down I would jump on a plane, dragging anyone and everyone with me to share in my love affair with it. Strangely enough, many of them didn't buy into my romantic vision – especially when the bus broke down in the hot afternoon sun in the desert on the way to Marrakesh, or we were robbed by knife-wielding boys, or else the food had everyone groaning and rushing for the toilet. You see, wherever I go, if I have a wonderful, life-enriching experience somewhere, I will keep going back, attemping to recreate that experience again and again. But of course it's never the same. It's like a slot machine: the returns are diminishing every time you play.

I once suggested 'Why don't we go to Morocco?' while sat at home with Huw Feather, feeling bored. Huw agreed, and we both packed within half an hour. We caught a flight to Casablanca two hours later, stayed the night, and took breakfast the next morning. But then we – or should I say I? – decided that we could be having a better time somewhere else. So we flew on to Tangiers, where we met Huw's girlfriend, Liz, and Jane, whom I'd invited and who had caught different flights. Having checked into the city's most expensive hotel, we ate – and noticed outside that it had begun to rain. What could we do? We checked out, went to the airport, and caught a flight to Marrakesh. Breakfast in Casablanca, tea in Tangiers, supper in Marrakesh. Always looking for that elusive better time that was to be had somewhere else, rarely finding happiness where I was. Whims were acted on at any opportunity – unless first class on the flights was full, or the best suites in a hotel were not available; then the whim would pass. My credit card was taking a hammering, and my accountant despaired as the bills came in and the coffers began to empty.

May 1984

Flights	£76,000
Hotels	£24,000
Restaurants	£11,465
Miscellaneous [no guessing what this is]	£19,000
Clothes	£2,908

Electricity/gas and telephone
– disconnected through non-payment

However, my love affair with Morocco was one day to end quite suddenly. I'd decided to drop half a tab of acid and take a walk from the hotel to explore the surrounding area. Not a good move. Within no time I was hopelessly lost and tripping on acid somewhere in Marrakesh.

Spotting a couple of soldiers, I decided to ask them for directions. At first they seemed extremely friendly, eager to help a foreigner in distress, and led me off in what seemed to be the direction of the hotel. Then, after we had been walking quite a while and it was beginning to get dark, I became a little concerned. We came to a waste ground, a little way from the street, where their friendly manner suddenly changed. They pushed me to the ground. I tried to call for help, but no one was around. I was afraid that they were going to kill me, or worse.

The acid was making me feel totally disorientated. As I lay there, helpless, I also became aware of dark shadows darting around me. The place was alive with rats! I loathe rats even more than journalists, and was frightened less of the soldiers than of the rats. I thought to myself, 'This is where it's going to end – on a waste ground in Marrakesh, beaten to death and eaten by rats.' I imagined the headlines. Oh God, what would my mother think of the headlines? The sky turned orange and the sound of the shouting soldiers echoed around my head as I hallucinated. All I kept thinking was what my mother would think of the headlines, and that if they killed me it would be quite a glamorous way to go – like Pasolini.

The soldiers made me empty my pockets, and I handed over my money. One of them then noticed my camera in my top pocket, and snatched it. Then the soldiers began to argue among themselves – heated voices raised in anger. I couldn't decide if they were arguing about the camera or about how they should kill me. As they began to push each other, I backed away, then turned and ran as fast as I could, my heart in my mouth, threatening to choke me. I ran and ran, turning back only when I reached a busy street, relieved to see they weren't chasing me. Suddenly I recognized the road, and ran all the way back to the hotel. When I got there Jane was sipping a cocktail, waiting, worried where I had got to. I told her about my lucky escape and that I wanted to go home and never return to Morocco ever again. The magic had well and truly worn off.

*

Jane and I took another trip later in 1984 – to Barcelona, at the invitation of the top Spanish concert promoter Pino Sagliaco. I'd met Pino the previous year, when he had wanted to promote the Soft Cell Spanish tour. He now wanted me to meet and work with a talented Spanish singer and musician he was managing, called Manolo García. Pino described him as Spain's answer to Matt Johnson of The The. I was intrigued. And I was thrilled to be returning, all expenses paid, to the Catalan capital that I had so fallen in love with. This time Pino promised to show us more of the city – especially the famous nightlife.

He took Jane and me to the bizarre drag cabarets and the traditional bars, outside of which sat the most garish prostitutes of all ages, fanning themselves while sat on small stools, cat-calling to customers. Bordellos were everywhere – whole streets were lined with neon-lit brothels. My favourite place became the notorious Baghdad club, where live sex cabarets and magic acts were performed. The shows featured many post- and pre-op transsexuals, a flamboyant homosexual Spanish comedian in sequins and thick white make-up, mutilated dwarfs, a black-and-white sex display, a rodeo porn queen called Vanessa, who rode upon a mechanical horse on which was strapped an enormous plastic phallus, and a weightlifter who lifted weights via hooks attached through his nipples and penis. The decor was wall-to-wall mirror tiles and red velvet flock, and the atmosphere was more kitsch than depraved or sexual. The velvet seats were only a few feet from the stage, allowing everyone a close-up view of the action, and the stage revolved to ensure that every angle could be observed closely. The sex displays took place to an over-amplified soundtrack of music and sexual moaning.

I visited the Baghdad club many times over the years – it was always a top choice when I wanted friends or journalists to sample the Barcelona nightlife. On one such visit Vanessa pulled me up on stage and insisted I ride behind her on the mechanical horse while she lovingly bounced up and down on a rubber appendage. I put my arms around her waist, but she insisted I hold on to her breasts – which were hard, perfectly round plastic implants. On a separate occasion I will never forget an embarrassed Annie Hogan being dragged across the stage on a go-cart attached to a hook on the end of the weightlifter's penis. On that same night another performer invited Jane to insert a knife through holes in his arms. Jane nervously inserted the knife incorrectly, and blood spurted all over her dress, leaving him bleeding profusely.

As Pino escorted Jane and me through the downtown nightlife of Barcelona, he introduced us to many interesting people – among them the acclaimed film-maker Pedro Almodovar, who became one of my favourite film directors. I wished I spoke better Spanish.

The night before I was to meet Manolo – the reason for the visit – I sat in my room and scribbled down ideas on subjects that I wanted to write songs about with him. I had had one idea for a song earlier in the year while watching a television programme about Andalusian farm boys who dream of bullfighting and sneak into the fields at night to look into the eyes of the bulls to glimpse their destiny. Loosely translated, this is called 'caping by moonlight'. Inspired by this, I now jotted down lyrics for a song. The next day the strangest of coincidences happened. I met Manolo, and we sat down and tried to communicate with each other, neither speaking the other's language very well. With Pino's help, he did, however, manage to convey his idea of a song that he wanted me to sing. The song was called '*Cara Cara*' ('Face to Face'), and to my amazement it was about a young Andalusian boy who had gone into the fields at night to face the bulls. As Manolo was from Andalusia, I guessed that his idea was based on personal experience. I was stunned. Did this have some spiritual significance? I explained to Manolo my idea, and Pino translated the lyrics that I showed them. Manolo was equally surprised.

'When did you have this idea?' Pino translated to me.

'Last night,' I said. 'It came to me in a dream.'

I decided to go with Manolo's song – after all, it was something he knew far more about than I, and when his Spanish lyrics were translated they were beautiful poetry. Manolo in fact had the whole song planned, and the players booked for the recording – a collection of the finest Spanish musicians, including a highly respected flamenco guitar player. In the end there was really no room for collaboration – but, hey, what the hell! I am not as egotistical as all that, and if someone has a better idea I'll happily go with it. At the end of the day, my voice is my trademark, and that is often enough – some people would say more than enough. We had no plans about what to do with the song, and it was never clear if Manolo wanted to give it to me or if it was for him to record himself.

Jane and I took the overnight boat to Ibiza, where we were to record the song in a beautiful studio up in the hills overlooking the sea. Manolo laid down the backing track and I sang, attempting my best Spanish intonation, though at times he grew a little impatient with me for not sounding authentically guttural. There is often a harsh, throaty quality to Spanish voices, due partly to the accent – a sound similar to that resulting from sixty cigarettes a day for twenty years – and my voice was just a little smooth to sound convincingly Spanish (although at this time I chain-smoked). I was pleased with the result, however, and it is without doubt a beautiful song. Unfortunately neither of us quite knew what to do with it, as it didn't fit in with my album ideas nor his; it ended up being relegated to a B-side on one of my singles. But there were also complex contractual complications, and I'm sure Stevo's tough negotiations probably had much to do with the track not being used at the time.

*

Back in England, bursting with inspiration, I began to think seriously about recording a new album. I felt it was important to do something soon – the music business has a very short memory, and I feared that unless I made a record promptly I'd be forgotten. The only problem was that I still wasn't entirely sure what kind of album to make. As usual, my head was going off in all kinds of directions. I'd collected ideas for lyrics in Los Angeles, New York, Tijuana and Morocco, and by now there was no shortage of material. I just wasn't sure what the music should sound like. I wanted it to be big, glamorous, trashy, orchestral, acoustic, Broadway-musical, pop, underground and electro. In fact I wasn't sure what I wanted, so it ended up having elements of all those things but not enough of anything – it ended up too diverse, and not fully realized. Too hurried, too multifarious, too much. It would have benefited from more preparation time – and, of course, from the involvement of different people.

I loved the idea of the whole record being like a musical journey, with elements drawing on the inspiration of Bernstein's *West Side Story*. It wouldn't tell a story as such, it would be abstract; but all the songs would sound like they were part of an overall narrative or theme – an ode to trash and filth carrying on from where *This Last Night in Sodom* left off. I like to imagine most of my albums in this way, as soundtracks to an imaginary film or show, and when I write I think in visual terms. I suspect that's why there is an inherent theatricality in the structure of the songs. It stems from years of watching and collecting musical films and soundtracks, and of avidly seeing as much theatre as possible.

I love musicals – especially the ones where the characters inexplicably burst into song for no or little reason. I shy away from full-scale operas. I find the whole idea of the musical surreal and bizarre. Many people have often asked me why I don't write a musical or appear in one. On occasions I have been asked to, and one day I might, but so far none has felt quite right. In fact I've always wanted to write a musical based on my favourite book, *À Rebours* (*Against Nature*).

I had a title for my album – *Vermin in Ermine* – and the cover I envisaged would depict me as the Prince of the Garbage Heap. I'd obviously got my priorities right – I had a title and a cover long before deciding how the music would sound. I also knew the producer I wanted to work with. Mike Hedges. He had worked with many of the more original and interesting bands of the late seventies and early eighties – Siouxsie and the Banshees, the Cure and the Associates – all pioneers of glamorous Gothic twisted pop, and all with unconventional singers. I loved the sound of Mike's records, which was a mixture of dark experimentation and pop, combined with a twist of psychedelia and Phil Spector reverb. I adored the way the vocal was treated with the utmost respect – a jewel in a shimmering setting.

I went to visit Mike at a session he was doing for the Banshees' *Hyena* album at the Roundhouse Studios in Camden Town. I immediately liked the portly, red-headed producer, who seemed to have a mischievous (if boastful) sense of humour. For me, being able to take time out from the seriousness of making a record to laugh and have fun was becoming a priority. Making an album can be frustrating, tiring and emotional at the best of times, but overall it must be a joyful experience.

Mike showed me a brochure of a very luxurious studio set in the countryside of Bavaria, Germany, surrounded by pine forests and green fields, twenty miles from the nearest village. To Mike this seemed like heaven, but to me it seemed like the worst sort of hell. I am strictly a city person, and my music is rooted in urban themes – I have always found the countryside to be a creepy, depressing place. I have to be in a city, to soak up the life, the vibrancy – I need to be somewhere loud, fast, polluted. But Mike insisted, as producers do, that this was where he wanted to work, and since I wanted to work with him it left me no choice. I grimaced and gave way. Besides, I should be more positive: this would be a new experience – all that space, all that fresh air, all that rich Bavarian food. I didn't do a good job of convincing myself. I kept thinking we could have recorded anywhere – Rio, New York, the south of France. But Bavaria?

Haartman Digital Studios was an expensive state-of-the-art recording studio with live-in arrangements for the performers. We would have to fly the whole band over, even though Mike said he could bring in the cream of German musicians. This worried me – I had a fear of the album sounding like session musicians' work, and as I wanted a Latin feel to some tracks I couldn't imagine where German musicians could be of use. I could see huge expenses ahead – not to mention being cooped up with bored band members who at the best of times could act like small children.

I might add that I have found this to be a trait of many musicians, their development having been arrested in teenage years by seizing every opportunity to drink, take drugs and act irresponsibly in a business that rarely discourages immature behaviour. I know this because I was one such musician. Musicians are temperamental, and constantly need their egos cosseting. When you are the star (me) and your name is on the product (Marc Almond), and your voice and personality are selling the record, perhaps then you are entitled to stamp your foot a little. For God's sake, if the star can't be a diva now and then (so long as you balance it out by being a wonderful, kind and benevolent human being), who can? On the other hand, if you are a hired musician, paid to do a job, then you have no right to behave badly at all. I have also come to learn that the lesser the talent, the greater the sulk, the sickening temperament and the fragile ego. A professional comes in smiling, plays brilliantly, and gives you heart and creativity too. All right, he plays brilliantly – at least.

I could see that Mike had an extravagant side, just like me, and that he could be a big kid like me. In many ways Mike was just the right producer for me. But in other ways he wouldn't necessarily be the best producer to curb my excesses, either musical or personal.

On arriving at the Haartman studio after landing at an airport in the middle of nowhere on a freezing cold German night, and a long, winding drive through little villages and pitch-dark countryside, my worst fears were realized. I could not fault the studio – it was excellent – and our hosts couldn't have been more pleasant in making us welcome. But it was in the middle of nowhere. Really in the middle of nowhere.

The surrounding countryside was beautiful, but I didn't care. Though I like Germany and have had wonderful times in Berlin and Hamburg, there was something about this part of Germany that I didn't like. Bavaria gave me the creeps. As we drove through those quaint villages, I was imagining those little red and black flags – you know, the ones with the funny black crosses. I could see people turn as our car passed, old locals looking disapprovingly at us with that expression that I imagined said 'If only the Führer were alive.'

The house attached to the studio was comfortable in a pragmatic, sparse, German sort of way. There was a kitchen, a communal room and video lounge and a games room; the bedrooms were simple, and had those annoying blinds that let in all the sunlight at six in the morning, followed by a cacophony of birdsong, crowing cockerels and other intrusive natural sounds. For someone who likes to sleep in a darkened cold room until at least nine or ten this was torture. There seemed to be no escape from anyone either, unless you took a brisk walk to . . . well, nowhere really!

I hated it the moment we arrived, but I put on my professional face and thought of my fabulous new album, and kept telling myself how lucky I was. There were plenty of others to do my moaning for me. The boredom had started.

As the boredom quickly spread, it resulted in niggling, quarrelling, bitching, bickering and childish practical jokes. Actually, Mike was often an instigator of these pranks, and he loved nothing more than to wind everyone up – often to the point of tears. He thought that if he made them angry enough it might produce a great performance during the recording – which is an odd theory, I know. It never worked. With Annie and Billy it usually ended in tantrums and tears, despairing at Mike's attitude. I have to say that I actually loved all this and encouraged Mike at every opportunity. The more people sulked, the more it brought out Mike's and my sadistic nature. Mike thought, as I did, that no one had any excuse to be bored, that all spare time should be spent rehearsing and perfecting the songs. He thought that certain members of the group were spoilt and lazy.

Mike gave the young drummer Steve Humphries a particularly hard time. Steve was a little inexperienced, especially in timekeeping. He had been brought in by Annie and Billy to replace Zeke Manyika, the drummer from Orange Juice, who had played on our earlier sessions back in London. Zeke had other commitments and couldn't come to Germany. Steve had been hired for his youth and enthusiasm, and I was prepared to forgive a lot. He was a nice, easygoing young man with no ego problems, and grateful for the opportunity. It's fair to say that he improved immeasurably with time, always putting 100 per cent of himself into the playing. But at one point Mike wanted to send him home and replace him with someone more experienced. In fact, with the exception of Martin McCarrick, the talented and humorous cello player and multi-instrumentalist, Mike wanted to send everyone home. He eventually drafted in percussionist Martin Ditchum to spice up the erratic-sounding rhythm tracks and to hold the timing together. I worked with Martin many times over the years, and his professionalism was always a pleasure, adding class to any track. In one take he could make a ropy rhythm track sound brilliant.

When not in the producer's chair, Mike loved to take us out for excursions to the local supermarket, half an hour's drive away, where we would stock up on rich German yoghurts, cheeses and salami. It was no wonder everyone put on weight. Mike also loved to stock up with toys to amuse everyone – his favourite being a giant water pistol, with which he would mercilessly hound everyone. On one occasion we spotted some frilly pink and blue party frocks hanging on a rack. Mike bet us that we wouldn't spend an entire day wearing these dresses. Martin, Billy and I bought one each and walked around the studio in them for days, as if it was the most natural thing in the world. People visiting the studio were greeted by hairy-legged young men squeezed into girly little dresses. We tried to shock the locals whenever possible. Yes, it really was that boring.

Unfortunately I discovered German lager and the lethal schnapps, and once or twice ended up under the mixing-desk vomiting. With alcohol, as with drugs, I couldn't say 'Enough' until I was unable to take any more, and even then I'd have a damn good try. I had a constant hangover. The strong alcohol mixed badly with the Valium and the sleeping pills I was downing, the joints I was smoking and the cocaine I was still snorting. So much for the healthy Bavarian environment!

On one drinking evening we ended up in the studio having a jam session, playing obscene versions of Frankie Goes to Hollywood's 'Relax' and Culture Club's 'Karma Chameleon' – me lying on the floor to do the vocals, a bottle of alcohol in one hand and a joint in the other. Mike secretly taped this embarrassing debacle, and often joked that unless the record company paid him the money he asked for he would release it as a bootleg. (At least I hoped he was joking.)

During recording, my friend Jane Rollink telephoned me with the sad news that Wayne, the gentle and sensitive friend of Stuart, the heroin addict who had worked at Some Bizarre, had committed suicide. He had gone to the White Cliffs of Dover and thrown himself off. Jane was devastated, and I felt a terrible sadness at this news. At the time, I was working on the song 'You Have', and it became a song for Wayne. In a despairing line in the middle section, I sing, 'I'm wishing I was with you on the other side, / Maybe tomorrow I may join you in Paradise'. Like many of my songs, there is a subtext of death and mortality, and it seemed so relevant to Wayne; when it came to sing it I found it very difficult not to cry.

*

Eventually the album was completed, but I wasn't quite sure whether I was pleased with it or not. I could see that it was flawed, some of the songs not sounding fully realized, rushed out, tarted up. There were some good songs, like 'You Have' and 'Tenderness is a Weakness', but other tracks, like 'Shining Sinners' and 'Solo Adultos', were too long and repetitive. There was a lot I liked about the album, however: it had something of the glamorous trashiness that I'd wanted, and Mike had made my voice sound better than ever before. I thought I was finally starting to sound like the singer I wanted to be.

I had, of course, recorded too many songs – as usual. One track, an epic ten-minute blues song called 'Grey Veil of September', was heavily orchestrated but ended up on the shelf at an early stage. Other songs, such as 'Always' and 'Stories of Johnny', were put on one side for the future, which in retrospect was a mistake. They should have been on the album, just as 'Joey Demento' should have been – a song written in Morocco and inspired by William Burroughs's *The Wild Boys*, in which Marrakesh urchin gangs run wild in the city. It became a firm favourite.

'Shining Sinners' was the opening track of the album, and set the scene. I wrote it after being on the Lower East Side in New York one day and straying into the wrong neighbourhood. I was feeling very self-conscious, because I had a lot of money on me. (Usually I never displayed what streetwise people call the 'V' (for victim) and if threatened I acted a little crazy – which wasn't hard.) Suddenly I was surrounded by a Chicano gang who just stood watching me. I tried to act streetwise, even though my knees were knocking and my legs were like jelly. I reached the other end of the street safely and heaved a sigh of relief. The gang had probably been more amused than anything else. I imagined a more colourful scenario of me having to confront a gang such as the 'Warriors' from the film of the same name.

The other set piece, 'Solo Adultos', was written after reading about a murderer who was going across America killing young kids and Mexican orphans sold into slavery from child brothels. It is sung through the eyes of the owner of a 'chicken ranch' (a child brothel) where the madame practises *santeria*, Afro-Cuban voodoo magic, and prays to Chango, the god of fire and thunder. I remember that on the Soft Cell tour in Los Angeles I had watched a group of very young hustlers being rounded up on Santa Monica Boulevard by club-wielding cops and had thought about their vulnerability – and of how many of Los Angeles's rich and famous, even stars, had employed their services. 'Solo Adultos' was about the sickness in our society – especially in Los Angeles, in America. It is what makes America so horrible and yet compelling – the coexistence of your most wild and wonderful imaginings and your most fearsome nightmares.

'Tenderness is a Weakness' was inspired by the dramatic Latin ballads I'd seen drag queens perform at places like L'Esquilita, but, instead of the usual theme of allowing love into your life, I reversed the scenario. 'Love hurts, / Love makes me vulnerable, / Love stay away.'

'Crime Sublime' had an exotic Turkish flavour. 'The Boy Who Came Back' was a windswept tale, almost country in style, of longing and rediscovery, and was the perfect single for the album. I was, after all, the boy who came back.

'Uglyhead' was a cruel song about rejection, adolescent torment and loneliness. 'Hell was a City' and 'Pink Shack Blues' had a Tijuana-inspired trashiness, and 'Gutterhearts' was a glam-rock anthem to like-minded souls – one for the fans.

'You Have' is my favourite track on the album. Its middle section is pure rainswept Marc Almond imaginings.

There is no doubt that the album would have benefited from a more diverse set of musicians and a more inspirational recording environment, but at least it had given me a starting point – somewhere to progress from and a collection of songs to go out and perform live. I was yearning to get back to the stage for an adulation fix.

I debuted the Willing Sinners at a concert in London's Royal Festival Hall, and managed to lower the tone of the place suitably, dressed in a pink-sequinned jacket and a black-sequinned shirt made for the occasion by Liz Pugh. The set, lit by purple and pink street lamps, was designed by Huw Feather. It felt good to be back. And, to top it all, the reviews were extremely positive.

'The evening turned out to be a privileged peep into Marc's surprisingly fresh revamped cabaret. Despite his slight change of direction he is still the strumpet of misery, filth, grime, crime, loneliness and love, and this is just yet another angle to his divine ABC of immorality,' wrote Hasi Howell in *Record Mirror*.

'Marc Almond displays a wildman of pop tendency to regard the combined pop styles of the past fifty years as a well from which to draw water and put funny coloured dyes into. The material is held together by a voice that roves wildly up and down the scale like a dying Liza Minnelli,' wrote David Quanlick in the *NME*. And Rose Rouse in *Sounds* added, 'Thank goodness for little boys like Marc Almond – the world wouldn't be the same without his wicked and weird little ways.'

The evening was unfortunately marred by a group of heavyweight security, who thought that their job entailed beating and pushing the enthusiastic fans who rushed to the front of the stage.

I was relieved that I'd received such a warm and encouraging reception to the new material. But that was in London. On the subsequent tour of England reaction was mostly enthusiastic, though occasionally somewhat muted. When no Soft Cell songs were forthcoming the reception felt disappointing. I must admit it was hard work – some might even say a little foolhardy – going out and expecting an audience instantly to take to over an hour of new material. I didn't even perform Mamba songs. A few bars of 'Say Hello, Wave Goodbye' or even 'Black Heart' wouldn't have really hurt me, and would have rewarded the audience for their patience. But I was as determined as ever to do it my way, and in one city it really paid off. Nothing prepared me for the reception I received in Glasgow, which was nothing short of a returning-heroes riot. At times the stage and the hall merged together as bodies overflowed over the edge and sweat dripped from the ceiling. A review in *Sounds* went:

He is camp but lecherous in the extreme, the only performer currently capable of being Jacques Brel, Scott Walker, Eartha Kitt and Liberace rolled into one feeble, feasible and lovable human being. [I blush as I reread this.] His concern for the audience is rather touching as one after another is rescued from the compressed throng. He alleviates the problem by waiting or rearranging the set with slower songs such as 'Tenderness is a Weakness', 'Love for Sale' or 'Always', so the rakes and wenches show their appreciation by trying to tear his clothes off. Women are virtually climbing over each other to get to him.

We ended the tour at the Hammersmith Palais – the venue where I'd said goodbye. We opened the show with a mounting and accelerating seven-minute version of Tim Rose's 'Morning Dew', and the crowd went wild as if reacting to an old favourite. 'He is the Jim Reeves of the lost and lonely bedsit generation,' said Barry McIlheny in *Melody Maker*, adding:

> The Billy Butlin of pop in that he and Mr Happiness have given so much pleasure to thousands, nay millions through the sure-fire formula of giving us very special thrills to brighten up our increasingly desperate and monotonous lives. And like our camping hero he does it with style, a touch of lunacy, occasional extremism, warmth and not a little bit of what can only be described as pure genius.

So there you have it. I was back.

But, you surely ask, what about the doubters, the critics, the jealous hacks? Surely someone said something bad? Well, maybe they did. But this is my autobiography, and if I want to bask in a moment of glory then I will. There will be other times for self-flagellation.

The album was also received very warmly, though I'd braced myself for chilly reviews. The couple of weeks when an album is released are always stressful, what with interviews, promotion and reviews in the major music press. Your artistry and life are taken apart and regurgitated, everyone expressing their opinion about you, what worth or value you have, where you are now and where you might be going. Past crimes – real or alleged – are dragged up and held aloft, and peculiarities are pointed out and ridiculed. You are meat for the delectation of the starving and cynical readership, who love to see an artist trashed because it makes for juicy reading. You think, 'Am I going to get away with it for another year or so, or am I going to be consigned to the bin? Will I be found out?' My doubts and self-loathing had returned to plague me again. There is nothing more depressing than when bad, cruel or mean album reviews hit the street and you are tossed aside and dismissed – often with no way to answer back.

Of course, if you are me then you begin again to write hysterical missives to the hack concerned. 'Can't wait until you're back on the dole queue, where you'll surely end up', etc. But, as I should have learned, this is not always the most advisable course of action. I never learned. It's best just to seethe in private and plan for greater success – which we all know is top-notch revenge.

As you're trotted out to do the rounds of soul-searching interviews again, you try to justify your work and your whole reason for being with all kinds of pretentious quasi-mystical twaddle. When it comes to twaddle, I should have got a degree with honours – looking back at some past press pieces, I have ejaculated several precious pieces of grade-A tripe. But read most interviews with rock and pop stars and you'll see such tripe again and again. The writer asks the question he or she has asked before, to receive the answer he or she has heard before, which of course is the answer he or she wants to hear. The performer knows that, so he or she tries to elaborate on it, adding a flourish or sneer. Oh God, *you* try answering the same question with the same answer but in a different way each time! So you take the easy road and resort to a put-down of a fellow performer or an outrageous statement just to guarantee a headline or a quote in bold print. The writer wants good copy and the artist wants helpful copy, and usually it's at the expense of the truth. Truth rarely if ever has anything to do with it – pop has seldom been about truth. It is about what's cool, what's current, what looks good, what sounds good, what moves, excites, stimulates – all of which are so subjective that if truth gets told then it's only on the by and by.

Pop paints in broad brushstrokes, especially when attempting to be sincere, sad or sensitive.

Pop is about fantasy, and that rarely involves truth. The PR and marketing people hone this fantasy, collude with the media, filter, soft-focus and airbrush out the ugly truth. Pop is the result of groups of middle-aged people sitting around a table every Monday to figure out how they can sell their product to a trusting public. That isn't to say the product isn't heartfelt or soulful, or about real, serious or relevant issues, nor that it wasn't created with serious intent. But none of that is relevant at that stage to the record company. What they are dealing with is reduced to *product* or *unit*. In all probability the only time an artist or group is stripped of all the nonsense of the music business is when they are alone on stage, without a barrage of lights, dancers, special effects; then perhaps the truth can be revealed. Perhaps only then. The rest of the time they are party to the manipulation of marketing. So once again was I.

As I said, the album was received well. Chris Roberts in *Melody Maker* gave it five stars and said, 'and then there's glitter, Garland, garlands, grace, grime, graphics, gore, Gore, Gomorrah, gold, red and black go for it. And be grateful that in 1984 records can still be made by a real man who doesn't eat shit but probably would if it would wind you up. Marc the punk!'

Adrian Thrills, in his review headlined 'The Slime is Stirred Again', was also enthusiastic, if a little more critical:

> Certainly the lyrical obsessions lie with sexual and social depravity and sin and a questioning of conventional morality, at the end of the affair no great conclusions are drawn – Marc's garbled lyrical kerb crawling aside it works well on a purely musical level. Since Soft Cell the boy has been no slack in surrounding himself with a coterie of inventive competent musicians – an ever changing clan who imbue his songs with a brisk drive and resonant depth which has resulted here in some of his most immediate and accessible pop he has produced since *Non-Stop Erotic Cabaret*.

*

As I toured Britain and Europe with the new album, it was obvious that I'd got a hard core of devoted fans, even if the audiences were smaller than at the peak of Soft Cell. There would always be some who were purely Soft Cell fans, who had liked the electronic sound and the combination of Dave and me together. There was a danger that without Dave's solid presence and economical but tough musical sound everything would get a bit too camp and overwrought. With Soft Cell I had always held back the gay sensibility, acknowledging that, as well as half the duo being straight, most of our audience were too; I just liked to let a little bit slip through now and again. But by this time my lyrics were starting to develop more of a homoerotic edge, and that scared some people away – as did the glitter-jacket image and the flamboyant gestures. But I felt that this new direction had more to it.

I knew that to survive, to have any longevity, I had to constantly try to reinvent myself, always expressing a new side of my personality, a different image, while constantly remaining true to myself. (The only artist who I feel has successfully done this time after time after time is Madonna. However different her image, it is always intrinsically Madonna.) Back then I knew I had to be part chameleon, and that meant taking risks with my career. I wanted to see how far I could go. I wanted to take the camp aspect to an extreme, but still retain my fans – a precarious balancing act. It was all part of my attempting to be subversive, and at that time no one was presenting the dark side of camp. It wasn't really something I sat down and planned; it just seemed a very natural way to go.

To me, true camp has an innocent, detached quality, a naturally self-deluded belief. Looking back, I was truly deluded that I was a kind of Judy Garland. When I went to Spain that year to record a television concert special, the press hailed me as the Judy Garland of the Garbage Heap. It was the kind of comment I always choose to believe, because at the time it appealed to my vanity. I was quite unaware of the subtext within it. The irony, of course, was that my life *was* like Judy Garland's – full of pills and alcohol, pain and cravings. I was crying out for love, adoration and attention. I was just like Judy Garland in that I couldn't see the criticism for the praise; I couldn't see the reality for the delusion – and I wouldn't see myself, for I dared not look inward. True camp is part flamboyance, part delusion, part manner and part tragic. In all these ways maybe I was truly camp. It always amazes me when people have referred to bands like Erasure or the Pet Shop Boys as being camp: perhaps they are far too contrived, too knowing, to be camp. A glittering leotard on a grown man, or an over-the-top disco cover version is not camp: it might be invested with camp qualities, such as a tragic aspect, but it lacks the naive delusion. The former is closer to pantomime, and the latter to cynicism.

*

When my touring came to an end, in Berlin in the Christmas of 1984, Mike Hedges suggested that I join him, his girlfriend Jane, Horst (the owner of the Haartman studio) and his girlfriend on a skiing holiday in Saalbach, Austria. Mike has a way of making things sound enticing and brilliant when in fact the reality is rather different. I'd never been skiing before, and the prospect filled me with trepidation and excitement. After all, I had an excuse to buy a whole new set of clothes – all I had with me was a suitcase full of sequins.

I met Mike at Munich Airport, and as we travelled by car to Saalbach I wondered what the hell I was doing here and why I'd allowed myself to be talked into hurling myself down mountainsides at great speed. I was exhausted from the tour and all I wanted to do was sleep. Why wasn't I at home, looking forward to Christmas dinner?

Because I'd never skied before, I had to start at the ski school, where an instructor would teach me the ropes. I did quite nicely going round and round the little poles on the barely noticeable incline of the novice slope – until, that is, I caught one of my skis in the snow and fell face first down the slope, snow and ice finding their way down my neck and sleeves. That was it. I was sledging from now on.

Actually, I hardly saw Mike, or any of the others. They were accomplished skiers, off on the slopes, and when they eventually came back each day they were so tired that they went straight to bed. I was like the lonesome gooseberry, left on my own and to my own devices – which in Saalbach meant drifting through the fondue cafés. Christmas came with only a hint of a celebration at the hotel – a meagre Christmas dinner which everyone but me felt too exhausted to eat. The situation livened up only when Horst gave us all grams of cocaine each. I spent the next few days filling time until my next line, and trudging up the hill and sledging down, killing time.

Eventually enough was enough. The place was cold, miserable and full of Austrians. I said goodbye to Mike and Jane, and boarded a bus to take a train to take a taxi to a hotel in Salzburg, where I spent the night braving a major blizzard. The next day I managed to get a seat on a plane to London, arriving back on New Year's Eve. I quickly met up with my friend Dillon for a drug- and drink-fuelled celebration. Never had I been so glad to be back home. Being afraid of heights as I am, I can't believe that I ever imagined myself actually skiing. Let's just say that I am not the sporting type.

*

Three singles were released from the *Vermin in Ermine* album, all denting the lower regions of the chart. The first, 'The Boy Who Came Back', did the best of the three; it featured a video by Tim Pope which had me riding on a small horse against a painted backdrop.

The second, 'You Have', also had a video by Tim Pope, which to this day remains one of my favourites, though at the time it caused some controversy. In it I lay naked in the gutter, getting soaked by the rain – an experience which was extremely uncomfortable and left me with a serious bout of flu. However, it wasn't the tasteful nude shot of me that made people uncomfortable and complain: it was the two half-naked mud-smeared urchins playing trumpets while sitting in dustbins. TV stations thought it was unacceptable imagery.

A member of Phonogram's video department took me aside as I erupted into hysteria, trying to explain it to me.

'What the hell is wrong with it?' I shouted. 'It's just in their minds, not mine!'

'Well ... er you've ... always been a ... bit ... well sort of suspect ... Your imagery is ... well ... you know ... and we're sure there's nothing odd about ... well ... er these two boys in your video,' he stuttered and mumbled as I visibly became more and more angered. 'I mean, they're ... only sitting there playing instruments ... but TV shows are TV shows ... They have to be sure ... They have to be certain.'

He tied himself in knots trying not to offend me, but what he was suggesting was offensive. I thought how pathetic his explanation had been, and I felt distinctly uncomfortable the more I thought about it. But it was my image catching up with me again – with just the right dash of prejudice, homophobia and suspicion. I decided that in future I would blatantly use homoerotic imagery just to spite whoever I could, just for the hell of it. This was not a good move.

It was, however, interesting and enlightening to me to see how people perceived me, in so many different ways. And once in a while I found it extremely worrying.

Many years later I was watching game-show presenter Mark Lamarr, on *Never Mind the Buzzcocks* – a TV music quiz show. One of the questions involved a sample of lyrics taken from my song 'Contempt'. 'Who wrote these lyrics?' quizzed Lamarr: ' "You split me wide open and spill all my beans." ' Autocue sniggers. 'Why, Marc Almond of course.' Oooh eer, nudge nudge, cue homophobic innuendo. There were my lyrics, taken out of context and seemingly imbued with new meaning: a meaning that Mark Lamarr felt I had to have intended – anal sex, that thing that makes it so hard (whoops, sorry!) for heterosexual people to come (whoops again!) to terms with homosexuality. I suppose I am an open target for the likes of Mark Lamarr, because much of my work is open to misinterpretation.

The third single from *Vermin in Ermine* was 'Tenderness is a Weakness', and if nothing else I was glad for the opportunity it brought to work with the experimental film-maker Derek Jarman, whom I had asked to direct the video. I had enormous respect for this controversial artist, and had met him on numerous occasions.

Derek wasn't very happy with the situation that Huw Feather was to be involved, as naturally he had his own people he preferred to use, but Huw was now art director on most of the videos I made – to the despair of record companies and most video directors, who wanted to see a change of style, while naturally I wanted continuity. There was a little friction on the day of filming the video. However, we all loved the finished result, and it really is a great video. It is a little theatrical play in a theatre, complete with backdrops, a painted starry sky, street lamps, and Jane Rollink and Liz Pugh dressed and posed as two Romans statues on either side of the stage. Derek particularly loved one complete take where, dressed as a glittering lascivious devil, I performed the song while perched in a dustbin. He wanted to use this entire take for the video, explaining that the performance was so strong and entertaining it needed nothing else. I wasn't so sure. Eventually he decided to use it as his own personal alternative version.

Derek was one of the many talented artists who died of AIDS. He was an uncompromising and unique film-maker, hugely admired and far reaching in his influence. By working with him I was refusing to bend to commercial considerations, and it was obvious as the camp glittering dustbin devil that I wasn't going to get the video shown on *Top of the Pops* or any other mainstream television show that would have helped the single be a hit. The record company, who had enjoyed only moderate success with the album, decided to cut their losses. The writing was on the wall.

I could sense it was all over when I went into Phonogram and people deliberately avoided me, or else were overly kind and convivial. In these situations, when you try to speak to anyone higher up they are always 'at lunch' or 'just gone into a meeting'. All the energy and work is shifted across to another project that might stand a better chance of making money or breaking even. You've had your time; now it's time to move aside. The press department's enthusiasm – such as it was – had now entirely evaporated.

It wasn't long before I heard the news that my contract wasn't being renewed and that Phonogram were not taking up their option for another album. In short, I was dropped. Of course it's never put quite as bluntly as that – 'Passed on you this time, Marc' is the most considered, though equally dismissive, phrase. So it was that Phonogram 'passed' on their option. So it was that I was past.

Phonogram by this time had a substantial back catalogue of Soft Cell material, which had made money, and of the Mambas and Marc Almond, which had not. All those records would be repackaged and rushed out every bloody time I had a hit on another record label. Anyone else's record label – just not theirs.

It was proving quite difficult being a solo artist – especially one as uncompromising as Marc Almond. And especially when he needed a hit before anyone would sit up and take notice. But, what the hell, I was an artist, and I still believed I didn't need anyone's advice.

Yes, it was time for a change.

Except that nothing would change – only the name of the record company.

12

Forever the Same

Actually it didn't seem any time at all before Stevo had found me another deal – this time with Virgin Records. It happened so quickly that for a short while I still thought that I was with Phonogram and once or twice nearly went into the wrong company's offices. No one really bothered to sit and explain to me the ins and outs of the deal, but I knew one thing – it was for a ridiculously large amount of money. All Stevo's deals were. Back then, record companies couldn't resist him.

It was Simon Draper who actually signed me, and our first meetings were full of enthusiasm and positivity. New record contracts always started that way. I would be a new Marc Almond, full of humility and on my best behaviour, brimming with fresh ideas, a new attitude, amiable handshakes, approaching the obligatory dinners with an open mind. But, as the song says, what counts is not how you start but how you finish. Later, when things invariably went pear-shaped, I would whip away my mask of congeniality and – lo and behold – that old devil would pop out to say hello. Then it definitely became wave goodbye.

At first I did actually believe that I could change. I did want to get things right, make amends, have a successful record – if only to make everyone else happy. Life would be so much easier with a bit of success – and, besides, restaurateurs would then give me a better, if not the best, seat. Oh yes, it was all going to be so different this time – with the same band, the same record producer and a handful of tracks left over from the last session of *Vermin in Ermine*. So much for my idea of a new start.

Stevo reiterated what he had said before: 'Do another album with Mike Hedges as producer by all means, but work with other musicians, move on, use this chance to start afresh.' Once again I knew he was right, but my sense of guilt and loyalty still made me feel an obligation to the musicians I'd been working with for the last year. The stage show had developed, and I'd begun to have a rapport on stage with Annie Hogan and Richard Riley, the versatile guitarist. The audience seemed to enjoy having a band with a feeling of camaraderie, rather than just a group of faceless session musicians. It would take me a while to realize that it was me that people paid to see – as Stevo said, 'they don't really care who's playing the instruments behind you. They want *your* voice, *your* personality, *your* songs.' Many years later I would have the confidence to see that he was right.

Stevo loathed Annie, and the feeling was mutual. She even took to phoning the office with tirades of abuse and screaming. 'Why should I put up with it?' he asked me. 'I'm your manager, here to look after your interests,' he would tell me. He tried to make things as difficult as possible for the others by paying their invoices later, if at all. But they just got on the phone to me and in turn gave me a hard time. This went round and round for years, and drove me to despair. I hated myself for being so weak and insecure. But I didn't feel the band members had to be loyal to me: they could walk out at any time to find a better situation – and one that could pay them more money. Besides, if I was to replace them, who would I get instead? Another set of musicians who would want paying on time too! I hoped that one or two of them would just go away and save me the guilt of saying goodbye.

*

Once again I decided to take a holiday before starting to record a new album. Anita Sarko invited me to join her for the carnival in Brazil. It was February 1985. I felt tired and run-down, but I wanted this holiday so much, even though there was a great deal of travelling from place to place, with a series of long flights. We planned to go into the Amazon jungle and journey up the river – something which I'd always dreamed of doing. But by the time we arrived in Rio I felt totally exhausted and just wanted to sleep. I had no energy, and it was a struggle to show any enthusiasm for anything.

We checked into a little hotel, and were warned always to be pleasant to the chambermaids and never to leave hair in the hairbrushes. Brazilian macumba or voodoo is a strong belief and practised by a large percentage of the population. Voodoo is always something that fascinates me. I believe that it is something powerful and mysterious that shouldn't be messed with. My Brazilian housekeeper, Henrique, has a resolute belief in macumba, and all over my apartment he has placed statues of macumba spirits with offerings of candles, food and money to ward off evil and to protect me. Bless him! A psychic friend of Henrique told me that he could see a powerful demon standing behind me who wants to harm me, but over my head there is a cloud on which sits a protective god. I love this image of walking around all day with a god above my head watching over me.

We saw evidence of voodoo everywhere around Rio – white lilies and candles strewn across the Copacabana beach as some kind of love spell, and wax heads burning at the side of the road. It seemed, though, that the demon at my back was doing his best to get at me. I decided to take a swim in the sea, but before I realized it I found myself hundreds of yards from shore, pulled out on the undercurrent. A lifeguard had to leap in and retrieve me. We were the centre of attention on the beach for that incident – and for being so pale. All the beautiful brown bodies stood and pointed and loudly laughed at our pasty white physiques.

I began to feel more and more ill as the days went by, only able to take a short walk every now and then, drained of energy and feeling spaced out, nauseous and withdrawn – hardly a suitable holiday companion for Anita. The day before we were due to take a plane up-country and into the jungle, I knew it was time to make a decision. I found out that on the same day there was a plane back to London, and it was the last one with a spare seat for days. I was so ill I knew I had to return home – I didn't want to risk being in the middle of nowhere and becoming even more ill. I broke the news to Anita, feeling like the guiltiest person in the world. But of course she understood, being the friend she is, though I could sense she felt let down and disappointed. If it had been any other woman than Anita I would have been extremely concerned at leaving her alone in a country like Brazil; but I knew that she was self-sufficient, determined and strong, and used to taking herself off alone to exotic locations at far ends of the globe. I spent the ten-hour flight back to London sweating and shivering. I thought I was going to die – especially when I discovered the seat was in Economy – but I had made the right decision. Anita forgave me for deserting her, and sent me a postcard saying how she had taken an Ecstasy and gone swimming with piranhas in the Amazon river. I felt as jealous as hell.

Back in London, I moved into a small mews house off Portobello Road, thinking it to be a hideaway from the world. I was horrified when Virgin Records bought the entire block opposite. I felt as though I was living in the record company itself. I just couldn't find anywhere to feel settled.

Matters weren't helped when I returned home one Saturday afternoon from a shopping trip with Huw to discover the front door ajar. The lock had been forced. Tentatively we went in, and were immediately threatened by two youths brandishing my decorative

African spears at us. 'Don't run, don't call for help,' they warned, obviously nervous and agitated after being disturbed in mid-robbery. I turned and ran out of the door and towards the end of the mews and the busy Saturday market around the corner, where I intended to get help. But the youths caught up and overpowered me, and then one tried to stab me with the spear (fortunately I was wearing a tough leather jacket) while the other pushed me to the ground. Then they ran off around the corner and into the crowd. I was more angry than anything else. The house was in a mess, and the situation went from bad to worse when the police arrived and began to dust everything for prints. I kept thinking what they might find – like all the drug stashes.

The following week I was in New York when I received a worried phone call from Huw. The burglars had returned to the house, in mid-afternoon, and brazenly kicked in the door. They had removed the television, the video player and anything else they could get their hands on. Huw had arrived back probably only minutes after they had left. For that I was thankful. Who knows what might have happened if we had been in the house, and Huw was not exactly the type to fare well in such a situation. I then had grilles and iron bars put up at the windows and doors, but it inevitably felt like they were to keep me in as much as to keep anyone out.

*

An interesting offer came into the Some Bizarre office early that year which stood out from all the other offers (which invariably would be answered with a 'thanks but no thanks'). The singer Jimmy Somerville and his group Bronski Beat asked if I was willing to duet with Jimmy on a cover version of the Donna Summer hit 'I Feel Love'. Jimmy had said before that I was one of his favourite singers and that Bronski Beat were influenced by Soft Cell, even down to using Mike Thorne as their current producer. They'd had a couple of major hits with the songs 'Smalltown Boy' and 'Why', and were openly gay – especially Jimmy, who voiced his political and sexual opinions at every opportunity.

I have a great deal of respect for Jimmy and his views, even though they differ greatly from mine. But I knew that doing the song would have both pluses and minuses. It would, for me, be certainly the gayest statement I had ever made – more than I felt comfortable with – and might be seen as some sort of 'outing'. I wasn't sure whether I wanted that, or if I could handle it. I was coming up against prejudice already, and was looking for a closet to climb back into, not out of. But it was the 'in your face' aspect that ultimately drew me in – it would be outrageous, brave, and a response to a thoughtless statement that Donna Summer had made about AIDS and God. Oh yes, and it was bound to be a massive hit. Stevo brought that fact home to me again and again. 'You've gotta do this Marc,' he said. 'You need a hit badly – if only to show Phonogram they were wrong and to instil some confidence into Virgin.'

So I agreed to do it. I thought about how I could both be involved but somehow be distanced from it at the same time – basically so I wouldn't come across as quite as 'out' as Jimmy. There was also another point that made me feel uneasy: the duet meant having to work with Mike Thorne again, and I wasn't entirely sure how to feel about him because I didn't know how he felt about me. Actually, I needn't have worried about working with Mike. He isn't a person who harbours a grudge; in fact it was pleasant to see him again, as he was as easygoing as ever.

The backing track, however, was recorded in too low a key for me. It gave Jimmy the chance to sing in his usual falsetto style, and I was going to contrast this by giving a deeper performance – but it was almost too low for me to give any performance at all. I was handed the lyrics, and gave them all the passion I could muster – which wasn't that much, actually. It was only much later that I found out the lyrics were wrong. I was singing 'Oooh, what'll it be, what'll it be, you and me?' when in fact I should have been singing 'Falling free, Falling free, Falling free', which is a much better lyric altogether and would have been easier to sing. Even though the original was one of my favourite records of all time, I had never actually listened to the lyrics before.

The song was interestingly segued into another favourite of mine, 'Johnny Remember Me'. I was a big fan of Joe Meek, the innovative producer from the sixties who had shot himself. He had written the track, which in the sixties had been a hit for John Leyton. This middle section gave Jimmy and me the chance to trade vocals, though Jimmy won that battle, his distinctive voice cutting through much more than mine. But, what the hell – I put on my professional face, smiled and did the job. Only afterwards did I spend sleepless nights worrying that it wasn't good enough, whether it was the right thing to have done, what would my mother's amateur-dramatic group think?

We filmed a video for the track in which each member of the band had a love fantasy with his ideal man. I balked at this, and insisted that I just perform the song with Jimmy. No touching either! After-wards a bullfighter twirling his cape was inserted into the video, and

I assume he was meant to be my fantasy. I cringed. The video is really terrible. I haven't a clue what it's about, and nor do I care any longer.

We performed the song on *Top of the Pops*, me singing uncomfortably while Jimmy camped it up, wanting full-on arms around each other to make a truly 'gay statement'. I tried to pretend I wasn't there, as I saw what I had left of my image going down the pan. Of course the record became a hit, reaching number three in the charts, and was to give my career the boost Stevo informed me it so desperately needed. I was grateful to Jimmy and the guys for that.

However, things weren't plain sailing. It was during this period that Jimmy decided to split from Bronski Beat – in fact just as we all set out to do the Montreux Music Festival together in Switzerland. The atmosphere was extremely uncomfortable, and I found myself caught between two camps – so to speak. To make the situation worse, the organizers, as usual on these European meat-market pop shows, treated everyone with indifference or contempt, never allowing rehearsals or full sound checks. I remember looking out of my hotel window in the early crisp morning, across the picturesque lake at the snow-covered peaks, and thinking, 'I hate fucking Switzerland!' When Jimmy left the band officially a short time later, the newspapers announced that I was to replace him in Bronski Beat. I couldn't think of a worse fate.

As it turned out, I ended up having a public feud with Jimmy that was as childish as they come. A journalist likened it to the Divine Feud – the one between Bette Davis and Joan Crawford. I wondered which one I might be. It all began, as these things do, through a so-called best friend telling you what your best friends don't tell you. Jimmy had allegedly said that 'Marc Almond doesn't do anything for the gay community, he's just a closet case.' Which was fair comment, but I couldn't leave it at that. Not then I couldn't. I responded in an interview, 'Jimmy Somerville doesn't think I do anything for the gay community. Well I would like to do something for it – strangle him.' After that it was handbags at fifty paces, and Jimmy seemed to be bad-mouthing me whenever he was given the opportunity. Of course I'm pleased to say that he and I are now on friendly terms again, and we even performed 'I Feel Love' one more time together – years later at the Love Ball, an AIDS charity event in Vienna. On that occasion I think we both really enjoyed ourselves: there's nothing like a charity event for going over the top and being as outrageous as you want – it's beyond criticism, you see.

*

So it all began again – my first album for Virgin Records in London, with Mike Hedges producing again and the same band line-up as before (you know, the people I spent half the last chapter complaining about). And, guess what? We finished the album once again at Haartman Digital Studios in Bavaria – that obscure, desolate backwater of a fascist stronghold I swore never to go back to in the last chapter. And, guess what? Relationships became strained again, with everyone restless and bored, bored and restless, and Mike and I trying to alleviate our boredom with the same old routines and wind-ups. Oh God, haven't I written this chapter? No. This is a new chapter – and a new Marc Almond, with a new record company and luckily, I'm told, another chance for me.

Let me give an example of how bored we were. Mike Hedges felt like sushi, but of course there are no restaurants in Bavaria other than hog rotisseries. So what did we do? We flew back to London for the night to go to our favourite sushi restaurant, and the next morning we flew back to Bavaria. It took four plane journeys, and probably ended up being one of the most expensive sushi meals ever. But when you have to have sushi you just have to. No wonder the band were getting pissed off. But I distinctly remember paying for the sushi soirée, just as I remember Mike inviting me to Maxim's one night. After washing down the meal with champagne and top-quality brandy, the meal came to £500. Strangely enough, even though it had been Mike's invite, I think I ended up paying – and I'll never know how he managed it. That was one of the great things about him.

It was my twenty-eighth birthday during the Haartman sessions, and Mike decided it would be amusing to invite the cream of Nuremberg's gay club society to the studio for a sauna party. You know when something is just not a good idea, but straight people think you'll really like it? When a gaggle of effeminate German queens turned up, we spent the entire evening on one side of the room and they on the other. One took a particular shine to Billy, who was terrified.

'C'mon then,' shouted Mike who thought the whole scenario was hilarious. 'Last one in the sauna is a sissy!'

Mike blames me for introducing him and Jane, his girlfriend, to the drug Ecstasy. I'd found a regular supplier in London – a young American guy who made fortnightly trips to New York. As far as I knew, he was the only one selling it at that time, to a select group of people. I always made sure that I had plenty for myself and my friends. I gave some to Mike and Jane at the Haartman studio and to the percussionist Martin Ditchum, who then disappeared for the rest of the evening. Mike and I heard him later making the strangest noises, which sounded like howling; the next day he was as normal as ever. So Mike liked Ecstasy. In fact he couldn't get enough of it.

Ecstasy was still relatively unknown in England, and still unclassified. In fact it was during the sessions for the album that I read a newspaper article about it – the first I'd ever seen. The piece talked about a new drug that had begun to appear in London clubs, and said the government were thinking of making it Class A. They said its dangers were unknown, and that it was a drug originally used as early as the fifties in trials between couples displaying violence, anger or an inability to communicate – it had made them open up, talk to each other, and even love each other, for a short while at least. What was wrong with that, I thought? But what better reason is there for banning something than that people have fun taking it? After all, fun is a dangerous thing. I gave almost everyone in the studio an Ecstasy, and work ground to a halt as everyone loved each other again, for a short while at least. That was something that made me feel very uncomfortable. Maybe drugs were a bad thing after all! Steve Humphries just sat at his drums and drummed a hypnotic beat in time to a strobe light for over two hours. I was conducting my own guinea-pig experiments.

On returning to England Mike went and bought thirty Ecstasy and locked himself in his flat for a week with Jane. She ended up believing she was being sucked into a vortex in the kitchen ceiling, while Mike collapsed on the floor through a pleasure overdose. He told me many years later it was the beginning of a downward spiral for him and that I was squarely to blame. I told him that in rehab you learn to blame no one but yourself. And, besides, look at Mike now. He's one of the country's most sought-after and acclaimed producers.

*

The *Stories of Johnny* album I regard as my 'behaving myself' album, far safer and more subtly sophisticated than *Vermin in Ermine*. I was in a dilemma – caught between being the me everyone wanted me to be (meaning more successful) and the me I wanted to be, darker and edgier (meaning less commercial). Actually, I wanted to be both. I wanted the acceptance and the success, yet at the same time to be less mainstream. I ended up somewhere in the middle ground – which occasionally meant I had an element of both, but more often than not meant I ended up with neither. Even the cover of the album depicted a cleaner, make-up-free (well almost) Marc Almond sat in white shirt alongside a stuffed hornbill which actually looked like a caricature of me. I never entirely understood the photo I chose for the cover, but then I never entirely understood many things then.

Vocally, though, I sounded the best I ever had, and the songs had a glistening sheen of production like never before. There was more of a romantic element within the lyrics, the songs dealing with the search for love and the feelings of love itself, the sleaze and tales of the gutter temporarily put to one side. This was because I had at that time met someone who would become a very special part of my life and my one true soulmate, someone who was to play a major part in my life from now on, but who requested that he not appear by name in this book – a desire I feel I must respect. This makes it all very difficult for you, the reader, for this person appears in many of the subsequent pages of the book and features in many of the future stories and scenarios but will not be referred to by name. Nor is this person's role to be taken lightly, for it was he who restored and maintained the balance in my life that was lacking, and inspired me to go on when times were at the lowest.

In many ways, *Stories of Johnny* was a direct progression from *Vermin in Ermine*. A couple of songs, 'Always' and the title track, had been written and recorded for the earlier album but somehow seemed too tender for that paean to the gutter.

'Love Letter' was a rather self-conscious and clumsy attempt to write an Abba-style pop song, but has about it a certain poignancy. 'I Who Never' is a song about losing love and looking for it again out in the streets. 'Contempt' is about love gone sour – perhaps love turning to hate and exorcizing past demons.

'My Candle Burns' is based on a poem by Edna St Vincent Millay, and is perhaps the most appropriate summary of my life then:

> My candle burns at both ends;
> It will not last the night;
> But ah, my foes, and oh, my friends –
> It gives a lovely light!

The confessional passion of 'Love and Little White Lies' is self-explanatory. 'Traumas, Traumas, Traumas' is a fight, a dramatic argument between two lovers; on the track the vocal is slowed down to create a Scott Walker feel – that Valium effect. 'This House is Haunted (By the Echo of Your Last Goodbye)' was one of my favourite songs, a torch song once covered by the great Mel Tormé.

Andy Catlin shot the cover photo, as well as the inner pictures of me lying in the arms of a statue of an angel inside St Paul's Cathedral – reflective and beautifully shot pictures.

The reviews for the album reflected that this was possibly a happier, more mellow, Marc Almond, who was emerging from his darkest days. Nancy Culp in *Record Mirror* wrote:

> The single 'Stories of Johnny' was merely a taster to prepare the way for a fuller yet softer sound. The rasping bitterness that made so much of his earlier work so difficult to live with has subsided somewhere along the line, the warmer more mellow side of Marc Almond has at long last been fully allowed to come out from under the covers.
>
> I guess you know the score by now – luscious, pouting Marc Almond avidly exposing his nightmares to the world while gutter-hearts swoon, record companies curse and mere mortals try to make sense of it all. Well, playmates, I have news for you, Marc may have been to Hell but he's back. No more valley of death, no more inner turmoil, no more suicide Sam, no more lovesick blues. 'The hour is darkest just before dawn,' he writes on the sleeve and apart from being a line from a Mamas and Papas hit it seems pretty fair appraisal of his approach to this album. If *Vermin in Ermine* was the dark then this is the dawn.

It seemed to all as if this was the emergence of an acceptable Marc, a contented Marc, a mature Marc. But you know better by now. It was all just a smokescreen for what was really going on. Instead of a dawn from a dark age, it was the dawn to a darker age. It wasn't the end of the beginning, it was the beginning of the end. Despite every positive thing in my life – my record deal, my new relationship, homes, money in the bank, a career and freedom – I just couldn't find it within myself to be happy. In interviews I would say, 'I'm happy – of course I'm happy. Never been happier, I now know what happiness is. Sure, yes, I'm happy.' But I knew the lady did protest too much. I thought if I kept telling everyone how happy I was then I might convince myself that I was, that I would be, or even that I might be. But I never really felt that I could be.

So why wasn't I happy? Because the self-doubt, self-loathing and lack of self-worth still remained, clinging like rust. I always believed I could never be the artist I wanted to be; however many good reviews there were, I would always focus on the negative. The bad reviews would be the ones I would take to heart, the ones I always thought were right, and they fuelled my insecurity and lack of confidence. If I was called a 'pop' artist I hated it; I wanted to be underground. If I was unsuccessful, I wanted to be the pop star again. But there was something far worse, and it had to do with fame and the nature of fame. All the time I was getting older, becoming an old pop star, yesterday's favourite. I couldn't understand then that trying to compete on the same level is not necessary. I never understood how to change as an artist or how to mature with my audience. I couldn't understand that perhaps my pop-star days were over, and that I had to accept where I was and who I had become. I looked out of the barred windows of my house and constantly felt imprisoned, trapped by my life as this famous person who was still recognizable but was not moving on – not evolving as a mature artist should.

So there I sat, in my expensive home, surrounded by the trappings of success and wealth. Bored and boring. Sat at home, day after day after day. Taking line after line of cocaine until it was time to go to bed. Then I'd take one final line, follow it down with Halcion and Valium, try to sleep, wake, get up, begin again. And that would be my life for almost a year. The dealer would arrive at the same time, knock on the door: 'I've got a bit of rock for you today' or 'You'll thank me for this, you will – pure Peruvian flake.' Two or three grams a day. Every day.

If I could get myself together, I would go down to the nightclub Heaven and buy a bottle of Dom Perignon, which I would drink myself, staggering about the club swinging the bottle wildly. Usually I had to be escorted out by the understanding doorman and put into a taxi.

I was lost, and I was unhappy. But I'm not searching for sympathy, because, for all that, I have to agree with Burt Reynolds, who said, 'I've been poor and miserable and I've been rich and miserable, and rich and miserable is better.'

'Stories of Johnny' was released as a single and entered the Top Thirty. Everything looked promising until I made a disastrous television appearance, coked up, and coaxed on by the record company. Somebody had the bright idea that I should appear on Terry Wogan's early-evening show singing 'Stories of Johnny', but with a different twist to it. An alternative version of the song was recorded, and I had to sing with a school choir of thirty children, a twelve-year-old alto taking the lead with me. Now bear in mind that the song was a tale of heroin addiction (I'd written it one evening after watching a documentary about boys on housing estates 'chasing the dragon'). The lyric 'My smoky lover will close my eyes for ever' refers to his escape in death. I cannot plead entire innocence in this matter, since Mike and I had already thought of using a chorister's voice on a version of the record, to add an ethereal quality. But this was the Wogan show, and the record company said they wanted the choral version as they felt that children accompanying my performance would appeal to the teatime family audience. There was just one snag: right in the middle of this choir of scrubbed, angelic children was going to be me – Marc Almond. I tried to look as sincere as I could, but the irony of the occasion wasn't entirely lost on me as I sat on a stool singing, surrounded by thirty boys in school uniform. I had to stop myself from laughing during filming. Julie Burchill wrote in her column that she thought it was the most outrageous piece of camp she had seen on television.

The public must have felt equally uncomfortable with it, and responded by not buying the record which plummeted out of the chart. So much for that brilliant idea! The subsequent singles made a dent in the chart, but, despite the exceptional videos directed by the ex-Throbbing Gristle member Peter Christopherson, were not really successful. The album followed, as did a tour.

The receptions and the reviews of the tour were fine, but my heart was not in it. Once more I felt as I had so many years earlier: that I was just going through the motions. What on the record had sounded textured and almost orchestral in parts was now beginning to sound live like (horror of horrors!) rock music – right down to each musician having their own solo, which if nothing else gave me a chance to have a cup of tea. I just couldn't take the touring seriously as Richard, the guitarist, went into solo after solo. It was my own fault. I was allowing everyone to indulge themselves, just as I was indulging myself in the worst rock 'n' roll excesses. At least on tour you could always get good drugs – the roadies and crew always have the best suppliers.

*

I knew what it was time to do. It was time for a rethink. So what did I do? I did what I always did, and ran away – first to New York. A new club had opened on Fourteenth Street. The Palladium was the latest high-tech temple to hedonism, owned by the infamous Steve Rubell of Studio 54 fame. A vast space inside a cavernous old theatre, it had different levels and rooms for dancing and excess. Anita Sarko had been made hostess of her own room – 'The Mike Todd Room'. Swagged with drapes and hung with glittering chandeliers, it was the VIP lounge for the glitterati, the famous, the freaks and the wannabes, and it was there that I hung out each night, not quite sure which category I fitted into – maybe all of them.

In my coke and Ecstasy haze, I found myself sharing different tables each night with the rich, the famous and the downright pretentious. One night it would be Andy Warhol who sat with me, reading comics, pretending he was oblivious to the constant parade of coke-addled celebrities who flitted around him. Another night it might be the eleven-year-old Drew Barrymore, who barked at her long-suffering family that she was a star, that she called the shots, and that no one would tell her what to take or drink, or what she should or shouldn't do. Often she exited in a hurry, and the family would gather themselves up and follow her like a line of ducklings.

Anita stood behind the decks spinning an eclectic selection of eighties electro, old soul and bizarre kitsch – fending off anyone who bothered her for requests with a sharp retort. I remember that once a furious Prince (long before he was the artist formerly known as) marched up to Anita's turntable and knocked the needle across the record. It was a Rick James record, and Prince hated it – or maybe he just thought he might be caught out as to just where his inspiration came from. But Anita took it all in her stride – she was like a den mother, and all the naughty celebrities were her wayward children.

For one of her pyjama nights in the Mike Todd Room I bought a sheer black baby-doll outfit, complete with red sequinned nipple pasties and jockstrap, and wore it with my new Mohican haircut and Doc Marten boots. I was photoed nestling my head into the ample bosom of Diane Brill, with the inevitable press headline 'What a Pair!' What a pair indeed! What I was on or what I was doing that night I cannot even imagine. My companion in New York at this time was a young punk guy who was known as Spring – my constant companion at the time, now a longtime friend, and incidentally the wayward son of a famous Conservative MP. An occasional film star and chronic heroin junkie, he consumed more drugs than anyone I knew, and spent most of those Palladium nights laid under the table.

When I became bored with New York, I would spend my time ensconced in the Hotel Colón in Barcelona, opposite the beautiful Cathedral Square. The first time I arrived at the hotel I was greeted by a scene that made me think I'd walked into a Hollywood film set. A man lay bleeding to death in the hotel foyer. He had been shot. A crying woman cradled his head as he lay dying, and other silent figures milled around, all splattered with blood. Camera bulbs flashed, but no one spoke. I walked straight into the scene and looked around for a movie film crew or cameras, but of course there were none. This was real. The staff tried their best to remain calm as I checked in, and never did explain to me exactly what had happened.

Barcelona became my city for a while, and it provided the perfect setting for writing lyrics and poems, for planning a new album which I wanted to take in a new direction, away from what was becoming dangerously rock 'n' roll. I wanted to get back to the essence of

Jacques Brel, Edith Piaf and *chansons* – something that I felt was truer to my heart. Barcelona, with its networks of narrow dark streets, its little cabaret bars, its brothels and its sense of danger, provided an apt atmosphere.

In the daytime I lay naked on the beach at Barcelonetta or swam in the crumbling white art-deco outdoor pool at San Sebastian, which was always deserted but for a handful of transvestites and gigolos, who danced the flamenco to tunes from old transistors. Sometimes the transvestites who worked the ice-cream kiosks brought out a microphone and karaoke machine and performed a cabaret show while I soaked up the sun. There I felt free; few people knew me, and I could do what I wanted because no one cared. However, I avoided the nude beach after one particular incident when I opened my eyes and found a group of Spanish fans proffering albums to sign and taking photos. I'd been spotted by someone, and word had spread that I often went there in the afernoon to swim and sunbathe. On that occasion I didn't quite know where to put myself. And the swimming in the sea ceased for me when I developed a terrible fungal rash all over my body. The doctor told me it was caused by the waste that was pumped out from a chemical plant along the coast.

At night Barcelona was a magic place – a place made for drug-taking. Among the bars with charming names like Bar Darling and Bar La Concha was a little absinthe bar called Bar Marsella. It was tucked away in the Barriochino, near the Chinese area, and was said to be the only remaining bar openly selling absinthe. It was full of the strangest old characters, who had no doubt lived through so many changes – revolution, war, a second revolution, Franco and now the post-dictatorship era. Many seemed to have partaken of too much absinthe themselves, their eyes wild, chatting and chattering, dancing to music that no longer played.

I asked for a glass of the greenish-yellow liquid, which was served to me in a small tumbler, with a spoon laid across the top and a sugar lump balanced on the bridge. A drop of water poured on to the sugar allowed it to dissolve and drip into the absinthe, creating clouds and shapes within it, stirring the goddess from her sleep in the liquor. The taste was not unlike pastis, though much woodier – the worm-wood, the mind-altering poison contained in it, yielding a bitter undertaste. It took effect quickly. A second glass and the lighting became muted, the sound blurred, colours iridescent, shimmering and glowing, dancing in the night air. It made me want to laugh and dance and walk fearlessly through the dangerous streets. Barcelona and absinthe. Goth and Gaudí. I drank a third glass, and the world turned upside down, under water, phosphorescent fish swimming around my head, air bubbles in my ears. Then I was lost.

But nothing on earth prepares you for the day after. My stomach cramped and my head pounded. I felt sweaty and sick, and close to death. For the whole day my stomach lining felt sore and swollen, and my appetite had gone. But you know me by now. This didn't stop me from returning for more, and even taking bottles of it back to England. It just had to be done – all part of the preparation for my new album. Anyway, I had already learned that for every pleasure there had to be pain, for otherwise how would we measure the intensity of each?

Barcelona was not without other dramas, for above all it was a dangerous city then. One evening, accompanied by a friend, I found myself in the most dangerous street of all, called San Ramon. It was full of drug dealers, pimps and the roughest prostitutes imaginable. We were trying to buy drugs – hash, I think. When one particular dealer quoted too high a price we moved away. But too late. He began to harass us, pulling out a knife. As he was getting increasingly threatening, we walked away, not daring to turn back. Just as he was closing on us with several of his colleagues, we reached the end of the street, hailed a taxi and climbed in. As it pulled away he was upon it and banging on the window, shouting at the driver to let him have us. Another man ran in front of the taxi and forced it to stop. We suspected this might be the end. Now a group of dealers and prostitutes were banging on the glass and shouting. But the driver was having none of it. Regardless of who was in the way, he kept driving and we escaped. We stayed away from the area for a while, for we had no desire to meet that dealer again, ever. Next time we might not be so lucky.

Another time I was surrounded by a gang of Spanish skinheads while leaving a club one evening. Two of them pulled my legs from under me, and I fell to the floor. I thought, 'This is it, Marc. This is where you make the headlines.' These gangs were notorious for beating up and stabbing foreigners. I was actually thankful that earlier I had taken an Ecstasy and was very relaxed about the whole situation. One of them put his foot on my neck, and then I realized what they wanted. (Stop right there – don't even entertain the thought.) They wanted my prized new Doc Marten boots, which they removed and disappeared with into the night. I spent the rest of the night barefoot. I've read many contact ads placed by people who would have paid good money to find themselves under the boots of a skinhead gang. It takes all sorts.

Drugs made me behave recklessly and stupidly on countless occasions. One New Year's Eve a couple of friends accompanied me to Barcelona from London, a supply of Ecstasy in my suitcase. When I arrived at the airport and stood at the luggage carousel, my case never appeared. The airline said there had been some sort of security problem with the case and I was to return the next day to pick it up. I spent all that night in a state of hysterical paranoia. What if the suitcase had been searched and the drugs found, and they wanted me to identify the relevant case so they could arrest me? Then a worse thought occurred to me: what if we had to celebrate New Year's Eve with no Ecstasy? The following day a message arrived at the hotel – our suitcase had arrived at the airport and they wanted me to collect it. Surely it was a trick. What if they were waiting to pounce when I got there? I was getting increasingly panicky. We were acting as if the suitcase was stuffed with bags of cocaine, not a dozen Ecstasy. Then I had an inspired idea. I sent the unsuspecting hotel concierge to pick it up. But then we waited in fear that he would explain the situation and bring the police back to arrest us all. Then the knock on the door came and we all jumped out of our skin. The concierge handed us the case, and there inside, imaginatively tucked into the lining, were the Ecstasy, intact. I was overjoyed that they were still there. We all agreed 'never again' again.

Back in London, my cocaine and Ecstasy intake worsened. I lost so much weight I resembled a nose on a stick, and with my skinhead haircut I looked emaciated and permanently ill. My skinny tattooed arms poked out of a black vest, and my legs, clad in tight black jeans, resembled sticks of liquorice, ending in ungainly, large Doc Martens. A strange look, and not a good one for the fans to copy – but copy it they did, with alarming results.

*

I was by this time sick and tired. I was sick of everything. Sick of my career, sick of my life, sick of being sick. Still, I had money, and I wasn't sick of spending it. At least that made me feel something – though what I don't know. But even that slight euphoria didn't last – primarily because I had everything I needed. What excitement was there in buying another outfit or piece of furniture? It was in this state that, while walking down Park Lane one day, I noticed a car showroom. In the window was a brand-new, gleaming black Merce-des 500 SEC coupé. So I went in and bought it. Its main attraction was that it had a telephone in it, and – get this – in the boot a fridge, for chilling champagne I suppose. I just had to have it, so I wrote out a cheque there and then. But there was one catch – I couldn't drive. So I gave the car to a friend, who promised to drive me around. Ronnie Harris, my accountant, despaired and nearly quit when he discovered the bill. But I must say it was great to be driven around, and we got two years' use out of the car – even driving all over Europe. Eventually, though, we grew tired of being pulled up by police officers suspicious of two scruffy people in such an expensive car; then they would recognize me – 'Oh sorry, Mr Almond, we didn't realize it was you. By the way, we love "Tainted Love".' If only they'd bothered to look in the glove compartment, which was always stuffed with drugs! After two years we traded the car in for a Range Rover, but that was really boring so we traded it for a TVR. When that promptly fell to pieces, I swapped it for 100 Ecstasy tablets. Talk about diminishing returns!

Despite all this, the remainder of 1985 through to 1986 was probably one of my most prolific years artistically. I was bursting with songs and ideas, which sent Some Bizarre and Virgin crazy with the endless recording invoices submitted. I decided to record a mini-album of cover versions, and went into the studio with Mike Hedges again.

The resulting album was an odd collection of songs ranging from Procol Harum's 'Salty Dog' to Johnny Ray's 'The Little White Cloud That Cried', with a nod to Lee Hazlewood, Eartha Kitt, Scott Walker and Peter Hammill on the way. Given the cringe-making title *Some Songs to Take to the Tomb Volume One* (letting everyone know that more could be on the way), the album featured Huw Feather's worst sleeve artwork. Musically it seemed rushed and incomplete. Even so, a couple of the tracks sparkle with some of Mike's best production work. I'd intended to record a dozen songs but the project was stopped for going overbudget. A song I desperately wanted to cover was Gene Pitney's 'Something's Gotten Hold of My Heart', but I wasn't allowed to.

A single was released called 'A Woman's Story', which was written by Phil Spector and originally sung by Cher. It's a brilliant song about a woman who sleeps around and through it finds true love as a result. I didn't bother to change the gender but just sang it like it was, which gave it a different and – dare I say it? – gay twist, though that was not my original intention. I thought that, as a singer who tells stories through song, I ought to be able to put myself in the role of the woman, tell it through her eyes. The single was accompanied by a video – one of my favourites – directed by Peter Christopherson. An actress played the part of the promiscuous woman, while a selection of young men (personally screened by Peter and me) undressed for her. Meanwhile I sang the song from a spinning bed.

I was surprised when the single reached number forty-one, as I thought it would have gone higher. Radio play had been good, and reaction favourable. Someone suggested that Virgin were not behind the single; perhaps no one cared, and everyone hated me. At least that was what I was led to believe, and, coked out as I was, it fuelled my paranoia and in turn anger. Then I began to feel that invisible forces were perhaps out to get me. I'd just have another line and then I'd know for sure. Just one more line. One more. Then I believed for sure that everyone *was* out to get me.

*

When studio sessions started for the *Mother Fist* album, I began knocking out songs like they were going out of fashion – I was frantic and insane from my cocaine abuse. Note that I haven't used the word 'addiction', because naturally addicts were other sad people, not me. Definitely not me. No, I could control the drugs.

The songs had a delicate acoustic flavour, and multi-instrumentalist Martin McCarrick became the central musician, with his accordion, cello and strange exotic oriental instrument the *j'ang t'chin* (strings beaten with little sticks) key components in the whole sound. With Nigel Eaton on the hurdy-gurdy and Enrico Tomasso on trumpets and trombone, the album had a warm, folkish bar-room sound – the perfect setting for the lyrics that told stories of hustlers, faded boxers, deluded drag queens, desperate women and masturbation fantasies. If Virgin had thought they could curb my excesses, they were sadly mistaken – I used every hour to record more and more songs.

Annie Hogan wrote some beautiful tunes for the album, such as 'The Room Below', written about the basement flat below a brothel where I used to live back in my Leeds art-college days. The song 'The Hustler' was based on a book by John Henry Mackay about a young male prostitute in Berlin. My favourite track on the album is a hymn to destructive divas and drag queens, the dark 'Saint Judy' – which refers, of course, to the most destructive diva and role model for tormented homosexuals everywhere, Judy Garland. Apart from the songs that actually made the album, there were many extra ones that didn't, instead finding their way on to B-sides and eventually a compilation that Virgin put together called *The Virgin's Tales – Volumes 1 and 2*. Yes, that's how many I recorded.

The track 'Anarcoma' was based on a cartoon character by the

Catalan artist Nazario. Anarcoma is a muscular transvestite who gets into all sorts of adventures with her super-hung robot boyfriend. The track was too long for *Mother Fist*, as was 'Jackal Jackal', about murder in Marrakesh. 'Broken-Hearted and Beautiful' is the story of an older woman's affair with a younger man. All these tracks were intended by me to be part of one album, certainly not split up. This would have meant a double album (remember the last ones?) but both Virgin and Stevo were adamant that it should be a single one. As well as working on all these songs, I also recorded a couple of Brecht/Weill songs that were originally written for women – 'Surabaya Johnny' and 'Pirate Jenny'. To further complicate the whole process, I also began working on several Brel songs, which I intended to develop at a later stage. It was around this time that I sensed Virgin beginning to get very nervous.

All through these sessions I snorted up gram after gram of coke (which I was now buying by the ounce, as I figured that gave much better value for money) while I directed the proceedings like an incoherent Führer, stamping my foot and shouting at frazzled musicians who were trying to get their musical heads round the umpteenth idea of the day. It was the Mambas all over again. But despite it all – or because of it – everybody put a great deal into the material. Looking back on this volume of work, I really feel it is some of my best.

The record was vocalled, finished and mixed at Abbey Road. But I never found the control room overlooking the huge studio used by the Beatles to record *Abbey Road* at all inspiring. So Mike Hedges and I found a shop nearby that sold beautiful antique red velvet and satin cushions and gorgeous embroidered curtains – all of which we hired at enormous expense (courtesy of Virgin) – and with these we decorated the studio like a luxurious opium den, which certainly made things more inspiring.

I was smoking sixty cigarettes a day – lighting one after another – snorting coke, downing Valium and knocking back champagne. I'm now amazed that I did any singing at all. It was a struggle, though, and for many of the songs I had to do take after take after take. On some of the recordings I sound like I'm full of a cold – a 'rock 'n' roll cold' I believe it's called – and my sinuses were screaming for a break. But if I stopped taking the cocaine my nose just bunged up – so it seemed best to keep taking it, just until the album was finished.

I did manage to stop smoking, though. I felt so bronchial that one day I picked up a cigarette and it tasted like hell, so I stopped. I never picked one up again. Then a short time later I did the same with alcohol. I just stopped drinking. I convinced myself that it must be the alcohol that was making me feel so bad of a morning, hung over and foggy – and besides it didn't mix well with the sleeping pills – so I downed one last bottle of Dom Perignon, and from then on never picked up another glass again. That was 1986, and, apart from a couple of minor relapses that lasted no more than a night, I've stuck to my resolve. I was as tired as everyone else of the outrageous behaviour and pathetic tears that always went along with the drink. I'd think, 'Who was that tragic drunk dancing on the table with his trousers round his ankles last night? It was me, wasn't it?' I haven't missed alcohol once, though stopping it had a negative effect in that I increased my drug intake. You see, I always thought that alcohol was my problem, always feared I'd end up an alcoholic like my father. So, naturally, when I managed to kick drinking altogether, hey, I convinced myself that I didn't have a problem, that I could stop anything if I wanted to. Chop out another line of cocaine, would you?

The first single from the album was a track called 'Ruby Red' – an exotic pop track and an ode to all things . . . well, red actually. Blood and rubies and brothel lamps and red velvet – you know the sort of thing. In all honesty I didn't really have a clue what it was about, but the record company told me it was the most commercial track on the album, and it has remained one of my favourite singles. I planned yet another video with Peter Christopherson that was to reinforce old prejudices at TV and radio and put the writing on the wall as far as my contract with Virgin was concerned. 'Ruby Red' was one of the milestone videos in my career, and proved to be a suicidal career move. It stunned and shocked the staff at Virgin, wound everyone else up, and all things considered was not the wisest of moves. But I was so strung out on cocaine that I didn't have any grip on reality. I would do anything if it seemed like a good idea at the time; only later, in the cold light of sobriety, would I see how incredibly foolish it was. I always seemed to be working with producers or video directors who brought out my worse excesses.

So what was the problem with the video of 'Ruby Red'? Where to begin? It featured writhing naked devils, scantily clad dancing sailors, disturbing drag queens, and all kinds of homoerotic nonsense. In one scene a sailor writhes masturbatory style on a bed, revealing his knuckles tattooed with 'Love' and 'Hate'. In another scene a trashy transvestite throws bags of red paint (meant to be blood) at the walls. When I'm not dancing through the song in Lycra cycling shorts and a sailor's hat – slyly revealing my ruby-covered nipples – then I'm dressed as Nosferatu, complete with skullcap, pointed ears and full red eye lenses made especially for me. At the end, individual bodies are indiscernible as they writhe around in a kaleidoscopic orgy. Now you don't have to try too hard to imagine the reaction of the record company (Virgin were banned from the set and editing) to all this. For ever afterwards, whichever record company I was signed to, they always ensured that there was someone present to monitor the filming – to restrict the 'camp quota' and 'kinkiness'.

I had successfully made an expensive video that would not be shown on television anywhere. The record company put their heads in their hands and despaired. Then, after talking openly about the theme of the song being masturbation and blood, I wondered why radio stations had stopped playing it. I complained that Radio 1 was singling me out to be ignored, and in a major interview damned its DJs to hell – which was quite unfair, as they had been very supportive up till then. This was still an extremely conservative period for the media, and there I was being more in your face than ever, sticking up two fingers at the mainstream. But of course I thought it was all part of the conspiracy – you know the one: to condemn me, to attack me, to bury me, or – worse – to just ignore me and hope I would go away. I stormed around the country on a promotional tour refusing to do interviews and only rarely meeting people. I would walk into radio stations, hear Soft Cell playing, and walk straight out again.

When I eventually was coaxed or coerced into interviews, they would ask me, 'So, Marc, your new album, *Mother Fist* – what's the title about?'

'Masturbation.' Silence.

The title *Mother Fist and her Five Daughters* was taken from a story by Truman Capote, but on the mainstream pop shows I ended up sounding pretentious if I talked about that. 'So who's Truman Capote, then? Is he one of the musicians you work with?' enquired a provincial DJ. I just couldn't be bothered to explain. I would just get up and leave.

'Hey, Marc, we haven't taken any callers' questions yet!'

I felt trapped. Caught between a rock and a hard place. I complained to Stevo that I was promoting the album on all the wrong shows, talking to the wrong people, but his attitude was 'Do everything, do anything. What harm can it do?' It did a great deal of harm. The record company would complain to Stevo, and he'd get on the phone to shout at me. The trouble was I was too pop for the underground shows, and not pop enough for the rest. It was soul-destroying.

Only when I finally started to tour again did the weight of it all lift a little. In April 1976 I set off on a tour of Italy, Spain and Germany which, as it turned out, would be one of the most enjoyable tours I had ever undertaken. The new songs seemed to come to life in concert. Martin added dashes of colour with his accordion, and as the tour progressed the songs developed and the audience seemed to react to and love my change of direction. In Italy I was escorted at all times by security who took macho pride in showing me their guns at every opportunity. At the shows, the crowd chanted 'Marco, Marco, Marcello' and lit candles. In Spain too the show was a success, and when I sang 'If You Go Away' many members of the straight male audience cried. The song became a tour de force live. Beautiful girls gave me paintings and jewellery, and I found it all very moving.

The *Mother Fist* tour eventually took me back to Barcelona, the city from which I had gathered so much inspiration for the album, and gave me another chance to sample the night life I had come to love. I returned to my favourite bar, called Kike, located down a narrow alley just off the Rambla. It was always inhabited by a diverse cross-section of people – junkies, artists, dealers, transvestites. There I met Lindsey Kemp, the famous mime artist who had inspired Bowie and later Kate Bush. Lindsey was always to be seen around the bars and the Placa Reial, a beautiful square off which he lived. He was invariably drunk, but now part of the local colour. In Barcelona everyone was drunk.

Dave Kentish, a lovely and dear man, was my security person throughout the tour and for years afterwards. It was during this visit that he himself was mugged. He always insisted on walking around decked in gold-nugget chains and sovereign rings. This was worrying: if my security had been mugged, what hope was there for any of us? Sadly, Dave died a few years ago. He is greatly missed.

In Madrid I headlined a show before 200,000 people. I normally refuse to play festivals, as a certain percentage of the audience is an unknown element, and on this occasion a brick was thrown at the stage, just missing the guitarist. I thought it best to just keep singing. Then when I sang an unaccompanied version of '*Cara Cara*' in Spanish I had the audience in the palm of my hand. After that the only missiles were red roses. As I left the stage the largest firework display illuminated the Madrid sky.

The tour ended in Holland, at the Paradiso in Amsterdam. There, while singing an a cappella version of a song called 'The Lockman' (an intense song, with complicated lyric arrangements), I suddenly went dry. All eyes were on me. My heart pounded, and I was frozen with fear. In front of all those people I had forgotten the song. I tried hard to remember it, but my mind was empty, sweat pouring from my face. I mention this because it was not the first time this had happened – it was beginning to happen again and again with frightening regularity – but because it was by far the worst. I tried to start the song again, and lost it again. It took several attempts before I finally got going.

Nor was it just songs that I was forgetting. Plans, people's names, places, jobs, and more frequently sentences would be left incomplete. I would go into a room to fetch something, and by the time I got there I would have forgotten my purpose. But it was on stage that my memory started to worry me intensely. As I increasingly forgot songs, my foul-ups had to be disguised. This was not too difficult in the up-tempo songs, where the backing singers would assist me, but lapses in the piano numbers were impossible to cover up. On more than one occasion I would have to leave the stage to collect my thoughts. Then the audience would stamp their feet and go crazy. When I eventually plucked up enough confidence and courage to go back out, the applause would ease me on. But I knew what was causing this. I knew that it was the Halcion sleeping tablets. These tablets should not be prescribed for longer than three months, but I was by then in my fourth year of taking them daily.

After the Amsterdam show, after going on for almost forty minutes longer than usual in a bid to make up for the fiasco in the middle, I was exhausted and my voice was strained. Throughout the tour I had been well behaved, not drinking or taking drugs ('Prescription drugs didn't count'), but after the show I was greeted backstage by a familiar Dutch cocaine dealer. I snorted and snorted. The next day my voice was wasted, and I still had a Rotterdam show to perform. I spent the day trying every trick to get my voice back, and managed to just make it through the show, singing as little as possible and cutting the difficult numbers. It was an emotional show, and the end of an era.

Martin McCarrick informed me that day that he was leaving to join Siouxsie and the Banshees. I was bitterly hurt, but also pleased for him. He was a brilliant musician, and I'd known that sooner or later he would move on. I also knew how much of a Banshees fan he was so it was a good opportunity for him. I put on my brave professional face and shook his hand, wishing him well. Afterwards we parted by taking so much cocaine that I ended up crawling along the hotel corridor to my room.

I couldn't sleep and dawn arrived with a grey depression. It was the end of the *Mother Fist* period whether I liked it or not. Future dates had to be turned down until I found a replacement for Martin, or rethought the whole thing afresh. Whereas I could normally rise to such a challenge, this time I felt crushed, caring little about what happened from now on.

What did happen was that I was dropped from the Virgin label.

First, however, they gave me one last shot and sent me off to Barcelona to film videos for the singles 'Melancholy Rose' and 'Mother Fist', allowing me to work with Peter Christopherson again – surprisingly after the 'Ruby Red' video. I suspect Virgin must have decided by then that they were going to drop me; perhaps they thought, 'What the hell – let him do what he wants now.' 'Melancholy Rose' was filmed in Bar Marsella (the absinthe bar) and featured many of its regular patrons and locals dancing and singing. 'Mother Fist' we filmed on a replica of Columbus's ship that was moored in the port. These videos are special to me, not only because they document my Barcelona period but because their settings are no longer there. Bar Marsella has changed, and the Barriochino has been pulled down to make way for a new shopping mall. I guess there just aren't enough Gaps, Body Shops and Tie Racks in the world already. The locals, who survived a revolution and Franco, have been defeated by the tide of mediocrity disguised as progress which threatens to engulf us all. Traditionalism is swept away, as we are told we all need the same things in this new global village; we are all statistics in a mass marketing plan. Francis Ford Coppola once commented that he thought the future would be neither good nor bad, just mediocre.

The Victorian grandeur of San Sebastian was bulldozed for the 1992 Olympic Village, and the family restaurants that had for generations plied their trade went with it. Bar Kike and others like it were closed by the police in case the new wave of tourists took offence at the colourful clientele, who might send out the wrong image of the new Barcelona. Even the replica of Columbus's ship was removed and replaced by a better one, with a fast-food outlet built into the side of it, and surrounded by 'designer' coffee bars. Columbus had discovered America, and now America was staking its claim to Spain. The Baghdad club, Bar Kike, all the tradition and colour, the character and spirit, were cleared away or demolished. The poor were exiled to one of those hinterlands, where such undesirables are sent in times of 'clean-up'. Barcelona is still a beautiful city, but much of why I loved it so intensely has gone. So it is with much of our past – remembered fondly and lost for ever.

*

Back in London, in the real world, I was once again without a record company – punished for not conforming, for making uncommercial records and videos, for committing the ultimate corporate sin: not having a hit.

In addition, I was now beginning to have a new problem, which I hadn't experienced since college. Money. So much money had gone on houses I didn't live in, cars I couldn't drive and people I couldn't stand. How much went on alcohol or tablets washed down with it? How much went up my nose? There's a question! Suddenly, quite out of the blue, there was talk of bankruptcy. I was spared this by selling my New York apartment, which I'd entirely forgotten I had. I'd never lived there; the dream of leaving England and moving to New York never came to fruition. The apartment was sold at an enormous profit, which immediately went towards paying tax.

I tried all I could during this time to give up Valium and sleeping pills, but failed. One day, while walking down Westbourne Grove in London, I suddenly felt incredibly detached and strange. I found myself unable to breathe, and the ground beneath me began to sway and rock. It felt like my feet were unstable, as though there was a mild earthquake. I couldn't stand up. I staggered to a phonebox and cowered inside, suddenly afraid to be in the open, afraid of not being at home, of being so far from where I lived (yet it was only a quarter of a mile away).

During the next hour, through tiny movements and controlled breathing, I made my way back, staggering as though drunk. The short walk seemed to take for ever. Once there, I rushed upstairs and called the doctor. 'I've got to have some Valium now, please, doctor!' I stuttered, sweat breaking out on my forehead.

Hearing my state of panic, the doctor didn't think more Valium was a good idea. He suggested this might be a good opportunity to try to stop. He told me to try to relax and make myself a cup of tea. He knew what was happening to me – I was having a panic attack as a direct result of the years and years of repeat prescriptions he had given me.

'I don't want a cup of fucking tea. I want some fucking Valium right now!'

I screamed until my voice was hoarse. He agreed – 'Just this once.'

I sent a taxi to collect the prescription.

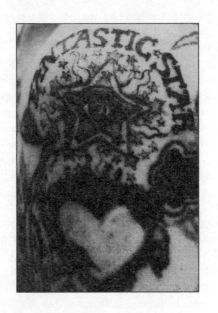

13

Seeing Stars

1988 saw me in my worst state of health. My face was bloated, my skin pale and translucent, and I had perpetual dark shadows under my eyes. I constantly felt tired, run-down and ill. I topped off my anaemic look with a sculpted Elvis-type quiff moulded with thick grease that ran down my face, making it shiny and sweaty. Altogether not a good look. I had been hospitalized for two weeks with appendicitis and the added complication of peritonitis, from which I almost died. I sat in the Cromwell Hospital in London feeling despondent, at an all-time low, and cried daily. In addition to all this, I had had to cancel a lucrative Japanese tour, which made matters worse. My last tour there with the *Stories of Johnny* album had been immensely successful, and I couldn't wait to get back. But, as I had had to cancel the new tour just one week before it was due to start, the Japanese promoters were so angry I suspected they would never ask me again.

The Valium and Halcion I took every night never truly had a chance to wear off the following day, and I was permanently in a state of drowsiness, feeling like I was existing in a fog, with everything distanced and obscure. The previous two years' events blurred into each other. People spoke to me, but I didn't really hear them. In fact the tablets at their present dose had ceased working effectively and, fearful of increasing the dose, I slept a shallow, unsatisfactory sleep that left me exhausted. Such was the vicious circle I was trapped in.

I would have some days that were better than others – even good weeks occasionally – and during those times I would convince myself that there was nothing wrong. Then I began to get all sorts of bizarre and deluded ideas about what songs I should sing or what my next record should sound like, or spend hours deciding what to wear for photo sessions. But I had no record deal, and there were no photo sessions outside my imagination. I lived for the weekends, when I would go out and take Ecstasy and cocaine, and then spend the week trying to recover in time for the next weekend. There was hardly a day when I was completely lucid.

For Stevo, though, it was business as usual. I don't remember how it happened or how long it took exactly, but Stevo phoned me up one day and told me he had done a deal with EMI Records. Subsequently I found myself in a room with a bunch of well-wishing and smiling people, raising glasses of champagne and toasting the future. I signed on the dotted line, bemusedly smirked, and took the cheque. I once again had a strange sense of déjà vu. If my confidence was at an all-time low, Stevo made me feel much better by telling me that I was signed to EMI only because they were so keen on him; I was apparently just the by-product of a deal that enabled the company to work with the legendary Stevo. He told me this so that I would be grateful, thankful and beholden to him for once again having saved me from the scrap heap and obtained me another chance. Naturally this had the opposite effect to what Stevo had anticipated, and simply made me resentful towards him.

The period between Virgin and EMI had been several months, during which Stevo held out for the largest amount of cash he could negotiate. Time on my hands, which meant time to be reckless – day after day filled with cocaine, overdraft-funded shopping sprees and flights around the world, trying hard to escape from myself. All that time I just wanted to be playing live or recording in a studio. If I was working I wasn't spending. The more money I received from a deal, the more miserable and the more under the controlling thumb of the record company I was. Record companies want to see a return on their enormous outlay. I didn't want the massive deals Stevo was negotiating for me, as they just meant more pressure. I really wanted a record-company home, less money but more freedom to make the records I wanted to make. And I wanted to be on tour – forever on tour was my ideal, not having to be in one place, not having to stand still.

But a side of me wanted success too. There lies one of so many paradoxes. I wanted freedom and credibility, and I wanted success and hit records. I'd had the critical success, but that was never enough, and now the big hits seemed to elude me. The singles always made a mark, sometimes in the Top Thirty, occasionally in the Top Twenty, but more often than not reaching number forty-one – a number that was plaguing me. I thought if only I could have a big hit then everyone would leave me alone, and I would also be able to crow at all those people who'd written me off. Crow again. Actually it was surprising how few people had written me off, but this was all part of my increasing paranoia and lack of self-worth.

You remember that conspiracy theory that dogged me – whereby everyone was out to get me, radio and TV had banned me, and critics were out to destroy me? Yes, that conspiracy theory. I remember when this actually began to form in my mind. *Smash Hits* had run an interview by Tom Hibbert about how people seemed to either love me or hate me. The headline ran, 'Do You Hate This Man?' Naturally enough, I had focused on the word 'hate'. Then I got to thinking, 'Do people hate me?' Why? Why didn't they love me? I couldn't see that Tom Hibbert was saying in his piece that people both loved and hated me; I just saw the word 'hate'. Hate. HATE. Then I thought of Gary Bushell's comment 'I can't wait for Marc Almond's suicide attempt'. How many times might I have put his waiting to an end! But, if anything, comments like this made me more determined to keep going; ironically, Gary probably saved my life. However, they also kept the conspiracy theory alive in my head. I sat at home and seethed all day long, listening to chattering voices telling me an assortment of half-truths and fabrications. The fog was thickening.

As I was handed the cheque in the EMI office, my accountant leaned over and snatched it away from me. It was going to pay the tax bills that I just couldn't seem to catch up with. Anything left over would of course have been frittered away in the usual fashion on extravagant trips abroad, clothes, gifts – anything to fill that hole in my life. Clothes I would never wear, records I would never play, books I would never read, art I would never even unpack, and tons and tons of fifties kitsch bric-a-brac that would fill room after room after room. For some bizarre reason I had developed an obsession with collecting lamps – a strange pastime for someone who shuns the light. Kept in boxes, they gathered dust and took up space. Another collecting obsession was stuffed animals and medical rarities, until the whole house was full of freakish Victorian creatures – two-headed calves, deformed lambs, pickled pigs and aardvarks, and even a preserved human baby I called Lionel (dated 1868). This latter collectable disturbed me so much in the end that I gave it away to Peter and Jeff (ex-Pyschic TV members), who appreciated it more than I did. The house became a cluttered, morbid place of death and nostalgia – not unlike Lydia Lunch's apartment that I had visited years earlier. When I grew tired of such things or space ran out, I simply gave them away.

As the weeks passed, my spirits lifted. I became more and more thrilled to be signed to EMI, for it seemed to me like a proper record company, steeped in history. A history of the Beatles and Cliff Richard. Er, well ... the Beatles. I had been signed by Clive Black, the son of Don Black, the respected lyricist of so many great songs – John Barry's among them. Clive is one of my favourite people in the music business, and had a cheeky, roguish charm reminiscent of a child in a sweetshop. He could twist me around his little finger (well, almost).

Tris Penna was my marketing/A & R person, and he was another great individual with whom I got on extremely well, both in friendship and in our working relationship. Tris was a fan before I'd signed to the label, and he had a vision of how he thought things should look, never afraid to say what he believed. He saw me as a serious artist and songwriter with a touch of Sinatra (Frank, not Nancy) and Brel – a classic singer not unlike the ones from the fifties and sixties he admired so much. It was this side of me that Clive and Tris wanted to bring out, and together they would help me make my most successful solo album, *The Stars We Are*.

My last album, *Mother Fist*, though critically acclaimed all over Europe, had not, in record company terms, performed. The general opinion was that it was too gay in its presentation. The sleeve depiction of me as a sad carnival performer was deemed too strange and uncomfortable an image for the public. (Nobody tells you this at the time.) The inner sleeve, with its drawings of sailors, and the 'rent boy in a sailor's cap' pose I had adopted in the photos were considered too camp. Add too much make-up and the over-the-top videos and the result was a festival of homo imagery. To sum it all up, it demeaned the music, I was later told. Too many of the ideas had come from my own deluded mind, and no one had dared contradict. Now, on EMI, Tris was not going to let that happen again. He appreciated the gay sensibility, but knew just how far to take it.

It was Tris who had masterminded the whole Pet Shop Boys campaign. Subtlety was everything. It is not that the public are particularly anti-gay, but there is a limit to what they can stand before it passes the 'uncomfortable' threshold. Most gay artists can't resist the call of camp or kitsch, and often attempt to shock or subvert, but the public don't readily grasp the in-jokes of gay culture. Why would they? Most gay artists need someone to hold them back, to check the reality and say, 'Wait a minute.' Tris Penna was such a person for me. In the past when I was left to my own devices it was a recipe for trouble.

The upside of the *Mother Fist* album was that in Europe I was now considered a serious songwriter/performer and likened to Jacques Brel, Scott Walker and French *chanson* singers – all artists who dealt in the substrata of our society, singing with feeling and with passion for life and love. And many of them also addicts. Piaf was an alcoholic and sex addict, the pain in her life showing through in the songs. Comparisons to Scott Walker, however, I have always felt a need to deny. Journalists describe any crooning voice backed by a string section as sounding like Scott Walker. Obviously they have never really listened to him, or they wouldn't make such flippant remarks, or be so generous with their accolades. I have of course always been a great admirer of Scott, but I have no desire to be like him. I would much rather people say that as a singer I sound like Marc Almond – that I have my own style and sound that is instantly recognizable. When I was asked to write the sleevenotes for a Scott Walker album *Boy Child* I was flattered to do it. I said, 'There is only one Scott Walker, the rest of us can just watch from the sidelines.' It is true that he is one of the greatest and most memorable of singers. But I feel I have earned the right to be my own singer, and to take my own place in the scheme of things, whatever that may be. When I was also asked to write the foreword to Scott Walker's biography I declined. Not through arrogance, or because my opinion of him had altered, but because I felt it was someone else's turn – hopefully from a new generation of artists who could understand Scott's contribution to contemporary music. I was more than flattered when I was told that Scott himself had praised me as a 'great singer' while talking on a radio show. Whether this quote was entirely true I was not able to confirm, but I had it on very good authority, and it is something I would rather believe than not.

*

I don't remember an official start to *The Stars We Are*. There was no preplanning or meetings with producers, no talk of budgets. One day I started doing demos, and the next thing I knew they had evolved into a finished album. I took up residence at the Matrix Studio off Little Russell Street in London's West End. The studio is lovingly dubbed 'The Ashtray', as it's underground, feels damp and dirty, and water pours from the ceiling when it rains. There's a perpetual smell of cigarette smoke and marijuana, as there is no adequate ventilation. While I was working there, the eccentric reggae artist Lee Scratch Perry was often found in the toilet, comatose on the lavatory, a half-smoked gigantic spliff hanging from his mouth. When he came round he would mutter cosmic nonsense to all who would listen. From another studio next door the ear-splitting sounds of producer Adrian Sherwood's latest mixes blasted out across the communal lounge. For two months this would be my home. The equipment was old and constantly breaking down, but despite all this everyone loved the place. A selection of gold discs on its walls testify to the enduring appeal it has had over the years. And hadn't

Marianne Faithfull recorded *Broken English* there. What more could I say?

The engineer on the sessions was a talented young guy called Dave Pine – otherwise known as Deptford Dave – a raving Millwall supporter who kept things going in the darkest moments with his leery sense of humour. But of course the most difficult thing remained – the same old musicians I just couldn't let go of. So too did the political problems between musicians in a band, especially during the long periods of boredom when recording an album. My motto became 'Anything for a quiet life.' Physically I remained weak, tired and run-down. I just wanted to get on with making the album. I wanted at all costs to avoid the fights that constantly threatened to come between Annie Hogan and myself. I just couldn't say no, and I despised myself for it. The tension increased, and so did the turmoil and stress. I should have put my foot down and done what Stevo had suggested years earlier: moved on. With Martin McCarrick gone I felt the heart of the sound had left with him. I should have taken the opportunity to let go. Clive Black was very unhappy that I'd chosen to continue working with Annie and Billy. Nor were EMI amused when both of them shouted down the phone for instant payment. Stevo grudgingly organized a good deal for them, but he was not happy about it. He fought them all the way, and they fought back. Wait a minute, guys, I'm trying to record a hit album here!

It became a nightmare of back-biting and bitching, screaming and complaining. I retreated into my world even further, often just falling asleep on the sofa while the arguments continued. Even though I was producing my own album, one day Annie and Billy quietly took me aside and explained that they felt they should get a production credit. I agreed – anything for a quiet life. Annie, who had formed her own group by this time, called Cactus Rain, suggested the void left by Martin could be filled by her keyboard and accordion player, a young guy called Teddy Edwards, and that her girlfriend should become our back-line roadie. I agreed – anything for a quiet life. Then suddenly I felt like the tail was wagging the dog. I felt like an outsider in my own group, which I had dubbed (somewhat ironically as it turned out) La Magia (Spanish for magic).

Though I was buzzing with ideas of my own, in an attempt to placate Annie and create some musical chemistry I asked her for music that I could write some lyrics to. I would never normally do that – usually I wrote the lyrics first, created the melody and all the ideas of how the song would sound, including the beat, and then sat down with the musicians who would make my vision a reality. The process would be conducted by me until the song sounded the way it had in my head. It would always be understood that it was my song. To work in this way you have to feel totally at ease with a musician, to have an understanding and a rapport. If and when that rapport has gone, it is impossible to feel comfortable and convey your ideas successfully. My lack of confidence generally combined with a lack of formal musical training means that whoever I work with has to be patient.

During the sessions for *The Stars We Are* I would sit down with Annie and try to sing my songs. She would tut and sigh and run her fingers impatiently along the piano keys, appearing to want to be somewhere else. It was no longer enough for her to be Marc Almond's keyboard player any more – though she always welcomed the pay cheques. Trying to involve her, I asked her for one of her tunes that she had played me. She declined at first, explaining that she wanted to keep her best ideas for herself, but I was having none of that and pestered her. She eventually gave me the song, which I adored and which became 'Only the Moment'.

There was also a power struggle developing between Annie and Billy. He was uncomfortable that so many of her friends were now involved in the project, and either he or Annie was forever storming out. Dave, the engineer, didn't know what to do when recording was held up again and again. I thought to myself, 'Hey, I'm the star here. Isn't this my record? Don't I call the shots?' It seemed not.

Eventually even I had had enough of it. When Annie demanded I sack the drummer, Steve Humphries, I put my foot down. Steve was the least trouble of all. 'He's just not good enough. Let's get someone else,' she said. Alarm bells rang – did she have someone in mind? I suspected she did. I wish that I'd known what to do about the situation and had had the nerve to do it. I felt isolated in the music business. I didn't know any other musicians, and Stevo, who would have gladly sacked the band, had no suggestions for replacements. Clive Black just assumed I was happy, because I never told him otherwise. When I thought, 'I must be ruthless, I must do something', I would get to the studio and be racked with guilt and unable to do it. After all, Annie had at one time been such a close friend. I needed her, as I needed Huw Feather, who was still designing for me. I didn't want to lose my friends – after all, I didn't have that many. Best just grit my teeth and keep things the way they are. Anything for a quiet life.

One of the songs I had written for the album was a Gothic torch song called 'Your Kisses Burn'. I'd written it as a duet, and I knew just who I wanted to sing it with. I contacted the German singer Nico through my record company, who had tracked her down to

Manchester. I had been such a fan of the former Velvet Underground singer since my schooldays, having bought all her albums – from the John Cale-produced *Chelsea Girl* and *Marble Index* through to the Brian Eno-produced *The End*, on which she sings the most chilling version of that famous Doors track. I had even bought the album on which she covers Bowie, *Heroes*. She was mysterious and enigmatic, beautiful and shrouded in myth and history. She was also an infamous heroin addict, who had on many occasions threatened to destroy her life. Now she was living a frugal life in Manchester and touring regularly with local musicians. I sent her a tape of the song, and it was an exuberant Nico I spoke to on the phone a short time later when she agreed to sing it. She made her demands – cash, hotel of her choice, and first-class travel for her and the management. She wasn't EMI's first choice for a duet, as I suspect Clive didn't know who she was, but at my insistence they agreed to all her demands. 'She is a legend, and I want her on my album,' I said.

I was extremely nervous about meeting Nico, especially as I'd been warned how difficult she could be. But I wouldn't expect any less from a legend. The woman I met was a complete surprise to me. Not tall, as I had supposed her to be, she came into the studio smiling, extremely pretty, with the aura of a young girl. Of course she had lines on her face, but they were the lines of life – a hard-lived life, a life of heroin and rich excess. But she was still beautiful. Clad in leather trousers and a woollen top, she perched on a stool and lit a cigarette, sucking on it and displaying those famous cheekbones. A spirit of Dietrich in her manner. She was laughing and smiling, tossing back her long auburn hair. I guessed she was playing a little at being the Nico we wanted her to be. She talked to me of Jim Morrison, whom she told me she had loved and a lock of whose hair she kept. Then she showed me a photo of her beautiful son Harry, whom she had conceived with French film heart-throb Alain Delon. She was all I wanted her to be . . . at first.

Then quietly her manager took me aside. 'Just get any vocal you can down and piece it together later,' he said. 'She won't get better with more takes. Just get what you can.' It was good advice.

It was obvious she was nervous and that she hadn't learned the song as she claimed she had. But once in the studio the voice that boomed down the microphone was unmistakable, sending chills down my spine.

We recorded everything we could, but it became a frustrating experience because successive takes were worse and worse. The situation was not helped by a prolonged visit to the bathroom, where she took the heroin substitute methadone. She became more detached and deflated, and then sad. As the afternoon wore on, perhaps I was seeing the real Nico – a desperately unhappy and bitter woman, lost to herself, enclosed in memories and cocooned from reality by addiction. I too began to feel crushed and depressed at witnessing this. It wasn't an easy song by any means, with its strange time changes and unconventional arrangements, and eventually I saw the chance of her singing it fading away altogether. When it became apparent that there was no point continuing, I called a halt. The engineer and I felt we might just have enough vocal recordings to piece it together. A photographer arrived courtesy of EMI to record the event.

'I want to be photographed playing pool,' said Nico. 'It will be something unexpected and different,' she explained. So together we picked up pool cues and posed as though playing a game. Apparently she loves to play it. Nico plays pool? Certainly not how I visualized her! Then, sat together on stools for portrait shots, it was obvious to me how vulnerable she felt about her looks, trying to hide her face with her hair and sucking in her cheeks until her eyes almost popped out. She swayed back and forth from the effects of the methadone, and I tried my best to make her feel comfortable and relaxed. Even then I was amazed at her beauty. Afterwards, the song and the photos out of the way, she relaxed much more and we talked further. She asked me if I would be interested in writing songs for an album she was planning, even suggesting we could write together. I hugged her and thanked her; then she was gone.

Within months she was dead, tragically killed in a cycling accident in Ibiza. After a lifetime of drug abuse, it had been an accident that killed her – such are life's twisted ironies.

I had a chilling moment when months later I was playing the final mix of 'Your Kisses Burn'. The engineer, Dave, had performed miracles with the vocals and it sounded like a great Nico performance. The sound on the TV was turned down, and as I put on the track an ad for the American television series *Nico* flashed up the word 'Nico' on the screen in red. Perhaps it was a good omen, I thought – either that or she was telling me she hated the mix.

I was hurt when a few years later I read a badly researched book on the singer by the writer Dick Witts. He claimed that I had exploited her with a few hundred pounds, and quoted her as saying 'Your Kisses Burn' was 'a horrible song by a horrible person'. Only later did someone who had been close to her explain that this was untrue. Apparently the biographer was not a fan of mine. Nor did he bother to ask for my account of the meeting or the recording. But whether Nico said what he claimed or not is of no relevance now – my meeting with her was special, and for me his quote does not fit with the time I spent with her. If she did say it, then perhaps it was as much the addict talking as anyone – I should know: I have said so many things that I have come to regret or consider mean-spirited later.

In my defence, I was interested in Nico when nobody else was; I gave her everything she asked for; and I spent the next year promoting the album and saying wonderful things about her, turning many of my fans on to her music. The only regret I have now is that at the time I let the quotes from the book affect me and I stopped saying pleasant things about Nico. The book had come at a time in my own life when I was emotionally low. But, after reassurances from people who knew her and understanding much more of how things really were, I couldn't not be an admirer for long. It was to be the last song she ever recorded – a song about death and our own fragile mortality. It was also cited by the critics as one of the best songs on the album, in reviews that were generally good.

The second of three duets that were recorded for *The Stars We Are* was with a unique and fascinating artiste called Agnes Burnelle. I first became aware of her when watching her perform a song on the Terry Wogan show, of all places. She had just released an album produced by the brilliant Elvis Costello and Philip Chevron from the Irish group the Pogues. It had an intriguing title – *Father's Lying Dead on the Ironing Board*. Backed by a Balkan folk trio, she sang in a world-weary laconic style with a dash of black humour and decadence, wielding a cigarette and wrapped in a feather boa. I knew I just had to record with her. So I sat down with Billy McGee and wrote a mini musical operetta called 'Kept Boy', for me to sing the gigolo part and in the hope that Agnes would sing the part of the rich woman who kept him on a metaphorical leash. In the song he tries to poison her and get her wealth, but she beats him to it and turns the tables. It was a slice of macabre vaudeville kitsch, or whatever you want to call it.

I eventually tracked Agnes down, but unfortunately she was hospitalized, undergoing an operation for a brain tumour. Everyone was extremely worried about her. I sent her a gigantic bouquet of flowers with a message to get well and that I was desperate to work with her. She had no idea who I was, but my message of concern moved her. Recovering from the operation, she agreed to record the song. I flew her to London from her home in Dublin for the recording. I had no idea where the song would go or even if it would fit on to my album, but decided to worry about that later.

Agnes was thrilled with the song and gave a great performance, incorporating her acting skill into the interpretation. For me, as far as cabaret performers go, no one had better credentials or delivery than her – especially when performing Brecht and Weill, both of whom she had known as a child in Berlin. Not only that, but Marlene Dietrich had been her nanny! In that genre only Marianne Faithfull comes close, because she too has lived a life full of vivid experiences that she can put into songs. I've met Marianne on several occasions, once bumping into each other in a TV dressing room. We caught each other's eye in the mirror while making up and swiftly embraced, both saying simultaneously 'Oh, I love you! and your music!', and when leaving we promised to sing together one day. Don't you just love show business?

'Kept Boy' with Agnes was eventually released as a special collectors' single with the album. It was such a self-contained song that it belonged on its own. Over the years, I performed it a number of times with Agnes for special occasions – once at the Dublin Olympia theatre. The fans loved it when she and I archly acted out the parts, camping it up with the necessary flair. It was interesting that when I was on an extensive promotional tour of America after the release of *The Stars We Are* the song many radio stations wanted to play and talk about was 'Kept Boy'.

I eventually persuaded Stevo to sign Agnes to Some Bizarre, but was upset that he refused to allow me to produce her album. I suppose, however, that I already had too much work on, and he felt that I should concentrate on that. Instead the production honours went to Charles Gray, who did an excellent job in bringing out the surreality of the songs. Agnes called the album *Mother the Wardrobe is Full of Infantry Men*, after a poem by the Liverpudlian poet Roger McGough. I wrote another song for the album, again with Billy McGee – yet another mini operetta, called 'It was Me'. It's simply a song about the Devil's wife, and how she is really the instigator of all evil deeds yet receives no credit for them.

Sadly, Agnes died in February 1999, after a long bout of bad health. She had always seemed such a tough soul, younger than her years, the kind of person who would be around for ever. I had talked to her on the phone just before Christmas, and she seemed on the road to recovery, even talking of future plans, although her voice sounded frail. I was devastated when I heard the news. I was unable to attend her funeral, partly because of other commitments but partly through choice: I find funerals difficult to deal with. I prefer to remember Agnes as still around somewhere, it's just that we've lost touch. I prefer to remember her as she was, and to imagine that she'll phone me out of the blue one rainy day.

Another artist whom I approached with a view to collaboration was the singer/songwriter Peter Hammill, but with no success. I had long been a fan of his songs, ever since I saw him perform with the band Van der Graaff Generator in my schooldays. He is a unique writer and performer with a disquieting voice – one that has a Gothic operatic quality, with lyrics that range from the personal and introspective to the dark and obscure. John Lydon cites Peter Hammill as an influence, especially his album *Nadir's Last Chance*, which preceded the whole punk movement, its distorted thrash sounds describing the rise and fall of a proto-punk rock star. In fact I had covered two of Peter's songs previously – 'Vision' and 'Just Good Friends' – both of which were personal to Peter but had also acquired a special meaning for me and many of my fans.

When Peter invited me to his studio in Bath to play me some tracks I was flattered. But I was in the midst of a deep depression when I took the train with Jane Rollink to meet him. I felt a little overawed and lost for words at the meeting, but thankfully Jane, with her northern forwardness, filled in the silences. As well as playing me some tracks that he thought I might cover, he also played me some excerpts from an epic gothic opera he was working on, called *The Fall of the House of Usher* – the Edgar Allan Poe story. I thought it sounded brilliant but totally uncommercial. I was flattered to be considered to take part in it, and of course said that I would be delighted and honoured to do so, telling him to contact me when he wanted the vocal done.

Never great at meeting people, I wished afterwards that I had been more jovial and conversational. Perhaps he thought I was insufficiently enthusiastic because a while later Stevo informed me that he had been approached by Peter to release the album of the opera.

'No, surely not,' I said. Peter had never contacted me to do the vocal part. I knew that some time had passed, but was aware how long these things take. I took a copy of the album from Stevo and read the credits. Peter had given the part to Andy Bell, the flamboyant singer from Erasure. He was having a great deal of chart success at that time, and perhaps Peter thought he was the more commercial bet. I was choked and hurt, especially as I suspected Peter Hammill meant nothing to Andy Bell.

'Shall I release it?' Stevo asked me. I swallowed my pride and told him that I thought he ought to, because I knew how important it was to Peter and that he would find it near impossible to get it released anywhere else, it being a triple album and all.

I have found it hard to listen to Peter's music since then and, though I sang 'Vision' at my Albert Hall concert, I obstinately refused to meet him afterwards. Mind you, as you will later discover, I was in no mood to meet anyone after that concert.

I had at one point also wanted the legendary singer Yma Sumac to guest on a track with me, and I flew to New York to meet her, catch her show, and chat afterwards. Yma Sumac was probably in her sixties, a rare-voiced singer who claimed to have a five-octave range. According to her Hollywood press release at the time, she was the star of several movies, descended from Incan royalty (whatever that is in the twentieth century) and a princess to boot. On the other hand, rumour said that she was born Amy Camus in Brooklyn, of mixed parentage (her father being South American), and that Yma Sumac is simply her real name reversed. Of course I dismissed this rumour and chose to believe the press release because . . . well, I like to believe there is still magic. Yma had made a number of exotic albums during the fifties, and at one time even attempted a rock album (in the seventies, of course). Her extraordinary voice growled, shrilled, trilled and ultimately thrilled.

Sitting in the front row with Anita Sarko at the barely half-full Ballroom, it was hard to contain our laughter as Yma berated her backing band for playing out of time when it seemed to those present that it was she that was unable to keep in tempo or key. She seemed a little oiled. Her face was a death mask of make-up, her lips lurid red, and black hair was swept up on her head. Bulges protruded from an over-tight, ill-fitting green dress. Unable to reach the high notes of her heyday, she would struggle and then turn around and scream and shout at the nervous musicians.

Afterwards, when I went to talk with her, I noticed an almost empty bottle of vodka on the dressing table and a smell of alcohol as she drew me close, the black wig on the table beside her, and wispy grey hair protruding from a skullcap. Close up she resembled a strange drag queen – part tragedy, part memory, part brilliance and all camp.

'I would love to sing with you,' I said, almost dizzy with the fabulousness of being so close to this formidable creature.

'It will be marvellous!' she cried, plainly not having a clue who I was. 'It will be the most wonderful, wonderful thing.'

She signed my CDs, offered me some vodka, and poured the remainder for herself. As she lifted her head and widened her eyes, I was reminded of Gloria Swanson in *Sunset Boulevard*.

Subsequent attempts to get in touch with her proved very difficult; her manager confessed that even he had problems getting any replies from her for anything.

'Yma refuses to have a phone or a fax, and can only be contacted through a letter. Things take for ever,' he explained with a sigh of exasperation. Yma had become a recluse, and at one point demanded $50,000 to participate in anything. She had seen that Madonna was commanding huge amounts of money, and felt that she could rightly ask for a similar amount. Like so many stars of yesteryear, she was still back in her glory days – except now more deluded and unreasonable than ever. I imagined myself in the future – sat in the darkened house, clutching a vodka bottle, drinking to an accursed world. When people say to me, 'Weren't you big at one time?' I'll reply, 'I still am – it's just the charts have gotten small.'

Yma was truly wonderful and a real star, and even though we never worked together she taught me something that I've always adhered to: if you make a mistake while performing, blame the bloody band.

The album was finished at Sarm Studios with a young producer called Bob Kraushar, who added the final production touches – the flair, the fairy dust and the solid mixes. I was happy with the result – a collection of beautiful string-driven songs and exotic ballads that had a feel of the sixties and a mood of lounge exotica. I dubbed the album 'electro lounge' when the Americans asked me to describe it. Vocally I had never sounded better; there was a warmer yet older sound to my voice. Tris Penna and Clive Black thought that it was Sinatra for our generation, whoever that may be. More importantly, it was pop-oriented. They were grateful that I hadn't delivered an album of the bloody Brel stuff. (I had that waiting in the wings.)

The closing track, 'She Took My Soul in Istanbul', was co-written with Billy McGee, and was a complicated opera epic – Billy found it impossible to write simple, minimal songs. Although I loved the track, the problem was I couldn't sing it properly. I actually duetted with myself on it, my alter ego, called Soraya Ahmed, being my voice speeded up. Journalists around the world thought Ahmed was a Turkish torch singer and wanted to know more. In fact I had originally wanted to get one of Turkey's famous transsexual torch singers, either Bulent Ersoy or Zeki Müren, to sing with me, but was unable to track them down in time. Zeki Müren in particular is a favourite of mine and has influenced me.

I had at this point never been to Turkey, but I thought after writing a song about Istanbul I'd better go there and then at least I could claim the song had been inspired by it. I grabbed Jane Rollink and boarded a plane. After checking into the fabulous Agatha Christie suite in the Pera Palace Hotel, we hit the city's nightlife – a whirlwind of cheap belly-dancing cabarets and dangerous clubs. Jane wondered what on earth she was doing there after the umpteenth belly dancer had wobbled her flabby stomach in her face. Jane was also desperate to smoke a joint, but hadn't dared bring any hash with her – 'I've seen *Midnight Express*,' she said.

We decided to visit Istanbul's premier gay club, strangely called VAT 69. (Don't ask.) On entering, we were pulled into a dim back room while a man tried to close the door behind us. Panicking, we struggled against several men who were trying to push us, and turned back towards the door. They planned either to fleece us or to give us a special Turkish massage – which I suspect amount to the same thing. As we struggled back into the street, a group of Turkish men tried to pull me back in, shouting and waving their arms. As Jane and I ran off and found a taxi, several Turks shouted 'Come back – good time inside!' I'm sure.

I wanted to have my photo taken in front of the Blue Mosque for the lyric sleeve; then, after a quick photo session, we took the plane back to London. Istanbul hadn't been quite how I'd imagined it – there were so many buildings being pulled down that the whole place resembled a construction site. I'm sure there are beautiful palaces being pulled down to build shopping malls as we speak. (You may have gathered that shopping malls are one of my personal hates.)

'She Took My Soul in Istanbul' actually went to number one in the Turkish chart, which I found strange because it was never a single.

*

The Stars We Are was released in a simple, stylish sleeve depicting me as . . . well . . . me! Gone was the glitter and make-up; I looked almost hard in a denim jacket and black T-shirt, with a vacant stare. The photo was taken by Andy Catlin, and no doubt contributed to making the album the success it was. Marketing even won an award for the design.

'Tears Run Rings' was the first record to be accompanied by a new phenomenon – the dance mix. I'll explain what I mean by this. Record companies discovered the dance market was a cost-effective vehicle to get a record noticed, air play or whatever – which is not unreasonable. But then they decided that whatever the record is – a ballad, a guitar-based record, whatever – there has to be a dance mix. Don't get me wrong: I love dance music. I worked in a disco, and Dave Ball and I were early pioneers of techno music. What bothers me is the obsession record companies have developed for turning everything into a dance mix, butchering songs that realistically have no relation to dance or that market at all, trying to fashion them into something they just are not. The vocal is sometimes completely removed, and what remains of the original song is barely recognizable. I have a suspicion that in some cases you get no more than the remixers' ideas that have been hanging around waiting for a project they can be applied to. Then there is the money – trendy (whatever that means nowadays) remixers can demand huge amounts of money. And all this, as the dance department of any record company will candidly explain, is meant to bring you to a different audience, a younger audience.

But in this world the DJ and the mixer are king, not the artist. Let's face it, when you're off your head on Ecstasy or whatever, dancing on a Saturday night, you're not going to give a toss whether it's a Marc Almond record playing or not – and even if you do like it there's little chance you're going to remember anything on Monday morning, let alone one particular record. And, finally, a Marc Almond record is probably not the hippest thing to play in any trendy techno club. Conversely why would a Marc Almond fan want to buy a vocal-less Marc Almond track?

Am I on a rant? Don't stop me now! I am the one who over the years has had a barrage of complaints laid on me by fans coerced into buying obscure mixes disguised as collectors' editions. Worst of all are the mixes where they don't leave off my vocal, but speed it up until I sound like I am on helium. Is it me or what is going on? Are they crap? If this is sounding like an old git, then so be it. I love cutting-edge dance music, techno, trance, hip-hop and trip-hop. I'm even partial to the odd hands-in-the-air handbag Euro disco. It's just that I personally don't want to hear myself sounding like fucking Mickey Mouse.

Now, as far as dance mixes go (which isn't very far), the 'Tears Run Rings' twelve-inch mix by Justin Strauss was quite good and, to come close to contradicting myself entirely, it went a long way to breaking the song in the United States. It reached number one in the dance charts, and headed somewhat reluctantly to the main chart. I was sent off to America for a gruelling promotional tour from coast to coast. I did countless interviews with faceless journalists, all asking the same mundane questions. I sat in radio stations answering even more mundane questions, and appeared on a couple of television shows. I would smile and take it all in my stride as interviewer upon interviewer would say, 'Hey, Marc Almond! Soft Cell! Remember this tune?' Da dink dink. I was back in hell.

In America, Soft Cell – and especially that song – had made such an impact that everybody needed reminding just who Marc Almond solo artist was. I was known only as the singer with Soft Cell; I hadn't had the recorded output or success I had enjoyed in Europe. There was no point being pretentious or arty either – Jacques Brel meant jack shit to the American radio jocks, who talked only in sound-bites. They would ask you a question but not listen to the answer, as they were lining up the next middle-of-the-road adult-orientated-rock record.

'Hey, that's great. So, where's Dave Ball?'

'That's real funny. So what are you doing now?'

'That's great. Do you really drink tea with milk in England?'

'Hey, England – the Queen, Marmite, fish and chips!'

'Hey, do you like REO Speedwagon? They're really something, aren't they?'

'Are Air Supply cool or what?'

It was a sobering process, and if you went on a pretentious 'out on a pedestal' trip you were soon knocked off. You have to play the game, because you're given such a tiny amount of space in the media that if you don't you're lost. You have to switch on your 'I'm on American radio and TV' persona and play along – fighting it is pointless. The American press, on the other hand, are quite different to the British press – far more serious and soul-searching. They seek an in-depth soul-revealing artist who conforms to all their tortured expectations. So you slip into that mode that is not too cheesy and not too serious. Hour after hour, one journalist after another traipses into the interview room, turns on his tape, looks you in the eye and says,

'Music is the antidote to this disease we call life – discuss.' 'Where do you go in your dreams?' 'Are you a tortured soul?'

In addition to all this, my very name caused confusion. In the seventies there was a band made up of two musicians with the surnames Mark and Almond, and they were imaginatively called the Mark Almond band. The number of times I was greeted with 'I am such a huge fan. I love all your work, especially the albums in the seventies'! Christ, how old did I look? I love the way they are always huge fans and yet don't even know what the group look like.

In America they don't have pop stars per se. They have rock stars. It's rock 'n' roll, and you're a rock star – and are expected to behave like one. It's all part of the entertainment market. I discovered it was especially appreciated if you sneer, look like you're on drugs and answer with one syllable. The main thing against me then was that I never had long hair – long hair is good, especially in LA. Short hair looks gay if you're not in the military, whereas long hair looks straight. People said how much they missed my long hair of the Soft Cell phase. 'You always had great hair. Out there hair.'

Then, as if this hell wasn't bad enough, there was something else. Record-store in-house signings. These are really nerve-racking and particularly unpleasant. I always think of the scene in the film *Spinal Tap* when nobody turns up to their band's signing, and the company rep proffers his ass to be kicked. I was most surprised when people did turn up, when queues went all around the block and people waited dutifully with their records to get them signed, with the album playing over and over and over again in the background – ad nauseam.

In Los Angeles I was besieged by fans at the radio stations and the signings. I remember one attractive girl bared her breasts for me to sign, and I scrawled my autograph across them. To my horror, she returned an hour later. She had quickly gone to a tattooist who had gone over my signature, disfiguring both her breasts. If I'd known I would have taken more care.

But the descent into hell was not yet complete, and downward we went. Promotional tours also involved meeting the staff at the record pressing and packing factories, meeting the people who shrink-wrap the album, and posing with them all for snapshots. Factory after factory. It was stressed over and over how important it was to do this bit of promotion, and looking at the photos on the wall of Michael Jackson and Billy Joel it seemed no one escaped this banal duty. But worst of all – the final ground-floor stop in hell – was having to go out for dinner and entertain the heads of the record-manufacturing factories. I would sit beside these people and we would all try to chat, but the smallness of the talk was beyond belief. On one memorable occasion in Texas I had to sit down with the boss of the distribution plant. It was a strange sight – this seven-foot Texan redneck, complete with cowboy boots and stetson, tucking into half a side of cow while I sat nibbling on a salad, trying to make chummy conversation. He asked me what I thought of American football, baseball, country music, Ronald Reagan, fucking communists and cattle steerage. Quite a few subjects there that I'm tuned into!

All this promotion took a month, and I saw it through. I was exhausted, but it seemed to pay off. *The Stars We Are* sold the most records I had ever sold in the States, and the single 'Tears Run Rings' went into the chart. It looked so promising that I was told to make a second video, as the original was too stylized (meaning too arty). The original was directed by the late Tim Broad, but was deemed unsuitable for MTV. Peter Christopherson was brought in to make something more appropriate, which involved me and a woman with large breasts being driven around in the back of a limousine picking up hitchhikers whom we encouraged to have sex in front of us. The car drove through a desolate orange and red landscape that looked very post-apocalyptic. Don't ask what that was about. Answers on a postcard, please.

Around this time I celebrated my 31st birthday. To mark it, I decided to do something a little different. I took myself off to Hamburg's notorious Reeperbahn for an experience with a female prostitute. Well, why not? In an underground car park lit up by neon and ultraviolet lights were women of all shapes and sizes standing around the concrete pillars in white leotards beckoning, grabbing and blowing kisses. I was eventually led off by a tall blonde lady who led me up a labyrinth of stairways to a sparsely furnished room.

The ritual of what you could have and what it would cost went on for ever and ever. She kept going off and coming back; each time I handed her more and more money, which she'd take off to some unseen place about ten minutes away. It all seemed designed to be as unsexy as possible, executed with a clinicalness that Germans seem to excel at. The act itself? Well, yes, it did happen – through about three layers of condoms, I should add. It was kind of exciting, but in a cold way. I enjoyed the experience enough to want to try it again, especially in Amsterdam where the prostitutes sit in windows and you can shop for the one you like.

The fact that it was all so easy, so uncomplicated, I found it exciting. I have no qualms about sex being a commodity if both parties are of age and consenting. It's a simple transaction, and can be enjoyable for both concerned – very nineties. Isn't everybody at it? I think it's the safest form of sex. The way I look at it, the sex is actually free; you pay for the luxury of being able to leave at will or have them leave.

The second single in Britain was the track 'Bittersweet', an up-tempo, bouncy affair. I was on tour in Germany at the time of release. The tour for *The Stars We Are* was one of the most successful tours that year, and I was enjoying playing to ecstatic packed houses, despite still having to deal with Annie and Billy's temperamental sulks. I was halfway through the tour when I was offered a spot on Jimmy Tarbuck's *Sunday Night at the London Palladium* to promote the track. I didn't want to do it, but the record company were insistent, so I flew back to England. I felt very uncomfortable about the whole affair as I joined a dismal line-up of stars and performed.

Jimmy Tarbuck was suitably pleasant, and matter-of-factly shook my hand. Because I was still having problems remembering lyrics, it was decided that it would be safer if I mimed to the track – something I prefer not to do. When Jim Davidson (I told you it was a dismal line-up) came on to do his alleged 'comedy' routine, he berated singers who mimed. I thought, 'You sanctimonious git!' but smiled all the same and trooped on for the final wave goodbye. All showbiz pals together.

'Bittersweet' didn't do as well as 'Tears Run Rings', and wasn't helped by a terrible video. It was a return to working with Tim Pope, but our hearts weren't in it. We had to film overnight in a catacomb just outside Crystal Palace. It was cold, and I was tired and miserable, shivering with flu. I just wanted to get the bloody thing over with. Tim, who had moved into commercials by this time, was also annoyed at having to do an overnight shoot in the freezing cold.

The song that really made *The Stars We Are* a huge success was 'Something's Gotten Hold of My Heart' – a cover of the sixties Gene Pitney classic. It was during a live performance at the London Astoria for a Japanese TV special that I first performed the song, and as soon as Clive Black heard it he knew it was possibly a hit, and insisted I record it for the album. If Clive was excited, so was I. I rearranged the song to add an Elvis Vegas-style 'you, you, you' section, and Billy arranged a stunning string section. We wanted to get it absolutely right, so Bob Kraushar was brought in to produce the track as he had already done such a fine job with the rest of the album. Bob set about the task with serious determination, brandishing an ever-present Evian bottle and refusing to tolerate any tantrums from musicians. Annie complained over and over that she couldn't do it and stormed out. She made it clear she had no time for Bob. The feeling was mutual. Bob hauled her over the coals. 'You're a bloody piano player – that's what you do – so play it, or I'll have someone else in here within the hour to play it.' Annie understood, and played her heart out. Bob pushed me too, making me sing again and again until I hit the right notes.

I can't clearly remember how the idea for the song to be a duet came about. I think I dropped a flippant remark about it to Clive Black, who took it seriously. At that time Gene Pitney was touring Britain. Perhaps I'd said he might come in and sing a few bars with me. But I'd never thought Clive would take me seriously. After all, I thought, why would Gene Pitney want to sing with me on a record that he had made famous? I was concerned he might be offended. But Clive had the chutzpah to ask him. Gene was delighted to oblige. As it turned out, his son was a fan of mine, and Gene himself liked

'Tainted Love'. It's surprising what you can get just by asking. A week later I went to see Gene in concert at Bow Town Hall in the East End of London. The venue was two-thirds full, and the audience was made up almost entirely of ageing housewives with bottle-blonde rinses and fox-fur coats. He looked great, the consummate performer – cool, professional, and sounding like he always did. 'Why isn't he performing at a major London venue?' I asked myself. People needed to be reminded of him. We all need a bit of that from time to time.

I was still on tour when Gene went into the studio to record his parts. He graciously acknowledged that it was my version, my record, and was happy to let me lead. Apparently he removed his shirt and sang bare-chested. When I was presented with the finished track I was thrilled. I had always been a huge fan of his, ever since, as a child, I had watched him on television singing 'Twenty-four Hours from Tulsa' on *Ready Steady Go!* And he was on my record! He has such an instantly recognizable voice, and a career that spans so many impeccable songs – such as 'I'm Gonna be Strong', 'Backstage', 'A Street Called Hope' and 'Mecca'. I could have quite happily recorded a Marc Almond tribute album to Gene covering them all.

I was first told of the song charting while I was doing a showcase for a record-company conference in Germany. I was furious with Stevo for putting me up for this event, performing as light entertainment while record-company executives wined and dined. It was so demeaning. 'You've got to play along,' said Stevo. 'It's all part of the music business.' Was this Stevo the rebel, the anarchist? Not any more. He had become one of the boys; he was kissing ass more than any of us. He was the record-company friend – corporate Stevo. Maybe it *was* him the record companies wanted. After all, I hadn't played the game – and where had it got me? Dumped . . . er sorry . . . correction: passed over from one record company to the next. Maybe it was time for me to kiss a few asses. Time to be the good, professional Marc Almond, to be part of the music business and stop shooting myself in the foot. Would it really matter if I became a corporate puppet? Well, yes it would – to me. Still, I liked everyone at EMI, and I was happy, so I conformed somewhat. I listened and tried to understand. I tried.

Clive Black knocked on my hotel door and broke the good news that the single was a new entry at number twenty in the chart, and getting massive radio play. It looked like it might be on the way up. After he left, I tried to locate some feelings of joy or excitement, but just felt numb. Everyone seemed to be a lot more excited than I was. The following week the record moved up to number ten. Then, the next week, bad news: the midweek position (which record companies love to find out) indicated a drop to number eleven. Still, I had some TV appearances; on the Thursday (*Top of the Pops*) and the Friday (*Pebble Mill* and *Wogan*), and everyone was optimistic these would prevent it falling any faster. Surely Saturday's sales would make a difference.

On Sunday, when the chart was revealed, no one called me. It was nearly seven, so I knew the record must have gone down. Then Stevo called and told me for the second time in my career that my record was number one. It seemed to be not real, to be happening to someone else and I was just looking on. I acted the part of being overwhelmed and excited, but the truth was more to do with shock, and then bewilderment and finally anxiety. I was back on that flimsy tightrope and, I felt, about to fall into a pit of trouble. I knew that all that mainstream glory would bring unwanted attention. Then came the doubts that the record was untypical and unrepresentative of me as an artist, and finally that it had taken another cover version to get me a number one. All these things nagged away at me.

In one way, though, success is better the second time around. If nothing else, it would buy me time, make everyone kiss my ass for a while and indulge me further. But it wasn't going to invite a lasting reappraisal of me as an artist. It started to feel as if the public were prepared to accept me as a singer of other people's songs, but were suspicious or indifferent towards me as a songwriter. They seemed able to deal with me as a singer, when there was no excess baggage to digest, but not as an artist. I had to reconcile myself to the possibility that it might only be cover versions that would get me the massive hits. While I do enjoy bringing my own interpretations to other people's songs, I naturally love having success with my own songs. If I was to abandon writing my own material then I would probably have had far more success in a middle-of-the-road market. But not only is writing a real pleasure, it makes sense on a business level too – it's where a great deal of my income is generated. I suppose one side helps the other: cover versions of songs already embedded in the public's consciousness have a good chance of success, raise your profile, and make people aware of your own work too. Yet if you hadn't had a distinctive approach, the cover wouldn't have intrigued them much!

Where was I? Oh yes, so the record is at number one, and all those people who had written me off can eat their fucking words. Revenge can be so rewarding! But wait a minute. You remember that stupid mistake with 'Tainted Love' – you know, the one about not putting my own composition on the B-side and losing approximately £1.7 million in publishing royalties? Guess what? The record company, along with my management, never put my own composition on the B-side of 'Something's Gotten Hold of My Heart' either, thereby losing me still more money. Twice in one career is pretty amazing. The B-side was my solo version of the A-side of the same song, thereby allowing the songwriters to be paid twice for the same record. This, the company explained, was in case Gene was unable to promote the record. But Gene was a businessman and he was certainly ready to promote, and promote, and promote.

As if to make life easier, the ever-thoughtful *News of the World* printed an old art college photo of me in a white frilly dress two sizes too small and curly wig, a hybrid between Susan Hayward and Baby Jane Hudson. It had doubtless been supplied by an old art college 'friend' for a fee. I prayed that Gene wouldn't see it.

The first time I met Gene in person was when we filmed the video together in Las Vegas in November 1988. We went out there for a week to film two videos – one for 'Something's Gotten Hold of My Heart' and another for an anticipated single 'The Stars We Are'. The two videos were to loosely tell a story of me travelling to Las Vegas to find my dream, picking up a car full of performers on the way – a showgirl, a hermaphrodite, a magician and of course an Elvis impersonator. In the 'Something's Gotten Hold of My Heart' video I arrive in Vegas, meet Gene Pitney, and end up performing with him. Unfortunately when the videos were finally released as part of a compilation they were put the wrong way round. Isn't that just typical? One more careless cock-up in a catalogue of career cock-ups!

It was freezing in Las Vegas that night when we filmed – a bitter wind cutting through you, burning your face and penetrating your clothing. Still, as I looked down at the lights of the strip from my hotel-room window, I loved the place. This was the end of an era in Las Vegas, when the last of the famous hotels of the seventies still remained. We were staying at the Sands; it still had that feel of Frank and Dean and Sammy – and Caesar's Palace, magnificently surreal, still dominated the strip. Permission had just been granted for the building of many of the new hotels that would change Las Vegas into a family attraction, remove the sleaze and reputation of the Mafia once and for all.

Vegas by day is such a strange and sad place. The concrete façades – masked at night by neon – are bare and cold against the sweltering desert midday heat. The hotel rooms – with fake teak and purple walls, all the televisions refusing to tune in properly, everything gloomy – are designed to deter you from spending too much time in them when you should be gambling. The metal bars at the hotel windows – to prevent suicides after heavy losses in the casino – are depressing reminders of a grim reality. It was, I thought, the perfect place to meet Gene for the first time and to make a video. Surprisingly, it had never been used for a video before.

Gene arrived in town, walked into the hotel lobby, put a quarter in the fruit machine, and immediately won $2,000. He felt it was a good omen. As it turned out the record would be an international number one and he was right.

I was taken to meet him in his Winnebago. It was a strange meeting between two artists from different worlds – he a clean-cut family man, and me with greasy hair, a rockabilly quiff and a dubious reputation. I was clutching a bundle of records of his for him to sign, like a star-struck fan. Smaller and dumpier than I'd expected, he was friendly and polite – always the professional. I couldn't believe he was here for me, on my record. I said to a journalist who had accompanied us to cover the story, 'Who would have thought that Marc Almond from Southport would watch a singer on *Ready Steady Go!* in his youth and years later would be in Las Vegas with that singer who was guesting on his record.' My mind was boggled.

Of course, both of us had to play our star bit. We naturally each had our own Winnebego, with our own make-up artists, hairdressers and managers catering to our own particular whims. Gene was brilliant, though one sensed that he expected utmost professionalism or else. I respect people who do. I was informed by his manager that he was not entirely comfortable with the white tuxedo and red cummerbund that Huw had dressed him in. I naturally sided with Gene, but he relented and agreed to wear it. I was in a black tuxedo and he in a white one – contrasting and conflicting. Our climaxing verse was filmed in what was a neon graveyard in the desert – a haunted place where half the neons of yesteryear's glamorous locations had ended up, half still working, headily symbolic of the changing Las Vegas. It was blowing a storm with dust everywhere, and we were freezing as we were led from our trailers, like boxers about to fight, to sing the final verse. Three takes only and then we were out of there. It was pure magic.

Gene came over to Europe for the rounds of promotion, a *Top of the Pops* appearance, and various other TV shows, including the *Wogan* show. Terry Wogan wanted to interview Gene and me together about the record, but I was having none of it and gave the stage to Gene, allowing him to do the interview alone. But such graciousness had an ulterior motive. Obviously I felt uncomfortable about television interviews anyway, but I also wanted to remain mysterious and aloof. And my presence might have inhibited Gene in his flattery of me. So it was that Gene did the interview and said all the things I had hoped he would say and more, reminding everyone of what a star I was. A living legend flattering me – I ask you!

The TV appearances and the constant radio play ensured the record stayed at number one for four weeks, until I became completely blasé about the whole thing – even bored. It just meant having to hide myself away for longer in my house from people who had started to shout 'Marc, where's Gene?' At least it made a change from the usual 'Marc – "Tainted Love".'

So there it was. Another number one. I'd begun the eighties with one and I'd closed the eighties with another. Not bad going. I'd perhaps crossed the barrier from being an eighties artist to being a nineties one. This time, I told myself, I would be more humble, more grateful for what I had. It would all be plain sailing from now on. Who was I fooling? Myself for one.

'Something's Gotten Hold of My Heart' went to number one all over Europe, but in Holland it was to mark the end of my Dutch TV career. The record was at number five in Holland, and I was booked on to a show that I was told would ensure it would go to number one the following week. The show was called *You Bet*. It was a Saturday-night family show, in which morons placed bets on feats of ridiculousness their families were encouraged to do. Throughout the show they had several musical interludes. This crap television is the same the world over. I was sitting in my dressing room when I was informed that our song had to be cut in half because of time restrictions, and most of Gene's part would have to go. I was furious. I stormed up to the producer of the show – the most powerful man in Dutch television (according to his press release). I aired my grievance. He dismissed me with a wave of his hand and told me the song was going to be cut and that was that.

'This show is called *You Bet*, and I'd like to bet you that if you insist on cutting our song we won't do the show.'

We didn't do the show.

Gene never said a word throughout. It was hard to know if he agreed with my actions. The Dutch record company thought it great that I had stood up to this producer, and the next day it hit the headlines in the Dutch papers that I had made some disparaging remarks about him (I'd been unaware of him sitting within earshot when I'd made them). I was the hero of the moment with many people, but the reality is that I have never been asked back on to Dutch television.

Gene benefited from the hit record. His greatest hits were reissued, and on his next tour he was playing at West End theatres. I went to see him, and took a bow from the box. And later that evening I had one of the most frightening experiences of my life involving people going out of control.

As the Pitney show finished in the Dominion Theatre and everyone was exiting through the packed foyer, I was jammed in the middle. Suddenly people started to recognize me, and began to turn around. As more and more people at the front turned back to see me, and those behind began to push forward, I became separated from my security man. People reached out to touch me, and suddenly hands were all over, trying to pull off rings and pushing paper and pens for autographs. A woman tried to pull off my jacket, and people had hold of me. I could see my security man trying to get me, but in-between were Essex women in boob tubes or foxfurs scrabbling at me, bejewelled hands outstretched. Finally the security man pulled me out from the mass of hysterical Chigwell housewives.

A couple of years later, when I was performing a retrospective show at the Albert Hall, I was sorry when Gene didn't join me on stage to sing 'Something's Gotten Hold of My Heart'. He was in London at the time, but said he had a bad back. I felt a little let down in one way, because I know he would have brought the house down.

Sometimes everything comes at once. I can sit around for months waiting for something to happen, left to my own devices (which usually means misbehaving myself and getting into trouble), then suddenly offers come in and things start happening. But you can only be in one place at the one time, and some offers have to be turned down. That can hurt! Just before 'Something's Gotten Hold of My Heart' was released, I was offered a part in a movie by the horror and fantasy writer Clive Barker. I'd met him on a couple of occasions, and he'd just been acclaimed for his directorial debut with *Hellraiser*. I was flattered to be asked to be in his new film, *Nightbreed*, about an underground city of freaks, rejects and strange fantastical creatures. I was to be a tattooed hermaphrodite, a speaking part. I spent a strange day at Pinewood Studios being plaster cast for a prosthetic body suit that would feature a beautiful, perfect pair of breasts. I was also shown round the set, a strange inverted Tower of Babel. I was excited: this was a whole new experience for me, and that this was a movie by someone as cult and well thought-of as Clive made it even more special.

But as 'Something's Gotten Hold of My Heart' headed towards its number one slot I was given an ultimatum by EMI: the film, or the record. Filming dates coincided with the promotional schedules that would guarantee the record a top chart placing. I chose the record.

Clive Barker was furious, and I felt very guilty about the whole thing, especially as the prosthetic suit, which had cost a lot of money, was useless to anyone else. My replacement wasn't given the suit, and was merely tattooed. But it turned out to be the right decision for me. 'Something's Gotten Hold of My Heart' went to number one across Europe, and *Nightbreed*, while not a bad film, was poorly received and didn't live up to Clive's previous success with *Hellraiser*.

*

I returned to America for a tour of the West Coast, accompanied by my new friend Sean, with whom I was having one of my stormy affairs. It was his first time in America and the culture shock left him feeling despondent, lost to the whole situation of me doing promotion and touring. Though the pair of us felt distant and jet-lagged, we were determined to play the part of tacky tourists, taking in all the sights. Yet all the time I found it hard to concentrate my mind on the work at hand. During the tour I played two nights at the beautiful Pantages Theatre in Los Angeles. The tour was sold out, but the shows were confusing for the American audience, who didn't get the European references and the Jacques Brel songs – especially with me bizarrely dressed in black rubber and leather. Though the songs from *The Stars We Are* were welcomed much more, they were all waiting for a Soft Cell song. But I never played one; I refused.

Those nights on stage I couldn't concentrate. The drugs – prescription and non-prescription – were taking their toll. It had all caught up with me. At one point I felt out of my body, watching myself from the back of the stalls. Then I collapsed, then slowly managed to stand and regain a little composure. The songs seemed unfamiliar, the audience distant, as though behind glass. I swayed about the stage like a sad Aznavour, looking faintly ridiculous, singing a slurring a cappella version of 'My Way' to an audience that seemed at best a tad uncomfortable and confused. The tension was thick in the air. It was a cruel cabaret, and had I not been performing but watching I am sure I would have found it all tragically, horribly fascinating. But it was me. I was doing it. And worse of all I was believing it.

What planet was I on?

14

Dis-Enchanted

During 1990 I began to understand for the first time that my life was slowly spiralling out of control, that it was gradually coming apart. But, though I knew it in my heart, I pushed this reality to the back of my mind and did what all addicts do – adopted a mask of denial. My addiction – though I never acknowledged it as that – remained something I always believed I could deal with in the future, and of course the future drifted further and further away from my present. I could think of a thousand reasons why I didn't have a problem, and then a thousand more why I couldn't deal with it right now anyhow. I began a life of lies and secrets – towards those around me and also, of course, to myself. I grew defensive when close friends pointed out that my sleeping-pill intake might be causing me to act bizarrely and irrationally, responsible for the extreme mood swings I was prone to and the amnesia which had become so acute that conversations and plans made one day would be forgotten the next. This in turn fuelled anxiety, doubts and paranoia, which led to darker feelings: violent thoughts about those who doubted or criticized me seethed inside my head, swirling around in the cesspool of my personal delusion.

I was seeing the world from behind glassy eyes. On occasions – which became more and more frequent – the demons slipped their restraints and raged against the world, and then it became clear to other people that all really was not well. If friends expressed concern or suggested I get help I would naturally distance myself from them, as addicts do, and in so doing would become isolated and then careless in my choice of companions. I preferred the company of other addicts – emotionally disturbed, fractured people clinging on to other dysfunctional people, adrift on our sea of aberration with no sight of land.

All through the eighties I had sought out people with problems of their own, so I could play the helper or carer, averting the glare from myself. But now my choice of companions took a darker turn, and I gravitated towards the morally bankrupt and the thoroughly danger-ous. Of all my old friends, only my soulmate remained, prepared to suffer my misjudgements, constantly trying to curb my excesses or foolishness, long-suffering and patient. He stayed with me through it all, but he found himself unable to curb my behaviour.

And then it became far worse. At night I would forget I had taken my sleeping pills. I would take them hours before intending to sleep (enjoying the mild buzz before I passed out), but an hour or so later I would take them again, and perhaps again even later. The consequences of this became very dangerous over a very short period. On a German tour Gerard, a lover at the time, had to talk me around one night when I was on the verge of slipping out of consciousness. I didn't thank him. On that same tour I took so much cocaine after a concert in Amsterdam that I nearly died. The next day we were due to leave, and there was still a great deal of coke remaining. As the car waited outside the hotel, Gerard and I took line after line until we were completely rigid, and then I went to the sink and washed away the remainder.

This is typical behaviour of an addict: the need to be able to throw drugs away is all part of the behavioural pattern of addiction. Over the years I have flushed so much down the lavatory, usually late at night after an excessive binge. This has a twofold effect. First, you are convincing yourself that you don't really need it, which of course is not true. You can make the gesture at *that* moment, because you don't actually need any more right then. But how many times have I spent the next day phoning dealer after dealer to get more, filled with anger at myself for throwing it away. Second, throwing drugs away is always accompanied by the notion that that is the last time you are going to use them. Filled with guilt, self-loathing and resolve, it's the addict's ultimate gesture of self-control: that is definitely it, you tell yourself in an act of defiance over your addiction. But it never works.

I was losing weight, which I could ill afford. I would lose my temper over the slightest thing, often screaming the most hurtful abuse I could. The anger was also directed inwards and eroded my self-esteem, especially when I would buy so and so a car, give them money or holidays, and then discover they were not thankful – no, that I was not able to control them. I would reproach myself for being so weak and manipulated, and then turn my anger on them, tell them to get out of my life. It was all part of the addict's controlling trip – while I thought I was in control I was actually being controlled, and ultimately it was my addiction that was in the driving seat.

I embarked on a string of relationships in the early nineties which always ended in tears – inevitably mine. Love and relationships were just another example of the addict's neediness. But if this all sounds too depressing – like a Narcotics Anonymous or Alcoholics Anonymous recital – you should be aware that in fact it was not all bad. There were so many good times that they made me refuse to consider the implications of the bad ones. The good times are essential to all addicts, as they fuel and reinforce the denial. It is only when the balance is tipped completely to one side that addicts are forced to recognize their addiction and act on it. But for now that had not happened to me. Yet every time I had a good time I was unable to recognize when I had taken enough, unable to stop, always going too far. *One line is too many and a thousand never enough.*

The delusional thinking was that I was untouchable, and worse still that I was exceptional, brilliant, gifted, a case of 'terminal uniqueness'. That I was an artist, and was experimenting in such extremes for my art. I insisted on doing my interviews in bizarre situations: my favourite was being interviewed in a rowing boat going around the island in the middle of the Regent's Park lake. In the majority of interviews I would spout about the virtues of drugs, and that only creative people know how to use them to positive effect. After all, I was one of those creative people and I was using drugs in a good way. Wasn't I?

Exercise too became an obsession – which many might say was positive. Even though I felt physically exhausted all the time, I still went to the gym and swam length after length in the pool. It is disheartening to learn that, whatever we do, psychiatrists and psychologists have already given a name to it, and that we are as predictable as the next patient. Going to the gym obsessively is recognized as just another sympton of addiction – to improve our body so we can take more drugs, to alleviate the guilt of taking the drugs, to mistakenly think the improvement outwardly will improve us inwardly, to be physically more attractive and so perhaps more likable to others and ultimately to ourselves. Then, of course, there is the production of endorphins by the body when exercising, which gives another type of euphoria, another feeling other than nothing. Besides all that jargon, I had another reason to go to the gym – I had a glamorous trainer, the porn star Aiden Shaw, who put me through my paces on the push-ups. It all seemed so fabulous I couldn't get over myself. For a brief time something quite strange happened to me – I started to feel good about myself.

I had stopped alcohol and cigarettes quite a while ago, and was trying to stop cocaine. Because I found I could go weeks without coke, I'd convinced myself that I didn't have a problem. I was only taking Ecstasy at weekends, and of course the daily prescription pills didn't count. But we all know they did count. You see, I could never imagine stopping them: the thought of a sleepless night literally terrified me. I read that prolonged abuse would have corroded my natural sleep pattern, and that without them I would be unable to fall asleep. I couldn't ever entertain the idea of not sleeping; I just kept repeating the prescriptions and taking the tablets. I know now that they contributed to my most fearful delusion: I had convinced myself that there would be a nuclear war. I became obsessed about it, and terrified that I might survive and not have any sleeping pills. So naturally I began to hoard, seeing several Harley Street doctors in the same day and getting repeat prescriptions from each. My house might be blown away in a nuclear holocaust, my friends be killed, my skin be burnt off, and I might suffer from radiation sickness, but at least I would get a bloody good night's sleep! Anyone for insane behaviour?

Drugged up, deluded and worked out, I was feeling fabulous. So I bought a beautiful new flat in a mansion block overlooking a leafy square in Earls Court and proceeded to fill it with the same kitsch crap I filled all my homes with. Then I knew what it was time to do. Record a new album.

*

I was still with EMI and flush from a number-one single. I was beyond reproach. So my new album began. It was during the recording of the first track, 'A Lover Spurned', that things finally came to a head with Annie Hogan. I was in the new Some Bizarre offices in Cavendish Street when I received a call from the producer, Stephen Hague, who was working on the track at Advision Studios around the corner. Apparently Annie and Billy were storming out of the sessions, each demanding payments of £2,000 before they would continue. I was furious at their unprofessional behaviour and went round there. I told them they were both fired and to leave the studio immediately. God knows what Stephen thought of it all. He was a mild-mannered American producer responsible for many major hits of the late eighties, and was just trying to get on with the job at hand. But after all the nonsense and stupidity I was free of both Billy and Annie. Stevo rejoiced.

'A Lover Spurned' was already turning out to be one of the most expensive singles of all time, costing the price of an album. It was originally recorded for *The Stars We Are*, but was deemed unsatisfactory and had been put aside. Now we had returned to it. The song was recorded in two or three different keys so I could find one that I felt comfortable with – I just couldn't decide. Eventually a forty-eight piece orchestra was brought in to record the backing. Around this time I can recall no one else using large orchestras on tracks – and, given the expense, I can understand why. The cost of such orchestras was to cause my fall from grace with the record company, but for now I could do what I wanted, and moderation wasn't it.

Money went into a bottomless pit. Stephen Hague spent two weeks in pre-production on the single, and he is by no means cheap; he is a perfectionist, and had me sing the vocal around sixty times before piecing it together word by word. It was not that I couldn't sing it, but that I couldn't sing it absolutely perfectly for his ear. Besides, if you're a top producer then that's what you do, I suppose. The track was eventually finished, and with its Latin-ballad dramatics and John Barry-type strings is a sublime piece of high-gloss kitsch. To complete the effect I brought in the acclaimed actress Julie T. Wallace, who had recently starred in an adaptation of Fay Weldon's master-piece *The Life and Loves of a She-Devil*, to speak the narration in the middle of the song. It has to be one of my preferred tracks.

We allowed Annie to finish her work on it before leaving, and I stupidly reinstated Billy – after all, he had done a wonderful job on the arrangement. He explained that it had been all Annie's idea to mutiny. This provided me the justification or excuse I needed to part company with her for good. As if I really needed one! In all honesty, I couldn't have parted with Billy then, because I wanted the album to be string-orientated and, though temperamental, he was also a very talented string arranger and I really wanted his arrangements on the album. I thought that with the departure of Annie everything would be all right. How wrong I was!

Unfortunately it wasn't quite the end of the Annie saga either. We were booked to do a tour of Italy as special guests of Robert Smith's band the Cure. I had misgivings about this from the outset. I naturally hate being the support (sorry, special guests) on anyone's tour but Stevo had assured me it was necessary promotion for *The Stars We Are*. It was too late to back out, so Annie consented to do the tour. But it was to be a major mistake.

It started promisingly enough in Rimini, with a passionate crowd of fans, but as the tour progressed it became obvious that even my following of fans was dwarfed in a stadium full of Cure supporters. I grew more despondent as the tour plodded on. There had been no time for proper rehearsals, and the atmosphere on stage was frosty to say the least. Annie and I never spoke to each other throughout. There was no feedback or chemistry from the audience – just miser-able Italians waiting for the Cure, watching depressed musicians going through the motions. To make things worse, we went on stage while it was still daylight, so there was no lighting to help the mood. I felt uncomfortable, exposed and vulnerable. The sets became shorter and shorter, the material less and less appropriate. In Rome, Depeche Mode came to the show and, as the audience threw coins, I was transported back to that concert all those years ago in Rayleigh, Essex, when Soft Cell had played. I tried everything on those shows. Bob Smith was really understanding when I asked him if I could miss out a show. He is a sweet, kind guy.

At the final show, in Milan – a place where I had usually gone down a storm – I announced that this was the last La Magia show (as if anyone cared) and afterwards jumped into a car with Huw Feather, our faces a mix of defeat, exhaustion and relief. It had been a gruelling and debilitating experience, and one that I would never repeat. I haven't seen Annie Hogan since that night, nor have I played another show in Italy.

Huw Feather and I were still friends, but I told him that I no longer wanted to work with him. I also felt it was time to move on. I hoped our friendship would survive this – after all, we had known each other since school, been through so many good times, and loved each other as only good friends can. He was hurt by my decision, applied some Jewish guilt – which he was adept at – but in the end accepted it. It was for me the end of an era. I felt a weight lift from my shoulders. At last I had artistic freedom, and could work with whom I wanted.

*

One of the reasons why 'A Lover Spurned' is such a special record to me is that it was the first time that I met and worked with the French artists Pierre et Gilles, who were to become my dear friends. I had read a magazine article about these artists, one a photographer, the other a painter, who worked together to create beautiful retouched photographs that were unique, erotic and mysterious, and iconized their subjects. I showed the article to Tris Penna, who coincidentally had seen the very same article himself, and had had ideas along the same lines. I was desperate to work with them for the sleeve of the single, and for them to direct the video for 'A Lover Spurned'. Tris thought they would be perfect for me, and flew them both to London.

I was incredibly nervous about meeting these two Frenchmen, and I broke out in a sweat when I entered the record company's office to see them. Even the fact that they lived in Paris intimidated me – I knew how some Parisians could behave: that they could be arrogant and disorganized, aloof and preoccupied with fashion. When I saw them both sat there with Tris – Gilles the blond angel with a sweet,

Performing 'A Lover Spurned' in a Bangkok go-go bar.

Above: 'High Roller' Stevo with the luscious Cleo Rocos. *(Jay Eff)*

Right: Initiation in the Church of Satan – Anton LaVey sent his ordained high priest Boyd Rice.

Below: With Cynthia Payne backstage after my concert at the Liverpool Philharmonic.

Above: Barbara Windsor and me on holiday in Fire Island, guests of John Addy and Nicky Marsh.

Right: With my style guru and international designer Roland Mouret at Fire Island.

Sandwiched between Raven O and Joey Arias at Freedom.

Left: 'The Legend' P. J. Proby signing to EMI.

Below: 'What the fuck am I doing this for?' With Zig and Zag.

Opposite page: Photo by Mike Owen.

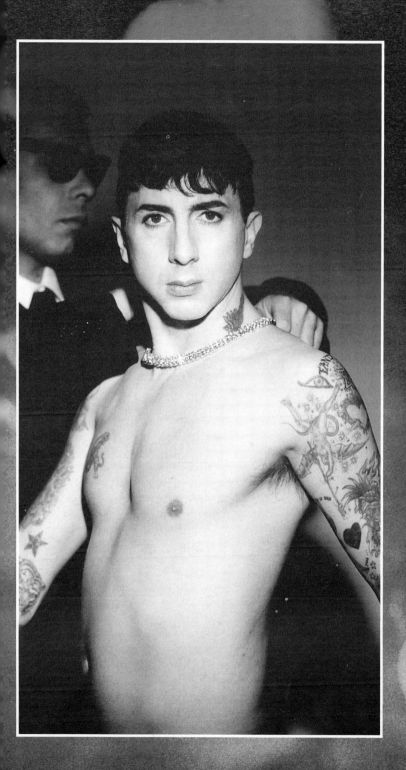

Some of the women in my life . . .

Bette, Molly, Courtney, Patsy and Edina . . .

... and, of course, some of the men in my life.

Right: Chris Eubank – philosophical moment and such a great fighter.

Below left: Jeff Stryker – 'Hot'.

Below right: Russian poet Slava and film-maker Bruce La Bruce.

Happiest of all when on stage.

Photo by Helen Marsden.

sensitive smile and Pierre the dark devilish one with an air of mischievous eroticism, contrasting and striking, identically dressed in army combat gear – I was pleasantly surprised by their masculinity and informality. (I had almost expected two effete fashion types.) I liked them immediately.

Tris took the meeting. 'I don't want Marc to look too gay,' he said (bless him), and I wondered quite how Pierre et Gilles were going to make me look masculine when their art seemed to be the very antithesis of such a thing. They both seemed bewildered at Tris's attempts to point out that they should not let me appear camp or effeminate: to them it must have seemed such a contradiction. But Tris was concerned that once we all got together, away from his watchful eye, we might create a festival of outrageous camparama. With my past record, he was right to be worried.

So Pierre et Gilles were commissioned to do the sleeve for the single and to direct the accompanying video, and I flew to Paris for the photo session for the sleeve. The session was to take place at their studio and workshop. The walls of the place were adorned in brightly coloured art and photo-montages of pop stars, Indian film stars, trashy pictures and postcards, and assorted memorabilia from their worldly travels. I fell in love with them both, just as I did with their ever-present assistant, Tomah, and it was to be the start of a very special friendship.

Since that first photo session I have been their model many times over the years. Once as a sad devil in a garden of innocence, another time as an absinthe-drinking Verlaine, and even once with the cabaret singer Marie France, perched together atop a wedding cake as newly-weds framed in a heart of flowers. And their introducing me to Marie France formed another friendship. Marie France starred alongside me as the jilted lover in the video for 'A Love Spurned'. A performer herself in the colourful Parisienne cabarets, a film star and arch beauty, her mysterious past concerned Tris somewhat. But his concern was unfounded. He was only looking after me, though, and he worried too much because he cared too much about his acts, cared deeply about his projects.

Pierre et Gilles flew to England to direct the video. If Tris had hoped it would not portray me as too camp, he was sadly disappointed. The video is filmed in a style of sweet naivety, with bright colours, sequins and bubbles, and the overall effect is hauntingly beautiful. In many ways it parodies kitsch, transcending it and emerging as a piece of stylized art. It has been copied many times in videos and commercials since, but never with quite the charm and humour of the original. Together Pierre et Gilles have influenced pop culture enormously over the past decade, and have spawned countless imitations. (REM's video for 'Losing My Religion' is clearly influenced by Pierre et Gilles' still-life paintings.) But their work remains unique, and few have attained their level of execution or perfection. They are the only artists that I have worked with with whom I have felt truly comfortable, whom I have trusted totally and never interfered with feeling completely in tune with their ideas, sources and inspiration. I hope that working together we have inspired each other.

I can think of few other artists for whom I have such high regard. Whenever I pose for them I know the outcome will be something quite special, magical. Each photograph is a theatrical adventure involving props, costumes, make-up and attitude. They know from the outset the image they require, and insist on perfection in even the tiniest detail. A few critics have dismissed their work as kitsch, but it is not. Kitsch means tawdry, vulgarized or pretentious, none of which applies to Pierre et Gilles. Their work is beautiful, evocative, erotic and sensual. It is a deeply nostalgic yearning for lost innocence, a search for naivety and for the richness of storytelling. In their paintings, saints and sinners are one – each appears free of sin, free of that terrible obstacle that mankind has devised. We look at their work and employ our own imagination upon it, or at the very least allow its aesthetic to sweep us away.

It was Pierre and Gilles who restored my love of Paris. Together, many times, we explored the Paris night (often helped on by Ecstasy) visiting the drag cabarets and the sequinned striptease of the *Folies Bergère*, the secret underworld spots, cruising areas and red-light zones. Once, after a party, they took me to an underground tunnel near the Pont d'Austerlitz, lit only by the lights of the cars passing above. Gay men had sex in the eerie darkness, in silence. On another occasion we toured bars, discos and sex clubs, where they were constantly surrounded by the most beautiful of Paris's people. Through them I made many friends in Paris – in particular Ken, an attractive Vietnamese American boy who also modelled for their portraits. I always hoped we could become lovers, but living in different cities in different countries made this rather difficult.

During the rest of the decade I would meet up with Pierre and Gilles in many cities throughout the world, from New York to Bangkok, and we would share many special times. In Bangkok in 1991, while on holiday to escape the depression that had settled over Europe owing to the Gulf War, I performed a special show for them in a Thai go-go bar. I had a glittering gold-lamé outfit made by a Thai tailor. Surrounded on stage by muscled go-go boys and stunning lady-boys, I performed a special version of 'A Lover Spurned' for them, miming to a bootleg tape I'd found on one of the many stalls in the night market Patpong. It was a magical moment – one of so many that I have shared with them both.

Working with Pierre and Gilles was the beginning of what I call my French period. I had always been influenced and inspired by French *chanson*, but Pierre and Gilles reinforced my love for that music and for the more esoteric intellectual music of such Left Bank singers as Juliette Greco and Barbara. They also turned me on to a wide range of French popular singers such as Dalida and Claude François. Dalida's favourite restaurant, Graziano's, is covered in portraits of the diminutive French icon, and became a regular haunt of mine.

'A Lover Spurned' became one of the most popular singles all over Europe, and made the Top Thirty in England. I have to thank Pierre et Gilles for much of its success because the video created so much interest. Their photos of me have been seen all over the world and have made me an icon many times over. I have also watched their own success grow as stars have lined up to have their portraits taken by them – they have worked with no less than Madonna, Jean-Paul Gaultier, Kylie Minogue, Catherine Deneuve, Sylvie Vartan, Jeff Stryker and Nina Hagen, to name but a few.

Marie France too became a special part of my life. I wrote a couple of songs for her – 'The Flame' and 'Sheherazade' – and also sang on two duets with her – '*À quoi ça sert l'amour*' (a famous Piaf song) and 'Autumn Leaves'. These songs were made available as a collectors' CD called *Marie et Marc*. In addition we have performed together in both Paris and London.

*

I had started in 1986 a Jacques Brel tribute album, and this was finally released on Rough Trade records at the beginning of the nineties, after what had started as a labour of love had ended up driving me to the point of despair and tears. It is hard now to remember how it had initially come about, but during the recording of the *Mother Fist* album I had contacted the writer Paul Buck with a view to his translating some of Brel's songs that English singers had not recorded before. Paul and I had kept in touch since I had performed at his tribute show to Georges Bataille. Paul was another person who excited my interest in French music and literature, sending me tapes of Juliette Greco, Barbara and Leo Ferrer, and books of Baudelaire and Verlaine. He had a genuine passion and understanding of this music, and I thought that he, if anyone, would have the qualifications to translate the Brel songs, and perhaps some of the songs of Greco and Barbara too. I felt it would be wrong for me to sing them in French, as I wanted fully to understand what I was singing about, and be able to draw on the appropriate feelings. Just as artists I had respected had turned me on to Brel, I wanted to inspire some of my audience, so that through me perhaps they too could discover the brilliance of him as an artist.

Paul rose to the occasion and worked furiously and passionately on the translations. I would telephone him and say how I'd love to do such and such a song. When I received the translation, I would record a rough demo, rearranging the structure if necessary to aid the rhythm. I was excited by the poetry of the words and by the rich subject matter – themes of death, incest, taboo and passion for life. I kept the arrangements of the songs as bare as possible, sometimes using only percussion and piano, but listening to them now, years later, some of them sound a little too cabaret for me, too serious and not personal enough. For the most part, what I had failed to understand in the songs is that, whatever the subject matter, they are intensely celebratory and optimistic; even songs filled with regret at the passing of life are about the rapture of self-realization and discovery.

I worked on so many songs that there was enough for a double album, or in this case two albums. And EMI had no problem with my Brel album – as long as it had nothing to do with them. Meanwhile, along with the volume of work, invoices mounted up from studios and musicians. People may share your passion for the art, but never the expenses, and I never stopped to consider that other people had lives and bills of their own to meet. It started to turn into a financial nightmare – as is almost always the case when I indulge in personal projects – and I was left with a double album of half-finished songs.

On top of that there was the complex publishing aspect to sort out – permission to use the translations, approvals from the writers, and deals to be done. All this I left to Paul. Fortunately for me he was working even more from love than I was. He was a man in his element, and in his numerous letters told me that that was what I should be focusing on in my career, and not that pop stuff (which he considered was beneath me). Beneath me or not, I could ill afford to ignore the pop stuff, and this issue was eventually to cause us to fall out.

Paul felt he had to send me page after page of critique whenever I performed on television or made a video. He would expound on every negative detail – such as how old I looked (not a good idea to tell me that), how bad the lighting was, or how terrible I sounded. In fact it seemed that Paul didn't like anything unless it was the Brel or French material, and in no uncertain terms he told me so. Then it came to my attention that he was writing to fans, giving them his personal opinion of my career (and then later, allegedly, of my personal life too). I was infuriated, and what had been a productive working relationship quickly deteriorated. I tried to repay him for much of the work he had undertaken, contributing money and working on backing vocals for an album by his protégée Melinda Miel, a sweet, talented girl whom he wanted to fashion into his vision of a torch singer.

The Brel recordings were eventually polished up by producer and maestro Charles Gray (who had worked on the Agnes Burnelle album), and were received ecstatically around Europe, with glowing reviews. The French paper *Libération* called my singing *écorché* – a term applied to *chanson* singers which means 'flayed, guts exposed, stripped naked to reveal the bone'. I think it's a compliment. I was even hailed as the new Brel – ridiculous I know, but I'm just telling you it like it was – and Brel's estate praised the album as one of the best interpretations of his work in years. (I'm sure the fact that they owned the publishing rights didn't influence their enthusiasm.) Most British reviews of *Jacques* were less generous, however, a few dismissing me as self-indulgent for believing I could sing Brel's hallowed songs. What credentials did I have? Actually, more than most. But Paul Buck hadn't helped the situation with his over-impassioned sleeve notes that hinted that I was the reincarnation of Brel himself. That was inviting trouble. Brel is, of course, still considered a European thing, and any English speaker who dares to venture into that territory (Scott Walker may be the sole exemption) is deemed a cabaret poseur.

The album did very well in Germany – a country that has always been supportive of me as an artist – and to accompany it I did a small tour of strip clubs and theatres playing the whole album live – nothing more, nothing less – accompanied by just a piano and percussion.

Listened to now, the album seems a very flawed and frustrating body of work. It could have been so much better, so much fuller and rounded, if I had taken the time to record it properly, given it my full attention and worked in *conjunction* with a producer. Instead I snatched time when I could, recording it in dribs and drabs between other commitments. And it would have been better if I had deconstructed the songs, and recorded them with a more relaxed delivery instead of treating them so preciously – hey, if I had just thought about it properly!

Yet, despite all that, there are some real moments of magic on it. Paul Buck's translations are beautiful and creative, more often than not finding the inner soul of the song and relaying it through a richly imaginative use of language. 'J'arrive' translated as 'I'm Coming', a song about death – 'from chrysanthemums to chrysanthemums' I sing, the flowers of death. The chorus becomes an emotive plea for deliverance, and inspired one journalist's puerile comment that the song must be about Brompton Cemetery (an infamous cruising ground for gay men) – if he had been better educated he might have seen the irony of his comment. 'The Devil OK' and 'Litany for a Return' are another two of the more successful tracks. But once again I had destroyed the song 'If You Go Away'. What had become a ritual tour de force in live concerts failed miserably when committed to disc, as for some reason I had gone for a lightweight pop interpretation complete with hamfisted chorus.

This time around the criticisms didn't hurt me too much, as I'd prepared myself for them – knowing in my heart of hearts they might just ring true. I did, however, remain steadfast in my belief that I was qualified to sing Brel songs, of singing them as well as anyone else – even if this album was not the one to prove it.

Much more successful on an artistic level was a second album of French songs, which I called *Absinthe*. It was begun at the same time as the Brel songs, but was not finished and released until 1993. It is a much better sounding album and a complete vision, though the vocals still seem too theatrical as I tried too hard. Part of the problem was the translations: they were just too wordy and complicated. In French the songs seem to flow effortlessly, floating on the rhythm and sound of the language, whereas the English equivalents sounded clipped and cluttered.

My favourite moments are such songs as 'The Slave' – a song found for me by Pierre et Gilles, in which the narrator not only dreams of being sodomized by a well-endowed black man but also wishes he was a woman too, and one who wears purple eyeshadow and is displayed in a cage. My kind of song – and great subject matter for radio, as you can imagine.

Juliette Greco's 'Secret Child' is a breathtaking song, given an extra twist of perversity as I am singing about my pregnancy. Barbara's 'Incestuous Love', written for her son, is self-explanatory, as is the raunchy striptease version of Greco's 'Undress Me'. The latter song is a firm favourite on the catwalk soundtracks of fashion shows. Rimbaud's poem 'My Little Lovers' was set by Billy McGee to form a complex blend of words and music. With hindsight, only 'Yesterday When I was Young' seems out of place, but it is such a glorious song that I couldn't resist it.

The album was eventually finished in Paris with the cream of Parisian musicians and a young piano player who had replaced Annie Hogan called Martin Watkins. Martin was introduced to me through a friend as a troubled yet talented boy who needed a musical break. He proved to be an excellent arranger and player, and incredibly handsome too. Yet his life seemed fraught with problems and unhappiness, which always threatened to get in the way of his talent. For nearly three years we would work together and I was extremely fond of him. As well as finishing the French album, Martin undertook a series of acoustic shows around the world with me in the early nineties. We travelled to Japan, Europe and Russia, and our shared sense of humour made the shows memorable and fun at a time when both of us had troubles in our private lives.

One song that was eventually left off *Absinthe* was a version of the Verlaine poem 'A Thousand and Three' which I'd set to music. It's a poem which is to be found in his volume of erotic verse entitled *Hommes et femmes*, and it refers to all the different lovers he had had, whom he describes in vivid detail. When I first recorded the song the tabloid paper the *Sun* ran a story with the headline 'Almond sings Pornographic Gay Songs'. It went on, 'Pop star Marc Almond has recorded an album of explicitly pornographic love songs . . .' It was a cringe-inducing piece of journalism, made all the worse because it was true – the song '1003' was as bold as any singer of my status has ever been in dealing with such taboo subject matter. I performed it a few times in concert, but was eventually persuaded to leave it off the album as no distributor would touch it. It would have ended up overshadowing everything else, and might have been misconstrued as being shocking or titillating. (As if I'd want that!) I thought back to the 'Sex Dwarf' video and the tiresome 'eight pints of what's your tipple' rumour, and thought, 'What do I expect if I persist in releasing songs like this?' As it turned out, no one cared about the album anyway – I could have been photographed on the cover swinging naked from a chandelier with a cheese roll shoved up my backside and no one would have noticed. France's press was less generous with its praise this time round, asking how dare I defile sacred French songs by translating them into English. I suppose I could have just as easily defiled them in French. Make that a French baguette shoved up my backside.

Stevo was suspiciously supportive of both these albums and

insisted they must be regarded as works of art. Personally I'd reached the stage where I just wanted to make another pop record. Paul Buck – as brilliant as he is and as grateful to him as I was – had driven me crazy with his French obsessions. Annie Hogan and the musicians had nearly ruined me and Some Bizarre with their invoices. (In fact Annie continued for several years to submit invoices, until the Musicians Union intervened and confirmed that she had been paid in full.) I had lost friends, my health had deteriorated, my reputation was tarnished, and no one noticed the album when it came out anyway. Art – you can keep it! It doesn't pay the rent.

*

After the 'A Lover Spurned' single charted, I began work on what was to be the album *Enchanted*. I felt curiously detached from the whole proceedings. Bob Kraushar had taken over the production, as he had made 'Something's Gotten Hold of My Heart' such a huge success, and he worked with the programmer Gary Maughn. Billy McGee was still aboard as keyboard player and arranger, but it was obvious to me that this was going to be a computerized album recorded in a sterile studio situation, and from the outset there was conflict between Bob and me about this. Bob wanted a synthesized, polished album, but I wanted a more organic album featuring orchestras, Egyptian percussion and strange, exotic instruments.

The process became extremely drawn-out. Hour upon hour, day after day was spent finding a particular sound or twiddling and fine-tuning until it all became a laborious, joyless exercise. This was Bob's first major production, and understandably he wanted to create something perfect. I, on the other hand, wanted instant results – spontaneity and surprise, passion and grit. I wanted excitement in the studio, chemistry at any cost: conflicts, rows, dramas, sweat – all those ingredients that make for an interesting recording. I wanted to be the conductor, waving my baton as musicians came in and out, brandishing strange instruments that created exotic sounds. But none of that happened. I wanted to be Phil Spector brandishing a gun and shouting orders to add to the creative process of making my album. But Bob was having none of it. I would stand in front of the microphone singing a line over and over again while he became increasingly frustrated because he felt it was never perfect enough. He was a technophile, and would have happily replaced everyone with the passionless dependability of his computer if he could. I would sing my heart out, give everything I could and even a little more, and he would simply say, 'Well, that will just have to do.'

I don't think Bob understood my songs. He thought them too complicated, too unconventional, too not-pop. He couldn't hear that big hit. And – you know what? – he was right. The arrangements were all too fussy, far too complex to be commercial. I wanted to hear and feel real strings, musicians playing their utmost and filling my songs with sweeping emotion like the songs from my youth – those of Gene or Scott or P. J. Proby. Bob just wanted to bring it all back to some kind of simplicity and minimalism. String arrangements were still considered not hip then, too muso. Now, of course, such arrangements are in vogue. Obviously I was too far ahead of my time. It probably needed a Dave Ball in there sorting the whole mess out.

When I brought in Hossam Ramzy, one of the most acclaimed percussionists in Egypt, if not the world, Bob was lost for words, horrified at my attempt to inject some reality into his vision. Hassam has played for the likes of Peter Gabriel and Plant & Page, and has toured extensively under his own name. He played on two tracks, 'Orpheus in Red Velvet' and 'Widow Weeds', and I felt he brought the sessions to life, that at last things were happening as I wanted them to. But it was not to be. His work was clipped, snipped, sampled and put into the computer until there was barely anything left of it. Again – and I hate to concede it – Bob was in part right. Left to my own devices I would have thrown so much into the mix that I would have buried myself in the process. It was never that Bob was wrong, just that we came from different places and had quite separate visions.

In the end of what seemed for ever the album was finished. I look on *Enchanted* as my 'world' album. It's an exotic journey around the world and through it, a journey into myself. It certainly reflected the type of music I was listening to at that time. It is part Spanish, part Arabic, even part Turkish. There are Indian bhangra influences on the track 'Death's Diary', Middle Eastern influences on 'Orpheus in Red Velvet', Brazilian lambada on 'Carnival of Life', Celtic flavourings on 'The Sea Still Sings', and Latin drama in 'A Lover Spurned'. The richly varied themes are encompassed in the cover picture, once again by Pierre et Gilles, who portrayed me as a sea-god swimming with a mermaid. It's my favourite album cover.

At the time, though, I felt disappointed with the result – perhaps because I was at such a low in my life, and had felt so detached from the recording process. Making an album is a lot like having sex: if bells don't ring you feel deflated, and then the critics tell you how it was for them. Often you listen to the result and find you've contracted that old music-business disease demoitis – meaning that you yearn for the feelings the demos invoked in you, those feelings that have been lost in the rerecording. A year later I played the album and loved it. Bob Kraushar had produced a highly polished, wonderful-sounding album, which at the time I just couldn't hear. But at that time I was doubting and dismissing everything. 'Oh for Christ's sake, Marc,' you're saying – 'get over it.' But self-doubt equals self-loathing equals self-destruction equals more self-doubt. Try getting out of that one.

Mind you, the reviews were good to excellent throughout Europe, which could only mean one thing – poor sales. Perhaps there was too long a period between the release of the first single and the album. *Enchanted* sold to hardcore fans, but was largely ignored by the general public. My American record company, Capitol, felt the album sounded too European (meaning too arty) and were disappointed that it didn't sound like the last album. Nor did they understand the cover, which they deemed to be spooky. It was an album they felt had no place in the American market.

This whole period of European-styled music, which had included my Brel album and *Absinthe*, was something I just had to get out of my system if I was to move on. I know it would have been more sensible (meaning more commercial) to steer away from it, but you know me by now. I had no more feet to shoot, and I felt I had to be true to my heart – which does after all contain the word 'art'. Many of my fans rate the Brel and *Absinthe* albums as some of my best and truest work, but the music business frown, considering them to be tainted with the dreaded 'C' word – 'cabaret'. (There are two other words which they dread more, both four-letter 'F' words – 'folk' and 'funk'.) Cabaret is not commercial. Cabaret is not cutting-edge. Cabaret is fringe (another dreaded 'F' word). So all too soon you find yourself marginalized and isolated. The press dismiss you. You start to get invited on TV shows that have the word 'Cabaret' in the title, or 'Edinburgh', and then the offers of 'fringe theatre' start coming in. This is fine if you're an older artist without a record deal, but suicide in the pop market, and flat out on the mortician's slab if you want to be cutting-edge. Record companies might indulge you for a while – especially after a recent number one – but their patience quickly wears thin. They they take you aside and quietly say, 'No more of that French stuff, do you understand? No more.'

Part of the trouble I had in shaking off this particular phase of my career was that I had begun to believe my own press. Only the good press, of course. And in particular the pieces that hailed me in Europe as Britain's premier torch singer, the new Jacques Brel. And especially the ones that said I was a genius. 'Yes,' I told myself, 'that's me. That's what I am. They're right!' Hmm. I had well and truly lost the plot.

But suddenly friends took me aside and told me a few home truths, and for a short while reawakened some sense of reality. I had to renounce all the *chanson* and Brel stuff and (as a record-company pointed out) get back to being a pop singer while I still had it in me to be one. (But did I have it in me?) Then I was told the *chanson* stuff was making me look pretentious, highbrow, pedantic and – worst of all for me – old. I went on a television show and sang the Aznavour song 'Yesterday When I was Young', which I was told was ridiculous for someone to attempt while still in their thirties. But the song said a great deal about the way I was feeling about myself. I felt old, tired, jaded – an old whore past her prime, just like the ones who touted for trade down the back alleys in Barcelona. It was all becoming too tragic to be ironic, and the parody was parodying itself. I was dying inside.

*

My grandfather died in 1991. My mother told me over the phone, and after an initial numb feeling I felt a sense of relief. The reality was that for me he had died a few years earlier, after he was admitted to a home which could care for Alzheimer's sufferers. The tall Norwegian whom I had called Papa, who had walked me down the beach during my asthma attacks, ended his days being spoon-fed while he cried at the burden he had become. When my tears came for him, they came for myself, for the realization that I too was growing old, that all those things I had loved in my childhood were gone, though in some ways nearer than ever. Would he have been proud of the mess I was making of my life, despite all the superficial success?

When I went to his funeral, it was of course my grandmother I felt sad for. How hard it is for the living to cope with the burden of loss! In fact she seemed a little relieved, almost hyperactively caught up in the occasion. But I knew that would disappear. At least she could console herself that her husband had at last found peace, and that the strong man she had loved for so many years would not grow more debilitated and unrecognizable to her; that at least part of her memory of him remained unspoiled.

I was shocked at how small the coffin was, unable to relate it to his seven-foot frame. I decided then that I would never attend another funeral, that I would have my memories and feelings remain unsullied by such surreal occasions.

*

Life goes on.

Life went on, and it seemed to me then to matter so little. Two more singles were released from the album *Enchanted* – the Spanish-flavoured 'Desperate Hours' and the ballad 'Waifs and Strays'. Neither did particularly well in the charts, but at least they gave me the opportunity to work with the talented film-maker John Maybury, who directed both videos.

I had met John on a couple of occasions before. The first time was back in the Soft Cell period. I was at the Camden Palace when I was accosted by a young man brandishing a camera and spotlight in my face. Wherever I went he followed, filming me all the while. On acid at the time, I grew increasingly agitated and ended up attacking him. Still he filmed me. I grabbed his hand and bent back his fingers, almost breaking them. Still the camera rolled. 'You shit,' he said, 'I've bought all your records.'

The second time I met him was years later. I don't think he was even aware of my presence. It was at a party in a New York skyscraper for the fashion designers Body Map. He was lying semi-naked and comatose across a bed; beside him a couple of fashion-world acolytes were placing raw pieces of meat on his body. It was some private performance piece. My colleague looked at me and raised an eyebrow. 'Only in New York,' We left soon after.

Working with John was a completely new experience for me. We hit it off immediately, and enjoyed ourselves making what I still consider to be two great videos. John appealed to my vanity by making me look fabulous in a beautiful embroidered toreador out-fit, with gorgeous people dancing and posing around me. That was the video for 'Desperate Hours'. And, in complete contrast, the video for 'Waifs and Strays' had me looking terrific with gor-geous people dancing and posing around me. Yes, that's right, the needle was all the way over in the dangerous red zone of the campometer.

John and I adored the videos, but the record company – princi-pally Tris Penna – were hearing alarm bells. Tris immediately did a severe re-edit on John's version of 'Waifs and Strays', which under-standably upset John. There was just too much gayness in it, explained Tris. Perhaps Tris was right, for, beautiful as the video was, it was just not TV-friendly.

That was the last time I worked with John Maybury – though not through choice. He went on to make many great videos, including the award-winning Sinead O'Connor video for 'Nothing Compares 2 U', and more recently his feature-film biopic about Francis Bacon,

Love is The Devil, won him critical accolades. He really deserves such success, and I am glad to have worked with him.

*

I was in America doing a promotional tour for *Enchanted* (which was a totally pointless exercise, since the album wasn't released there) when I received a telephone call from Stevo. Not having a band at that point meant that no tour could be arranged, which overjoyed Stevo. It meant I had much more time to embark on interviews and promotion.

Stevo had some bad news for me. My option was up with EMI and they had to decide whether they wanted to renew or not. EMI wanted to keep me, but they wanted to renegotiate the contract, to make it more realistic and in keeping with my sales. *Enchanted* had been an expensive album for them, and the single 'A Lover Spurned' had cost over £40,000 just to record. I was £1.5 million in debt to them. To accept me for a third album they would have had to pay me £300,000, so understandably they wanted to renegotiate.

Taking advantage of their faltering, and his chance to wheel and deal, Stevo seized the moment. He told me that EMI had lost faith in me and that WEA (Warner Bros.) were ready to do an immediate deal. 'Head of Warners Rob Dickens wants to sign you right now,' he claimed.

I didn't want to leave EMI, and would have stayed even if it meant renegotiating the contract. I had loved working with Clive Black and especially Tris Penna and Murray. I had at last felt a kind of home and stability with people who cared – in a life that was fraught with insecurity. Stevo, however, was having none of it, making me believe I wasn't wanted. It seemed to me that he had mainly his own interests at heart and wanted to secure a lucrative deal with WEA. But he ranted on as only he can, and eventually I gave way and put the phone down, deflated and unsure once more of the future.

I had just started a promotional tour for Capitol and I still had ten days to get through, putting on a brave face for a record company that I was no longer on, for EMI and Capitol were linked. Ten days of interviews with that bombshell hanging over my head.

I didn't want to go to WEA. I had been down this Stevo-with-his-bright-ideas road before. I made a sorrowful call to Clive and Tris to thank them and tell them how much I had enjoyed working with them. It was a dark day when I packed my suitcase and waved a tear-stained goodbye to EMI. I was signed to a new record company before you could say déjà vu.

15

Unfinished Symphony

Rob Dickens, chairman of WEA, sat me down in his office for one of those 'honest talks' that you know is well meant but is laden with home truths that have you reaching for the razor blade. You know, the great confidence-building stuff like the world doesn't need another Marc Almond record (well, he did have a point there), that I looked like a circus freak (well, he had a point there too), and that I should write a song as good as 'People are People' by Depeche Mode (he didn't have a point there at all), which he proceeded to sing to me. He said that he judged a record by whether his girlfriend liked it and how it sounded in his car. 'Listen to this,' he said, putting on the new record by Enya (his discovery), and suddenly he was momentarily lost in his own world of self-congratulatory unit-moving brilliance.

Now don't get me wrong. I like and respect Rob Dickens immensely. I'm even a bit of a closet Enya fan, too. But what is good for her might not necessarily be good for me. I tried to see where the conversation was going.

Rob had a vision. God, did he have a vision – right down to the title of the album, *Tenement Symphony*, which he had taken from a favourite song featured in an old Marx Brothers movie. (Worrying or what?) He had it all planned – even what the cover would look like. He was personally taking over this project, my career, determined the next Marc Almond album would be done his way. I felt so emotionally destroyed at this point that I would have agreed to anything (even 'Knees up Mother Brown'). 'Give me a beat,' I thought, 'and I'll sing it.' I resigned myself to the situation, and surrendered meekly to the Master.

I had already recorded a number of tracks, mostly just demos, which included a couple with Dave Ball. One good thing that had come out of the *Enchanted* album was that it had at least reunited Dave and me. It had been hoped that 'Waifs and Strays' would be the single that might break the album; and, as it was very Soft Cellish, Stevo had suggested that Dave should do a dance mix. Dave was having success of his own as one half of the Grid, as well as producing and remixing other people's work. He agreed to take it on, but his mix came in too late, the single being released the very week that I left EMI for WEA. There was no hope of any promotion for that record, as I was with a new company by then. But it had broken the ice with Dave and me.

I now wanted to write with him again and I went to visit his studio and met his partner, Richard Norris. In the instant I walked in it was as if the last eight years of being apart had not happened. He was still the same old Dave, and it was great to see him again. In the time we were together we wrote three tracks – the extremely Soft Cell-sounding 'Meet Me in Your Dreams', the dark 'I've Never Seen Your Face' and the killer ballad with huge potential 'My Hand over My Heart'. It was a return to a sparse, dark pop sound – the magic combination of Almond and Ball – and it invoked excitement about music in me once again.

I had also recorded a handful of tracks with Billy McGee, but the sessions were fraught with tension and problems. Things were just not happening between us. I blew up one day at Billy; he had been given studio time to work on ideas and, rightly or wrongly, I felt the results were mediocre. I berated him for not being the songwriter he could be – or, more to the point, the one I needed. As an arranger he was second to none, but I felt he never could write a pop song. It all ended in tears after that, as it was bound to do one day. When Billy found out I was working with other people, he decided to sue me for songwriting credits and production credits. He wanted 50 per cent of the publishing during our working relationship together, although I felt he had not contributed 50 per cent on the songwriting. The very way I work – creating the melody, selecting the tempo, and writing the lyrics – leaves very little for anyone else to do but arrangement, which can never amount to an equal writing relationship. The only exceptions I make to this are when I'm working with Dave Ball.

Of course neither of us could agree, and we soon reached an impasse, both of us equally stubborn. I always felt I had been more than fair with credits, but Billy refused to accept it. Exhausted by the whole legal proceedings, and fearful of the legal aid he had been given, WEA settled with him just to close the whole issue. I deeply resented the implications of that. And, worse still, I was saddened that such a long working relationship had ended this way. I never saw or heard from Billy again, except through lawyers. It is so often the way, and so sad.

Shortly afterwards I found a co-writer to work with who was exciting and fresh – a young producer called John Coxon. John used R & B samples, trip-hop, break beats and soul grooves, and in him I felt I had found the partner I had been looking for. He was invigorating, dedicated and nineties-sounding. It was a soulful direction I felt I should be moving towards, and he was cutting-edge in that field.

But this had no place in Rob Dickens's vision, and he swept it all aside. Whereas he felt the material with Dave was good, and even the material with Billy was acceptable, the work I did with John Coxon he didn't get one iota. He felt it was all too 'small'. He wanted something grander – something that would surprise people, make them sit up and take notice, 'blow them away'.

'I know what you should do,' he exclaimed excitedly one day – ' "Jacky". You know, that Scott Walker song!' I did know. I felt indignation rising up inside of me and the words 'Fuck you' stuck in my throat, but I swallowed them back down quickly. Hadn't I just moved away from all that Brel stuff, at last got it out of my system? Was I about to take several paces backwards?

'That is a really great idea,' I said to him. I was confused. Hadn't Rob been vehemently against what he termed my 'cabaret persona'? Hadn't he said he'd hated that TV appearance when I sang Aznavour's 'Yesterday When I was Young'? I smiled, thinking it was a terrible idea. I felt that 'Jacky' was for Brel alone – it was his theme song, if you like. Of course Scott Walker's version had been outstanding, and it was obvious that Walker's version was the one Rob wanted me to revitalize. I smiled again at Rob. 'That's a great idea,' I repeated.

I was really worried. I thought that the public wouldn't understand who Jacky was or what I was singing about. I thought people might think I was calling myself by a girl's name, or, worse, that people would think it was a 'gay thing'. As much as I adore Jacques Brel, and acknowledge his influence on me, I just wanted to move on. But Rob was sold on the idea, and that was that. I quelled the despair I felt inside, swallowed my pride, and decided that if life throws you a lemon it's time to make lemonade. But then Rob threw me a sweetener.

'Trevor Horn will produce it. That's who you should work with. I'll ring him straight away and arrange for you both to have dinner.'

'Oh God,' I thought, 'I hate meeting people.'

'That's a great idea,' I said.

'It's better than great.'

At least Rob was a visionary, I kept telling myself, and hadn't I always admired people who were passionate? So I was finally beaten into corporate submission. I decided to accept it all as part of this journey that I called my career. Perhaps it would all work out for the best, just drifting on the current of other people's ideas, handing yourself over to the highest power, and seeing what happens.

But Rob was on a roll. 'I know what. The song "Eloise",' he then suggested.

'No. The Damned have just covered it!' I had to make a stand.

'What about . . .' Rob's mind was working overtime – ' "Thoughts of Emmerlist Davjack" by the sixties group the Nice?'

'No, too obscure. And, besides, the lyrics wouldn't suit me. Why would I want to sing a song by the Nice?'

Before he could suggest anything else, I quickly put forward a suggestion of my own – 'The Days of Pearly Spencer'. I had loved the song by David McWilliams ever since I'd listened to it in my teens.

Rob seemed to like the idea. It seemed to fit into his idea of a suite of orchestrated 'grand' songs, which would become one side of an album, while all the tracks I had co-written would be relegated to the other side. 'It will be the two sides of Marc Almond – the grit and the glitter,' he announced to me. Rob was only interested in the glitter side – especially now he envisaged Trevor Horn at the helm.

I must say I was beginning to warm to the idea. 'Warm,' I said.

I met Trevor Horn for lunch soon after, to discuss working together. I was a nervous wreck at meeting this legendary figure whose reputation was as over the top as his production work. Trevor started sounding me out over the appetizer, trying to decide if he wanted to spend his heavily-in-demand time working with a supposedly uncompromising and difficult artist (I'm talking about me) – an artist who wrote dark (meaning weird) lyrics and put self-expression (creative suicide) before commerciality (hits). In Trevor's world commercial success came first, and he had an unblemished reputation that he didn't want to risk soiling on me if he sensed difficulty. There would be no room for art, of course, but he was open to the odd suggestion or two.

I liked him. We found that we shared many musical tastes, including the huge production numbers of the sixties pop era and the kitsch, overblown records known as pocket operas – 'Johnny Remember Me', 'Excerpt from a Teenage Opera' and 'Eloise' – all records I loved from my youth. Trevor seemed set on doing 'Jacky' too, and 'Pearly Spencer', as well as his own production job on one of the new songs I had co-written with Dave Ball, 'My Hand over My Heart'. So we shook hands. It began.

Working with Trevor Horn was an exciting experience, at first. He would have all of his studios in Notting Hill on the go at the same time, engineers, tape ops and mixing producers all beavering away at his bidding. In one studio someone would be reprogramming a track in a different key simply so Trevor could choose which he preferred; in another studio he'd have the American remixer Brian Malouf doing nine mixes of a track just so Trevor could edit between them; and in yet another studio I would be vocalling a track over and over and over. In the case of 'My Hand over My Heart', so many mixes were done that I lost count. As time passed Trevor would get increasingly frustrated at not being able to take something where he wanted – wherever that was. He acted like a man obsessed, and on several occasions dramatically called the whole thing off. Then it was on again.

One day I arrived to find him admiring some new acquisitions – countless old instruments – Hammond organs, timpani, mellotrons – all new toys to be played with and then be stored away. He looked up at me. 'You know, I don't think I can do what I want with the song "Pearly Spencer", so I'm calling it all off.' I panicked. Of all the songs, I believed that would be the biggest hit. 'I need that extra twist,' he said, 'and I'm just not feeling it.'

That extra twist came when he audaciously suggested I should write an extra verse for the song, to finish the story. I tentatively obliged, Trevor liked it, and the whole thing was back on. Then off again. Then on again. Trevor added thunder effects, and flew from LA Prince's guitarists Wendy and Lisa to play on one of the tracks, though unbelievably their parts ended up not being used. Money was being spent at a fantastic rate.

For 'Jacky', Trevor wanted to get a heavy electro sound for the basic track, so he took a sample from a German band called Sun Electric. (Coincidentally, they were signed to his own record label, ZTT.) He couldn't get the sample to fit into his scheme of the track, so of course he flew to Berlin and had the band play the piece live to his exacting requirements. He topped everything off with a seventy-piece orchestra and choir, fabulously arranged by the Oscar-winning arranger and composer Anne Dudley.

When I eventually heard the finished tracks I was floored. Camp perhaps, but they were extraordinary. I was enthralled. I wasn't so thrilled, however, by the track that had obviously been included as a sweetener in the deal – a Trevor Horn/Stephen Wooley composition called 'What is Love?' It's a good song, but far too eighties for where I wanted to be then and just not my style at all. I felt it was out of place on the album, and would have much rather written something original or at least picked another classic to cover. But the song was to be included regardless. That's business. Unfortunately, however, this meant that I had failed to write the required number of tracks to fulfil my publishing agreement with Warner Chappell (WEA's publishing arm), which meant I owed WEA another album. This should have been my last.

I felt 'Jacky' was just a little too near to Scott Walker's version for comfort, and my vocal too mannered and West End. I wondered what Brel would have thought of my treatment which certainly veered into some kind of camp, however sincerely I tried to sing it – probably *because* of how sincerely I tried to sing it. I certainly got a huge kick out of performing it, though, and it became a huge audience favourite. I also wondered what Brel might have thought of the subsequent video and TV appearances to promote it as a single, complete with dancing girls surrounding me. It was on the *Wogan* show that I felt the most uncomfortable and wooden, trying desperately to execute the rehearsed dance routines. It was all too stagey.

The video, on the other hand, by the French director Philippe Gaultier, is one of my finest moments. In it I stand on a lectern in front of a giant portrait of myself – a reference to *Citizen Kane* – my megalomania and self-obsession clearly emphasized. In other parts of the performance I ham it up in front of an audience, approving their sycophantic adulation. As one person pointed out the Aznavour reference, another insisted acid-house Aznavour. Only a French director could have come up with something so stylish and beautifully paced.

'Jacky' was released as a single and made the Top Twenty. I was pleased that it got higher than Scott's version – at least I think I was pleased. In Europe, although it did well, many critics thought it was too overblown for the true spirit of Brel. I responded by saying that I had done the understated cabaret Brel and now here was the pop star Brel. I was happy that I had brought his work back into the charts, even though a great many gay people considered it a song about a drag artist!

'My Hand over My Heart' is one of my favourite singles from *Tenement Symphony*, and very much an Almond–Ball collaboration. It has a glorious string arrangement, and the finale always brings a tear to my eye. I was sorry that it didn't make it higher than number thirty in the chart. In the video, also directed by Philippe Gaultier, I sing in the rain dressed in sequins, accompanied by an exquisite dancer in a Thierry Mugler outfit. Looking at it now, I suspect it was again just too camp for the mass public's taste – or at least that is what WEA's marketing people told me.

'The Days of Pearly Spencer' was the biggest hit off the album, getting to number four and bringing my first *Top of the Pops* appearance for several years. A bloody cover version yet again had got me a major hit – and, to top it all, with one of the worst videos I have ever made! The less I like something, the more successful it is. What does that say to you? Not that I disliked the song. After all, I chose it. I think it's great, and fits perfectly into my world. I was told the composer, David McWilliams, ordinarily a shy, retiring man, had to go into hiding to evade whatever momentary spotlight it cast on him. Though it was my biggest hit in Europe for quite a while, when the American record company heard the song they dismissed it: 'It's like an Irish jig. Don't get it. Is this a joke?' Oh well, thankfully not everything crosses the Atlantic successfully.

The follow-up single to 'Pearly Spencer' was to be 'What is Love?' (the Trevor Horn composition – naturally). I was not happy about this, much preferring 'I've Never Seen Your Face' to be released and remixed as a club-only dance single. I preferred to end the album campaign on a high with a major hit. I had never liked Trevor's song – it just wasn't me – and I couldn't bring my heart and soul to it. When I heard a remix that Trevor had done, with most of my vocal excluded, I put my foot down and refused to allow it to be a single. My patience had worn through and I was having no more of company politics. The track sounded like the worst of Europop! WEA expressed anger, then disappointment, and decided there and then to call a halt to the whole campaign. And I thought I could be childish! But wait a minute, where was my manager? Busy ingratiating himself with the record company.

The cover of the album was another thing I hated with a vengeance – a cutesy-looking photo of me, with a graphic design to make it seem like the traditional classical-music cover so beloved of the seventies. I much preferred a shot of a tall, glamorous female model carrying me in her arms – it reminded me of early Roxy Music. But the photo was Rob's decision, and that wasn't part of his vision.

On the whole, the album was a long way from my true direction at this time – I wanted a scratchy, sampled, R & B soul album with the producer John Coxon, and, as I have pointed out many times since in interviews, it was the album I felt most excluded from in the making. Trevor Horn would have had me phone in my performance if he could, and Rob Dickens believed that the one thing spoiling his Marc Almond album was me. God knows how we must frustrate record companies – if they could just get rid of those annoying people called artists and be left to get on with it! I felt for the most part like an unwanted guest on my own recording. I am naturally grateful (is that the right word?) that Rob gave me the opportunity to work with such a legendary producer as Trevor Horn, and helped me get some major hits into the bargain, but enough already! All right, my profile was raised and the album received great reviews, but what matters in the end is what matters as an artist.

Caren Myers in *Melody Maker* wrote:

> It's hard not to love Marc Almond – his extravagances, his operatic gestures, his sordid past, his guilt, his glitter – he's the sort of romantic for whom the adjective 'hopeless' was created. And even if it is part affection (he is after all a born performer) his desire to make a big gaudy splash in the still waters of pop is, despite all odds, still thrilling. *Tenement Symphony* is a gorgeous piece of indulgence.

Another reviewer said, 'Nothing less than Lorca meets Don Juan in the bar of Barry Manilow's Copacabana.' I'm not so sure about that one.

*

On a personal front, I awoke one morning with my usual hangover to what was for me shattering news. Overnight, the government had banned the prescription drug Halcion – that little blue tablet that had for the past seven years controlled my life. It had been proved that people were suffering terrible addiction problems after one year's use, and the result was memory loss, aggressive behaviour and violent episodes (in one case allegedly leading to murder). And here was I, in 1992, having taken them for seven years. Not that I necessarily knew what year it actually was then!

All the symptoms struck a horrible chord, but that didn't concern me. All that bothered me was where I would get some more. I had only the previous day exchanged a new prescription and, with my hoard, had just over a month's supply. Then what would I do? Panic consumed me. I decided to plan several trips abroad, where the tablets were still available. It was quite out of the question to give the drug up, though the situation made me consider it. I even rang a helpline, who sent me a book on withdrawal. Having read it, stopping taking Halcion seemed too horrible to contemplate, so instead I took a flight to Thailand and in the chemists in downtown Bangkok I bought boxes and boxes of the tablets. A few months later I flew to New York with the same task in mind, an American doctor obliging me. I would fly to Switzerland or other European destinations for the same purpose. And this went on for three years – three long years of feeding my addiction, suppressing the fear of insomnia, of panic attacks, of the hallucinations of withdrawal.

Slowly, almost imperceptibly, my life began to finally unravel completely. Whatever sanity there was that had seen me through this far was now fragmenting. I thought that without Halcion I would die a slow, painful death. My addiction had at last taken over, and now completely controlled my life. Whatever I did or planned, the consideration of supply would be foremost in my mind. And so that addiction led on, as all addictions do, to extreme behaviour on other fronts.

For three years I found myself caught up at the London techno clubs FF and later Trade on many Saturday and Sunday nights. It was a close friend of mine who had actually discovered the club Turnmill's, then a paltry wine bar doing no business, and opened FF there. It was named after a satirical magazine that he wrote and put out every month. FF struggled but eventually picked up, and then Trade opened and went on to become one of the most successful techno clubs in the country. Night after night I started once more to take E – by now the most popular drug in Britain. Millions were taking it every month, and it became synonymous with techno and rave culture. But you know all this.

It seemed such a long time ago that Cindy had introduced me to it, and it was hard to believe that this drug, which had once been the secret of an elite few, had become a common recreation for so many. But soon it was barely recognizable as the Ecstasy I knew – perhaps because the demand was too great, it was mixed with other drugs, cheaper ones such as amphetamine, LSD or even heroin. Later still it would be mixed with the drug called Special K, and eventually so adulterated that a whole generation would speak of Ecstasy but never have really had it.

Invariably the clubs I went to were filled with sweating, twitching, gurning clubbers who just couldn't stop telling you how much they loved you – over and over and over again. At its height, Ecstasy fever absorbed everything – everyone was sucked into the vortex, and a good few became casualties of it. The price was as high as the euphoria.

The FF club held many fond memories and strange sights. Strangest of all were the rough, hard, laddish boys who under the influence of Ecstasy opened up their emotions and kissed and caressed their best friends (who they had perhaps met only moments earlier). Love thugs – once football supporters, hooligans, ready to beat anyone up that differed from them – were now transformed by Ecstasy into loving rogues and embraced gays, blacks and anyone else on their

Ecstasy level. They were decadent times. My close friend Jane Rollink
had even metamorphosed herself into the DJ Mrs Woods – London's
first and most successful female techno DJ. Our Jane – could you
believe it? She had become the ruling force of the FF club, the diva of
the twisted night. Every drug was tried, and parties went on for days.
Make that weeks! After the clubs were the parties, and after those the
chill-outs – somebody's house or apartment, a select few smoking
joints, levelling out, snorting coke, bonding, listening to ambient
music, talking rubbish. But it made sense, to you or them, at the time.
Then it was forgotten. Forgotten rubbish.

These chill-out parties were almost always at my apartment. More
often than not I didn't know who the hell anyone was – strangers lay
around, lines of coke, lines of nonsense being spoken, gibberish,
babbling, prattling. Tablets were bitten on, chipped bits passed
around. Speed. Rambling. Acid drops placed on strangers' tongues.
Strangers talking ten to a dozen. Chattering. Blurting. Bragging.
Barely able to focus. You can hear them saying how much they've
taken. Five Es. No, more than that. Three grams, at least, in one
night. Boasting braggarts. Romancing. Bullshitting. Lying. Anyone
for a cup of tea? This went on for days.

More often than not it would get out of hand. Too much Ecstasy,
acid, cocaine, alcohol. Someone would say something. A harmless
remark would be taken the wrong way, misheard, misconstrued,
misread, misunderstood. Tension. And you're on edge. Tense. You're
out of it, unsure, nervous, anxious, vulnerable. Someone taunts
someone else, or do they? An argument ensues. Visual signals.
Shouting. Then fighting. How many nasty incidents through too
many drugs? How many people on the edge? Over the edge? How
many hours patiently talking people down, away from the precipice?

On one occasion I awoke to find the lounge taken over by cocaine
and Ecstasy dealers counting and weighing their wares on scales, or
into plastic bags. I suddenly caught myself seeing myself and the
situation I had allowed myself to be in. Who they were, I never found
out. The same can be said of some of the people I woke up in bed
with after three-day drug binges.

As the drugs on the scene fluctuated in quality and strength, so
the mood of the clubs' patrons changed too, and so did the music.
Ecstasy was so cut that it was no longer Ecstasy, and whatever
cocktail it was proved to be an ugly one. Whereas Ecstasy had opened
people up and allowed them to communicate, this new drug posing
as Ecstasy did quite the opposite. People retreated into themselves,
isolated and solitary. How do I know this? Because I was one of the
people taking this drug. There came a point towards the latter years

of the FF club when people were taken out each week on stretchers, almost always the result of the Special K cut into or sold as Ecstasy.

Special K, with its innocuous name, is one of the worst drugs I have ever tried, and fearsomely unpleasant. I first tried it in the early eighties in New York with Anita Sarko, while watching a *Star Trek* movie. I snorted a large pile up my nose and . . . collapsed on the pavement outside the cinema. I cannot describe the effect exactly but it is very much about detachment, imagining yourself shrinking into yourself, and then someone coshing you over the head until you are virtually comatose and incapacitated. That is called the approach to the K hole. The K hole itself induces the effect of everything looking solarized, like a cheap seventies effect on *Top of the Pops*. This is considered by some – though not me – as the ultimate in fun.

With the rise of drug culture, came a rise in HIV infection – perhaps attributable to the recklessness of youth combined with lowered inhibitions from the drugs taken. The prevalent attitude was that AIDS was a disease that affected older gay men, and that one could tell if someone had AIDS – a sad and misguided belief I had personally encountered in many young gay people then. But this is not to damn the culture of techno or of drugs. People should be free to make their own informed choice. And I still believe the most dangerous drug of all is alcohol, which I have seen destroy more lives than anything else. People don't need telling what not to do, but they do need information which makes the risks clear. Holland has the right idea – even allowing people the chance to test the purity of the drugs they are taking.

I say all this because I don't want this chapter to seem like a sermon on the evil of drugs. My problem with drugs came about because of an insatiable addiction that needed a fix. It could have been alcohol, and nearly was. It could have been food, or love. It was in part shopping, work and exercise. It was mainly illegal drugs such as Ecstasy and cocaine. It was finally prescription drugs. Whatever it was, it was never enough to fill that void inside me – the void that is addiction. Of course not everyone is an addict. Most people can handle drink or drugs or any combination of them at a sensible level. It may affect their health or finances, but it doesn't mean they're addicts. They may even become addicted to one or more particular drugs. But, difficult though it is to grasp, addiction is not the same as being an addict. The very act of living is dangerous, just as the very act of sex has never been safe. These are not recent concepts.

If I wasn't lying semi-conscious on the floor with strangers listening to techno music, I was being driven around town in limousines, taking acid, listening to techno music. London, New York, Barcelona

– the view is much the same from inside a smoked-glass limo. Still with me were the people I hardly knew, flitting in and out of my half-life – people willing to repeat the things I wanted to hear, which were never the truth. The close friends in my life – few as they were – were pushed to the margins for my fear of them telling me what I didn't want to hear.

*

It was around this time that I met one of the most interesting and glamorous characters in my life, and we became close friends – some might say partners in crime. I shall call him 'Gangster Max', because I do not know, even to this day, what his real name was. He used several aliases, for he was a gangster in every sense. I first met him at the FF club one night; decidedly Italian in appearance, he had a thick fake tan and a black quiff, a touch of Robert de Niro and a dash of Alec Baldwin, a fierce signature tattoo and a leather jacket. He was the companion of a famous film star – in fact, I was to learn, of many famous film stars. His jacket was open to reveal a worked-out body as tanned as his face. The hair was dyed and the smile entirely capped. It all added to the intrigue, and revealed him to be older than he claimed. (Well, who isn't?) Max liked to collect people, and, since I did too, we collected each other.

He was the most inexhaustible person I had ever met, with what seemed like an endless supply of money to indulge himself and his friends. I guessed at what he did, but didn't want to know. I never asked questions, for I knew that what is not known cannot be repeated. More often than not his stories – wrapped carefully in euphemisms – seemed so far-fetched as to be lifted from movies, but I knew from the people that he worked with that they were true. He took on a role of protector towards me, and with that came the protection of a South London gang to a member of which he was a loyal bodyguard. On one of many occasions in America he was forced to go into hiding from the Russian mafia and gave me a gun for safe keeping. I kept it hidden in a box until he asked for its return. It was all so glamorous that I never stopped to think about how out of my depth I was, swimming with sharks.

Together we would explore the dark side of life around New York or Amsterdam. Most of the time he was straight, often with two girlfriends in tow, but occasionally he crossed over and dabbled. He especially loved to visit the annual Amsterdam Love Ball, an enormous gathering of S & M enthusiasts from all over Europe, and from there he would move on to the underground fetish parties of Berlin or Rotterdam or other red-light districts of Europe. I went with him as his companion on these twilight sojourns – he was always paying, and always saying. It was thrilling and exciting. He wanted a life full of diverse experience and adventure, free of the constraints of morality. To him people were playthings, toys for amusement until he became bored with them and needed fresh people to spoil or impress, and ultimately control. Famous dress designers, models, writers, actors, film stars, prostitutes, dominatrices and club kids all drifted in and out of his life. I lasted longer than most because I suppose I was only prepared to be owned up to a point and we never had an intimate relationship – and we shared a jaded sense of humour. Most of the time I could match his energy, though often even I would have to retreat.

But he played a dangerous and twisted game – partly to test people, and partly because he had created a life suffused with mistrust and paranoia. I had seen him set people up, test them and discard them, and I didn't want to be one of those people. I knew he would eventually get bored with me, so for periods of time I made myself scarce, got on with my own life – after all, I still had a semblance of a career, and what was left of it had to have my attention. In fact it was a miracle I managed to keep any of my professional commitments, but keep them somehow I did. I was on the *Wogan* show one evening, Bruce Forsyth the following evening, and the next night out of my head on drugs at Max's party, surrounded by naked guys and girls.

In 1993 I left my apartment in Earls Court, partly because the other residents had petitioned against the endless noise and damage I created and wanted me out, but partly because I had found a fabulous new property. I bought and moved into a converted church in Chelsea. It was still only a raw space.

A few days after exchanging contracts, Max turned up out of the blue. I opened the front door to be greeted by the sight of a huge black BMW with tinted windows, driven by his full-time bodyguard. Max opened the back door, I climbed in, and he began to have sex with a young woman waiting there. He wanted me to join in. Instead, we all fell out on to the pavement in various states of undress.

Afterwards, when Max came into the church, he was hit with the idea of using my new premises for one of his parties. I wasn't too enthralled by the idea. I don't mind a small gathering, but my heart sank when he mentioned two hundred people. I hoped he would forget the whole thing, but there was no chance of that – this would secure his reputation as 'King Swinger'. The church was an inspiring and vast space, large enough for a nightclub let alone a party, but it was my home – or soon to be. Max started making calls, and then getting invitations printed.

'For God's sake don't tell anyone it's my place,' I told him, fearful of more tabloid nonsense; I knew just what Max had in mind – he loved the whole straight swing scene: wife-swapping, suburban orgies, S & M and pussy parties. He had told me so many times about these events, and as many times urged me to attend with him. Now I was going to have no choice. I had always been curious, but it just wasn't my scene. Then Max told me how many stars he had invited to this party he was going to have at my home, and how many of them I just couldn't believe would attend such an event. The party was going to coincide with his birthday, and he wanted an occasion to remember. I just wanted it all over and done with. I felt that my house was going to be violated, destroyed, abused – whatever. But nothing prepared me for the onslaught to come.

On the day of the party, the house was decked out with thousands of fairy lights and psychedelic oil wheels, and a massive sound system was set up. Fortunately, because it had been a church, it was relatively soundproof. We piled all the furniture in a spare side room which we then sealed off – this was where I was to spend most of the evening. Security men surrounded the building, and others stood at the front door to ensure that only invitees could get in. But even I wasn't prepared for the four hundred people he had invited – people in fetish outfits, black leather, rubber, bare-breasted, men in just jockstraps, some naked, all cavorting, drinking and queuing down towards the Fulham Road while waiting to get into my home. I thought I was going to die of shame as neighbours came out of their houses. I expected the police to turn up any minute – a thought that intensified as waitresses took around mirror trays with hundreds of lines of cocaine cut out on them, while others handed out joints, acid and Ecstasy as people entered. Then I just thought 'What the hell' and joined in.

It all slowly became like a surreal scene from a Fellini film. Max had hired erotic dancers, strippers and prostitutes, who performed on the stairs. In the bedrooms, couples were putting on live sex shows while voyeurs masturbated furiously, a select few being encouraged to join in. It was the Hellfire Club all over again – except it was in Chelsea, and it was in my house. I spent most of the time hiding, taking cocaine and pills and wishing the whole thing would go away – especially when I thought I'd seen a tabloid journalist among the guests. Now don't worry, I hadn't suddenly become puritanical, but it really does change your views when it's all happening so blatantly, noisily and colourfully in your own house, and by now spilling out into the street.

I found Max sitting where we'd stored the furniture, looking thoroughly miserable. He had taken so much cocaine that he could barely talk, and on top of that had taken Ecstasy, which he rarely did. I tried to calm myself, having taken so much myself moments earlier, and sat by him. Then suddenly he burst into tears. 'It's all over, it's all over,' he sobbed.

I tried to reassure him that this was just a feeling everyone gets on their birthday – being that bit older and all.

'No,' he said, 'they're going to come tonight. They're going to arrest me here. I'm just waiting for them to arrive.'

'What?' I asked. He then explained that a deal he had done had gone horribly wrong and someone wanted revenge on him. Either the police would have been called, or worse.

I tried to stay calm. 'What do you mean "worse"?'

He was still sobbing as he explained that a rival gang might turn up and blow his head off.

Regardless of the drugs I'd taken, this news had quite a sobering effect on me I can tell you. Outwardly I remained calm, but inside I was going into panic overdrive. I tried to calm Max down. I tried to calm myself down. This couldn't be happening. Not in my house. Not in Chelsea. Not with a tabloid journalist outside.

Suddenly a group of party-goers burst in and frightened the life out of me. I yelled at them to get out as I tried to calm Max once more. It was unclear to me if this was real, or if he was imagining it, or if it was real cocaine paranoia with some truth to it, or if I was imagining it. Everything was so edgy, weird, strange. I tried to gather him up, but cocaine fell out of his pockets – packets of it, all over the floor. Now in my head the sound outside in the main party sounded like panic, laughter, screaming, shouting, sniggering.

Throughout the party we sat in our separated-off area, neurotic and miserable. Max wanted it all to end, for everyone to leave. Hour after hour passed. Gradually, one by one, people began to disappear, leaving a trail of empty bottles, broken glass, joint stubs, used condoms and vomit, until there was only a handful of us left – Paul (a top rave promoter), his girlfriend Wendy, Max, his loyal, handsome black bodyguard and myself. Suddenly, in an effort to cheer us all up, the bodyguard volunteered to show us his party trick. This involved him inserting a Coca-Cola can into his anus and, through muscular contractions, expelling it across the room. (I joke not!) 'Has it come to this?' I thought to myself.

To hide from the oncoming daylight, which had started to peep through the stained-glass windows of the church, we locked ourselves in a blacked-out bedroom. Suddenly there was loud banging on the door and we all froze. Who was it? The police? Max's enemies come for him at last? I slowly went downstairs. It was another drug dealer with a new supply. 'The door downstairs was open,' he explained, 'so I just walked in.'

The dealer had everything except heroin, which is what Paul and his girlfriend had wanted. (Some people are never happy.) So they made phone calls and soon enough the shadiest-looking dealer turned up at the door, complete with dark glasses. Where do these people come from? He might as well have had a sign saying 'Drug dealer' on his back. By now I felt that my life had reached a new low. I spent the whole day sprawled on the floor, covered in sweat after shooting up cocaine. I had at last crossed that personal barrier I had sworn never to cross and had started using needles.

*

During this two-year period when my life had become overcast with a dark cloud of madness, drugs, gangsters, guns, swingers' parties, techno chill-outs and even murder attempts (wait, I'll get to that one), by complete contrast my career had taken an even weirder turn. I was presented as respectable and clean-living by the record company. They even had me cover my tattoos, which they hated.

Over the years my tattoos had become another obsession. For a while, each city I visited meant adding another tattoo, and when I was in London I would regularly visit the tattooist Lal Hardy in Muswell Hill. It's interesting how tattoos have become mainstream fashion accessories and almost commonplace – certainly among gay men. I particularly love extreme tattoos – full-body statements that set a person apart. It's the dinky, cute tattoos that I find so annoying – the faux butch ones of the scene queens and pop stars. Whereas I thought of tattoos as beautiful, erotic, provocative and evocative, however, the record company considered them to be sleazy, wayward and criminal-looking, and went to extraordinary lengths to cover them up, making me wear suits or airbrushing them out entirely. I agreed to cover them up because I didn't want that particular image to be too obtrusive. I put on a front of respectability – as much as Marc Almond could (which many might consider was too late in the day; the horse had not only bolted but was now in the glue factory).

All this was part of my surrender to WEA. Inside I cared deeply about the lie I was living, and this served to intensify my self-loathing and led to further destructive behaviour. But the skin to cover up was also one to hide in. Perhaps when the marketing department talked to me of respectability, of normality, I really wanted it. But in the pretence I again lost track of the real me. I tried to tell myself that I was reinventing myself as a Vegas crooner, but the real Marc Almond lay dormant inside. I felt like a devil in disguise. I said, 'Show me the image you want and I'll wear it. Play me the song and I'll sing it. Just leave me alone.'

There was no point asking Stevo for support, as he was allied to the record company. Besides, he agreed that the real Marc Almond was a scary person, frightening to all those normal people who'd bought the Gene Pitney record and 'The Days of Pearly Spencer'. (Who were those normal people? I had no idea.) Stevo was now clean and serene (or at least clean), and heading dangerously close to respectability. He dressed in polo outfits and seersucker, spats, cloaks and canes; he frequented Claridge's, Mayfair restaurants and gentlemen's clubs. One day he proudly showed me his wardrobe, which consisted of row upon row of cashmere sweaters, fur coats, suits and accessories made from every species of endangered creature – ivory-topped canes, alligator shoes, snakeskin bags. That wardrobe probably contributed to the extinction of several species of animal. What had happened to him? He was still trying not to be that working-class lad from the East End; he thought that being ostentatious and flamboyant was a way of showing the world what he was not.

Amidst all this madness, I had to do live concerts, which meant collecting myself together and presenting myself to the world.

Stevo hated concerts, though he acknowledged they were a way of generating revenue. Having no band, it had been a couple of years since I'd played a proper show, but Stevo had during that time seen how popular the acoustic shows were. He also realized how cheaply the acoustic show could tour, and decided that I should go on a world tour with it. Accompanied by just Martin Watkins on piano, we had already done successful shows in Greece (in a beautiful open-air amphitheatre in the hills overlooking Athens), in a church in Berlin, and even throughout Japan.

Earlier in the year, the opportunity to tour on the west coast of America arose, but the dates clashed with Trevor Horn's schedule. It was pointed out to me that Trevor could not change his busy timetable and I would have to fit around his requirements. I was devastated. Then the LA riots ensued, and Stevo happily cancelled everything. American fans complained in droves. I felt pathetic that we had used the excuse of the riots when it normally would have taken a full-scale war to stop me performing. But what did Stevo care about the fans? He was contemptuous towards them.

To Stevo the acoustic shows were an economic joy and revelation, yet I personally never saw any money from them. But I enjoyed the challenge they presented – to go on stage, stripped of props and production, to entertain an audience for two hours with just a piano accompaniment, was always demanding but exhilarating. I had to make the shows work. If I could do that, I knew that anything else would be simple. I felt that I had the repertoire of songs, and I had the right chemistry with Martin. Also, performing gave me a chance to release all the tension I felt in my life, to let it all out and give my all. My pain was exorcized on stage, even though being alone in the spotlight could be terrifying. Often audiences would need coaxing, cajoling, winning over, and it could be an uphill struggle; but on all but a few occasions I would succeed and be rewarded with a standing ovation. You see, it is not over until they stand! Even if it takes all night.

The critics, however, remained mixed in their response. Some thought the shows meant I had no more to do with pop music, as if that was a condemnation of my work. But they were the most popular shows I ever undertook, so in one way they were pop. (Isn't 'pop' short for 'popular'?) Night after night I was out there, alone and giving my soul – and if that is nothing to do with pop then bugger it.

Then I was offered the chance to do an acoustic tour of Russia, including Siberia, sponsored by the Russian government, and, for a reason that I could never fathom, I agreed. I was warned it would be difficult: Russia in 1992 was a country in turmoil after the collapse of communism, a country in rebirth. But I was sure it was something that I wanted to experience – and, besides, it would get me away from England. I wanted to feel like an artist again, and what better opportunity?

The *Sun* had just printed a half-page photo of me shambling along in an old camouflage jacket carrying two Marks & Spencer's bags, unshaven and destitute in appearance – 'The Daze of Marc's and Spencer' was the wittier than usual headline.

Re-Marcable Millionaire Marc Almond dresses like a tramp to escape fans. [Do I?] Marc, at number 6 with 'The Days of Pearly Spencer' in the charts, has ditched his leather stage gear for a camouflage jacket, tracksuit bottoms and old trainers. A pal of the ex-Soft Cell star said, 'He was fed up with being mobbed, this way he never gets noticed.'

I wondered who the pal was. I also imagined myself schlepping around M & S in my leather stage gear. What was I supposed to wear when I went shopping? I imagined telephoto lenses following my every move – photographing the daily visits by dealers to my house.

Then an altogether more disturbing tabloid attempted a story on me. I was told that every known gay star was being approached and told they had been seen at an HIV clinic. I duly received a call. The caller claimed to have seen me coming out of a Harley Street clinic and that it was known that I was seeing a specialist in AIDS. Of course I knew this was lies. They were trying to provoke a reaction that would give them a grain of a story. In my case they were disappointed. I had just been given a clean bill of health on that front, but I do know that the tactic induced another well-known celebrity to break the news of his infection. Lovely journalism there from the tabloids.

I thought that Russia was as far away as I could get from all this, so off I went.

Siberia was our first destination. I couldn't wait to arrive. But if I thought I had experienced insanity at home, nothing – absolutely nothing – prepared me for the two weeks in Russia. We were a party of five; the tour manager Lee Kavanagh (a girl who worked at Some Bizarre), Mark as assistant on the tour and also filming it, Martin Watkins playing piano, and a friend of Martin's called Josh, who wanted to come along as a kind of recuperation holiday. He had just had a serious illness, but by this time he felt well enough to travel and was enthusiastic for this once-in-a lifetime trip. I had been reluctant to let him come, but Martin said it was just the break he needed. As it turned out it was not exactly the break he needed. In addition, Lee was several months pregnant, which she said would not be a problem. It turned out to be a major problem. For Josh, taking the trip proved to be a fatal decision and he tragically died a short time after returning. And Lee came near to losing her baby.

To describe the Russian tour in detail would take a book in itself, so I have included only highlights taken directly from the diary I kept each day throughout.

Day 1

Arrived in Moscow at 10.00 a.m. The flight was full. TV crew waiting at baggage claim and a girl from British Council with bunch of roses. Nick Hobbs, the promoter, was waiting to sort out our visas and passports. Customs was virtually non-existent, everything seems in chaos. TV presenter Art Trotsky interviewed me in airport for Russian TV channel and asked me questions. 'Was I afraid?' 'How did I feel to be in Russia?' 'Did I know anything about Russian music?' Answers: 'No', 'Great', 'Not much'. Kept thinking about the question *Was I afraid*? What did he mean? Cameras followed me everywhere, transmitting live to millions of Russian homes. Felt uneasy.

Took a long van drive through the city, choking on the leaking exhaust fumes in the back. Our connection for the flight to Siberia was from an airport at other side of the city. The flight was delayed for six hours. Josh doesn't look well: I think the exhaust fumes have affected him. The airport had no food except bread and salami – not a good meal for vegetarians. We're all hungry and tired. Plane so delayed we drove back into Red Square and took a walk. Saw the Kremlin and St Basil's all lit up, spotlit through the shining mist. It's so cold – minus 19. The streets are deserted and it's so eerie.

Went back to airport, which was like hell on earth. Plane still delayed. They told us it had left Siberia but turned back because of leaking fuel. I'm feeling really uneasy about this. Couldn't believe there is no bag check-in and we had to carry all our luggage on to the plane. Passed bags through an X-ray machine that was not switched on – the security woman was pretending to look at the screen, which was blank. Everyone seems to be pretending to work, going through the motions but doing nothing.

Plane turned up nine hours late. Promoter had to bribe an official to get us all seats, and then we had to drag our cases across tarmac and climb a ladder into the plane. Last week, the promoter laughingly told us, there was a gunfight between passengers fighting for seats. It's unbelievable. Passengers without seats are made to sit in the aisles. There are no seat belts, no food and no toilets on board.

The plane has just taken off on our six-hour flight to Siberia. I'm worried about Lee now. She looks tired and is holding her stomach. Josh is coughing badly and complaining of a pain in his head.

Arrived in Siberia. It's cold and raining. It's so bleak and all the trees are dead, the buildings disused and burnt out. We board a minibus and are told it will be a four-hour drive to Barnaul. Still no food or drink. We cross the seventh time zone. I feel disorientated and tired. Christ knows how everyone else feels. The road almost disappears at times, only a mud track as we pass through small towns. No lights in the houses, past cemeteries with plastic headstones, and grey skies forever. I'm beginning to see the worst in everything.

It's taken twenty-five hours from leaving London to arriving here, wherever here is. It's the OB sanatorium in Barnaul where we're staying. The house is quite pleasant and warm, and is the summer retreat of Boris Yeltsin. I'm given his bedroom. How bloody weird is that? He slept in this bed only a few months back. I bet I'll find that quite amusing one day. Due to the delays, I only have an hour before the first show. Washed and changed, had a cup of M & S tea (thank God I brought some teabags) and I feel sort of ready to perform.

No food, no sleep, no soundcheck and straight on.

Done the performance. The hall looked austere from the outside but inside was quite cosy. Sang 'Fun City' through to 'What Makes a Man a Man' – just over an hour. That was enough for me. The audience were seated – didn't know how to react to them, or them to me. Weird mix of people – old and young, soldiers, a couple of gay men, children. Surprisingly, they knew many of the songs. A favourite with them seemed to be 'A Lover Spurned', which I was told is a big Siberian hit (whatever that means). When I sang 'What Makes a Man' a couple of people applauded at the intro – Aznavour is probably in their dusty collection. Wore black trousers and leather shirt – I must have looked like something from another planet, which I suppose I am. They liked the tuneful, upbeat songs best – 'Jacky', 'The Flame', 'Toreador in the Rain'.

Had first food for twenty-eight hours in dressing room – delicious home-made bread and honey. Fans queued outside afterwards for autographs and kisses – I obliged, especially the soldiers. Felt like Marlene entertaining the troops on the front line. Lifted my spirits a bit.

Back at sanatorium, Russian idea of vegetarian spread is uneatable, everything full of onions and dry salted fish. Big old Russian babushka took a shine to me and pushed my head into her bosom, stroked my face and talked excitedly in Russian – translator Nick said she wanted to arrange marriage for me. Fell asleep in Boris Yeltsin's bed.

Day 2

Awoke to a pale Siberian sunshine. Stunning views across a lake. Russian breakfast consisted of sweet cheese, rice pudding and blinis with plum sauce. Four-hour drive in minibus again. Arrived at university campus where we are to stay for next two days. It's basic and seventies. Black-and-white TV shows only vase of flowers while classical music plays for hours, occasionally interrupted by news bulletins. There's a fridge, though we had nothing to put in it. Went to local supermarket, which was just rows of empty shelves. At one point though a bell rang and queues formed for a new delivery of cucumbers; a few minutes later another bell and a delivery of bread. This is really sad. Outside on the way back a small riot of people fighting to buy tins of marrowfat peas. Bought an apple off a woman for $5. What is this place?

At the soundcheck, Martin and I rehearsed a couple of new songs – 'Black Heart' and 'Tenderness is a Weakness', and an upbeat version of 'Mr Sad' they can clap along to. We found an old wooden frame backstage covered in glitter and coloured light bulbs to use on stage. The promoter suggested it might be too kitsch. He obviously hasn't seen us before.

Sound problems all the way through the show. Eventually sound broke down completely and so I sang a cappella to the crowd, who lit matches and passed me a bottle of vodka. It turned into a drunken sing-along, and everyone invaded the stage for autographs. No bloody security. Crowd seemed to recognize many songs. Afterwards in the press conference I was surrounded by drunken Russian sailors.

Evening meal was barely edible – stringy chicken (I think it was chicken, though it looked like it had a ribcage – do chickens have ribs?) and rice. I feel so bad about not being able to eat, because everyone is trying to make us welcome and giving us the best of what there is. Starting to feel really hungry all the time. Josh's health is deteriorating and he's looking worse, just wants to stay in bed all the time. He asked Mark to get him a doctor, but the promoter said there wasn't even aspirin out here. I'm worried.

Learned some Russian words – 'good evening', 'goodbye', 'thank you' and 'please'. They should get me through.

Day 3

Had lunch of broiled fish and potatoes in the hotel canteen. Having to force myself to eat now. Managed to find hotel in town, as we can't stay here any more – students party all night and bang on the fucking door. The whole town is sparse and depressing, buildings all look the same – what would this country have done without concrete? Beginning to feel this tour was not the best idea. We are having problems we never envisaged. Lee being pregnant means she cannot risk drinking the unpasteurized milk, and none of us can drink the untreated water. The bottled water is only carbonated and tastes salty. Josh is bedridden now, he is so ill, and Martin is beginning to get really anxious over his condition. He shouldn't have come, but what can we do out here? What the fuck are we doing?

Show was great. The audience clapped and joined in at all the right places. Rearranged set worked much better. At the end I lay on the piano and pretended to sleep. Girls threw flowers, and a guy jumped on to the stage and danced wildly. Walked on to stage with my trouser fly down and had to manoeuvre myself – not easy in the spotlight. There were real bananas in the dressing room – we couldn't believe it. Food is really scarce, and if any comes along we're learning to hoard it. While changing afterwards, live television cameras burst into the dressing room and filmed me in my underpants to 15 million homes.

Ate one banana before going to sleep.

Day 4

Woke to another miserable grey day in Novosibirsk. Went out early to join bread queue at bakery. There are no roads, just deep mud tracks everywhere, and it is so cold with biting wind. Everybody quiet and hungry now. Bread had sold out before I reached the counter. It's getting very depressing. The hotel has no food. The promoter laid on dinner tonight of broiled fish and cucumber. Concert supposed to be outside, but due to rain they've apparently moved it indoors. The temperature is minus 9 and had they seriously expected us to perform outside? The whole arrangement sounds ominous.

Arrived at venue to discover they had set up the stage in a narrow corridor. No soundcheck and the piano is broken – half the keys are missing. Martin was thrown out for smoking. Sat in the dressing room, I can hear student rock bands playing irritating, meandering progressive rock. Tiredness, hunger and the complete disorganization have caught up with me. I was prepared to lower my standards, but not this far. Lost my temper and threw a major wobbler. Martin laughed through despair, and Mark just kept recording everything on his camera till I made him turn it off. I couldn't do this concert – not in a corridor. We left.

Just had dinner and no one is speaking to us because we cancelled. Fishcakes and guess what – cucumber.

Mark took me for a walk to show me his discovery. We walked across the mud in the rain to the main railway station, and down enormous spiral stairs into a vast ballroom below the station platforms. Huge chandeliers and gold statues decorated a cavernous room, while drunken sailors, prostitutes and barefoot boys waltzed around to the sound of a bored dance band on the stage. In the midst of all of this I couldn't believe it – a scene from a forgotten era.

Day 5

It's 5.30 in the morning, diary. The plane to Moscow is due to leave at 8.00.

Standing outside in the rain waiting for the minibus, Josh was barely able to stand he is so ill. He hasn't eaten for four days, and the pain in his head has worsened. All he can say is that he wants to go home. He looked so frail and ghostlike. We tried to look after him, but could get no medical help or medication. Our only reassurance is that we are going back to Moscow. I caught Lee off guard and saw her clutching her stomach and crying. This whole thing is becoming a terrible ordeal for all of us.

The aircraft was delayed by four hours. Lugging cases on to the plane, Mark and I had to do most of it while Martin took care of the others. I just keep thinking, 'This is not happening! Is this what my career has come to?' The only seats we could get on the plane were broken; one had no back on it. The hostess brought around a bucket of revolting chicken floating in brine, and pieces of diced cucumber. FUCKING CUCUMBER! Most of the passengers were drunk on vodka. The hostesses were having sex in the toilet with passengers for money. Then at one point a hostess trolley was wheeled proudly down the aisle displaying one Mars bar and one Snickers bar. The asking price was $5 hard currency – no rouble price. No takers there. As the plane landed, drunk people fell down the aisles. This place is insane. The promoter explained that internal Russian flights are not governed by international aviation rules – I don't know if he thought this information was reassuring or what.

Outside the airport I bought two bananas for $10. Josh had to be carried by two of us to the waiting car. Even the healthiest of us are getting run-down.

Everything has suddenly changed. An hour after leaving the airport we are all sitting drinking tea with milk in a spacious white apartment of the British consulate, overlooking the whole of Moscow. It belongs to a woman working for the British consul. She explains that everything is available to her through the consul. Her fridge is full of food, and she cooks us the best meal I have ever eaten.

Josh is laid out in bed and Lee relaxes as best she can. When they're both asleep, Mark and I go out to see the sights. Went to the Kremlin to see the crypts of the tsars, whose decaying dried bodies are displayed beneath glass lids. Outside I posed for photos with a group of bemused Russian sailors. Afterwards we're taken to Russian sauna. Mafia cars with black windows lined up out-side. The sauna is at the top of a hotel on the twenty-eighth floor – down dark corridor, turn left, knock on door and ask for Ivan. Giant fat Russian man gave me backbreaking, neck-cracking massage.

Visit the theatre I'm due to play in a few days' time. It's a mini version of the Bolshoi, beautiful and opulent, with white, red and gold ornate decoration. Taken to secret restaurant which had real food.

It's been agreed that Josh and Lee should return to England. The British consul is arranging their flights and we had to leave them. I want to be going home. I don't want to be here any more. Now there are only Mark, Martin and I. 'Then there were three.'

Took a flight to Minsk in Belorussia. Greeted by TV cameras with all the usual questions. Martin made joke about Moldavia and if Joan Collins was still queen. Only we laughed. A limousine was waiting outside, but of course it didn't work properly. Nick Hobbs is still with us, but everything is wearing a bit thin with him. He's used to this madness, but even he is getting stressed.

Martin is desperately worried about Josh, and we all are over Lee. She had wanted to carry on, but it would have been stupid to let her with her pregnancy.

This place is grim. The hotel is monstrous. The foyer is full of prostitutes. The first room I was shown had no electricity. The room I take is crawling with cockroaches, and the curtains have been almost completely eaten by moths. All the clocks read different times, and none of the keys seem to work. Nothing works. No one does anything. I'm hungry again and there's no food. Why the fuck didn't I leave when we were in Moscow? There is an old woman assigned to every floor to prevent prosti-tutes coming up, but she doesn't. Women prowl the corridors. This is the best hotel in town – God help us!

Day 6

Gloomy Monday. I don't know what to tell you that you don't already know, diary. I am hungry, tired and emotional after a sleepless night. I kept waking up with cockroaches crawling on my face, and am bitten all over by mosquitoes and bedbugs. Nobody bothers to tell you Russia is full of mosquitoes – it didn't mention that in the Thomson's brochure. I can't make tea because I've lost the kettle adaptor, and I have to eat my cereal with sour ewes' milk on it.

Lunch is a disaster, which is a pleasant surprise. Everything looks great but nothing is edible. Red meat and onions and cucumber. I was given dried salt fish, which was revolting, so I tried one of the many variations of cucumber dishes – sliced in vinegar, diced in vinegar, fanned in vinegar, pickled in vinegar, even fried in vinegar. Fried cucumber – now there's something for Delia! The mineral water is cloudy with salty sediments in it – straight from Chernobyl, which we are told is reassuringly close by. The tap water is not recommended for drinking or bathing in, which sort of limits its use.

Hungry and thirsty after lunch I made my excuses and left the meal – offending the host, who, our translator explained, considered it a feast. I try not to be rude, but it isn't easy. I felt guilty afterwards. Spent all afternoon in the hotel room reading *The Shrine of Jeffrey Dahmer* by Brian Masters just to cheer myself up – but all the cooking he's doing in it has made me hungry. Used the book to kill cockroaches.

The theatre for the show is quite nice, so I tried to psych myself up a bit, but it's not easy. The concert turned out to be great, and I got a standing ovation – which I didn't really deserve, because I raced through the set. After the show, people clamoured for autographs and the TV cameras again asked me how I enjoyed being in Minsk. I lied and put on my professional face. Then they took us to a restaurant. The menu had only red meat and onion dishes, so Martin and I despaired. A band played the Charleston.

This has ceased to be amusing. I think one day I might laugh about the whole thing, but that's hard to imagine right now.

Day 7

Drive to Vilnius in Lithuania in the limousine that doesn't work properly. It breaks down, once for two hours while people fiddle under the bonnet and pretend to know what they're doing.

Argument breaks out between us, all over who'd eaten the last half of the emergency rations (half a Mars bar). I'm really angry about it. I know it wasn't me because it wasn't; and we're all in this together and there's a principle at stake. Personally I think Mark ate it, but I can't be sure. No one speaks to each other for the whole journey because of it. What's happening to us?

Arrive in Vilnius, which is really beautiful. The hotel is small but comfortable, previously used by the heads of the Communist Party – one standard for them and all that. People here seem to have had far more Western exposure and influence since their independence from Russia, and food – yes, food – is actually available. We're taken to a restaurant which suspiciously claims to have an Egon Ronay recommendation, but at least it has Evian – thank God! I eat caviar blinis, crab with spaghetti, chicken with grapes, and buy thirty bottles of water and stack them in the limo.

The concert was a high point, very energetic on stage due to me having eaten properly I suspect. Fans held out copies of the records to sign, and each song got an enthusiastic response. I sat on the edge of the stage and sang 'Say Hello, Wave Goodbye' at the end, and was joined by two boys from the audience who accompanied me in the chorus. The audience loved it, and I loved them loving it. Afterwards a TV and press conference – all the same questions and professional Marc Almond face.

Day 8

We drive for four hours across the border to Latvia and arrive in Riga. It's hot and sticky weather, and the hotel is a concrete monstrosity. The best in town. Some hotel, some town! No air conditioning (like who gives a fuck any more really?), but no shortage of cockroaches. Mark had to remove one from the bath which was nearly three inches long – I'd like to know where it was getting its food from. We try to eat the hotel meal but cannot.

Concert was a disaster. Only 250 people showed up. Apparently no promotion. The people who were there were almost all over seventy years old – like a Liberace audience. Cold concrete modern concert hall. No lighting. To top it all, TV cameras filmed the show for live TV. It was impossible to create any atmosphere, and you could hear a pin drop. Polite applause after each song, but at the end they all erupted into wild applause. Maybe because it had finished and they could get home to their ewes'-milk Horlicks. A woman from the consulate said, 'They loved you from the beginning, they always act like this in Riga. If you think this is bad, wait till you get to Estonia.' Great. I didn't give them an encore.

Day 9

Another drive – six hours this time, through the border to Estonia. At the border we were kept waiting for an hour. Some sort of problem. A moustached guard came out and asked if I was Marc Almond. Marc Almond from Soft Cell? (No, Marc Almond from the Beverly Sisters.) 'My brother is your biggest fan,' he said. 'He has all your CDs.' I signed autographs to his brother, and then for all the other guards and all their brothers and families. Then we sped through.

I can't tell you anything else today because I'm hungry, bored, tired, depressed, sad, worried and not wanting to be here any more. I hate my manager for sending me here, and I'm going to shoot him when I get back.

Did a concert about an hour ago. You don't want to know. Like the audience, I've forgotten it already.

Day 10

A major fuck-up. Problem. We crossed the border and left Estonia to return to Russia. Between the borders we are waiting. The driver is Lithuanian. Leaving Estonia he gave in his exit visa, but he has not got an entry visa for Russia. We can't go forward and now we can't go back. I'm writing this from the back of the limo stuck in what is essentially no man's land between borders. The time is ticking away and no one knows what to do, and St Petersburg is three hours away and I am due on stage in seven hours.

Still sitting here waiting. Six hours. Boring.

Still sitting. Three hours.

Still sat here feeling tired and emotional, and can't stop crying. I'm due on stage in one hour and we're still sat here. The concert has to be cancelled because there is no way we can get there as we're still sat in-between borders.

Word is sent to the concert hall and to the fans that we cannot get into the country for the show, and – this is the exciting bit – an actual riot has broken out outside the theatre and it's on the television. Of course we can't see that because we are still sat here in the fucking limo between the borders of these godforsaken countries. Then the guards call us to their hut and point at their

TV, ranting away in whatever language they speak here and show us the rioting fans on the news. This is insane. Then the promoter has the bright idea of bribing the guard, but unfortunately picks the only person in the whole of Russia who is unbribable and appalled at our Western behaviour. The Russian guards then force the Estonian guards at gunpoint to take us back and eventually, fourteen hours later, let us go back into Estonia, where we drive four more hours back to the hotel that we left twenty-two hours earlier. So that was a nice day out.

The concert is rescheduled the following night, which is sensible because time is running out on us again. The only option is to fly to Helsinki in Finland, change planes, and fly back into Russia.

What a fucking ordeal! Arrived at St Petersburg airport to be greeted by the apologetic mayor, if that's what he was. TV cameras and journalists vying for space as we try to push past.

In St Petersburg at last – it's amazing. The show is in a beautiful old decaying ballroom decorated in gold splendour. No real amplification, and just one spotlight with someone holding coloured gels over it.

Done the show. One of the best on the tour. I love St Petersburg. The architecture is unbelievable. Everything is so grand, opulent and decaying. Tonight the sky was brilliant pinks and reds. Outside there is a Communist demonstration – you think they'd have had enough of it by now – people calling for its return. From the top-floor balcony of the hotel, watched a fireworks display against the illuminated skies (weird how these poor countries can always afford fireworks). Everywhere there are bored drunk soldiers and sailors, arm in arm with each other. You can see the influences of Tom of Finland – the men are incredible-looking. Gold spires and churches glitter in the distance – it's the most magical of places. The streetlights, like in Venice, are lit by gas and glow green in the damp night air.

Meet many interesting Russian artists – Vladek Monroe, who was the first person to appear in drag on Russian television – as a consequence, he told me, the appearance led to his incarceration in an asylum for sexual correction. Met artist Afrika, and his girlfriend Irene, a beautiful actress. Hotel was just a glorified brothel – prostitutes everywhere. Got eaten alive by mosquitoes and bedbugs again. Still starving!

Day 11

Flew back to Moscow. The last show of the tour. The promoters have booked us into a dormitory outside the city. I put my foot down and booked us all into the Metropole, an incredible five-star hotel across from the theatre. This is an amazing hotel. I just needed some room service. They even have BBC on the television.

The concert was a really moving experience in the most beautiful theatre I have ever performed in. The show was trans-mitted live on Russian television. (How many more Marc Almond televised concerts can these people take?) Made speech at the end and said I wished for a tolerant Russia with room for different ideas, views and sexuality, and how it would contribute to a greater Russia. I sang 'What Makes a Man' while walking among the audience. People cried and held my hand. It was too emotional after two weeks of this hardship.

Day 12

Posed for photos in a silver sequin outfit in front of the Kremlin in Red Square. Caught plane back to London. I am tired, run-down and ill. Never again.

The Russian tour had been horrendous at the time, but I now look back on it as worthwhile and enriching. It's true that I'd kissed the tarmac at Heathrow so pleased was I to be back, true that I'd lost half a stone and my face was covered in boils and bites, but it was worth it – and it was to make me appreciate my own life so much more. Russia is one of my favourite places in the world, and I've been back with a full band and in much more comfortable circumstances, and each time I love it more and more. The Russian people are a testament to the indomitable human spirit. It's a brilliant, insane, exciting and beautiful place, full of paradoxes and history, cruelty, hardship and understanding.

*

Shortly after arriving back in England I was approached with an intriguing offer: to star in a West End musical version of *The Picture of Dorian Grey* – a version co-written by producer Mike Leander (famous for his work with Marc Bolan). I was interested. I was willing to be coaxed. I received a copy of the script and a tape of some of the working songs, which I thought, as musicals go, were not bad at all – a couple of dark ballads which I could easily imagine myself singing (though admittedly a couple of others I could not).

I went to meet Mike Leander and to demo a couple of the songs. Mike was not in the best of health, but worked patiently with me until he felt I had the required emotion and tone. I was thrilled to be working with someone who had made so many records that I loved. I was keyed up to play the part, and so the wheels began to turn slowly.

Linda Duff, a tabloid journalist, reported my interest in the role in her usual spot-on fashion:

> Former Soft Cell singer Marc Almond is taking a break from his music career in a dramatic move to follow ritual teen favourite Jason Donovan on to the West End stage. [It had been a long time since I was a teen favourite!] Marc, 29 [cough], has landed the lead role in a multi million-pound stage version of Oscar Wilde's scary story *The Picture of Dorian Grey*. Now Marc and Jason are lined up for a showbiz showdown to see who will win the battle of the box office. Marc said, 'I just told them I am Dorian Grey.' [Did I?] Soft Cell's keyboard player Dave Ball and top Madonna remixer Richard Norris helped to write the show. [Where on earth does Linda get her information from?] Tattooed Marc, whose pop videos include shocking scenes of bondage and fake blood, added to the new trend of casting top pop idols in top West End shows.

Then one day I awoke and looked in the mirror. I had all the years of late nights under my eyes – permanent black bags – and was pasty, spotty and thin. The only thing I really had in common with Dorian Grey was my hair. If I was going to play this part I needed to get my priorities right, so I booked straight into a cosmetic surgeon's for corrective surgery. Two weeks later, as I left the hospital I looked like I'd been hit in the face with a brick, racked with discomfort and pain, I went home and recovered. That was the best £3,000 I ever spent. I'd undergone a blepharoplasty – to you and me, the removal of under-eye bags.

But even that never helped. I thought long and hard about the role of Dorian Grey and who was I fooling. I felt I was just a little old and too short to play the part. It would have been all too easy, and I sense disastrous, to accept it just out of vanity – though rather ironic too. Mike Leander was disappointed. I may have had the voice and the persona, but I didn't have the looks. I do, however, have a portrait in my attic.

It wasn't the last time I was offered involvement in musicals, which I always declined. I was asked by Andrew Lloyd Webber to sing songs for *Phantom of the Opera*, *Sunset Boulevard* and *Whistle Down the Wind*, all of which for one reason or another never happened – timing, money or just the fact that I never felt entirely comfortable moving into that genre. But I was flattered – who wouldn't be? Like him or not, Andrew Lloyd Webber is an important part of theatrical popular culture, and only the ignorant or arrogant would dismiss his body of work. But in Britain 'popular' equates with critical ridicule or contempt, and that's part of the burden we all have to bear.

I was also put forward for a role in a major Broadway production based on the music of Charles Aznavour; I was invited to take part in workshop rehearsals in New York. But prior commitments prevented that too. Since then the show has been postponed for two years.

So, Marc, what are your opinions on musicals? Well, I'm glad you asked that. I have mixed feelings about them. Though they're not something I strongly desire to do while I still have a musical career of my own, I'm always open to ideas. But they rarely add credibility to any artist's career. Then, of course, there is the commitment – six months or even twelve months performing nightly (strictly no matinees), involved in a show that may not do well and still having to go out each night. It's another world – and one that leaves me sceptical.

*

In September 1992 I presented a retrospective concert financially supported by WEA for a live album and by the BBC for a film. A celebration of my music so far, it was called *Twelve Years of Tears*. The show was at the Albert Hall in London, and featured dancers (choreographed by Les Child, who later worked on the spectacular shows of PSB and Erasure) and a forty-piece orchestra, as well as my regular band. The inspiration for it was Elvis's 1968 comeback special, and a night at the *Folies Bergère*. Everyone close to me was there – Pierre et Gilles, Anita Sarko, my family and my nearest friends. Only one person missed it – Dave Ball. Encircled by dancers, being held aloft and carried on stage was one of the most exciting moments of my life.

During the three-hour show, I sang songs from *Tenement Symphony*, did an acoustic selection of Jacques Brel, and played hit after hit, single after single, including for the first time in eight years Soft Cell songs such as 'Bedsitter', 'Torch', 'Soul Inside' and of course 'Tainted Love'. When I sang these, I dedicated them to Dave. I was reconciling myself with the past, dressed in gold lamé and feathers, and at one with a sold-out audience that clapped and cried for more.

A catwalk had been built from the main stage out to a smaller stage in the middle of the audience. There, at the end of the show, I just sat on a stool, in denim jacket and jeans, alone in the spotlight, and sang 'What Makes a Man'. As the waves of love flowed over me, I realized that this is what makes it all worthwhile – those fragile moments that carry us away and imprint our memories with such worth.

Sat in the dressing room half an hour before the show, however, I'd been absolutely petrified, questioning what I was doing, why I put myself through such things, thinking about all the what ifs that might happen. When that knock on the door comes for you to go to the stage, the adrenalin and nerves are overwhelming. But then when you're there – in the spotlight – you know why you do it, why any performer does it. It's about being someone. That's all. Proving something. It no longer really matters what or to whom other than yourself. Proving something to yourself in the hope that it becomes proof. Proof that you're no longer in that playground. Proof that the applause means you're loved and special – the applause that conceals the sound downstairs of your father shouting and hitting your mother. Proof that you would have made your grandfather proud as you walk together along the Southport beach, him singing 'A Stranger in Paradise'. Proof that it's time for some new clichés.

Reviews were ecstatic, and the concert came to represent a crowning moment in my career. Everett True, when reviewing the resulting live album in *Melody Maker*, said, 'One of Marc's strongest points is his ability to communicate with glitter, the way he can make everyday life seem warm and glamorous all the while referring to what in lesser hands would be the humdrum – let's not wash the tears away for ever.' And he admitted he hadn't even been there.

The only reviewer who wrote in a sour tone was my old friend Betty Page. (Isn't it always the old friends?) I wondered what I had done to upset her, as only recently I'd had dinner with her. Now married, with her S & M days behind her, she was probably eager to bury the past. As so many journalists do, she mistook vitriol for wit. 'Poor old Marc, he'd like to be Liza Minnelli but he can't hit the high notes,' she wrote. I sent a bunch of flowers to her at *NME* with a note that I hoped she'd be feeling better soon. Poor old Betty Page had so wanted to be the glamour icon her pseudonym suggested, but no matter how hard she tried she was always just plain old Beverley from suburbia.

Now, contrary to what you may think, not all went smoothly

with the Albert Hall show. It would mark the end of my long friendship with Huw Feather. I hadn't worked with him for a couple of years, but, as this was such a special show, I'd wanted him involved with it – after all he'd been there with me through most of the career it was looking back on. During the rehearsals, the pressure got to both of us and we flared up into an argument in front of the crew (never argue in front of the crew!) over something like batteries for the torch. On the night of the concert, both of us still tense, we fell out again. At the end of the show my name in lights was supposed to descend from the ceiling, but Huw was still putting it together as the audience were coming in. In the interval I insisted on it being tested, and to my dismay the M didn't work. Thank God it was tested – the BBC film would have had the word 'ARC' descend from the ceiling behind me! Afterwards we argued bitterly, allowing such a petty thing to get in the way of an otherwise successful and triumphant show – and, more importantly, in the way of our long and significant friendship. From that day we didn't speak to each other for seven years, which saddens me immensely. But both of us are so proud. Or is it arrogant, or is it stupid?

*

It's ironic that during a time of such personal turmoil – of drug abuse, disastrous affairs, self-destructiveness and unhappiness – and despite the fact that I wasn't following my own personal artistic path (or perhaps because of it), I was between 1990 and 1993 to have one of my most successful periods. Hit records, critical success and acclaimed live performances, as well as other offers of projects and work. I had so much to be happy about, so much to build on and take to new heights. I had finally been acknowledged in many ways as the solo artist I'd worked so hard to become during the eighties. But it was all to end as my career and my life took the final nosedive – to rock bottom.

16

Fallen Star

In 1993 I started work on songs for the album that I'd wanted to do before *Tenement Symphony* had got in the way and given me so much bloody success. Now that was done with, I could get on with fulfilling myself creatively. I wanted to do an album of twisted techno blues, glam rock, electronic dance beats, drugged-out noises and trashy, twisted New York Dolls-style guitars, but all with an under-current of soul and R & B. Of course *I* knew what I was talking about, though no one else did.

I returned to work with John Coxon, and we started to write songs around some great R & B samples that he'd discovered. He also presented me with a great cover song called 'Smiling Faces (Sometimes)'. I forget who it's by, but the title summed up my relationship with WEA – or any record company for that matter. Once again Rob Dickens didn't understand what I was doing, and nor did my new A & R man, Steve Allen.

Steve had come in to replace Michael Rosenblatt, who had tired of England and wanted to return to America. I had known Michael from Soft Cell on Sire records in America, and he was always sympathetic to my artistic needs. I knew of Steve Allen (not personally though) from his days in the group Deaf School – I'd liked them, and even bought their album back in my art-college days. But to have him as my A & R man and telling me what I should be doing with my career made me uncomfortable. Still, he made some sense; he was full of energy and seemed genuinely interested, even though I considered most of his ideas off the mark. But I am thankful that he pursued one suggestion that had originally come from Rob Dickens: that I should work with Neal X, the former guitarist of the eighties glam techno punk band Sigue Sigue Sputnik. Neal was looking for someone to write with, Rob said, and so was I, so maybe I should call him.

At first I dismissed the idea, quite simply because it wasn't mine. I dismissed everything at first. I would go away and think about it, and later come back to it as though it was my idea from the start. So it was with Neal X. I thought about him, remembering him from the mid-eighties in the VIP bar at Limelight, that haven for so many eighties artists. I remembered when Sigue Sigue Sputnik had first emerged, on the cover of every music paper, the next pop sensation. I remembered that at the time I'd been as intrigued as everyone else – their concept a kind of fucked-up amalgamation of Eddie Cochran, Marc Bolan and Giorgio Moroder. I loved the concept and the record 'Love Missile F1-11' – they looked great, had attitude, and for me were what pop was all about, as much to do with the Monkees and the Sex Pistols as with anyone. I remembered too how soon the music papers had turned against them, as papers tend to do. Listening to them now, and watching the videos once again, they were so ahead of their time, and I would argue with anyone who claims otherwise. Futuristic glam punk disco, using samples before anyone else, they played the roles of obnoxious pop brats brilliantly. They were pop art.

But I was also caught up in their bad press and sceptical of working with Neal X, imagining him to be a drunken lout who couldn't play a note. Thankfully I put my prejudice aside and decided to meet up with him in a small studio in the East End of London, and to try to write some desperately needed 'pop' songs. I had to write with someone who had a pop sensibility, who shared my influences – someone whom I could bounce ideas off.

When I met Neal I was pleasantly surprised. As I came to know him, I discovered he is one of the most positive, friendly, sincere and uplifting people I have ever met. And, despite his old guitar poses, pop-star stances and rock 'n' roll yearnings (he just can't help himself), he is also one of the most ego-free and talented musicians around. Those who know him love him. He is an excellent guitarist and producer, bringing such enthusiasm to even the most mundane musical tasks. We hit it off straight away. His knowledge of pop and musical trivia, combined with his dedication, made him a breath of fresh air. So there we were. Together we wrote a bunch of songs – 'Rise', 'Mr Midnight Sun', 'The Idol' and 'Childstar'. I was delighted that I had found someone so enjoyable to work with.

When I occasionally read disparaging remarks about Neal in some reviews of our live appearances it makes me sad. People should understand that Neal came along in one of the worst periods of my life and made it bearable, exciting, adding much-needed laughter. And for that I am grateful. Anyone who cares about my music or about me as an artist should thank him for being a positive influence in a mire of negativity. To some he committed the crime of being in Sigue Sigue Sputnik, but there is so much more to him than that.

So it began promisingly enough. The new album that is. The new album that would turn out to be a disastrous adventure. The album of new and invigorating ideas that should have taken no more than a couple of months to record but which finally took three years, five producers, three A & R men, two record companies, countless months of recording and re-recording in five cities and three countries – of remixes, re-edits and re-re-re-recording – until every bit of freshness or enthusiasm for it was squeezed out. It would end up an acrimonious exercise in self-indulgence by everyone concerned (not least me), with half a million pounds down the drain and me in a rehabilitation clinic. It would be the near-finish of my career in the music business, and the end of my fifteen-year relationship with my manager, Stevo. The only good thing that stayed the course was my writing relationship with Neal.

The album began with the title *Urban Velvet* and ended up being called *Fantastic Star* – a defiant, against-all-the-odds, two-fingered gesture of a title that would become the final irony. Instead of 'fantastic', words such as 'fake', 'fallen', 'faded' or 'forgotten' might have been more appropriate.

There were so many twists and turns in the plot of making this album that to detail all of them would tie you up in knots, as they did me, and ultimately bore you with their sheer futility. After all, if you've read this far, you've seen it all before in earlier chapters – except that this time it was worse than you can imagine and than I can remember. But, before we start on the edited highlights, back to the delusion I called my real life – a phrase that never meant anything in reality terms.

*

My drug intake rose dramatically, until at points I nearly overdosed. My eyes were closed, literally – I often passed out either in clubs or on the kitchen floor, semi-conscious or comatose, my eyes rolling back into my head, techno music pounding in the back of my mind. I was in disco hell. I spent messy nights with messed up people. The phone calls, the appeals to long-suffering friends, became more regular – 'Help me, I'm in a mess.'

After taking a bad cocktail of acid and Special K my face became paralysed for three days. As I lay in bed, unable to move at all, all I could think of was that I should paint the room red. In a moment of physical crisis, interior decorating was foremost in my mind!

I seriously thought I had caused myself brain damage. I seriously thought about stopping. But when my speech and movement returned the motivation to stop drugs disappeared.

Incident followed incident – vomiting in public, falling down stairs in nightclubs, lying in corridors barely able to function, ending up at strange houses with strange people taking stranger drugs. I'd even got a bit of a reputation as being an impromptu transatlantic floorshow. I write this with feelings of despair at what I had become. I was heading onwards and downwards with no end in sight. It had all long since ceased to be fun. It was now a routine, habit – no fun at all.

To make the going easier, I am going to cite just two incidents, out of many, that brought the situation to a head. The first involved my criminal friend Max, who was having a party at his luxury flat – a far smaller affair than he'd organized at my home. Two club kids – a beautiful young couple (a club DJ and his junkie girlfriend) – had brought with them from Amsterdam a cache of drugs, among which was a small book full of acid tabs, each one embossed with an image and each one soaked in LSD. There were about a dozen people at the gathering, and we were all handed a stamp of acid to take.

Of all the acid I had tried, this was by far the strongest. As it began to take effect, I tried to keep a façade of normality, but the more I tried the more detached I felt, the more neurotic I became, and the more traumatic were the feelings of panic sweeping over me. Suddenly I felt my body begin to spasm. My vision clouded, and then shapes became images which dissolved into colours and my consciousness floated outside of myself and I became terrified. Still trying to remain calm, I tried to reassure myself, to stay cool. But by this time the other guests appeared to be changing, their faces dissolving into their heads. I felt myself falling into myself and sat on the bed, clinging to the headboard. I was spinning through space, through time, barely aware that everyone else was having similar feelings to me.

Then paranoia set in, I mean *really* set in. As I looked around, I noticed people watching me, chatting, laughing, all motion slowed down to imperceptible movements, chattering, pointing at me. Someone would say something which couldn't be understood or was misconstrued and then they would feel stupid, or you would feel excluded, and the paranoia would sweep around the room. While being massaged by a topless girl, I began to imagine myself turning into Arnold Schwarzenegger, imagining every muscle protruding from my body and vying for attention. Then all attention turned to Max's bodyguard, who we were told had never taken acid before. He had fallen asleep just after taking it and had then suddenly awoken, struggling with the new reality the drug had produced. His face said it all. He watched us watching him. Trying not to induce paranoia in him, we found ourselves trying to not let him see us watching him.

Then suddenly in this mental chaos Max lost his temper, lost control, focusing his anger on his girlfriend, who had by this time convinced herself she was a witch and had taken to crawling around on the floor, whispering spells, peeping around doors or over armchairs. Max grabbed her and threw her out naked into the street. He then phoned a cab to come and collect her, while all the time we could hear her screaming outside the door, pleading to be let in. I just sat there, afraid to intervene for fear that it may be misconstrued or that I might myself have misconstrued things, retreating further into my own world.

Then Max announced that he was going to telephone a drug dealer to bring over a couple of ounces of cocaine. Max and his bodyguard donned dark glasses and then, to my absolute horror, took out guns from a bag behind the sofa. 'Just in case anything should go wrong,' said Max. Oh dear God! Panic turned to fear turned to hysteria, but I just kept still, said nothing. They had guns. These people who were paranoid, neurotic, out of their heads actually had real guns – actually here in the room with us. But still I sat there, saying nothing, trying to keep myself from going over the edge.

A short while later three dealers – black guys in dark glasses, two in suits and one in a long white robe – arrived and Max and the bodyguard disappeared into the other room. We all waited quietly, the intense silence pressing hard into the eardrum, half expecting gunshots. I wished I was somewhere else, wanted to be not there, to be anywhere in the world but there. I wanted to get out, but how could I? What if I tried to leave and someone misjudged my actions? What the fuck was I doing here? I couldn't stop myself shaking.

Eventually they came back into the room with an ounce of cocaine, and the three black men left. 'It got a bit heavy in there for a while,' said Max, laughing and waving the gun around, jokingly pointing it at each of us in turn. I was not feeling good about this.

Then Max takes out the bag of cocaine and asks someone to test it for him. I try to shrink out of sight. Damien, the cocaine expert on hand, imparts his wisdom. 'There's only one way to test it for sure,' he announces, 'I'll have to shoot some up.' I'm thinking there must be an easier way to test it than that, but I just keep quiet. What do I know? Then he volunteers me to help him. 'Why me?' I'm thinking. All eyes turn to me. The gun is still out, being waved around, and everyone's waiting for me to answer, so I say, 'OK. Yes. That seems like a really good idea.' To my utter relief, helping him means only holding the needle, not actually having to take it. Moments later, everyone's looking on, I'm tripping, and Damien injects himself with the mixture into a vein in his foot. Without warning he immediately seems to turn pale yellow, with sweat pouring off him. 'It's good –

very good,' he declares as he slumps to the floor. 'Well, that's good,' I'm thinking. 'I mean, what if it hadn't been good? What then?'

So, Damien not being dead, everyone chops out lines and starts snorting. The acid seems to be lasting for ever, and now everyone's taking cocaine. I don't want any, trying to be sensible, but there's a line cut out for me and they've all taken theirs and someone asks whose line is left and everyone says not theirs and suddenly everyone's looking at me, waiting for me to take it, and Max is still waving the gun. So I take it. Up one nostril in one go. Eeeecckkk! Then the room, the ceiling, the furniture, everything begins to swirl around and around and is sucked into the television. As someone slides another line towards me, I run to the bathroom to be sick.

Almost twenty-four hours after the party had started, Damien is the first to leave to go to the FF club. The acid had worn down enough for a degree of safety to return. Finding a close friend to talk to, I sat and cried my eyes out. It had all been too much for me.

The second incident that comes to mind didn't involve junkies, dealers, gangsters or the like, but two people who were actually mentally unbalanced, though of course it involved me being on drugs. The expression 'If you lie down with dogs you catch fleas' comes to mind. I was at times living in the kennel.

I'd met a man (who shall remain nameless) who in turn had a friend. I befriended them and put trust in them. They did the odd job for me – that sort of thing. (I was so out of my head most of the time I don't know what they did.) Then I began to suspect that I was being defrauded, in more ways than one; cheques with forged signatures had been cashed, and personal belongings went missing. In my constant drugged-out state, I must have been easy to rip off. Close friends warned me, but I ignored their advice.

Then one day I was told that a cheque for a substantial amount had been cashed. I went into a blind rage. I foolishly went round to pay my new 'friends' a visit at their high-rise flat in Islington. I should have taken someone with me, but I trusted them so I never thought to. I was so angry that I wasn't thinking straight. Besides, I was Marc Almond – well-known person. What could they do to me? They wouldn't dare!

I banged on their door, but they pretended they weren't in. Only when I threatened to get the police did they open up. I walked straight in and confronted them. At first came denials, but then, when I again threatened to get the police, one of them lunged at me and slammed the door shut. 'You're not going anywhere,' the other shouted menacingly.

A fight ensued as they suddenly attempted to drag me out on to the balcony and throw me over the edge. Six floors up. The window smashed and pictures and ornaments flew everywhere as I struggled for my life. 'Hit him with the lamp,' shouted one. 'Knock him out.'

As they continued to try to force me out and over, I fought with all my strength, throwing punches and kicking. Then one of them leaped on me and began to strangle me. I don't know how long it was before I blacked out. When I came to, a policeman was standing over me and a paramedic was talking quietly in my ear. Hearing the commotion, a neighbour had intervened while another had called the police.

'Do you want to press charges, sir?' The two of them sat there looking at me, their heads in their hands, afraid I would tell the truth.

'No,' I said. 'I just want to go home.' My eyes black and a deep gash across my head and face, I said it was an argument that had got out of hand. I imagined how this nightmare could become a far worse one if the press found out. Attempted murder. Marc Almond. Cheque fraud. Pressing charges would charge the tabloid press up. It would raise more questions than I would feel comfortable with.

I left with the two thugs apologizing and crying, but I ignored them. I was just thankful that I hadn't been thrown over the balcony. I could imagine the story: 'He just jumped. He was unbalanced. He was on drugs. We tried to stop him. We fought to stop him.' Isn't that what they would have said? Who would have known the truth? I *was* unbalanced. I *was* nearly always on drugs. I was insane. They were insane. It was all bloody insane.

Shock hit me later, and I had a short nervous breakdown. It affected me badly. All I could think of was how near I had come to the end. The desire for revenge and retribution consumed my every thought until it became more dangerous than the situation I'd earlier found myself in. Max wanted to teach the pair a South London gang lesson. I considered it, but I couldn't have let anything like that really happen. I heard later that the two had fallen out with each other, and in the fight between them one had had his ear bitten off. (I never found out which ear.) The biter ended up in a home, then later in prison for attacking a police officer. So, what becomes of us all in the end? Karma sweetly visits.

*

The two incidents I have just recalled made me change. Made me want to run away from London altogether. Doesn't the song say 'Sometimes I feel I've got to run away, get away.' Stevo packed me off to New York to work with Mike Thorne on my new album. I thought it was the best and worst idea ever. The best because it took me away; the worst because I wanted the album to reflect the changing London, which was currently hip and happening again, and wanted to record with new people, cutting-edge dance producers. But after arriving in New York and meeting Mike I settled down. Besides, I couldn't live in the church I'd bought, which was now no more than a rubble site thanks to an idiot posing as a builder who'd siphoned money off me at an exorbitant rate. Six weeks in New York in autumn of 1993. A big mistake.

It became clear that Mike Thorne had loved the Synclavier system so much that he'd bought the company, and he didn't see things quite the way I did. His recording technique had become burdened by the dated technology he preferred. The studio was like a small office with bits of old computers that made electronic farting noises after they'd been messed about with for half a day. I thought, 'At this rate, in six weeks' time I'll have an album that sounds like a bout of electronic wind.' We'd used this equipment to make the Soft Cell album, but times had moved on. Teenagers had better equipment than this in their bedrooms! I wanted to work with *them* – hungry young DJs and aspiring producers, eager to record and give their best work. I didn't want Mike to do my album. I wanted cute, young talent creating exciting dance beats over which I could add my touches of colour and flair. I was in New York, home of dance music, but stuck with an oversensitive middle-aged producer, bogged down with creaky old equipment. And me on the verge of a nervous breakdown. The process quickly became tired, laboured and difficult.

There was only one thing to do. 'Oh no!' you're thinking. 'No, please, not again!' Yes. Take drugs and escape to the bars and clubs. This time my preference was the bars down near Forty-second Street and the Port Authority Bus Terminal: bars like the Savoy and Tricks – those frequented by 'hustlers, hos and their johns', as Jerry Springer would say, by crack addicts and Puerto Rican gang members. I became friendly with members of the Spanish gang the Latin Kings, and when I wasn't frequenting the bars, buying drinks or drugs or even trying to play pool, they would all be round at my apartment smoking crack. I tried crack. I didn't like it at first, so you know what I did? I tried it again. You know if you don't like something at first . . . One evening I was around at the apartment of my Latin friend Frankie Diaz; the very next evening the police burst in and hoisted him and his transvestite room-mate off to Ryker's Island, the notorious New York prison, charged with possessing and supplying heroin and crack. If I'd been there then, I could be writing you a chapter all about my time in Ryker's, fending off some big black daddy.

So I'm in New York, filling the time, trying to record an album, but burdened with a producer who's interminably slow. So who turns up at my apartment? My friend Max – who'd thoughtfully flown to New York especially to see me – a bottle of cocaine and a chauffeur-driven limousine waiting outside. So whatever chance there was of my recording the album suddenly disappears. (Actually, I just thought I'd let Mike Thorne get on with it – there were electronic farts to program, and that could take weeks.) On the town with Max meant having to help him sneak out of one luxury hotel after another without paying, until he had the bright idea of moving into my apartment, and then the place was never without a visitor or ten.

The recording of the album was going spectacularly badly – I mean, much worse than anyone envisaged. A couple of tracks were sent back to Steve Allen at WEA in England, who responded with a curt fax – words to the effect of 'tired-sounding, lumbering, stale crap!' Actually, his summing up was spot on, but, encouraged by all around me, I responded with an obnoxious fax in which I told him in no uncertain terms where to get off, said he was a failed artist, and asked how he dared tell me (a successful artist?) what sounded good on my album. Now, you know that feeling when you've sent a fax and then suddenly you think, 'Hmm, maybe that wasn't the best thing to do', and then you think, 'I wish I'd thought that through a bit more'? The result of my fax was that all my money was stopped, the apartment was stopped, and I was immediately summoned back to WEA in London for a talking-to.

At the airport, I found I'd been booked into Economy, so I knew I was really in trouble. I created a commotion. 'I'm meant to be in First Class,' I explained, 'or at least Business.' I shouted at the desk clerk, 'Surely there's some mistake!'

She looked at me with contemptuous satisfaction. 'I'm afraid not, sir. But just let me check one last time. It is Mr Almond, isn't it? As in the nut . . .'

'How dare you?' I shouted.

Then she said, 'If you don't desist, I'll have security remove you.'

I was incensed.

'If you'd like to buy a first-class ticket, there are still three available on this flight,' she added, giving me the most disdainful smile.

'You know what? Yes, I would! That's fine.' As I whipped out my credit card, that grin left her face immediately.

I'm telling you this for no reason other than to illustrate how I hated everyone. I'd been called back to England like a badly behaved schoolboy and I was really pissed off. It hurt to pay for that ticket myself, and it hurt even more when WEA refused point-blank to reimburse me. I was in trouble, and had to see Rob Dickens immediately. He was furious about my fax to Steve Allen.

'Don't take it to heart, Rob,' I said. 'It was only a bit of fun. I like Steve, I really do.'

I really did like Steve, and I regretted my unpleasant fax (kind of) and tried furiously to back-pedal as I saw my chances of returning to New York fading fast. But in all honesty I didn't really want to go back there to work with Mike Thorne again, as it had been a mistake. Neal X backed me up and told Rob how disappointed he'd been with Mike's results on tracks like 'The Idol', how Mike had turned a groovy electro pop song into lumbering techno rock.

'Mike is too old-school,' said Neal.

'Exactly,' I said, 'I behaved badly, Rob, because I was frustrated. I so want to get this right for Warner.' I blamed the whole incident on Mike – which was unfair, but I was desperate.

Rob said he'd have to take time to decide what to do with me, and closed the meeting.

Once back in London, I was offered a New Year's Eve appearance at a party at the Astoria. I normally hate personal appearances in clubs, but even I can be bought when the money supply is running dangerously low. Ten thousand pounds for fifteen minutes. I thought about it, looked at my bank statement, looked at the rubble in my unfinished house, and agreed to do it.

On the night of the appearance, I took so much Ecstasy and cocaine before the show that I fell off stage. At one point I was so out of it that I didn't know where I was. After my spot I climbed into the back of a stretch limo I'd hired for the night (not a good move on New Year's Eve in the West End) and went from club to club taking drugs. At nine in the morning I ended up with a small group of us back at my place. When the drugs we had ran out, I sent my friend Jamie out to scour the clubs (which had reopened by then) for more, until the entire £10,000 had been spent. We had a chill-out that went on for two days until I took some Special K and ended up in a K hole, trying to climb out of the shag-pile carpet that threatened to eat me.

Happy New Year.

*

I went back to New York early in January 1994 to collect my things that I'd left at the apartment I'd been staying in, and there I fell ill with a fever. New York was gripped in the worst snowstorm for decades, and for two weeks my friend and I sat watching TV and movies. I felt subdued, beaten and depressed on the biggest drug comedown ever, and of course still chained to my Halcion and Valium. One of the reasons I had come back was to stock up on Halcion from my New York doctor.

Upon returning to England I was summoned to Stevo's house.

He sat me down.

'Warner Brothers and I feel that it is time for you to get help. We feel you should go into a treatment clinic for your addiction,' he said. He then explained how they all felt I had become a liability, but that Warner were prepared to pick up the bill for two months of treatment if I agreed to go immediately.

Stevo said all this with his most serious face and tone, so I knew it wasn't a joke. I couldn't believe that all this had been discussed in my absence and an arrangement agreed.

'I don't have a problem. It's everyone else that has a problem.'

But Stevo was having none of it.

So that was their solution to me. Me. The freak, the trouble-causer, the liability. Put him in a treatment centre. Stevo of all people was telling me that my life was out of control. All the fucking things he'd taken and done – right down to his acid trip on Radio 4! But of course he was reformed. He was the new Stevo, modified Stevo – and we all know what reformed people are like. I was to become one.

And I knew in my heart that what he said was true. I was numb and then resigned. I agreed to go.

Within a week I had seen a specialist and was taken to the Promis Treatment Centre, just outside Canterbury, run by the brilliant and comforting Dr Robert Lefever. Two close friends drove me there, and I felt like an empty shell, or worse, a vessel of badness, but also broken, miserable, no longer a real person. I'd been told I was lucky to have this opportunity. My life and my career were on hold, and my excuse for a life would be exchanged for another life, the old Marc exorcized to make way for a new Marc who would understand the needs of others and his caring record company – a selfless Marc, and one who would be appreciative. A Marc 2. But would I like this Marc, or would I hate him even more than the old one?

I felt bitter, angry and betrayed. Why me? Was I any worse than anyone else? And of course I was fearful. The purpose of the stay was to break my addiction to Halcion – the drug that I'd taken every night for the last twelve years and without which I couldn't sleep, or without which sleep would be just a light drifting punctuated with panic attacks, anxiety and sickness. This broken machine was going to the garage for a complete overhaul and service. But treatment centres, as I was to learn, don't deal just with specific addictions: they deal with the source and nature of the addict's proclivities.

As I sat in the registration lobby, surrounded by kindly, understanding people, I felt like a criminal. And I was a criminal. I was morally, socially and emotionally bankrupt. A Polaroid was taken of my swollen, scowling face, and my pockets were emptied, my pills confiscated. I was then body-searched and read the rules. The rules! Call it a clinic, a treatment centre, a retreat – for me it was a psychiatric hospital: I sheepishly waved goodbye to my two friends and began my penance for my life of excess. It was time to pay the piper.

I was shown around the building and introduced to everyone – an extremely friendly yet diverse assortment of people, each dealing as best they could with their own nightmares. I wanted so much to be special and different. I thought I was, but I was just like everyone else at the centre. No different at all. As I found out more about everyone in discussions, meetings and group therapy, I realized that I wasn't alone and that I could identify with other people. It's almost disappointing to learn that we're all coming from the same place, acting out the same behavioural patterns, sharing the same pain. I was very soon even picking up the language of rehab – 'identifying', 'acting out', 'sharing'. But as anyone who's gone through it will tell you: taking the talk was the easy part; I had to learn to walk the walk too.

I sent a close friend a letter which he has allowed me to use to show you my thoughts at that time:

Dear . . .

Just a quick letter to tell you I'm doing my best to fit in. It's only my second day, but already I feel more relaxed. I'm beginning to feel easier with people here and talking to them. It's a quite hard and regimented timetable, and sometimes it feels like I'm being punished and I'm in prison. The day starts at 6.45 with a wake-up call over the tannoy, and various meetings and therapy follow – some of them quite difficult and emotional, but I'm doing my best to contribute to the group sessions by speaking out.

I'm lucky to have my own room, and they may even give me a portable TV for insomnia. I had a sleepless night last night because bedtime was so early, but tonight my Valium will be taken away (only on alternate nights to start with) so I'll probably be climbing the walls alongside other people in here.

The people are really nice, and there are some really sad stories – people on methadone withdrawal, anorexia, alcoholics, sex addictions. In meetings I have to introduce myself as a drug addict. It's really hard to speak out, but there's no avoiding it.

Someone completed their course today and they had a ritual called 'a burning'. A bonfire is lit and the person has to burn all their notes, forms and psychoanalysis sheets – tons of it – with everyone saying a special prayer, first whispered and then shouted. A song is sung of choice, and then everyone has to do the hokey-cokey. It's so bizarre. I've refused to have anything to do with religion, which keeps sneaking in here and there. God, I'd love a cup of caffeinated tea!

Please send me some swimming trunks, as they have visits to the health club. I filled in my cross-addiction form, which indicates how addicted you are to various things, and sleeping pills and Valium seem to be the least of my problems – I'll probably never get out. Some people have been here for months and months. It'll take a long time of hard work to adjust both in here and when I get out.

Initially the one thing that put me on guard was the word 'God'. I suspected that I'd been duped and was surrounded by religious maniacs – that I might even end up being brainwashed, a glass-eyed Christian smiling and doing all the right things. No, I was Marc Almond. I dressed in black and sang about the darker side of life. Religion couldn't be my fate. I was fearful I would lose myself somewhere along the way, instead of finding myself. As everybody sat around, held hands and repeated the Serenity Prayer ('God give me strength to accept the things I cannot change . . .'), I felt very uncomfortable. But I found something soothing and calming in the mantra, and appealing in the phrase 'clean and serene'.

Over the following days, I began to understand what 'God' could mean for me. As one counsellor, Elizabeth, said, 'GOD stands for "Good Orderly Direction".' With the religious reference removed, the idea began to appeal to me. Good Orderly Direction. I came to understand that my lack of GOD simply meant I was powerless over my addiction, and that my life had become unmanageable. I read all about me in the Narcotics Anonymous books. I needed something to fill that space inside, the black hole that we try to fill to ease the pain. The hole was decidedly GOD-shaped. GOD could be nature, it could be music, it could be a group of like-minded people to share troubles with.

There was so much to get used to at the centre, to fit into a regime that was so unfamiliar. Morning started at 6.45, and strict rules were always respected and observed. Breaking the rules means you put other people at risk, you jeopardize their chances, and so it is that you are made to understand the needs of others, to acknowledge that other people have needs, that other people exist in the world.

After breakfast, household chores were followed by group therapy or one-on-one sessions, discussions and step exercise. The Promis programme is based on the twelve-step programme of Alcoholics Anonymous, supposedly the only real chance for an addict – not a cure, but a series of instructions for living your life by. I'd reached the point in my life where, although I wasn't responsible for being an addict, I had to be made to understand that I was responsible for the consequences of my addiction in terms of my behaviour and actions. I had to learn to deal with my anger, my self-loathing and of course me. I had to learn about myself from scratch, from scrutinizing and examining the past, and it was not a pleasant lesson.

Although bonding with one other individual was forbidden at Promis and carried with it the threat of expulsion, I did find one or two people whom I got on with – in particular a recovering alcoholic called Beverley, who, like me, also thought she was special and different. We were always hard on each other in our character critiques, probably because we saw too much of ourselves in each other. We shared a similar sense of humour, and made each other laugh through the difficult times.

The first week was the hardest. I was still resentful of being there, and was allowed no outside phone calls at all – I was totally isolated from the outside. But worse, of course, was the withdrawal from the benzodiazepine drugs. Weaning off them began on my second night, and stopped on the fourth. As long as I live, those nights will haunt me. I thought I was going to die. This had nothing to do with the GOD-shaped hole, or me as an addictive person, but was to do purely with physical addiction and withdrawal. During those first nights without the drug for all those years, I lay in bed, my heart pounding, fearful of the suffocating panic attacks that came every few minutes. I would constantly summon the nurse for reassurance in the difficult moments. I shook and went into spasm, my stomach cramped, and every noise intensified my headache. Then, during the third and fourth night, my senses started to reawaken and smells and touch felt alien. I had horrific dreams of murder, of murderers coming into my life, and then my room. I thought the trees were alive and began to hallucinate, and the wind turned into louder and louder wailing.

Each day, while suffering withdrawal, I was made to sit in group therapy alongside heroin addicts and chronic alcoholics. We had to observe each other, and through others ourselves, and suffer together. I was cold and sweaty and couldn't breathe properly. I would shake and cry, and my joints ached constantly. One of the worst aspects was the waking dreams – nightmares that I had suppressed would flash before my eyes and I would recoil in despair. Emotions that had for so long been locked away and forgotten began to emerge. This went on for days and nights: sleepless panic, black insomnia and utter depression, feeling psychotic or hyperactive or lethargic – from one to the other and then back again.

I began to eat and eat as my taste buds seemed to revive, but then I was put on observation for fear of my addiction switching to food.

After the second week I awoke one morning from some sleep and clouds began to clear in my head and I felt a bit better. I had slept unassisted by pills for the first time in ten or more years. I could smell the air, and I felt good – I actually felt alive. I had, however, been warned that I would to some degree always suffer the after-effects of withdrawal, the jolts, occasional insomnia, panic attacks, but they would get less and less over time, though they probably wouldn't disappear entirely.

By the end of the third week I began to enjoy being at the centre, and I looked forward to the group sessions and the lectures from Dr Lefever, who made all the pain and the reason for persevering make so much sense. I realized I owed so much to him and to the others I had come to know during the therapy. I had come to understand myself a little better, and I actually began to like myself (though not too much as yet). I looked healthier, fitter, and even put on a little weight for the first time in my life.

I passed my steps one to five only just in time, for suddenly one Sunday afternoon a man came into the clinic lounge. A tabloid newspaper had discovered that I was there and had posted a photographer with a telephoto lens by the gate. I was sickened and upset. I'd just under two weeks to go, but I was told that I couldn't stay there now. I'd wanted this time to be mine, my own private time for recovering, and now it had been spoiled. It turned out that a heroin addict who'd been at the centre and run away had needed money and gone to a tabloid. I didn't blame the addict – he was just doing the kind of thing addicts do out of desperation – but I was surprised that any tabloid was actually interested. I called Stevo, who turned up with a limousine (his usual discreet self), and we left the centre with me hiding on the car floor. I could never resist a dramatic exit.

*

Still in recovery and experiencing withdrawal symptoms, I was back out in the world – with all its temptations. Though I'd had to change,

I couldn't expect anyone else to – that would be up to them. I was going to have to cut myself off from many of my old cohorts, however hard it would be to do so. It was early days for the new me, and I had to avoid putting temptation in my way. I wasn't going to take drugs of any kind, for I'd learned that, as an addict, if I did I would lay myself open again to every type of drug. I knew I could be strong, and I was determined – I had to be. But even so I couldn't risk people taking drugs in front of me – it would have been stupid to place myself in such a situation.

At first it was easy, because being clean was in itself a new high, a new experience. I knew in my heart of hearts that I would never touch Halcion or Valium again after they'd been the cause of so much pain and insanity for me. But the danger comes when you feel that you're in control of your life – sufficiently in control to try other drugs again. I was still in denial about my cocaine addiction, because I binged on coke only sporadically and told myself I never really had a problem with it, despite all I'd learned in rehab. When a tabloid ran a story about me having treatment in a clinic for cocaine addiction, I was furious. 'My problem was prescription drugs, it was not cocaine.' But my problem was really everything. I preferred to choose prescription drugs as my problem because then it seemed to me that I was a victim. But I had no excuse for the cocaine, the Ecstasy . . . I'm not going to give you a list: you know what I took.

It was then that Stevo had one of his ideas, which were always worrying things. It was an idea that was to upset me and to contribute to our separation. Stevo led me to believe that the Sunday tabloids were going to do a piece about my rehab spell and relevant drug problems. He suggested that I should get in there first and make some money out of it. I didn't like this idea one bit.

Stevo's new obsession, I'd learned, was with the tabloids and the money he could make from them. He knew all too well what I thought of this. I wasn't anti the tabloids – which would have been hypocritical, since I read enough of them – but I felt they were dangerous territory and wanted nothing to do with them. To me, working with tabloids is a Faustian exchange from which there is only one winner. Besides, the stories sold to tabloids always struck me as sad and desperate, the people they concerned always eager to be celebrities. I hated the thought of being a celebrity more than anything, and had always gone out of my way not to be one. I am a singer. I don't do shows in which I don't sing, or if in exceptional circumstances I am interviewed it's only about my work. I would never appear on quiz shows or comedy sketches – it just isn't me.

But Stevo was having none of this. He explained carefully that if I didn't put my story to a journalist then someone else would – in a bad way, with a negative slant on it. I was worried, and so stupidly agreed to talk in an off-the-record meeting with two journalists to gauge whether I had a story worth buying. I found the whole affair creepy and unsettling. The journalists were two young, normal-looking people (I don't know what I expected), purposefully innocu-ous and suspiciously discreet-acting, but when I insisted on a positive story about the dangers of prescription drugs they lost interest. They wanted famous names, stories of drug orgies and addictions to sex. There wasn't any angle in it for them; mine was a story fit only for *Woman's Realm*. I was offered £5,000 for my paltry revelations, which Stevo thought an insult. I was delighted, because I didn't want to do the story anyhow, and now I had a reason to decline altogether.

Then I was offered £100,000 for a story if I had AIDS. I was even more pleased to disappoint that time. So that's the going price for terminal illness! I couldn't believe that Stevo even relayed that offer to me. As I've said, this was to mark the beginning of the end for Stevo and me. I was questioning his motives too often these days. Then it occurred to me that his insistence that I go into rehab might have been because he thought there could be a payout at the end of it. The most delicious irony of all is that Stevo made me go into rehab, and rehab opened my eyes to Stevo.

Now it has become almost de rigueur for a star to do a session in rehab – usually around the release of an album. In turn, rehab has become blurred with health farm, and anyone who has snorted a line or got drunk one time too many is now a case for rehab, which equates with public sympathy. Usually what is involved is just a couple of weeks in somewhere with not too many rules and very comfortable regimes. Rehab can even be part of the marketing spend these days – recording costs, photo sessions, advertising campaign, rehab and videos. The star comes out looking fresh and revitalized, armed with stories of 'Drugs Hell' or 'Cocaine Shame' for the new photo session. These stories are usually prompted by earlier press revelations after having been caught taking a line or two at a party, carelessly observed by a tabloid journalist. Penance, rehabilitation, repentance, album release, and the star is given an 'edge' – it's so important to have an edge in the nineties. Cynical? No, just realistic. My favourite headline, by the way, was 'Drugs Brought Me to My Knees'. Hmm.

Then I was told that Warner – who I should point out were incredibly supportive during my time in rehab, and paid the bill for it – said they wanted me to return to New York to finish the album with Mike Thorne. I was stunned. The last I had heard was that everyone hated what I had done with Mike – including me. But, knowing how important it was for me to stay away from my drug-taking friends and places of temptation (all centred around London at this time), I agreed to give recording in New York another try.

You may think I was only jumping out of the frying pan by going to New York, what with all its temptations available twenty-four hours a day, but at that time it was certainly the lesser of two evils. Besides, if you can resist drugs there, you can resist drugs anywhere. Can't you? It would be a test of my resolve and determination. I also thought that, with my new spirit, events might work out more creatively with Mike, and perhaps Warner did too. And it seemed that they did, to a degree – though it was still a technical hell. The sound was not quite what I had in mind, but certainly getting nearer to it – far more twisted techno and glam blues. I felt it had fire and energy that an odd remix would bring out fully.

The album was still called *Urban Velvet* for the time being, and it opened with a stomping version of 'Out There' – quite Iggy Pop at that stage, though later it would be mellowed out. 'Betrayal' was full of bitterness, and 'Lie' was full of anger, complete with shrieking guitars courtesy of the legendary Chris Spedding. There were three guitarists working on the album: Neal X adding glam twists and chords; Rick Shaffer, from New York's punk-influenced band the Reds, adding a razor's-edge slide and punk riffs; and of course the greasy rockabilly Chris Spedding. It was exhilarating when Chris plugged in his guitar, even though I thought he was going to keel over and die, he looked so wasted from life's excesses.

A techno blues of 'Adored and Explored' (again quite different from the final version on the album) had David Johansen of the New York Dolls playing a dirty, wailing blues harmonica. I had known David years before, and it was great to see him again. He has a wicked New York sense of humour that makes sessions such fun, and is such a talented musician. The most memorable days for me were the ones with David, Chris and John Cale playing piano. Together we recorded three songs – 'Love to Die for', 'Come in Sweet Assassin' and 'Sacrifice'. John Cale and I were the clean guys, drinking our mineral water, drug-free – a situation that seemed to irritate David. Perhaps he hated us reminding him of what he should be doing. Chris, on the other hand, didn't give a damn what anyone thought, and indulged himself. I felt privileged to be singing with these three musicians.

As we sat around afterwards eating sandwiches, we watched the news. Kurt Cobain had committed suicide – he had just shot himself. Everyone sat in silent contemplation for a while. It was such a strange day.

The album closed with a ten-minute track called 'Rise', an uplifting dance track that opened with the lines 'Out on another date with despair/ And I'm paying the bill once more.' The track ended with five minutes of pounding guitars and feedback with voodoo techno drums.

It was an intense album on the whole. The vocals, though laden with too much reverb, are delivered with bitterness, anger, sorrow and finally a new-found strength. It was cathartic – the last couple of years of my life exhumed and exorcized.

At Warner I was handed over to a new A & R man, my old EMI colleague Clive Black, who had just joined the company. I was delighted to be working with him again. It's so amusing how in the music business everything goes round and round. When the music stops they all move round – musical chairmen. I had more than once worked with the same person at several different companies, and was now to do so again. Clive had planned for 'Rise' (remixed, naturally) to be the first single from the album, and once again everything seemed to be on course. After all it had been Clive who had helped me get my second number one. But, just as things were taking shape, Stevo phoned me with news that by now seemed all too familiar.

He'd fallen out with Warner and wanted me to leave the label. He was at this time representing several other groups as well, all of whom were also signed to Warner, and wanted to take all of us away. He'd been informed at some point that if he wanted to leave he could, so he seized the opportunity, believing it to be another master stroke in his constant battle of one-up-manship. To have an artist like me with a finished album which he was free to take to another record company, sell to a new label, was a chance he wasn't going to pass up. 'You can stay if you want to,' he told me – 'it's up to you. But, if you do, Warner's will probably put your album out with no marketing spend. Or you could do as I suggest and I could get you a brand new deal with a fresh company who want you.' What choice did I have?

Stevo then went on to put forward more confidence-eroding arguments to persuade me that no one really wanted me at Warner anyhow. He always had a way with words. But it was never made clear to me why Warner would let all his bands go at the same time. Perhaps, of course, the common denominator was Stevo himself. Perhaps they'd had enough of him. Now that was something I could relate to. When I asked him for a full explanation, he told me it was all 'hush-hush'. He explained that, due to contractual obligations, he couldn't tell me everything and refused to go into it further. I was very suspicious. I couldn't imagine what poor Mike Thorne must have thought of all this – he'd worked hard, and the end-of-album celebrations were cut short as I suddenly had no record label.

*

It had been a strange time for me in New York. I was drug-free there for the first time in my life, and suddenly it seemed such a different place. I filled my time with cultural activities – galleries, the theatre, movies – and mixed with non-drug-taking friends. Which meant I spent most of my time alone. I kept myself very much to myself in my apartment on Madison Avenue and watched TV. I was still going through withdrawal symptoms and, worst of all, I was becoming that thing I'd always feared I would become: a reformed drug addict, with all the pompous speech and attitude that can entail. 'Hey, I feel so great now . . . You should try it . . . You know, drugs are no good for you . . . I was just like you . . . You know, if I can do it, so can you . . . I didn't know how much drugs were ruining my life.'

I'd started to walk the walk, and in turn talk the talk, and it scared me. This was all so new to me, and to reassure myself I had to tell people about it, to try to find someone to identify with. I tried not to impose myself on friends, who really didn't want to hear it over and over, so in New York I tried to find Narcotics Anonymous meetings to attend. But they all seemed too intimidating and specialized – 'Cocaine Abuse from Parental Abuse', 'Single Black Mothers on Crack', 'Amputee Codependents on Welfare Suffering Addiction'. I suspected most of them were created just because the acronym sounded great – like BLAST: 'Blacks and Latinos Addicted to Sexual Therapy'. I couldn't find one for me.

When I returned to London I tried to attend NA meetings there, but I never felt comfortable. I found that I knew too many people attending them, or else my shyness meant that I couldn't get a word in edgeways. 'What about me?' I would think, as meeting after meeting the same person told the same exhausting story. Sometimes it felt enough to drive you to drink. So I eventually gave up going. NA was just not for me. I muddled through and tried to lose myself in the arts or cinema, or dinner with friends. I tried to do anything that didn't involve thinking about drugs.

While in New York, though, I found there was no pressure on me – or, more to the point, no boredom. There was always something to be doing, something new to see or take part in. I kept myself so busy that I found myself not thinking about drugs – which I know is not the same as not wanting them – and by the evening I had exhausted myself so much that all I wanted to do was sleep. But that, of course, was not easy, and I still experienced panic attacks and muscular jolts. But the path that Dr Lefever had set me on, and which he assured me would lead to a better life, was in some ways beginning to pay off. I was enjoying life. I was even happy.

But that was in New York. Back in London life was far more difficult. The gloom of return – from the weather to the pressures of my career, now without a label – descended on me as soon as the plane landed. My house, still in a state of disrepair thanks to the cowboy builder who had worked on it and ripped me off, was now a worse problem than before I'd left for New York. Bills had not been paid, money was a worry, and I'd no career as such. Nevertheless, I was still drug free. But soon the pressures meant that I succumbed to temptation and relapsed into Ecstasy and cocaine binges. How many times? Maybe five at the most, but each time with diminishing pleasure and a burden of guilt. Drugs were just not doing it for me any more. I had just grown out of them, left them behind. Whereas before I had felt reckless and fearless when taking lines and pills, I would now think too much of the consequences, of how many people I was letting down and what a disappointment I had become to myself after going through so much. I wouldn't be able to relax and enjoy myself, to escape. I felt paranoid, edgy, sick, sweaty, dirty. I saw it all in a new light.

Tired of living alone, I invited someone to move in as a lodger. I had known Jamie for quite a while, and thought he would make a good companion. A friend of mine, who'd met him playing the fruit machine in the Copacabana Club, Earls Court, had introduced us. I came to know Jamie very well. He divided his time between his beautiful girlfriend Pepi, a rich elderly confidant and a central London casino. He always had a scam or an idea up his sleeve, and often returned to the house with a bundle of cash of which he gave me a share. He also introduced me to the joys of dog racing and the Arsenal football club. But when Jamie turned up yet again with bruises, stab wounds and elaborate stories I decided enough was enough, and asked him to leave. When Jamie and Pepi eventually split he went off the rails, turned down a chance to model for a top agency and hit the bottle. But that soft spot I had for him remains, and we are still friends. Years later he's still chasing the same things, as handsome as ever, a new girlfriend in tow and a first child on the way. I'm even going to be the godfather!

Life still threw me odd surprises, bizarre situations and interesting diversions – sometimes so wicked that it was impossible to say no. I received a telephone call from my old friends Jeff and 'Sleazy' (Peter Christopherson). Since Psychic TV had split acrimoniously and

Genesis P. Orridge had fled to America to escape scandal, Jeff and Sleazy had formed a new group called Coil. They had just recorded a couple of albums for Some Bizarre, on which I was a guest vocalist on two tracks. Those albums inspired such people as Trent Reznor of the band Nine Inch Nails, who was to later sign them to his own American label. Another collaborator with Coil was the musician, writer, performance artist and all-round Satanist Boyd Rice. Like all Satanists, terrorists, public enemies and the like, he was one of the nicest people you could wish to meet. Jeff said that Boyd was in town doing some work, and was I interested in meeting him and being initiated into Anton LaVey's Church of Satan? Boyd himself was an ordained minister in the church. (I knew that Anton was a fan of mine and, though I'd never met him, I had an open invitation to call him when in San Francisco.) Not being one to turn down a theatrical moment and a chance to be relegated to the bad book, I immediately said yes. The initiation was to take place in a small grotto in a wood at the home of Rose, the singer with the group Strawberry Switchblade, very near the place where the Hellfire Club used to meet in the last century.

On the day, I hired a long black limousine for the occasion and went to the appointed place at the prearranged time. Boyd, Jeff, Peter and Rose were waiting for me – Boyd wearing his dog collar, his black beard and piercing eyes suitably Satanic. The others took a short walk into the woods while Boyd said the secret words to me in private. I was thrilled, actually half expecting lightning to strike me down, and every hair on my neck stood on end and sweat broke out on my top lip. Afterwards I was given a badge and, lo and behold, I was then a member of the Church of Satan. Quite simple, really – no dancing naked, no bonfires, no blood sacrifice. I didn't really feel that different – well, maybe just a little wickeder.

Around this time my friend had opened a new bar in London's Soho, in which he gave me a share. It was called Freedom, and for a while it was the chicest place. Downstairs it had a small theatre, for which we brought over some of our favourite performers from New York: drag acts like Joey Arias, Coco Peru, Lady Bunny and the Duelling Bankheads – brilliant performers. We also put on torch singers such as Caroline Nin and Marie France, with whom I might perform impromptu. The bar had the brilliant creative team of Mark L, Heidi B and Roland Mouret behind it, and together they created a venue that was unparalleled in its innovative ideas and style. I poked my nose in at every opportunity, trying to fill my time – it was a diversion in which to indulge myself so I would think less and less about drugs. There was nothing like Freedom then, nor has been ever since.

It was the 1995 New Year's Eve party, when Freedom invited Pierre et Gilles over to decorate and host the bar, that would mark the end to my drug binges for good. I welcomed the year in a semi-conscious stupor, lolled between Pierre and Gilles, and that finally was it with drugs.

Yet the problem of too much time on my hands remained. Stevo was taking for ever to get me a new deal for the finished album, holding out for as much money as possible. I'd been on most major labels by now, so there weren't many left to choose from. Then Stevo seized upon the situation of my depleting funds and insisted that I part company with my accountant, Ronnie Harris, and my lawyer, David Glick. Stevo claimed he couldn't work with them. He gave me an ultimatum: it was either them or him. He knew I was counting on him to get me a new deal, and that at that point I couldn't do without him. So I made the wrong decision and chose him. But it was a move I didn't feel good about, and one that boded very ill for our relationship. And, as it turned out, it was a move that would cost me a fortune at a time when my finances were critical. But it was what Stevo wanted.

The end was in sight. The end of Stevo and I working together. But for one final time I allowed Stevo to manoeuvre me into a place where I didn't want to be.

I got together with Neal X again, and together we wrote a bunch of good pop tracks – 'upbeat', with a glam-rock feel about them. I was bored with the Mike Thorne album – in fact everyone was – so I hoped the new tracks would go a long way to helping Stevo secure me a new deal. I liked the techno blues of the Mike Thorne stuff, but I wanted to do some electro pop tracks, ballads, big orchestral numbers – in all honesty, I didn't know what the hell I wanted to do really. I just couldn't decide. So I did a bit of everything, as usual, which when added up comes to not much of anything.

The deal Stevo finally secured for me – a year after leaving Warner – was with Mercury Records, a subsidiary of Phonogram, my original label with Soft Cell and the Mambas. I had finally gone round full circle, even working with A & R man Dave Bates again, whom I knew from the old days, and Roger Aimes, now head of the company. It was a case of having déjà vus about my déjà-bloody-vus!

I took all the tracks I had recorded with Warner (which all but equalled an album) to be part of the deal with Mercury; a finished album ready to be released. But that would have been too simple. The album was remixed, rerecorded, rehashed, revocalled; new songs were added, others taken away and buried. At one point I found myself working with producer Martin Ware, formerly of the Human

League. He was such a lovely guy, and gave me some of the best vocal sounds I had ever had. At another point I worked again with producer Mike Hedges, first at Abbey Road and then later at his new chateau studio in France. Things were not only going full circle, they were spiralling in on themselves. Mercury Records, Mike Thorne, Clive Black, Roger Aimes, Mike Hedges – all I needed was Dave Ball and then things would really have imploded.

It was great, though, to see Mike Hedges again – as ginger, jovial and boastful as ever – just like the best of the old times (which they always are with hindsight). I recorded an EP with Mike consisting of four songs – 'Childstar', 'My Guardian Angel', 'The Edge of Heartache' and 'Christmas in Vegas' – and it's probably one of my favourites among all my recordings. 'Childstar' sounded fabulous, with Phil Spector touches and a huge orchestra – though I wasn't entirely pleased when, years later, Mike used all the same sounds and samples with his next project, the Manic Street Preachers, and they managed to have a big hit with them.

*

So the album was finished, again. And what a mishmash of songs and sounds it was. It's not that it's a bad album; it's just that it sounds like two albums merged into one. It has too much of everything except discipline. It sounds like a compilation album, and that in many ways is what it had become. No one knew what they were working towards, aimed at every possible market and so missed the target completely. It was a feathered fish. It was made before and after rehab, and the darker side contrasts too much with the lighter, more frivolous tracks. The final masterstroke of nonsense was the addition of a techno track, because, let's face it, that was the one thing it didn't have. So the sixteenth track was added – a bouncy collaboration with my old friend Jane Rollink, a.k.a. Mrs Woods. 'I'm like the sun shining brightly,' I sang, having at last taken my musical Prozac. Even the title, which until then was *Urban Velvet*, bored me. I couldn't think of a new one, so I just said to the marketing department, 'Call the bloody thing *Fantastic Star* and be done with it.' So they did. Cue the most disastrous album in my career.

To examine why it staggeringly underperformed would bore you rigid, and I suspect you're already becoming as jaded and tired as I am by this catalogue of disasters I call my career. But let's have a go at summing it up, because it is quite amusing.

Nearly four years since my last mainstream record release was too long a gap, since the public have difficulty remembering what or who you are after a month, and the album itself just wasn't worth the wait. You disagree? You're too kind.

The press for the album was done almost a year before its release, which was mind-bogglingly stupid. This was mainly because no one could decide what the single should be. In the music business everyone is indecisive – which translates as cautious – because everyone's job is always on the line, and major companies seem to equate paranoia with keeping everyone on their toes, though of course it has quite the opposite effect.

Eventually 'Adored and Explored' was released with good radio support, good(ish) reviews and a fabulous video by director Zana. The video, costing £60,000, was shot over two days and saw me acting out various roles such as Alice Cooper, Marc Bolan, David Bowie, Elvis, Liberace, a skinhead, a heavy-metal rocker and an Indian. And somewhere in there was me. TV liked it. I appeared on Cilla Black's *Surprise Surprise* – which I can't really believe I actually agreed to, but the record company and Stevo applied pressure so off I went to LWT. Then, as though that wasn't humiliation enough, I found myself cuddling up to Zig and Zag on their show, complete with name-tag and mock goofing around. Was that what I had worked so long for? Was that what my career, such as it was, had finally become?

It all added up to gross mismarketing for me. On *Surprise Surprise* and *Zig and Zag* I just looked out of place, and misguided. Fans told me they thought the appearances were cheap and tacky, and I was forced to agree. They didn't help sales of the record – in fact I think they helped to kill any chance it had. The record company told me all promotion is good, but that's not true. 'There's no such thing as bad publicity,' they kept reiterating. (Try telling Jeremy Thorpe that.) 'The more people see you, the better it is.' Untrue if it means more people see you making an ass of yourself, looking uncomfortable and out of place.

The record went into the Top Thirty. It missed *Top of the Pops* by one place. Fingers were pointed, blame was apportioned, heads rolled, the campaign began to collapse. Everything had been pinned on the *Top of the Pops* appearance, which struck me as stupid in itself. The momentum was lost.

Panic. Delay the album.

Another single: 'The Idol'. Another £60,000 video. Did they never learn? Then marketing felt the single needed a boost, a gimmick. Someone came up with the brilliant idea of giving away water pistols and black nail varnish with every single as part of the campaign. Is this how they saw me?

No one liked the video. In fact that's not strictly true; I liked it. But TV thought it was too like the last one, and MTV considered it too British (whatever that means).

Panic. The album was delayed.

The next single, 'Childstar', had, I thought, the best chance of any, and was due to be a Christmas single. It had another £60,000 Zana video (no, they don't learn), in which a talented kid played me as a child singing the song, intercut with my performance, both of us dressed by Alexander McQueen. Everyone seemed to like the video and the song. Radio picked it up and A-listed it. It was all going well, which always spells trouble, but then Mercury stalled its release, holding it back until one week before Christmas. Why? Who knows why. It was lost in the pre-Christmas market, buried, dead, turkey, stuffed.

As I sat in the car going home for Christmas, I listened as they announced the last new entry in the Top Forty countdown. I stiffened in anticipation . . . 'Steve Harley, "Come Up and Make Me Smile".' Where was 'Childstar'? New entry at number forty-one, of course. Where else? Happy Christmas.

Panic. The album was delayed.

The last single, 'Out There', had a £25,000 budget – note: reduced budget means flagging confidence. This time the video was shot on location in New York, with me as a taxi driver picking up friends as the track played. I loved the video, but the shooting of it ended in disaster. At the end of a long day's filming, the director and producer were wasting time in Times Square for so long that when we came to shoot it was so late all the Times Square neons had been turned off and they missed the last shot. I'd had enough. I walked back to my hotel, the Paramount around the corner, leaving them to argue among themselves. Then the American assistant director followed me.

'Hey come back,' he said, grabbing my arm.

'No, and let go of me,' I said.

'You're coming back to finish this video!' he shouted, and began to tug my arm.

'Get your hands off me!' I shouted.

Then, to my utter disbelief and shock, he jumped on me, punched me in the face, and twisted my arm behind my back. 'You're coming back to finish this video if I have to drag you back!'

This was just too surreal for me to handle. Here I was being attacked by the assistant director who was trying to force me back to the shoot to finish the video. I was the star, and what was this person doing?

Then he punched me again, and we began to brawl in the street as he tried to drag me back to the shoot. It wasn't a good move on his part, because at that point my friend Max pulled up (oh yes, he was back in New York, hanging around, staying at the Paramount), leaped out of his car, threw the assistant director into the road, grabbed him by the throat, and threatened to break his kneecaps and shoot him. I ask you, where are the video cameras when you really need them? That would have made a fabulous video.

So, was 'Out There' a hit? My giddy aunt it was. And when the album was resignedly released nobody noticed it. Even fans wrote in asking how they could get it, as shops didn't stock it. It was released and deleted within several months. The whole debacle had cost £515,000.

Still, it wasn't all bad; there were a few good laughs along the way. I got to work with great people like the brilliant Nicki Sanderson from TV and radio. She too thought it was the worst marketed album ever, but at least we got to fly to Graceland together to do a TV spot. And if nothing else – and there isn't really – it did get me back out on the road touring, with successful concerts around Europe. Some of the new tracks worked well live and sat comfortably with many of the old Soft Cell songs that I was playing again. I was enjoying myself.

'Shiny happy person having fun,' wrote Glyn Brown in the *Independent*:

He looks like a baby, not a veteran whose first single hit the number one spot 15 years ago – maybe it's the wavelets of kiss curls along his forehead, a new hairdo that gives him an Audrey Hepburn cute insouciance; maybe it's the music that makes his comeback, clubby glam pop replacing the introspective torch songs heavy with orchestration. Clutching a bouquet and emoting like Judy Garland, he kisses his fingertips and sweeps out. When it comes to theatrics at least, the man cannot be beaten.

John Ree in *NME* wrote:

The four-piece that includes Neal X (formerly of Sigue Sigue Sputnik) on guitar somehow seems to make perfect sense. This perhaps is the kind of set-up Sputnik dreamed of subverting pop with – a glam rock disco outfit but with songs and an idolized star singer. Brilliant, funny, crammed and sweaty, this show feels like the triumphant return of a lost star genius.

Sara Manning wrote in *Melody Maker*:

I start to feel sad that I've neglected him for so long and feel even sadder that nobody ever` acknowledges the debts that Jarvis Cocker and Jake Shillingford (of My Life Story) et al. owe Marc Almond. But mostly I feel sad that we both had to grow up. Now, like then, it was the best of times, it was the worst of times. I still love you, Marc!

Enough already. I was back . . .

You see, good can come out of even the most dire situations. Sometimes all you need is to add sugar to the sourest mouldy old lemons and make that lemonade.

I was drained after three years of making an album that after its eventual release had come and gone in less than a few months. I was still the magnet of both extremes: good luck and bad luck. Twice during that period I had almost died. Oh, haven't I told you about these? The first time was from a carbon-monoxide leak in my home, which made me very ill and hospitalized me. The second was when, while walking down Berwick Street in Soho, I heard a warning shout and then felt a crunch to the back of my head. Blood poured down my back and face. Looking down, I saw I'd been hit by a neon transformer (weighing forty pounds) which had fallen from the third floor of a building. It had caught the back of my head, splitting it open. I collapsed and was rushed to hospital. How perfect it would have been – to have spent a career singing about the world of neons and then been killed by one.

The doctors explained how lucky I was not to have died – don't they always say that? – when in fact they should have said how unlucky I was to have been hit in the first place. They stitched me up, sent me to the lawyers to talk about compensation, and two days later I was filming the 'Adored and Explored' video, donning wigs and hats, suffering literally for my art.

There was a guardian angel – there really was.

17

'There's a place for us . . .'

In the spring of 1996, after the calamity that was *Fantastic Star*, I was broke. The three years it had taken to record the album, which had then died a death, had left me financially crippled. Though often financially comfortable, I've never been the kind of artist who can take the luxury of three years to create an album, forfeiting advances for other projects in the process. Ideally I like to make an album every eighteen months, easing cash flow and alleviating my boredom – the two of which are directly linked. All through the nineties there had been periods of not working, recording or performing live, and they had cost me.

Other expenses, directly linked to Stevo, also drained my finances in this period, and the cost of changing accountants alone came to £25,000.

Money had been spent on good times which had long since become not so good times.

Money had been spent on recording projects of my own, principally to keep my creativity flowing.

The incompetent builder I'd employed to renovate the church had taken a large part of my money and had managed to make the place more uninhabitable than before he began. Doctors' bills, credit cards, VAT and of course the tax man all had to be paid. The small advance I'd received at the beginning from Mercury was thus whipped out of my hands, as was all my publishing advance. I was awarded a nominal amount of money for my head injury from the falling transformer, but I wished it had happened in America – I'd have been a millionaire.

Circumstances made me for the first time in my life stand back and evaluate where I was, and how I could try to get things into some sort of order.

The first thing I did was what I should have done a decade earlier: I sent a letter to Stevo terminating our relationship. There was a window in my contract with him, and I took advantage of it. It was the hardest letter I have ever had to write – words to the effect that we'd had good times together and successes for which I was grateful,

but it was time for both of us to move on. I sent it round to the Some
Bizarre office and waited with trepidation for his response. I knew
Stevo would consider me a traitor, ungrateful, and believe that I'd
change my mind – that it was just me 'stamping my stilettos' as he
liked to put it.

Maybe a few years earlier he would have been right, but not now.
As I have already said, Stevo had pushed me into rehab to clear my
head and get my act in order, and in so doing he'd made me realize
that I could no longer work with him. I'd worked hard for fifteen
years, making records, promoting, towing the line and 'pulling it off'
as he would reassuringly say, as if I'd just done a bank raid. I'd been
loyal when every other artist had abandoned him: through the
difficulties and pain, I'd tried to remain constant professionally (to
some extent) and to do what he told me. Do I sound guilty? I don't
mean to – after all, I really had nothing to feel guilty about. Like
codependents, we had helped each other. But he must have seen that
the relationship was now stale, no longer even a marriage of con-
venience; we were both fooling ourselves if we thought there was any
mileage left in it. But often it is easier to stay together than to face
the difficulty and uncertainty of letting go. Fifteen years, after all, is a
long time.

Amicable though I wanted the split to be, it was never going to
happen like that. It was an unpleasant divorce.

I'd become suspicious of Stevo and was now questioning his
motives all too often. I felt he'd lost his passion for the art and music,
and had become a hard-nosed, cynical businessman for whom
nothing but himself mattered. His ambitions had grown in a different
direction, and I couldn't perform accordingly. I didn't want to be a
mainstream celebrity singer guesting on tacky shows. I thought about
Tenement Symphony and *Fantastic Star* and all the crap he had urged
me to do – from Tarby to Zig and Zag. I wasn't presenting myself
honestly and I hated myself for it. Quite simply, we now had different
goals.

Looking back, the rot had set in around the early nineties, when
relations hit a sticky patch and for the first time Stevo had insisted I
sign a management agreement with him. The trust that had seen us
through so much now wasn't enough. At the time I didn't realize the
folly of having a manager who owned the record label I was signed
to. It can create a conflict of interests, and even though I am no
longer managed by Stevo he still retains control of many of my early
recordings, which he is free to exploit as he chooses. There is nothing
I can do about this situation – in fact it is so restrictive that he could
legally force me to comply with all the material he chooses to release.

For me, an artist who values the quality of his work, this remains a thorn in my side.

From the move to Warner I became disillusioned with him. I think he wanted me to make one huge sum of money and retire; I don't think he ever understood that my work was my life, playing to live audiences was my reward. Money had never been my motivation, and if you take that out of the artist/management relationship there often isn't much left.

On many occasions Stevo was unable even to name my newest release. He had more important things to do. Stevo loved deals, and towards the end he climbed in bed with the tabloids to earn money. Stevo and his beautiful girlfriend Cleo Rocos became regular fixtures in the tabloids. I recall one story splashed across the middle pages in which he announced their engagement and showed off an engagement ring allegedly costing £500,000. How could he afford that, I wondered, when I was broke? How much of that was paid for by my 20 per cent? I rang and asked him. 'None of your business,' he told me.

But it was my business: he was my manager. Of course the ring never cost as much as he claimed – that was just another exaggeration in a lifetime of them. That tabloid piece was just one of many – tacky and trashy: the type of thing I often enjoyed reading, but not when it was about my manager, and not when he was supposed to have some integrity, I thought.

The final straw that convinced me to leave him was a strange and sinister episode. On returning from a successful tour of Germany, I was on a high and ready to break the news to Stevo that our partnership was over. I phoned him at his office. As I began to talk, he suggested I go over to the office to see him. 'I need to discuss a private matter with you,' he said.

Surprised and wary of the serious tone in his voice I made my way over. When I arrived, he was waiting with my A & R man, Dave Bates, from Mercury Records.

Stevo told me that while I was away in Germany a Sunday tabloid had been planning to run a story about me, but he'd used his connections (meaning an associate within the tabloid's staff) to remove a tape and a photograph from the paper's newsroom to prevent it. He then explained that he'd paid a substantial amount of money for this favour. The record company had been alerted by a mystery phone call which prompted them to telephone the tabloid in question and ask whether a story about me was to be run. The tabloid confirmed that they were considering one. I listened partly in horror and partly in disbelief. I asked what the photograph and tape contained. The photo allegedly showed me kissing a young man outside a nightclub, and the tape was allegedly of me involved in a threesome with two people below the age of consent (though what that was supposed to have on it I couldn't imagine). My first reaction was to laugh. Then, when I asked Stevo where the tape and photo were, he told me they'd been destroyed. I asked him why. After all, these were important. I asked him what I was supposed to have said on the tape, but he'd never actually heard it. I asked him if there even was a tape – I mean, if you're paying a substantial amount of money for something, wouldn't you want to get hold of it, to know for sure it existed? He simply said it had been destroyed.

I'd heard enough and wanted the police called. Then it was explained that it had all been sorted.

I became hysterical. There was nothing to sort out. I hadn't done anything. If the tabloids had a story, then let them print it and prove it. There could well have been a photo of me kissing someone outside a club. But a tape? And of what? What would a tape of people having a threesome sound like? Besides, as you know, I was never much one for threesomes.

I was having none of it. The whole incident was beginning to disturb me. Stevo was claiming to have paid money to save my career (what career?), and now I was supposed to be thankful to him, indebted for whatever this piece of bilge was.

'We believe you that it didn't happen,' said Stevo in front of Dave Bates. 'We just had to be sure.'

'What is this thing you believe didn't happen?'

The whole thing stank. And I was surprised that I was still newsworthy anyhow.

What upset me more than anything was that my manager might be lying, or that there were two people out there with a grudge, out to make up a story about me. To me the tape was the answer – it would show that it was all lies. But of course the tape had been destroyed. There was no story in the paper because I knew that the truth was that there simply was no story.

More questions were raised than answered. Maybe it was just coincidence that this all happened just as our working relationship was being terminated. Stevo was the hero of the record company, but I was the bad artist, having to be bailed out by my manager, and as ungrateful as ever.

When it comes to the tabloids, my philosophy has always been to let them print what they want and let the lawyers take over after-wards. After all, I have a dreadful urban myth attached to me (which could be outdone only if I were caught fucking the Queen Mother's corgis), and Stevo did nothing in our long relationship to ever prevent that myth being reprinted. What upset me most was his claim that he'd paid somebody to prevent this story without even asking me if there was any truth in it first. But the most insulting thing of all was when Stevo then informed me that I would have to pay him back the money that he'd spent destroying the tape and photograph that none of us had seen or even knew for certain had existed at all. It was all hearsay and I suspected make-believe, and I'd had enough of it.

What had become of us all? What kind of world was I involved in where people were allegedly making accusations against me, where my manager was involved out of his depth, and everything that was said remained unsubstantiated and groundless? During this whole escapade Stevo had not thought to seek advice from my lawyer, who when he heard about it also thought the whole thing stank and was full of holes.

During the following weeks, the whole incident took its toll on me. I stopped trusting people, stopped going out and became even more reclusive and alone. Perhaps, though, that was a good thing, for from then on I toughened up, took a course in cynicism, and passed with flying colours. I told myself, 'NO MORE!' I saw the album promotion campaign through, and when that was over I completed my separation from Stevo and requested that Mercury release me. I sent a letter to Dave Bates asking him to please let me go. He obliged.

*

Once again without a record company. Without a manager. Broke. So broke, in fact, that I was forced to accept offers of personal appearances abroad – club performances tossing off a few hits in exchange for good sums of money. Thank God for those hits now, for they can pay the bills in these times of need! Thank God even for 'Tainted Love'! I hate these PA performances, but beggars can't exactly be choosers. Faced with mounting debts and dwindling finances, I decided to hold my head up high, do my best, and get out there and earn. Surprisingly, on many occasions I actually found it really enjoyable.

One such time I was invited to sing at a festival in Lebanon. The money was good and I accepted. I was surprised that I still had a following in the Middle East; on arriving at the airport I was treated like visiting royalty and whisked off to radio stations where they knew all about me. Inevitably at these things, part of the deal is that you have to spend time with the promoter as they show you off around town – which can be tiresome. But in my free time, along with my assistant, Sharon Ashley Hoffman, I set out to explore the city – or what remains of it. Years of war have left much of it devastated, but we found authentic old-world Lebanese restaurants with the most exquisite dishes. I met up with my old friend Jimmy Somerville, who was playing at the same festival, and together with a Lebanese friend we took a night tour of gay Beirut. When I say 'gay Beirut' don't get over excited and book your holiday immediately: there are no gay clubs or bars, simply dark streets where men cruise other men from their cars, and the Corniche promenade where they cruise on foot. I was surprised to see such an openness in the Middle East, and heartbroken a month later when I watched on TV the same promenade being bombed by Israeli aircraft. Why can't we just all get along?

Beirut is the most surreal place on earth. The buildings are almost flattened, and people live in the bombed-out shells of half-standing blocks. The roads have no speed limits or traffic lights, which is not the most sensible of combinations, and everywhere there are Syrian soldiers at blockades. To add to the surreality, I posed for a photo session in a long sequinned and velvet coat in front of the bombed-out Holiday Inn, surrounded by Lebanese children looking at me as though I was an alien from a distant planet – which of course I was.

In my short time there I felt a strong bond with the Lebanese people I met, and, as in Russia, the visit made me appreciate my life, and England, so much more.

*

It was time that I looked around for a new manager. I met some great people, all with their own visions, but eventually I decided to work with a lady who is something of a legend in the music business herself: Vicki Wickham. Tris Penna recommended her to me, and after meeting her I thought she had just the right eccentric touch to deal with me. Vicki has had a long and varied career in the business – one of the original producers of *Ready Steady Go!* and with a vast record of other media work, she has inspired many and managed such artists as the incredible Dusty Springfield, Patti Labelle, Cameo, Morrissey and Holly Johnson. She is also a lyricist, most notably of the very famous, 'You Don't Have to Say You Love Me'. But above all she is absolutely wonderful (darling). I was privileged that she wanted to work with me. I found her resolute, solid, and most of all reassuring. And she knew absolutely everyone (darling). With Vicki based in New York and a localized management company in London, I had a great team of people around me. So they began the arduous task of securing me a new record deal.

In the meantime I scouted around for other projects to keep me occupied. A chance remark by Neal X one day made me sit up as he recounted a story about the time he had been involved with some recording for the singer P. J. Proby. P. J. Proby was a big star in the sixties – he'd a ponytailed, frilled-shirt, highwayman image, and had a big hit with 'Somewhere' from *West Side Story*. He was one of my favourite childhood singers. I told Neal I wanted to meet him. I wanted to write a song for him, but secretly I wanted to sing with him.

Neal then played me a song that P. J. Proby had recorded a couple of years earlier with St Etienne which astounded me – especially how fantastic he sounded on such an understated song, delivered with tenderness and pain.

Neal was unsure about being involved with him, for P. J. Proby had a reputation – a very very bad one. Though he had a definite talent – flawed perhaps, but immense certainly – he was also known to shoot himself in the foot at any chance of success. His career peaked during the sixties, and he was then sucked into an ocean of alcohol and pills, until at his lowest point he was a road sweeper. At one point, so the story goes, he was sweeping the street outside the Hammersmith Odeon where years earlier he had played sold-out shows. Then he was rediscovered by a small independent record label which tried to revive his career by urging him to do a selection of cover versions – one of them being a wild and drunken version of 'Tainted Love'. The result had seemed like an exploitation of a broken genius (and, if P. J. Proby is to be believed, he was paid only with a case of Jack Daniels).

I thought Neal's mentioning him was fate. And it would be a challenge to work with this person who had such a reputation, who was infamous for splitting his trousers in the sixties and shocking the world with antics that ended his television career. There was, in all honesty, a great deal about him that I could relate to – although he was more impossible than I could ever hope to be. I'd heard that he'd stormed out of the sessions for the St Etienne record when Bob Stanley of the group had brought in a record player from which to sample a sound from an old disc. 'I only work with musicians, not fucking DJs,' said P.J. Proby. 'If you want to play the fucking records, then play them at home.' He then dramatically exited, and that was that.

P. J., of course, had little idea how records were made these days – no concept of sampling or mixing. He wanted the world that he knew and was familiar with, of real musicians playing real music together.

Neal arranged for me to go and watch P. J. at the theatre where he was starring in the play *Only the Lonely* to triumphant reviews. It was the Roy Orbison story, and he had a medley of his own hits in the show, playing himself. (Who else could?) He stole the show, and looked great too – distinguished grey hair, and still handsome. In his suit and with his manner he looked like an old roué as he crooned to the knicker-wetting housewives who gathered in the first row.

I knew then I wanted to make a record with him. I thought about a project, and later met him face to face. He was by this time playing the latter-day Elvis in the West End musical of the same name. Once again he stole the show, and on occasions distressed the producers and other players by ignoring the script and improvising for long periods. With each performance, P. J. was forgetting the part he was playing and allowing himself to take over. His personality seemed too large to be contained.

When I met him, he was one of the friendliest people you could wish to meet. And we talked and planned to make an album together – an album, not just a single. I insisted, though, that he would have to sing one of his own compositions – because I considered him a talented songwriter. He agreed.

With Chris Cook (who was acting for P. J. Proby as his manager) Neal and I set about finding him a deal. Several companies were interested, especially if the album would include a duet between P. J. and me (obviously not forgetting the last time I had dueted with a sixties star). But it was my old friend Tris Penna at EMI Premier whom we eventually went with – primarily because he seemed to understand what was required from the project. It was to be something neither party was going to thank me for.

All the while P. J. remained pleasant, friendly and charming. It was not until the contract had been signed and the advance had been handed over that his other side came out – the one we came to call the Devil in Red Velvet, after the famous red suits he wore in the sixties. In my time I too had played the devil with my career. But nothing quite prepared me for the devil in P. J. Proby. I suspect it arose as much as anything from fear, from not having the confidence to deliver, a feeling that events were moving too quickly and were out of *his* control. His uncertainty and isolation, his suppressed addiction and his obstinacy had left him worried – and that translated as difficult. I think he felt out of his depth with all the new recording techniques and the changed musical world, not to mention the limited time on a tight budget. Many artists have in their time felt the same, including myself. We bluff and bluster, trying to show ourselves as the artist we want to be, fearful that people may see our flaws or inadequacies. And then what do we do? We hit that self-destruct button. So it was with P. J.

The problem began with 'P. J. Proby is running late today.' Then 'P. J. Proby won't be able to make it to the studio today.' Then 'P. J. Proby can't sing today or tomorrow. He can't sing in the foreseeable future.'

Day after day, Neal and I sat around the studio wondering what on earth we had let ourselves in for. In turn, Tris at the record company became worried. As time and money ebbed away, P. J. was called into Tris's office and read the Riot Act – which, of course, never helps the situation as hoped. Quietly, though, I was loving it – all the high drama of making a P. J. Proby record – and a Marc Almond record, for that matter.

P. J. refused to give up his role in *Elvis: The Musical* in the West End while we recorded the album, which meant we could secure little if any time with him in the studio. Who can blame him? After so many lean years financially, he was now in a regular paying job and was determined to see it through. But that shortly came to an end when his behaviour in the show became too erratic. He would stop the performance and tell the audience of his dissatisfaction with the production. One night, while on stage in his Elvis garb, he told the audience to go to the box office and get a refund, as the show was so shoddy. On another occasion he stopped the music and shouted at the drummer in the orchestra, deriding his playing. The producers had had enough. He was not allowed to perform. But they couldn't fire him so long as he turned up and put on his costume, so night after night he would go to the theatre, make up, and sit in the dressing room. All this was going on while we were trying to record his album.

Then the choice of songs became another sore point. It was decided that, since he had recently been in the Orbison and Elvis shows, he should sing one song associated with each of them. I picked 'If I Can Dream', and the group St Etienne, who were now working with us on the project, picked 'Don't'. P. J. Proby picked the Orbison song given to him by Roy's widow, a stunning track called 'Crawling Back'. But P. J. was sick of Elvis (and especially hated the tribute show). He told us that he'd never got over the fact that Elvis, whom he knew personally, had thrown him out of Graceland for stealing his girlfriend. 'Fuck Elvis!' he said.

Though Neal and I were the main producers and coordinators of the album, EMI were paying and so they were saying. Tris had a clear vision of the type of song that P. J. Proby should be singing, and Neal and I agreed. But did P. J. agree? Absolutely not. He had his own list of songs, the bulk of which were country and western tracks. Days and nights of diplomacy lay before us. Eventually he gave way, and we learned to work quickly before he changed his mind.

Then came 'I don't want to sing in that SOMM-A-WHHERE voice.' He was referring to his famous sixties hit. 'I don't want that voice at all. You understand?' We understood.

The trouble was that P. J. didn't know what voice he did want to sing in. One day he would sound like Gene Pitney, another day Roy Orbison, another day Elvis – all of them brilliant, but none of them P. J. Proby. He was the best mimic I have ever heard, but he had trouble locating his own voice. He would step up to the mike, out would come a sound, and he would back off frustrated. 'I can't find myself today. I don't know where I am,' he would shout, curse, swear, and that would be that until I sat with him and cajoled him into trying again. Over and over and over. Or he would deliberately sing a take as badly as he could, so we couldn't use it.

We must have tried everything. In the end we would ask him to rehearse a number and deliberately leave the microphone switched on without him knowing. They would be our best takes. Then with no word of goodbye, he would just leave – off to torment another taxi driver (his pet hate) – while our long-suffering engineer, Ben Cape, tried to piece together whatever he could, working as much from love as any of us.

The album had a fair but tight budget, so Neal and I did all we could to pull in favours with top-class musicians and programmers. I had the idea of contacting Jake Shillingford, the singer with the band My Life Story, who were doing well in the charts at the time and getting great press. I knew Jake was a fan of P. J.'s and thought it might be great to have him on board. We did a deal with them to play on most of the album for a nominal sum and full credits. For P. J. Proby, of course, all this wasn't enough. 'I want eighty string players,' he bellowed – the nine players we had just didn't impress him one iota. But My Life Story worked hard, were young and fresh, and did a great job.

P. J. had by this time declared his own personal war on EMI. He claimed that they were trying to screw him, and an old grudge surfaced from years earlier when he claimed they had short-changed him on royalties. Personally I thought EMI were more than generous, and I knew they were excited by the project. But goodwill was soon eroded. 'Have you ever been in prison?' P. J. Proby shouted menacingly at Ben, the engineer. 'Because I have, and I've got a hand grenade at home and I'm going to take it to the EMI building and blow them up!' He was deadly serious, and I grew increasingly worried as he became increasingly volatile.

I suspect P. J. never wanted the album finished and that if he'd had his way we'd all still be there now. Day after day we'd listen to his ideas – many of them great, but totally unrealistic: 'A hundred-piece orchestra, that's what this track needs . . . a full gospel choir.' He'd keep coming in with new ideas, if he came in at all, each more elaborate than the last, like his stories.

Tris was just as insistent, as I was, that St Etienne should be featured on the album. As they were hip and credible, I thought this was important, but to P. J. Proby they meant very little and he had to be coaxed. As it turned out, however, on the day he was a pussycat with them, and when presented with the opportunity to show off in front of a room of awestruck fans he delivered heart-rending vocals to their songs. You can go through hell with him, but when it works it's pure magic that makes so much of it worthwhile.

Neal and I wrote three songs for P. J. One was a megalomaniac track called 'I'm Coming Back', with just a touch of his old hit 'Somewhere' leading into the song. 'Go and give God a load of money,/ Tell Him that I want it sunny,' he sang, with no sense of irony whatsoever.

'The Devil in Red Velvet' was a fifties tribute song, a lounge pastiche, a kind of theme tune for him which I couldn't resist penning. P. J. wasn't too keen on it at first, but then he imagined that it would be a song to grab that 'gay market'. (Don't ask.) The song is flamboyantly theatrical, just like 'I'm Coming Back'.

But it was the song 'Suburban Opera' that really excited him. It was almost a Soft Cell-type song, and I felt it to be one of my finest compositions for a long time. It's the story of a housewife tuning into a nostalgic radio station to hear the singers of her youth, and hearing P. J. Proby singing the chorus. It's a yearning for the songs and singers of yesterday – real voices singing real songs. 'They don't sing them like that any more,' sings P. J. Proby with genuine emotion. 'A voice can be adored in a modern world.' The performance was poignant and moving, and brought tears to both Tris's eyes and mine. 'Suburban Opera' (in which I was happy to name-check Richard and Judy from *This Morning* – no mean feat) was the song that had persuaded P. J. Proby to do the album in the first place. He wanted the whole album to sound like that – except, of course, BIGGER.

To find a suitable duet for P. J. Proby and I to sing proved extremely difficult. There are very few duets suitable for two male singers, and attempts to write one fell by the wayside. Originally 'Suburban Opera' was to be a duet, but P. J. Proby handled it so beautifully alone that I backed off. At one point we found a track called 'Child of Clay' by Maresca and Curtiss, originally sung by Jimmie Rogers – a very Marc Almond-type song, but not thought to be a suitable single. Then, after days of searching, Tris found a song in his record collection – an uplifting anthem to living for the moment by Cupid's Inspiration, called 'Yesterday has Gone'. More than a little irony there, we thought. I took the liberty of writing a middle eight to the song to hammer home (with a sledgehammer is always best) the message 'We gotta live for now'. While recording, P. J. insisted that we face each other when vocalling, as in a real perform-ance. He was right, and the result is magic.

The album was finished, at last, eventually – though as far as P. J. Proby was concerned it was simply as far as we could go and he wouldn't have described it as finished. But for the record company the difficulties were far from over. The single was to be the duet between us, 'Yesterday has Gone', and P. J. Proby went into the record company to talk about the campaign and to tell them his idea for a video treatment, which made me laugh a great deal.

Apparently he insisted the video should cost no less than £180,000 and be filmed in Wembley Stadium (to be filled with extras and our fans – obviously mainly extras). It would feature a game of American football, with P. J. and I leading opposing teams and dressed in the full gear (complete with padding, helmets, etc.). We would run on to the pitch leading our teams, and the crowds would be chanting 'P.J., P. J., P. J.,' Very young girls dressed as cheerleaders in very short skirts would be waving pompoms and jumping up and down. The game would begin. P. J. and I would run head to head, he would tackle me and run to score, and the song would start. (That's right: the song hasn't started yet.) Then I would tackle him, run and score, and then in turn he would again do the same. Cutting to the final whistle, P. J. would have won the game and would be presented with a trophy by the Queen. (Apparently he would settle for a look-alike.)

After telling them his treatment, he looked around at the EMI staff. Silence. He wasn't joking. 'If it is not done my way I am not making a video!' Moments later he stormed out.

But they all took it with good humour, and in the end it wasn't his demands that wound everyone up, it was his, shall we say, slight lack of political correctness. In fact this floored us all. Now P. J. had been born in Texas, where toleration is not high on the agenda, and was brought up at a time when people had black staff – 'servants', as he insisted they were. This was a place where women should look pretty and always remain in their place, and where it was acceptable to marry twelve-year-old girls, yet infidelity was punishable by prison. If you knew P. J., then you at best looked on the resulting attitudes as an eccentricity and tried your utmost to ignore them, but his views were deeply shocking and offensive. This meant the promotion was risky, which made the marketing and press department very nervous.

Chris Cook, who was meant to be acting as his manager, was fired, and so too was his P. J.'s agent. The record company was reluctant to deal with P. J. directly, and so the album was doomed from then on. Everyone was exhausted.

A video was eventually made – a modestly budgeted affair. P. J. was brilliant in it and looked great, but it wasn't his dream of what the video should be, and in the short process of making it he finally managed to alienate everyone completely. EMI didn't exactly feel like making P. J. Proby a priority in the end, and as I wasn't signed to the label the single wasn't exactly on the top of their priorities' list. It did well enough, however, hovering outside the Top Forty for a few weeks around the New Year of 1997. I sang the song at my Palladium concert that Christmas, and part of me hoped that P. J. would sing it with me. But he didn't show up – he lived up to his reputation. I saw him a few months later belting out songs with The Who during a performance of *Quadrophenia*. He was in perfect form.

It has been working with people like P. J. Proby that has made the music business so enjoyable for me and such an adventure. And my work on P. J. Proby's album *Legend* led to other offers, one of which was to submit songs for Shirley Bassey. But one call that came quite out of the blue was from Barbara Windsor.

I knew that familiar voice instantly, just as it is known to millions: 'Hello, darling – it's Barbara.' Barbara, who'd started her career as a singer in movies, was planning to make an album of her own, and she wanted some advice on what kind of record to make. She also wanted an original song that she might sing on a forthcoming BBC special celebrating her career.

I'd met Barbara on a couple of occasions, and had once spent three days on holiday with her in Fire Island, outside New York, guests of our mutual friends John Addy and Nicky Marsh, a flamboyant, generous and colourful pair. John is a multimillionaire, having made his money from among other things his 'poppers' business. Poppers – amyl nitrate – are infamous sex stimulants. John was the chief supplier and reigning King Popper. He and Nicky were friends to the stars, and when not in their mansion in Huddersfield they spent their colourful lives travelling the globe in search of sun. Each summer they hired a house in Fire Island, and that's where we met Barbara off the ferry. As she disembarked from the ferry in the twilight, accompanied by her charming boyfriend Scott, I could hear the click clack of her heels on the wooden pier and that famous dirty cackle – it was straight out a scene from Carry On. The house belonged to John Addy, who, in his overgenerous way, had also invited a selection of characters he had met on his worldly journeys, some of whom he'd forgotten, and they all decided to turn up that week. It became like a scene from the Mart Crowley play *The Boys in the Band*, the inclement weather forcing us all to remain indoors – the actress, the pop singer, the poppers tycoon, the drunken queens, the assorted boyfriends and unsuspecting guests. All of us trapped by an oncoming storm on an island. A day later the storm lulled and I seized my opportunity to return to New York, leaving Barbera trying to learn her new *Eastenders* scripts in vain. As I departed more people arrived and Barbera gave me that look – please take me with you.

From then Barbara and I have remained in touch. When she came to the Palladium show, I serenaded her with a version of 'Something's Gotten Hold of My Heart'.

I set about trying to write a song personal to Barbara – a kind of 'My Way' meets 'I Will Survive', with lyrics that related to her life. I came up with an over-the-top song called 'My Fantastic Impossible Life'. But when she heard it I think she thought it was too near the knuckle even for her (though I thought she could have carried it off). 'Darling,' she said, 'I love the song – I really do – but I just can't sing those words. Let's work on it together.' She was being tactful, but I think she didn't feel comfortable referring to herself as an icon. Nor did she really appreciate the middle section of the song – 'I've met some villains, loved a few, / Ronnie, Reggie, Ronnie too' – or the lines 'Kenny and the lovely Sid, / All the movies that we did.' I wanted Barbara to deliver them with a sense of comic burlesque, but I understood that they were too personal.

Barbara is a remarkable, sweet lady. While she is one of our biggest stars, she remains down-to-earth and immense fun to be with, even though it's difficult to not be conscious of who she is – she is, after all, Barbara Windsor! I might just add that she was one of the first naked women that I ever saw (taken as a child to the cinema to see a Carry On film), but I don't know if she'd find that flattering, knowing how I turned out.

I'm useless where famous people are concerned. I still seem to be unable not to be star-struck and tongue-tied, unable to think of anything to say, coy and embarrassed. Tragic really, isn't it? But peculiarly I meet people who feel the same about meeting me. When I encountered the American singer Courtney Love in a TV studio, it was Courtney who nearly fainted on bumping into me. 'Oh my God, it's Marc Almond! I can't believe it!' she said. I was actually about to go, 'Oh my God, it's Courtney Love!' I'm a huge fan of hers, and for a few minutes we held a meeting of an impromptu mutual appreciation society. We even sang a few verses of 'Say Hello, Wave Goodbye' together – and, believe me, nobody sings 'I can see the make-up sliding down' like she does.

Whenever people react to me in this way, with recognition or praise, I still find myself doubting their sincerity, or thinking they have mistaken me for someone else. When I read that I am a cult, an icon, a star or even on some misguided occasions a legend, I naturally feel they are talking about someone else. I guess, though, that I've reached that time in my life when I should just accept the accolades and praise that go with the life I've lived. Though when they say I'm an institution I think they mean that I should be in one.

Who else have I met? So many people – quite a few of whom I've mentioned already – many at parties or in passing, and most when I wished I'd been articulate or in a clear state of mind to remember more.

I met Gore Vidal and spent time with him. I'd like to tell you how we sparred intellectually, but alas I can't. Nor how I swapped humorous stories with Mel Brooks, or discussed philosophy in a hotel lobby with the boxer Chris Eubank. (I'm a fan of boxing and have seen Chris in the ring several times, so it was great to talk with the charming, eccentric sportsman.)

Even though I've managed to meet Madonna to Gainsbourg, Warhol to whoever, it's the so-called kitsch celebrities whom I adore – the ones that are notorious, or scandalous or famously strange, or even famous just for being famous. I was honoured when the celebrated brothel madam Cynthia Payne came to see one of my shows and visited me backstage, for it was like meeting an old friend. 'Have fun, Marc,' she said – 'if you can in this country.'

Chi Chi La Rue, the big drag-queen porno director, is one of my favourite people too. I loved to hang out with her at her shows in the now closed Eros porno theatre in New York, and then later at Cats, a Latino hustler bar.

And meeting Jeff Stryker, the legendary porno star, was such a thrill for me. He was appearing in an off-Broadway show in New York during which he ran around the audience and hit people over the head with his famous appendage. After the show I stood talking with him and noticed he was sweating profusely 'You're hot!' I said to him.

Jeff narrowed his eyes and tweaked his nipples, 'Yeah! Real hot!'

'No, Jeff, I meant you're sweating.' Something seemed to get lost in the translation.

Jeff seemed only to be able to think in sexual terms; but his fake tan, capped teeth, extensive cosmetic surgery and paunch all added to a faded glamour that intrigues me.

I've met very few pop stars apart from the ones I've mentioned, which is very few when you consider the duration of my career. I just don't feel comfortable hanging out with pop stars – I will even turn down TV shows if I have to sit and mingle with other pop performers.

I was dragged out to meet Morrissey for dinner once. A mutual friend of ours – Jill Smith, a journalist with the now defunct *Record Mirror* – wanted us to 'hook up' because she mistakenly thought we would have so much in common, what with our respective styles and lyrics. Early dinner in a London restaurant was arranged. I was my usual nervous self, but determined to see it through, and Jill was in her element, accompanied by her two favourite singers. So there we all sat, Morrissey across from me, and both of us guarded and reluctant to open up or chat. Morrissey was concerned with being Morrissey as much as I was concerned with being Marc Almond. The small talk remained so polite and charming that it was all but nonexistent, and there were long, long pauses, fake laughter, much lingering over the menu, much filling time. Jill proceeded to get so drunk that she ended up crying in the toilet, and Morrissey and I had to help her out. Snivelling and weeping, she was overcome with the experience of having dinner with the both of us. We loaded her into a taxi. Poor Jill! Morrissey and I at last managed to have a good laugh as she was driven away.

It is rare that I'm seen in the company of the famous. I rarely attend openings or premières, still more rarely go to parties or gatherings, and dread being perceived as a celebrity ligger – once known as that, your career is over! My friend Roland Mouret says that I should get out more, be seen, make people aware of me – that it's time I was more visible, accessible. (At the right functions, mind you!) God knows I get enough invites, but I always turn them down – which is probably why I get them. Maybe now *is* the time for a change. Roland pointed out that the reason I often find myself marginalized, or just overlooked, may be that out of sight really is out of mind.

*

I needed a new record deal. It wasn't easy to find one. Not that there wasn't interest in me – there was. It was just that at this stage in my career I had to find a company that I could call home, a company in which I could be settled, make albums for reasonable amounts, and generally be left to be creative. My management company and Vicki Wickham saw a variety of labels. Some passed on me, others had their own vision for what I should do – many worryingly so: one A & R man suggested I make an over-the-top dance album, whereas another suggested a soul angle. I didn't dismiss anyone's suggestions any more, and I was glad that people cared, but I wanted to make an album of my songs my way, and of course with a minimum amount of interference. In exchange for this freedom I was willing to forfeit my advance if necessary. It was necessary.

I settled with a relatively new label called Echo, a subsidiary of Chrysalis. They had an interesting roster of artists and were perceived in some ways to be cutting-edge. They sounded just right. I met with the MD, Steve Lewis, who seemed an honourable man, with integrity. But what swung the decision for me was the vibrant and attractive A & R woman, Ingrid Brandstatter, who believed in my project from the outset, and who had a vision of the new album that I shared – a cool late-night album with trip-hop and grooves, sexy, mature and passionate. Ingrid came from Southport, had gone to the same art college as me, and shared my Lancastrian sense of humour. She is cool and fun and clever, and we liked each other. I also seemed to get on very well with Steve Lewis, who was a no-nonsense man and had intriguing stories of pop history.

Having a new project also gave me a chance to work with another idol. I had first bumped into Siouxsie Sioux fifteen years earlier in the King's Road Market, both of us browsing sex goods and leather accoutrements at a specialist stall, and both of us enquiring about made-to-measure leather clothes. Mariella Frostrup had told me that Siouxsie was a Soft Cell fan, but meeting her I was the one who was star struck. She tapped me on the shoulder and said in that distinctive, husky voice, 'Hello, Marc.' She and I and her long-time companion Budgie, the Banshees' blond drummer and percussionist, small-talked and swapped phone numbers. I blushed and blurted at my usual inane chat, stuttering with nerves at actually meeting one of my heroes, but it was the start of a friendship.

We've met up over the years and commiserated with each other at how our record companies don't understand us or have fucked us over. We are both pretty uncompromising as artists, which translates as 'difficult' in record-company speak. Drunken birthday parties in Greek restaurants, smashing plates and dancing on the tables, or taking over the dance-floor at a small Kensington gay club called the Sombrero and dancing to 'You Make Me Feel' by Sylvester, much to the delight of the patrons, come back to mind. Such nights used to end up at the Portobello Hotel under the influence of some psychedelic substance, talking into the lonely hours in the bar until the sun streamed in to reveal us as bedraggled Gothic vampires, clad in our black leather, with jet hair and smudged eyeliner.

When Siouxsie and Budgie broke from the Banshees in the mid-nineties to dedicate themselves to their Creatures project they emerged rejuvenated. We met up at the former house of the artist Gustav Moreau in Paris in January 1999, full of enthusiasm for the future. It had taken until 1998 for us to work together, the Creatures duetting on a track, 'Threat of Love', for the new album.

I spent the end of 1997 and the beginning of 1998 writing, recording and producing what became *Open All Night* with a small team of people: engineer and co-producer Kenny Jones, Icelandic programmer and co-producer Oskar Paul, and a group of excellent musicians – including Neal, of course – all of whom worked beyond the call of duty, with Ingrid keeping a respectful eye on proceedings. It all went incredibly well. I was clean, happy making the records I wanted to, and by the end of summer 1998 the album was finished.

I premièred the songs and my new, more sophisticated, presentation with a series of shows at London's Almeida Theatre, receiving the best reviews of my career – and from the serious press. The first single, 'Black Kiss', was limited edition only and was premièred on Jools Holland's show *Later*, on which I even sang 'Say Hello, Wave Goodbye' with Jools at the piano. I was back – again. And then, guess what? Just at the finishing line it all fell apart. I know what you're thinking – it was all going too well.

In the autumn of 1998 Echo appointed a new MD, Jeremy Lascelles. Echo had had no success to speak of in the previous year, and a new visionary was required to oversee and overhaul the label. When Jeremy Lascelles was appointed, he made it clear that he was not a fan of mine and wanted to rush out the album with minimum marketing spend and get halfway to fulfilling Echo's commitments to me (I was on a two-album). My management were having none of it, and negotiated my release from the label with the significant proviso that we could take the finished album with us. Echo agreed.

Record labels are inconsequential really. When the dust settles, who really cares about them? Artists are all that matter, and labels are simply devices by which an artist can get his work across to the public. After all, who even knows or cares which film company made such and such a film, who manufactures the paint David Hockney uses, or which publisher releases Gore Vidal's books? Record companies come and go, but an artist's body of work remains long after.

So Jeremy Lascelles was not a fan of mine. That was less of a surprise to me than discovering when people *are* fans. What disappointed me most was that I had hoped Echo were not the same as other record companies; in the end they were. In one respect they were worse – playing at wanting to be cutting-edge, independent and left-of-centre, while all the time hankering to be a major. It was a hopeless contradiction. In that game of musical chairs, when the music stopped, I and quite a few other artists were left standing. Jeremy Lascelles, it seemed, had not taken on the challenge of making Echo's roster of artists successful, but had chosen instead to make it an entirely new record label altogether, replacing acts and staff, and taking it to that place he knew best – commercial pop: neither good nor bad, just mediocre. The vision of Echo that Steve Lewis had passionately espoused was handed over to accountants who viewed everything by the bottom line. I was glad to leave.

I decided then that enough was enough. If I was going to have any sort of future, then it was time, albeit very late in the day, to take charge of my career. I decided to form my own label, through which I could record and release my own work without the demands of a label to restrict or restrain me. By the time you read this, *Open All Night* will have come and gone – the first release on that new label, Blue Star Music. This tentative step to artistic freedom was taken as much through necessity as from choice, but at least I will have only myself to blame if it goes horribly wrong.

The album *Open All Night* was a success, and the press seemed to be unanimous in their praise. And you know what? I want to share my moments of critical acclaim with you, because if you've read this far you deserve it. As they say, that's enough about me, so what about the critics, what did they think of me?

'Selfishly we can only hope he continues to get stronger through the years, because this is another sheer drop into class, radiant-*noir*, ravishing brilliance'

– Uncut

'Almond has come up with probably the best work of his solo career'

– Independent

'His best album. One of the finest songwriters there has ever been'

– Gay Times

'*Open All Night* finds Almond back on the bar stool, doing what he does best – scorching, bluesy, sing-yer-heart-out torch'
                                                      – *Attitude*

'Still managing to prompt glorious shivers. *Open All Night*, a sensuous, profoundly lush record. Almond is in as fine voice as ever, tremulous, impassioned and just a little deranged'
                                                      – *What's On*

'Unique vision that should be treasured' – *Guardian*

'*Open All Night* is a pitch-black blend of R&B and pop – moody and introspective music at its best. Highly recommended'
                                                      – *FHM*

Excellent, fair and, might I say, balanced reviews. Of course, there were some that were so over the top I felt it would be too self-indulgent to print them. Anyway, as you can imagine I felt re-appraised and respected, engergized in music again. I had found a new voice, the melodramatic Almond of yesterday put to bed for a while at least. The album was just as well received in continental Europe and America as it was in the UK, and the prestigious French newspaper *Libération* dedicated a whole page to it, calling me the Sinatra of the backroom. You see I was back . . . yet again.

18

'Laughing in the face of adversity'

So here I am, in the *here and now* – spring 1999, as I write this.

Living in the here and now – a phrase I learned in rehab – is what I try to do. The future, as we all know, is uncertain, and the past is but a reminder of all that we cannot change. Maybe by writing this book I can finally draw a line underneath that past and move on. Part of the future is revisiting the past, and re-evaluating it, and now that's done. This chapter was the hardest to write of all, because it couldn't just be about what had been: it had to be about what I have learned (if anything) and where I might be going (if anywhere). In many ways it involved having to think carefully about what I'm doing with my life.

Writing an autobiography, you find yourself thinking that you don't want to sound patronizing or bitter, but the words don't always come out the way you want. Your editor and publisher scribble notes and comments over your work in an attempt to make you seem more intelligent, articulate or likeable. They ask, then plead, and eventually tell you to keep it simple, clear; they request more famous names, more anecdotes, more sex. Maybe I should have had that ghost writer I was offered. (Maybe you're thinking, 'He's right about that at least.')

Then the lawyers sit and peruse the manuscript in that long-drawn-out costly way that lawyers have. They slip in the words 'allegedly' and 'supposedly', and underline massive sections to be checked for accuracy. The words 'defamatory?' or 'grossly offensive?' are scribbled across paragraphs – always as a question, as though to say, 'This might be, but it's a grey area. Do you want to risk it? Don't say we never told you.' Told me what? Is it defamatory or isn't it? Who can say? Lawyers charge for their costly advice but without their advice it could be costly. But it's costly anyway. Aargh! Round and round in costly circles without actually securing anything definite, concrete, solid. I ask the lawyer, 'If I call someone a liar, is it defamatory?' It might be, if you can't prove it, but it might still be even if you can. Let's move on. Personal fear.

*

If I'm cursed with a long life, then I'm not yet at the halfway stage. Why do I use the word 'cursed'? Because of the effect old age has had on those around me. Having watched my grandfather suffer from Alzheimer's until he died, having visited my grandmother, whose active mind is trapped in a frail, useless body, and having passed by so many of the old people's homes that haunt the tree-lined streets of Southport, debilitation scares me. Still, I might have forty years to look forward to before that.

Forty years like the last? Definitely not.

It's strange to be that person who sees myself getting older, still unable to grasp that it happens to us. For it doesn't happen to us, it happens to other people, whereas we still feel young. When do any of us acknowledge that we are getting older? Or that we are old?

When you've lived a rich and varied life, with so many intense experiences at such an early age, it's hard to supplant old memories with new ones, better ones. And of course if you've been a public figure, had the past recorded in photos and videos, there's always a reminder that appears at the least welcome time of how you once were. Imagine not one but thousands of old passport photos with the terrible haircut and the dubious clothing you can't ever believe you chose to wear! I see myself singing on a TV appearance in 1981 and wonder whatever became of that person. He really thought he knew it all.

This isn't to say that the next stage of my life won't be interesting, full and productive; it's just time to do things a bit differently. I've become more conscious of time itself. Passing time. It's difficult in writing about the past to find the line between recognizing history and clinging on to nostalgia, but I feel compelled to try.

Financially the future looks comfortable. Thanks to my new management team and my new accountant, I've finally found myself solvent. Thanks to insightful accountancy earlier in my career, I've had money put away for my old age. There, I said it – old age. (I find myself agreeing with Cher when she confessed she could find nothing good in getting old.)

I've made more money than I expected in the past year or two – certainly from live shows. The work keeps coming in from different directions, and I'm still privileged enough to be able to turn work down. But it's strange that when you reach my stage in life you start to think far more about being comfortable, about getting older, about the decline in interest that may come from both the public and yourself. You suddenly become more business-minded. You say yes to a few more things.

That doesn't mean I've dropped my standards, thought less

about integrity – that bloody thing that gets in the way. I'm still far too choosy, too overprotective of my image, wary of selling out. Mind you, I suppose you have to have had something to sell to be accused of selling out, but, as some of my friends remind me, 'Does anyone really care?' Does anyone really care about anything that much?

I find myself caring about different things that matter to me personally. I care deeply about animals and their plight, and find myself speaking out about this. When I contribute to charities, they are usually animal shelters, or causes that alleviate animals' suffering. Or else HIV and AIDS charities. The battle against the disease seems never ending – on top of all the shit of having to be a gay person you then have AIDS to deal with. The worry for those around me, close to me; their strength a constant source of inspiration, of keeping what really matters in perspective. And the friends who never made it, their faces can still illuminate my darkest memories – 'when we die we're gonna go dancing/ at that nightclub in the sky'.

Where does Marc Almond go from here? I carry on. I am, after all is said and done, a singer – that's what I do. It's often amusing to hear people talking about the eighties or singers from the past who are still trying to perform and make a living – 'still making records'. But that is what they do, after all. Singers sing and musicians play, and it surprises me when people say it's really tragic that such and such is still trying to make a record. Why is it? Are performers supposed to sit at home and starve, or go back to college to learn a new trade, or just disappear altogether? The problem for many pop singers is they've had their time as pop stars; however, they can still be singers.

For anyone to succeed in *pop* culture, their approach and style have to feel contemporary and fresh. Pop has to be something we take in easily, effortlessly, not something we have to work on. The problem I encountered with *Fantastic Star* was that it was marketed as a pop album and me as a pop star. I was made to compete in a market where I no longer had a place.

When it comes down to it, I really don't want to devalue my current work by having it marketed as that of a pop star. I know a nineties teenager is unlikely to respond to my music as immediately and wholeheartedly as I responded to Bowie when I wore out *Aladdin Sane* on my turntable in the seventies. Many teenagers today would find my music a thankless toil. Pop music is about innocence, and eventually you have just too much history to respond or to participate in it. And that, I believe, is a good thing. For each generation, pop music is about how it feels when everything is new. No matter how barren it may look to us now, the pop music of today will be someone else's affectionate remembrance.

I just want to be a singer speaking to my generation. If other people also like it or learn that it can mean something to them, that's great – they might then also come to understand that current music and past music are all part of the same thing. Realistically, after Soft Cell finished, so too did my pop career – or it should have been allowed to. There was already a new generation of pop stars for the next generation of teenagers. But whenever I have tried to take my work far away from pop and into other realms, tried to be perceived as a singer and not a pop star, I have come up against resistance from record companies or management. Ironically, however, the times in my solo career when I have been allowed artistic freedom have been my most successful.

I have, as I have said, seen so much change. The sixties, the seventies, the eighties – I can say I was there. There when things were truly new to us all, rather than new to just one generation. I have made my living through the music business and watched it change: watched music become business, and finally seen the suited accountants take up their positions as MDs in companies. But during the next five years the business will change still more unrecognizably. Thanks to CDs, Minidiscs, reissues, 400 channels on cable and satellite, multiple-choice radio stations and most importantly the Internet, nothing will be the same again. To fill all these, everything from the past will be more widely available than ever, everything old will be reinvented and repackaged, and you'll be able to find it or buy it at any given time of day somewhere among the endless choice of channels. All that stuff, however good or bad (and a great deal of it was really bad), will be preserved for ever, when most of it, particularly the pop, was never intended to last longer than a few months.

I have respect for people like Rob Dickens, Clive Black, Seymour Stein, Roger Aimes and some of the other people I have been lucky enough to work with, because they were and are visionaries, benevolent dictators whose passion first and foremost was the music. Audacious, brash, colourful, they involved themselves wholly in the process of making a record – occasionally to the frustration of the artists. Such men are increasingly rare now that accountants are taking over. The result is that the cleverer musicians and artists are taking their careers into their own hands, away from companies and corporations, creating and releasing their work themselves. The Internet has made that possible, and will in time mark the end of the major record companies.

Maybe I should cash in on my past more. God knows, others have

– more than many other artists I've seen my back catalogue plundered and my image borrowed without due credit. I've been recycled so many times; and, though I try to smile and to accept it graciously, it can be frustrating. But I've also seen most of the new Marc Almonds disappear.

At this stage I'm simply pleased to have made music that has entertained and inspired others, which for me is what it's all about. I measure my success not in terms of the hits that I've had, but by the influential body of work I hope I've created. My career has taken me all over the world, into diverse areas of creativity, to meet interesting people and work with inspirational artists, and it's a continuing journey. Maybe the best you can hope for is just to get through, do your damnedest and give your most, learn, and have some laughs on the way. There must always be the laughs! My biggest fear was that I would be unable to create without drugs, that without them I couldn't be Marc Almond, wouldn't be suffering for my art. But I've found that drug-free I can create just as well as before, if not more so. I don't think I've lost my edge. Lucidity is my new drug – the only trouble is you have to wade through so much shit to get to it.

And the bigger picture? My fear remains that the world is becoming a monoculture, where every country will have the same consumer goods available in the same shops, everyone will listen to the same music and see the same films and television shows. In this global village, national identity will disappear. Having watched the New York I loved become a shrine to Disney – cleaned up and stripped of all character under the direction of a deranged mayor – and the old Barcelona I held in such affection bulldozed out of sight to make way for shopping malls, I hate the idea of that.

I recently went on a trip to Malaysia, into the rainforest in the north-eastern province of Sabah, to observe orang-utans in their natural habitat. Needless to say I never saw any. The rainforest is now no more than a small area of national park through which tourists are led down well-worn paths in the vague hope of glimpsing a rare ape or bird in its natural surroundings. The trip included a visit to a shopping mall close by the park, where visitors can purchase goods from Tie Rack, Body Shop and Gap. The same shops the world over, in malls that look the same.

Back in the hotel you can see the same films you saw on the plane or the same videos on MTV Asia hosted by presenters who appear as Western-looking as they physically can be while still being deemed Asian. You can go to Disneyland in Florida and in the course of several days visit all the capitals of the world, experience the flavour of each, visit Animal Kingdom, where you're guaranteed to see all the wildlife of the Serengeti (what's it matter if some of it is animatronic?), and still have time to buy the T-shirts. Experiences can be bought on a whim; there's no need to live them any more. And that's what I hate.

The truth is that in my life I have been very lucky: for an asthmatic from Southport with a speech impediment and learning difficulty I've not done so badly. Not the greatest singer in the world, not the best songwriter, certainly not the greatest looker, lets face it – a physically challenged homosexual from a broken home – I have nevertheless carved out a place which is mine and I have hung on in there through changing times.

I hate the word 'survivor'. Julie Burchill once said, 'It conjures up an image of someone desperately clinging to wreckage,' but I suppose that, as my life and career have been wreckages more often than not, I am some sort of survivor. I have been lucky to work with some of the best producers, artists and musicians, and a few of the most exciting people in the industry. Despite the tears, the self-indulgence, the debts, the difficulties and so much going wrong so often, I have been looked after by people both in and outside the industry who have believed in my talent and given me chance after chance – some would say far more than I deserve. But you can only fool some of the people some of the time; you need talent to fool some of the people all the time. Twenty years means the fooling ended a long time ago. The longevity of my career must be testament to that.

I'm sorry that with some of the people I worked with things didn't always turn out as intended – both for record companies and for colleagues who put their faith in me.

There is no sure-fire recipe for success in the music business. Whatever you do and however you do it, you always need that intangible X factor of time or place or talking to the right person, taking the right advice. Had 'Tainted Love' been first released today, perhaps it wouldn't be a hit – the fashion, the climate, all those sort of things might not be right now. It's that X factor that means that record companies, like Hollywood, can't find a formula that always works. God help us if they could!

You work to create an album for perhaps two years, investing your soul and passion. It can be your big chance, your next chance or so often your last chance. It can even be the greatest record you've ever made. But then you hand it over to other people – marketing, the record company, independent pluggers, you name it – and the success of that record can rest on so little. The slightest thing can mean failure. Like a missed *Top of the Pops* appearance, being omitted from the playlist, the video not being shown, general mismarketing, someone at the radio station not *getting* it, or not being a fan, or just feeling lousy that day. It happens. Then everyone dives for cover.

'Sorry, Marc, but think positively – this is great groundwork for the next single!'

'I just don't understand it. Maybe we should have gone for that gay market.'

'You did everything right, Marc, but regional radio got it too late.'

Excuses and regrets. I've had a few: but then again not too few to mention.

I wish I'd kept some of my friends and my work apart from each other, then maybe I would still have one or two of those people I miss for all those years.

I wish I'd been a stronger person and not allowed myself to be manipulated, and that I'd acquainted myself with the word NO sooner.

I wish that I'd learned some useful Yiddish words.

And the people in my life who have mattered? Stevo. It is hard not to still feel a liking and fondness for him. He too is a survivor, the archetypal lovable rogue – lovable as long as I'm not doing business with him, that is. I remember now why I liked him in the first place. He too was struggling against personal demons, trying to make something for himself. The music business has been a better place for his presence. He is a person who should never be underestimated, as many have learned to their detriment. I will always wish him well, though so often I wanted to kill him. I know that however hard or awkward he is, he is essentially a person with a good heart. Wait, am I being too kind?

My father. I blamed my father for what he put us through when I was a child, but, though there was once a time for bitterness, this book has exorcized the last of it. I don't feel it any more. I've learned that addiction is hereditary, and its actions and consequences are difficult to control. My father was sick – probably just as much as I was at times. But that doesn't mean that there is now a place for him in my life. It's too late for all that making up, too late to try to get to know a complete stranger.

As for my mother and the rest of my family, we have a good relationship in that we keep in touch, see each other regularly. But I'm sure this book will be as much a revelation to them as to anybody. We live our own lives, and when we meet we talk that cursory and sketchy talk that relatives do. I know my mother is proud of my achievements, and after all these years she is still able to embarrass me with her attentive nurturing. Mothers have a great deal to answer for!

And what of my friends these days? I have a small, close circle of friends whom I trust – a chosen family who protect me as much from myself as from the outside world – and I like it that way. Mark L, who sorts out the mess over and over and over again, and who through it all has remained constant and invaluable, and without whom I would not have made it – he alone has done so much that no words of gratitude can even come close to thanking him enough. Roland Mouret, who ensures that I am not committing any style felonies, offers words of solace, and makes sense of things in the way that only the French can. Jane Rollink, a.k.a. Mrs Woods, who is now a mother herself and at last understanding her demons. Dillon, my friend from Leeds, still working on his life and looking for happiness (we talk for hours on the phone and laugh about the old days). Anita Sarko, my old friend from New York (no longer a DJ but a writer with her own stories to tell). And of course my very special friends Pierre and Gilles.

Sean, a love affair that didn't end in tears, now has a successful business and a fulfilled life – something went right there. Huw Feather, my oldest friend, whom I rowed with after the Albert Hall show in 1992 and we fell out, neither of us speaking to the other for seven years, came to see me and we made up instantly, all those years apart seeming as though they were nothing. We resumed where we had left off, as close as ever, friends again and making up for lost time. It's strange how faces from the past appear again in your life – I put it down to the millennium, reassessing, looking back and making up. Tim and Stuart, my two school friends from Southport, with whom I started my first group, met up with me, now two butch skinheads (well, gay men with cropped hair). They both live nearby and we see each other regularly. Also from school, I recently met Tina Mitchell and Gillian Lax, who came to see me in concert, twenty-eight years after our school days. And then, of course, dear Molly Parkin, so like me in many ways. She fought and won her personal battles with addiction and emerged victorious. Our paths crossed nearly twenty years later on the King's Road, a short walk from where we had originally met. All those years and miles and there we were, laughing about our old selves over cherries and organic apple juice in her Chelsea studio.

Perhaps it is writing this autobiography that has made me gravitate towards old friends, open doors previously locked, and made me realize what is important. With real friends, no matter how much you argued or how long you stayed apart, it's astounding how easy it is to make up time, and surprising how silly it was not to keep in touch. Am I making you reach for the insulin yet?

Hey, but what about the others? What about the 'so called friends', who threatened you with the tabloids by concocting stories, or treated you like shit, or a meal ticket, or a fool? I've had my unfair share of those too. Those who use and abuse your position or generosity, or exploit your public position, who threaten you because of your sexuality. You know what I say? I just can't be bothered. Not anymore. I just hope I've learned to recognize such people a bit quicker, to be more cautious, more realistic. Some hope. As my French friend Roland tells me – 'it's not from a donkey you make a racing horse'. Don't you love the French? But I still look for the good in people, despite having my fingers burnt. So many of us came so far, and some travelled no distance at all. So many of us learned so much, and others, they stayed just the same.

I live a more sober life now. Offer me a line of cocaine and I'll turn it down, because I know that I'll want the whole gram and then some more. 'One is too many and a thousand never enough.' Keep telling yourself that. I know all the clichés – I've lived them. That doesn't mean that from time to time I've not weakened in my resolve. It would be dishonest to tell you otherwise, for as I am sure you know staying clean is a day-to-day thing. I still have that gap to fill, that GOD-shaped hole in my soul.

Did I mention religion? I'm still looking for one that fits. The perfect religion would be a concocted one – a little of this and not too much of that: whatever it takes to get me through.

I try to keep healthy, but that too can become an obsession. I look forward to my training sessions with my handsome trainer Patrick Topliss, who fills me in on all his exploits. Hey, and we have a laugh!

I no longer hang out in nightclubs out of my head, for without the drugs they're not the same places – just frustratingly full of people on drugs, with the only person to talk to being yourself. In all honesty, nightclubs are so unbearable that you have to take drugs to enjoy them. How you notice that when you're clean! But sometimes, once in a couple of months, I go to a club and dance for a few hours, just to check out the music. I can have a good time without drugs, but it's not the same. These days I leave before two o'clock and look forward to a night's sleep.

I've become more cocooned, with everything around me that I need. My addiction and obsessions manifest themselves in obsessive behaviour, compulsive rituals I have to go through every day to get from A to B. This drives close friends insane, but so long as it gets no worse they agree to put up with it: otherwise they'll make me get help. You know the sort of thing (or hopefully you don't): the cushions that can't be sat on because the creases will drive me crazy; the amount of time it takes to leave the house; going to the same restaurants, sitting in the same seats, eating the same one thing on the menu. Food rituals? Don't ask!

Then of course there is my personal war to arrest the disturbing effects of ageing – that war that so many of us fight, the one that keeps cosmetic surgeons and toupee makers in business. Time for more surgery? What do you think? Isn't that the kind of thing that Marc Almond would do? I'd hate to disappoint you – especially after you've read this far.

I try to keep my dreams small these days, my ambitions realistic – I might try to use old forms now, to make new feelings articulate. I know that the emotions I'm dealing with are those of someone my age – virtues, cravings, disappointments in love, or life, clarity.

What's left for me? To be in a movie, produce and write for other people, write a book (fiction), visit places I have never been to. You know – the sort of Miss World answers.

But music – the recording and performing of it – is my first love. Putting out my own work on my own small record label is my current venture – being allowed to do what I want. (Note how I used the phrase 'being allowed'. That says a great deal!) Music is my passion and, until I can find a spiritual substitute, it will remain my higher power. Who knows how long it's going to last? Who knows how long we have to live? (Please, no more!)

I think of the poignant words of the chorus of the song I sang with P. J. Proby:

> Yesterday has just departed,
> Yet tomorrow hasn't started,
> All that really matters is right now.
> Live a lifetime in each minute,
> Take the sweetness from within it,
> Yesterday has gone without a sound.

A blessed life? Maybe.
A charmed life? Certainly.
But most definitely a tainted life.

Epilogue

Dave Ball and I sat in the café drinking our tea and talking over the past. Laughing and remembering the good times, the madness; forgetting the bad times – they didn't matter any more. Hadn't they really all been good times, even the bad ones? If we weren't careful we might have become sentimental, but then Dave would mention Stevo and his face would cloud over, bringing us back to reality.

When had I seen Dave last? The year before, briefly. And the year before that. And each time we'd plan to do a project together. You know: write some songs, do an EP, whatever – full of enthusiasm, but never agreeing on how to proceed or what to call it, because of course we couldn't call it Soft Cell. Oh no. Definitely not. We didn't want all that again. Did we?

Over the years the projects we discussed never came to fruition, the timing never seemed quite right, there was always so much to get in the way, all those old ghosts never laid to rest. Now, here we were again, talking about working and recording together, writing songs, a project, something.

Neither of us had anything to prove any more, for in our own ways we had both had success in our solo careers. Dave with the Grid and then constantly in demand as a producer and remixer. And me? Well, you know all about me. There was no bitterness or dissatisfaction about where we were as artists. Time had made us equals once again. Feeling that, sat together in the café, we just wanted to write and record some songs, and the more we talked, the greater our sense of excitement and chemistry became.

'I'm not with Stevo any more,' I told him.

'I can't believe you stayed with him as long as you did,' he replied. 'It's time to make the effort this time – to work on something really great.'

I looked at him.

'But, Dave, we can call ourselves whatever, but when you and I work together there is only one thing that everyone wants. It frustrates the hell out of people, and it doesn't give us the chance we deserve.'

Dave looked down and thought for a moment.

'Why don't we just do a new Soft Cell album and be damned – but a really bloody great one?'

Dave thought on it. Stevo had always been the reason or the excuse that stopped us doing it before: Dave had never wanted to work with him again.

'Stevo wasn't around when we formed Soft Cell, and he's not around now.'

Dave thought on it again, and then smiled and nodded. The twenty years since we met vanished, and there we were again in the college canteen.

'But it has to be a brand new Soft Cell album. Twelve new tracks,' I said. 'Not a nostalgia retro trip. Totally brand new.'

What had been said was what we had both wanted to hear, though it had taken fourteen years for either of us to say it.

'You're right,' he said. 'Soft Cell it is!'

Outro

So the taxi driver goes on and on, and I switch off in the way I always do, hoping the journey will pass quickly. He asks the same questions; I smile, and answer as succinctly as possible. I don't want to be drawn into a conversation. I think of the Clint Eastwood film where he leans over to the driver and says, 'Shut up and drive!' But it doesn't take much just to smile and be pleasant, and to make his day. It's nice to be recognized, after all.

After I've spoken to his wife on the mobile, and he's finished telling me his views on the worsening traffic in London, the weather, the trouble with music today, and where he was when he first heard 'Tainted Love', he looks in the rear-view mirror.

'So, what you been doing these past few years?'

I smile and raise my eyebrows before looking out of the window.

'It would take too long to tell you.'

'Still singing?' he asks.

I laugh resignedly to myself.

'Yeah. Still singing.'

Acknowledgements

This book would not have been possible without Mark Langthorne to whom I am eternally grateful.

My special thanks to Gordon Wise @ Sidgwick & Jackson.

Thanks to my mother, to whom I owe so much and don't recall ever having thanked her.

To my sisters Julia and Sarah, my nephew Craig, Aunt Roma and the memory of my uncle Lawrie.

Thanks to Rob Collins, Jay Eff, Scott Ewalt, Brad Branson, Nick Timms, Lee Kavanagh, Helen Marsden, Peter Ashworth, Anton Corbijn, Paul Burston (for his enduring support), Kate and Michelle, all at Ellipsis, Henrique Da Silva, Flavio, Jorge and all of the brilliant Brazilian musicians and dancers that featured in some of my more spectacular performances, Lucy of Cellmates and Gutterhearts, Fernie Bubble, Marion, Kirk, Gordon Lewis, Ben Cape, Nigel @ Matrix, John Murray and Lou, Steve Baker, Jamie and Ricky Cummings, Simon Tebbutt, Darren Walsh, Nicky Timms, Francesco Piro, Johnny Holden, Michael Jelves, Steven Toyne.

Unfortunately, lack of time, space and a ruthless editor means that I have not been able to mention everybody I would have liked to by name. Many of you were present during the recounting of some of the stories – you know who you are – and if you have not been mentioned by name does not necessarily mean that that you weren't in my thoughts. There are also many faces that come to mind that I just cannot put names to, and for that I am sorry. I am sure when this book has reached the shelves I will think about you and feel guilty about it. Just as I will remember stories and anecdotes from my life that I should have mentioned, but under the pressure of delivering a book on time have forgotten. In forty years of life there are hundreds of such moments but, as you have read, life has been a little out of focus from time to time. To mention everybody who has ever crossed my life would take for ever. Don't take it that you weren't memorable or special – but of course there are one or two of you, if you read this book, who will be glad you aren't mentioned!

Thank you to the fans. To the Torch crowd in Germany and the Lust crowd in Holland.

Index